Lingo and Shockwave Sourcebook

Vineel Shah

John Musser

WILEY COMPUTER PUBLISHING

John Wiley & Sons, Inc.
New York • Chichester • Weinheim • Brisbane • Singapore • Toronto

Publisher: Katherine Schowalter
Editor: Tim Ryan
Assistant Editor: Kathryn A. Malm
Managing Editor: Carl Germann
Electronic Products, Associate Editor: Mike Green
Text Design & Composition: Benchmark Productions, Inc.

Library of Congress Cataloging-in-Publication Data:

Shah, Vineel, 1971-
   Lingo and shockwave sourcebook / Vineel Shah, John Musser.
      p.   cm.
   Includes bibliographical references.
   ISBN 0-471-16893-9 (pbk./CD-ROM : alk. paper)
   1. Lingo (Computer program language) 2. Shockwave (Computer file)
   3. Interactive multimedia. I. Musser, John, 1961- . II. Title.
   QA76.73.L22S48   1997
   005.13'3--dc21

                          96-47551
                           CIP

ISBN: 0-471-16893-9
Printed in the United States of America
10 9 8 7 6 5 4 3 2 1

Contents

Acknowledgments   **ix**

Introduction   **xi**

**Part One Jumping in with
a Boulder Tied to Both Feet**   **1**

Chapter 1 Dissecting Director   **3**

Chapter Objective   3
The Stage   4
The Cast   5
The Score   5
The Authoring Environment   5
The Runtime Engine   6
Lingo   7
The Lingo Elf   7
The Battle   7

Chapter 2 Navigation   **9**

Chapter Objective   9
Introduction to a Project: A Smiling Skull   9

Contents

Implementing "A Smiling Skull"   14
Chapter Summary   18

Chapter 3 Where to Stick Scripts   **21**

Chapter Objective   21
Introduction to Project: An Expressive Skull   21
Project: Understanding the Problems   27
Project: Solving the Problems   29
Chapter Summary   37

Chapter 4 Lingo Crash Course   **39**

Chapter Objective   39
Introduction to Project: Skull Sequencer   40
Exercise 1: Puppet Master   41
Exercise 2: Skulls and Cursors   47
Stop Exercising and Relax for a Minute   50
Exercise 3: What a Drag   51
Exercise 4: Getting the Picture   60
Exercise 5: Handling Handlers   79
Fixing the Second Problem with a Director Trick   97
Exercise 6: Skull Sequencer   102
Chapter Summary   111

Chapter 5 What I Didn't Tell You   **115**

Chapter Objective   115
What I Didn't Tell You About Navigation   115
What I Didn't Tell You About Puppets   121
What I Didn't Tell You About Conditions   124
The Parentheses Around the Condition Are Optional   124
What I Didn't Tell You About Repeat loops   127
What We Didn't Tell You About If..then   130
What I Didn't Tell You About Variables   133
What We Didn't Tell You About Custom Handlers   135
You Can Jump Out of a Handler at Any Time   142

Part Two Tricks of The Trade   **145**

Chapter 6 A Quicktime Player   **147**

Chapter Objective   147
Introduction to Project: A Quicktime Player   147
A Quick Quicktime Primer   149

Starting the Project: Setting Up the Quicktime Movie   155
Pixel Doubling: Playing Full-Screen Quicktime   181
Implementing the Slider-Bar   187
Implementing the Volume Knob   207
Chapter Summary   218

Chapter 7 Outline   **221**

Chapter Objective   221
Introduction to Project   222
Playing with the Kids   223
Rolling Over Kids   225
That Wacky Bird   243
Speaking the Words   250
Managing Your Memory   270
Under the Hood   274
CD-ROM Considerations   281
Chapter Summary   283

Chapter 8 A Small, Encarta-like Database   **287**

Chapter Objective   287
Introduction to Project: Musical Database   287
Text Containers   290
The Cast as Database   300
Bugs? What Bugs?   333
Director and Menus   344
Extending Director with Xtras   349
Chapter Summary   361

Part Three Shockwave   **363**

Chapter 9 Introducing Shockwave   **365**

Chapter Objective   365
The World Wide Web Before Shockwave (B.S.)   366
So What Is Shockwave?   368
Two Browsers, Two Flavors of Shockwave   372
HTML and Shockwave   376
Shockwave versus Java   378
Bandwidth, Evil Bandwidth   379
Online Resources   381
Chapter Summary   383

Chapter 10 Creating Shockwave Movies   **385**

Chapter Objective   385
The Shockwave Development Process   386
Shockwave Movie Project: The NavMan Navigation Bar   386
Movies on Fire (or Learning to Burn with Afterburner)   395
Loading It onto the Browser   402
NavMan 2: Using the gotoNetPage Command   408
Uploading and Testing Your Movie from a Server   411
Using HTML Frames with Lingo   412
Using the OBJECT Tag   415
Chapter Summary   420

Chapter 11 Advanced Shockwave   **423**

Chapter Objective   423
The Eight Types of NetLingo Commands   423
Understanding Asynchronous NetLingo Commands   425
Exercise 1: A "You Don't Know Jack"-like Trivia Game   428
Debugging Shockwave   441
Exercise 2: Adding Streaming Audio to the Game   444
Other Tips That Didn't Fit Anywhere Else   460
Chapter Summary   461

Part Four Shipping Your CD or Kiosk   **465**

Chapter 12 Projectors, Platforms, and Products   **467**

Chapter Objective   467
What's a Projector?   467

Part Five Conclusion   **481**

Chapter 13 Conclusion   **483**

Appendix A   **485**

Index   **489**

Acknowledgments

I'd like to thank my brother, Nigam Shah, who was my able assistant in this project, and who was responsible for most of the diagrams and screenshots. He put up with my stress and just-in-time writing style, and he crunched when we needed to crunch. In the process, he became a pretty darned decent Lingo programmer. I'd also like to thank Melissa Mackey, for keeping me somewhat sane.

I have to thank Regina Joseph and the gang at Engine.RDA, for putting up with, and actually encouraging, a Lead Software Engineer who often had his head (and maybe his body) in a consuming outside project.

Also, I would like to thank Tim Ryan and Kathryn Malm of John Wiley and Sons, who gave me this opportunity and didn't yell at me when I was late.

Finally, a student should always remember his teachers. I want to thank Jim Barr, my high school computer science teacher, and Ken Perlin and Allison Druin, two scientists who helped me understand the multimedia paradigm and gave me a hand with my career. Thanks, guys.

— *Vineel Shah*

I'd like to first thank Vineel for making this book a reality and for inviting my contribution. He's much more than a Lingo guru.

I would like to thank Carl Germann and Kathryn Malm at John Wiley and Sons for their assistance in guiding our book through the final editing and production.

I want to also acknowledge those wise and helpful folks from Downtown Digital who reviewed earlier drafts of the Shockwave chapters including Robert Moritz, Jim Berrettini, and Joe Lucca.

And most of all I'd like to thank my wife Beth for her encouragement, wisdom and support.

—John Musser

Dedications

To my parents, Vinrod and Neela, who fed my computer habit until I could feed it on my own.

—Vineel Shah

To my parents, John and Carolyn, and to my wife, Beth.

—John Musser

Introduction

Creating multimedia is a hugely imaginative, fulfilling, passionate, annoyingly detailed, tiring, often frustrating experience. It requires that you or someone on your team has expertise in several distinct disciplines: the content itself, graphic design, audio design, video design, media production, and yes, programming.

Our area of expertise is the often dreaded P-word. As we have worked in the multimedia industry, we have noticed how few people really understand programming. Do I need a pound of programming? Can it be done in a week? A month? Do I really need that weird programmer in the design meeting?

Some people get it right off the bat. They grab the Lingo manual off the shelf, dive into Director, and start making cool multimedia. Eventually, though, they hit a wall. They lack the programming background to decipher Puppet Sprites or parent-scripts or real-world simulation systems. Often, they don't have a programmer's practice to get their head around a concept and break it down into a programmable problem. This skill is something you have to learn from a programmer who has been there and done that. It's not something that you generally learn in class. It's not something you can learn from a manual. It's definitely not something you're born with.

The best way to get a handle on programming is by programming. If you want to understand programming but not necessarily program yourself, a few simple projects will help you get a feel. Once you have been through the emotional and dramatic process of giving birth to a program, you'll be amazed at how easy it is to relate to your programming staff. It absolutely will help you make informed decisions about the programming process.

Then again, if you want to become a true Lingo hacker, you've come to the right place. This book will help you get to whatever level you need to reach, in your own time, at your own pace.

This book is not a replacement for the *Lingo Dictionary* because it isn't a reference for commands and syntax. Instead, it is a learning tool designed to lead you through sets of real-world programming problems, to help you understand how to invent solutions based in what Director and Lingo can do.

Our Approach

There are eight professional-level multimedia projects in this book. We implement the programming in each of these projects, step by step, start to finish. We figure out what the problems are in making the projects happen, then we solve the problems. You and us, together.

Our goal, as authors and teachers, is to help you learn how to take an interactive multimedia idea, break it down into implementable problems, and solve those problems. Nobody is born with this skill; we all learn it as we go. You can, too.

As we progress through the projects, we explore new Director, Lingo, Shockwave, Internet, Quicktime, programming, and multimedia concepts and terms. We have tried to introduce new concepts **in context**, so you always have a pretty good idea **why** you are learning what you are learning. We strongly believe that, in a learning environment like a book, new concepts should always feel **relevant**. We also believe that multimedia, in any form, should be fun. We keep things as lighthearted and entertaining as we can (even though John can't dance).

What You Should Know

Before using this book, you should already know how to use Director as an animation or presentation tool. You should understand the Cast, the Score, the Stage, and how to use them to make a presentation.

You Do Not Need to Know How to Program

We wrote this book assuming that you are new to programming. We take you from your first steps in Lingo to that gray area between intermediate and professional Lingo programmer.

Who We Are

We, Vineel Shah and John Musser, are professional programmers who make multimedia for a living.

Vineel conceived of this book and wrote Parts I, II, and IV. He is the Lead Software Engineer at a multimedia developer called Engine.RDA in New York City, making CD-ROMs, Enhanced CDs, and Websites. He has also worked for Citibank, Imergy, and the Voyager Co. His favorite projects, so far, have been an Enhanced CD for Hootie and the Blowfish, the *Star Trek Omnipedia* CD-ROM, and the *This Is Spinal Tap* CD-ROM. He has also worked on almost a dozen other CD-ROMs.

His inspiration for this book comes from teaching beginning, intermediate, and advanced Lingo classes at the New York University Multimedia Center for Advanced Technology. Vineel holds a B.A. in Computer Science from NYU.

John stepped in, hero-like, and wrote all of the Shockwave sections, which make up Part III.

John currently builds Web sites for Downtown Digital in New York City (stop by its site and play some games at www.dtd.com). Over the past five years he's built multimedia CD-ROMs and computer games for a variety of existing and no-longer-existing companies including Imergy, Eidolon (an Electronic Arts affiliate), and SilverSun (America Online games). In a previous life he designed Wall Street trading systems but decided to have some fun instead.

He has written on multimedia programming for publications such as *The C++ Report* and *Dr. Dobbs Journal*. He's been a conference speaker on Internet-topics and has completed his M.A. in Computer Mediated Communications at NYU.

Multimedia is nothing without beautiful graphic design. The graphics in these projects were created by these expert designers:

- Chris Cappuzzo designed the backgrounds for Chapters 1, 2, 3, and 4 and all of the art for Chapters 6 and 8.

- Todd James designed and illustrated Chapter 7 and created the little surfer-guy in Chapter 10.

- Jane Howell drew the skull animations used in Chapters 1, 2, 3, and 4.

- Damion Clayton designed and edited the Quicktime movie in Chapter 6.

The Book

This book has four parts.

Part I: Jumping in with Boulder Tied to Both Feet

Chapters 1–3 gradually help you understand Lingo and how Lingo fits into the rest of Director. The projects are small and cute.

Chapter 4 shifts in high gear, picks you up by the scruff of the neck, and drags you into Lingo adulthood. The project involves everything from loops to puppets to variables to conditionals. After Chapter 4, you won't be a Lingo virgin any more.

To keep from overwhelming you, we don't fill your head with options, terms, and subtleties in Chapters 1–4. In Chapter 5, we give them all to you.

Part II: Tricks of the Trade

The projects in this part of the book embody three of the most popular types of screens you see in CD-ROMs: a Quicktime player screen, a Living Books-like animated page, and a small Microsoft Encarta-like database.

Chapter 6, the Quicktime Player, introduces you to Quicktime technology, how to control Quicktime from Director, and how to persuade Quicktime and Director to get along. We also implement two cool interface widgets: a slider and a rotating knob.

Chapter 7, the Living Books-like animated page, delves into rollovers, custom cursors, Lingo animation, and matching Quicktime to Lingo control. Along the way we also meet linear lists.

Chapter 8, the Microsoft Encarta-like database, explores Director's relationship with text, hypertext, movies-in-a-window, and file input/output using Xtras.

Chapter 9, Extra Credit, outlines some new directions for you to explore on your own, using the projects from this book.

Part III: Shockwave

This section takes your Lingo programming education into the online world.

Chapter 10 introduces you to multimedia on the World Wide Web. It shows how Shockwave, Afterburner, plug-ins, Active Shockwave, HTML, URLs, and browsers fit together to deliver Director movies online.

Chapter 11 takes you through the complete Shockwave development process, from soup to nuts. By the end of the chapter you'll have built a fully functional, animated Shockwave navigation bar.

Part IV: Shipping Your CD or Kiosk

Chapter 12 explores the vagaries, difficulties, and outright wacky things that happen when you make multimedia software for different machines. Nitty-gritty details about installation, the differences between platforms, and other end-game problems are covered.

Part V: Conclusion

Chapter 13 is a rousing and heartening pep talk to help you on your way.

The CD-ROM

The CD-ROM included with this book has all the projects in programmed and unprogrammed form. It also has a nice little multimedia interface that lets you play with the projects, like a normal multimedia CD-ROM. All of the projects, including the interface to the disc, are open to your exploration and examination.

The projects on the CD-ROM are put together like professional-level products that you might see on CD-ROMs, Enhanced CDs, CD +, or the World Wide Web. Spend some time playing with it; you'll be glad you did.

Windows versus Macintosh Issues

This is a cross-platform book, with a cross-platform CD-ROM. You will find all sorts of Macintosh-specific and Windows-specific tips throughout.

However, almost all of the screenshots were taken in Windows. In most cases, the Macintosh screens will look virtually the same, with stripes in the window's title bar. We'll admit it: We bowed to market pressure.

In the text, when we mention a mouse click or mouse button press, we always mean the **left** mouse button on multibutton mice.

The keyboards of a Macintosh and a Windows PC are a little different, and that difference takes a little explaining.

On the PC, both Enter keys do the same thing. On the Mac, the Return key (in the QWERTY section of the keyboard) and the Enter key (in the numeric keypad) often do different things. In the text, we usually say "press the Return key," which PC users should interpret as the Enter key.

On the Mac, special commands occur with the Command key (the one with the hollow apple icon). On the PC, the same special commands are triggered by the Ctrl key. We usually mention both in the text.

Typographic Conventions

The hardest part about reading a book like this is figuring out when the authors are talking in English and when they are talking in code.

In this book, we use...

this, plain old text font

when we are just talking. In the middle of book text might be a piece of code, like *go to frame 5*. Any code inside normal body text will be in italics.

When we list Lingo code, it will look like this...

```
on exitFrame

        go to the frame

end
```

Lingo code is always shown just the way you should type it. Finally, when we want to emphasize something, like **run, there's a fire!**, we'll make it bold.

Part One

Jumping in with A Boulder Tied to Both Feet

1

Dissecting Director

Chapter Objective

You should already know the difference between the Stage, the Score, and the Cast. The prerequisite for using this book is that you can use these elements of Director to create linear animations and presentations.

We'd like you to understand our own, personal spin on what these elements are all about. We'd also like to introduce you to a few less visible, more abstract elements of Director, like the Authoring Environment, the Runtime Engine, and Lingo.

And just wait until you meet the Lingo elf!

When you use a word processor or a spreadsheet, you feel very much like an armchair general. You point here and click there, and the troops, the pieces of the application, follow your orders and behave with relative discipline.

When you create a multimedia project in Director, you feel more like a field general caught in a raging battle. Events swirl all around you, processes march relentlessly on, and you try to maintain enough control to accomplish your objectives. It's tactile, tough, dirty work. But when you win, you have created a wonderful, interactive, multimedia title. It is probably worth it.

Before we begin the battle in Chapter 2, we thought you would want to meet your troops.

The Stage

The Stage is that fascinating rectangle on your screen where you see all the pretty graphics. It is a window, just like a window in a word processor.

The Director movie displays itself to the user through the Stage. The user interacts with the movie through the Stage (Figure 1.1).

Figure 1.1 The Stage.

The Cast

The Cast is a collection of **assets**. (An asset is a piece of media, like a graphic, sound, video, text, or Script.) Most of your assets live in the Cast (Figure 1.2).

You can browse the Cast through a special window called the Cast Window, in the Authoring Environment. Each asset takes up one slot, called a **Cast Member**, The members of the Cast are numbered, and they can optionally have names.

A Director movie can have more than one cast. Each cast can be contained inside the movie or linked from an external file. The projects in this book have only one, internal, cast per movie.

The Score

The Score is the basic, underlying structure of a Director movie. It is laid out like a timeline or a spreadsheet. Each column represents a frame of the movie. Each row represents a media asset on the Stage. Each frame can have up to 48 graphics or videos, plus two sounds, plus some other information like transitions, color palettes, temp, Lingo programming, and so on.

You can browse the Score through a special window called the Score Window, in the Authoring Environment. It looks something like Figure 1.3.

The Authoring Environment

The Authoring Environment is the aspect of Director that gives you all the wonderful windows, menus, and widgets that help you put together a Director movie. The

Figure 1.2 The Cast.

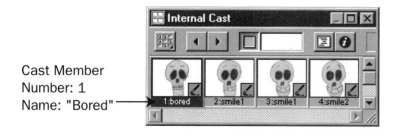

Cast Member
Number: 1
Name: "Bored"

Figure 1.3 The Score.

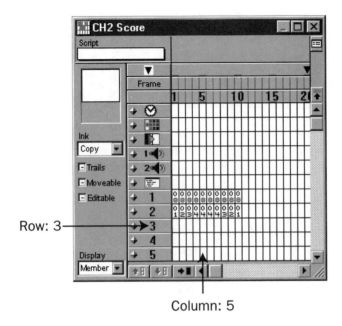

Row: 3

Column: 5

Score Window, the Cast Window, the File Menu, and most everything that you think of when you think "Director" are part of the Authoring Environment.

Think of the Authoring Environment as everything that you, the multimedia author, see but the end user of your product won't.

The Runtime Engine

The Runtime Engine might or might not really exist in the bowels of Director's code, but it's a really useful metaphor. Normally, you work in the Authoring Environment, importing Cast Members and laying them out in the Score. When you're ready, you press Play, and the Runtime Engine takes over.

The Runtime Engine looks at the Score in frame 1. It builds an image of everything that should be displayed in frame 1, then displays it on the Stage. Then it moves to frame 2 and does the same thing. This keeps up until the last frame in the movie.

Lingo

What was this book about? Oh, yeah. Lingo!

Lingo is the "scripting" language of Director. You will create sequences of Lingo commands that tell the Runtime Engine what to do. Simple commands might tell the Runtime Engine to display a certain frame. A complicated command might read a file from disk.

People used to argue about the difference between "scripting" languages and real "programming" languages. These people mostly got blue in the face and looked so weird that they lost their friends. In this book, a Script is a program is a Script, and don't worry about it.

The Lingo Elf

The Lingo elf is a character we made up (actually, we secretly believe that he's in there, somewhere.) The Runtime Engine can only execute one Lingo command at a time. The Lingo elf is the mythical figure that actually executes that command and determines which particular command is executing at the current moment. In traditional programming terms, the Lingo elf is called the "execution point."

The Battle

You might think of a Director movie as a battle for control of the Stage between the relentless forces of the Score versus the clever hero, the Lingo elf. (As in, "This is a job for the Lingo elf!")

The most powerful thing that Lingo can do is to make the Runtime Engine ignore what the Score dictates and do instead what your Lingo Script dictates. So, instead of playing through a linear animation, Lingo can make the Runtime Engine behave like an interactive multimedia title.

Keep your head down, your eyes open, and your powder dry.

Let's go.

2

Navigation

Chapter Objective

In this chapter, we slowly cover the basic concepts of Lingo, including events, navigation, and handlers. After finishing this chapter, you will start to understand the relationship between Lingo and the rest of Director.

If you already have a little experience with Lingo, this stuff will probably be old hat. You should still skim this chapter and read the summary at the end.

Introduction to a Project: A Smiling Skull

Don't worry; this isn't a hard project.

If there is one thing that Director does moderately well, it is animation. I thought it would be fitting, then, to make our first project about controlling animation. The first frame of the animation is shown in Figure 2.1.

Figure 2.1 First frame.

I know the skull looks bored now, but if you open file Ch2.dir from the Chapter2 folder on the CD-ROM, then press Play, you'll see him smile. Once.

(If he smiles repeatedly, you need to uncheck Play Looping from the Control menu.)

Our objective is to make him smile repeatedly, looping the animation until we press Stop. The easy way, of course, is to click the loop button in the Director Control Panel and use no scripting or programming at all. But you're here to learn Lingo. So roll up your sleeves, and get ready to rumble.

What Lingo Looks Like

Programming in a language like Lingo means typing in some text that the computer will understand as sequences of commands, which it will execute. Generally, each individual command is pretty simple and limited in power. By putting together interesting sequences of commands, though, we can make magic.

Programming in Lingo is sometimes called scripting. Scripting is the same as programming. Little bits and pieces of Lingo programs are called Scripts. Script is a euphemism for program, invented by somebody who thought you would be afraid of the p-word. Don't be.

Director gives us a place to play with Lingo commands and see immediate results—called the Message Window. So, open up Director and choose Message under the Window menu (Figure 2.2).

Reader, meet the Message Window. Message Window, meet the Reader.

Now it's time to try your first Lingo command. Type

beep

and press Return (Macintosh) or Enter (Windows).

Did you hear your computer's beep noise? I did. If you didn't hear anything, your computer probably isn't set up for sound, the volume is too low, or your speakers are turned off. Do whatever is necessary to get sound working, and try again.

As you have probably guessed, *beep* is a Lingo command that causes the system to beep. Now try typing

Figure 2.2 The Message Window.

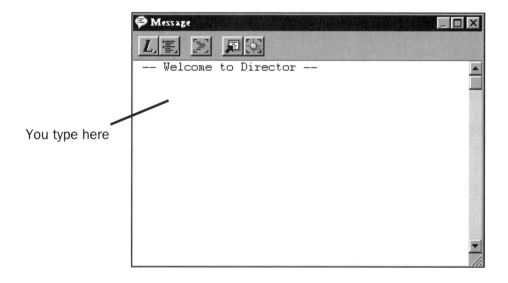

You type here

beep 3

Press Return (Macintosh) or Enter (Windows). Your computer should have beeped three times. We accomplished this by using the same command, *beep*, but giving it a little extra information, namely, the number 3. In this case, 3 is called an argument to the command *beep*.

A command is a verb, which tells Lingo to perform an action. An argument is like an adverb, which adds information that changes how the action should be performed. Some commands are made up of multiple words, and some take multiple arguments, as shown in Figure 2.3. We'll see examples of both in upcoming chapters.

Are you excited yet? OK, I'll admit it, the *beep* command isn't going to help you program Myst. Don't despair, though, because other simple commands will.

Navigation

If you closed the movie for this project, open it again. Now, take a look at the Score Window (choose Score from the Window menu, but you knew that).

See that little black rectangle in the upper left, next to the word Frame? That rectangle is the Playback Head (Figure 2.4). It determines which frame is currently displayed on the Stage. When you press Play, the Playback Head moves forward, one frame at a time.

Remember this —*The Playback Head likes to move forward*. When you hit Play in Director, the first frame appears. Then, the second frame appears. Then, the third, then, the fourth. These are followed by the fifth, the sixth, and on

---

Figure 2.3 Multiple-word command.

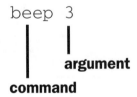

Figure 2.4 Score Window and Playback Head.

The Playback Head

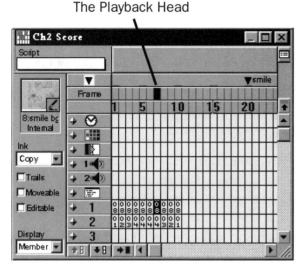

and on until you just want to scream. We are trapped in the doldrums of linearity.

Can anything be done? Can anyone save us?

Never fear, Lingo is here. (I don't believe I just wrote that.)

There is an incredibly powerful, amazingly simple Lingo command that lets you take control of the Playback Head. Director won't display a frame unless you, the Lingo programmer, lets it. The command is called *go to frame*. Let's play with it a bit.

Open the Message Window and position it so that you can see most of both it and the Score. Type the following into the Message Window:

```
go to frame 10
```

(From now on, assume we told you to press Return or Enter after you have typed a command.) Did you see it? Did you? The Playback Head immediately jumped to frame 10. You can bet it isn't used to being pushed around like this. It will be. Type

```
go to frame 5
```

This time, the Playback Head not only jumped a few frames, but it jumped backward. Wow.

Finding the right commands and the right arguments is essential to making Lingo bend to your will. We need to talk about one last aspect to slinging Lingo.

Events

So far, we have figured out how to tell Director **what** to do. Now we have to figure out how to tell Director **when** to do it.

Lingo is called an "event-driven" language. This means it executes specific bunches of commands when specific events occur. The mouse button being depressed is an event. This is an opportunity for a Lingo programmer, such as yourself, to insert some Lingo commands that will be executed whenever the user presses down the mouse button. The user's releasing the mouse button is another event, and another opportunity for inserting Lingo commands.

The simplest events are generated by the Playback Head. Whenever the Playback Head tries to leave a frame to go to the next one, it generates an event called, appropriately enough, *exitFrame*. An *exitFrame* event is a great place to use the *go to frame* command that we just talked about. In fact, this is the last thing we have to understand to complete the "A Smiling Skull" project.

The easiest way to understand this concept is to try it. The easiest way to try it is to do the chapter project. Isn't that convenient?

Implementing "A Smiling Skull"

This project is a slow and easy introduction to programming with Lingo. We'll use the basic Lingo that we've just seen, and learn how to integrate it with the Director movie.

Whenever a programmer sits down to write a new program, the first step she will take is to analyze the problem and understand it, deep in her bones. She will try to look at the problem in terms of things she already knows. Once she has worked through this stage, she will begin to implement the actual program.

"A Smiling Skull" and every other project in this book is set up in this format. We're hoping to get you used to this process, so you will follow it when you're programming on your own.

Understanding the Problem

Open the movie Ch2.dir from the Chapter2 folder again. If it is currently open and you have changed it, choose Revert from the File menu to get the clean version back.

Our task is to use Lingo to make Director continuously loop the animation of the smiling skull, which is laid out in the score from frame 1 to frame 10.

How should we do it? Well, let's review what we already know:

1. The Playback Head likes to move forward, displaying a frame at a time. This is how Director displays Score animations like the Smiling Skull.

2. We can use the *go to frame* command to manipulate the Playback Head's position.

3. The Playback Head generates an event called *exitFrame* that is a good place to use the *go to frame* command. (We'll see how to do this in a little while.)

Because these are the only Lingo things that we have really talked about, you can assume that there is a way to use them to complete the project.

The Solution

Ready for the solution? First, we let the Playback Head go forward, the way it likes to. When it displays the last frame of the animation, frame 10, it will try to leave and go to frame 11. In doing so, it will generate an *exitFrame* event. All we have to do is insert a *go to frame 1* command into this particular *exitFrame* event. This command will cause the Playback Head to jump directly to frame 1. From there, it will play forward, which it likes to do. Eventually, it will try to leave frame 10 again, which will generate an *exitFrame* event, which will execute *go to frame 1,* which will start the whole process over again.

Implementing the Solution

To put commands into the *exitFrame* event for frame 10, we first have to find frame 10. Open the Score Window, and make sure you can see the first 10 frames. If you can't see the Script Channel, scroll up a bit. The Script Channel is directly above Sprite Channel 1. (See Figure 2.5.)

Figure 2.5 The Scripting Channel.

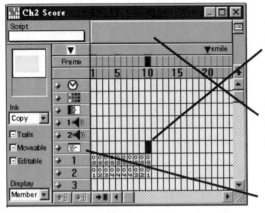

The Script Channel, in frame 10. Click here first.

The Script Preview Button. Click here second. This will pop open the Script Window.

The Script Channel. This is the normal place to capture Playback Head-related events like *exitFrame*.

Now, click in the Script Channel on frame 10. This is where our Script will be attached. Next, click on the Script Preview Button, the gray rectangle at the top of the Score Window, as shown in Figure 2.5. This will pop open the Script Window.

The Script Window

Welcome to the Script Window. This is a text window into which you will type many Lingo commands in the days to come.

The Script Window allows you to attach a bunch of Lingo commands to parts of your Director movie. In this case, we are attaching some Lingo to frame 10. More specifically, we are defining how Director should react to the *exitFrame* event in frame 10. The Script Window should look something like Figure 2.6. Don't worry yet about all the buttons and interface doo-dads. There's plenty of time for that later.

See the words *on exitFrame*? In Lingo, this is how you specify which event you want to deal with. If there were an event called *armageddon*, you would attach Lingo to it by starting with *on armageddon*.

The third line, *end*, is the last line of Lingo that will react to this event. All the commands you type in between *on exitFrame* and *end* will be executed whenever the *exitFrame* event occurs, which will be whenever the Playback Head tries to leave frame 10.

Figure 2.6 The Script Window.

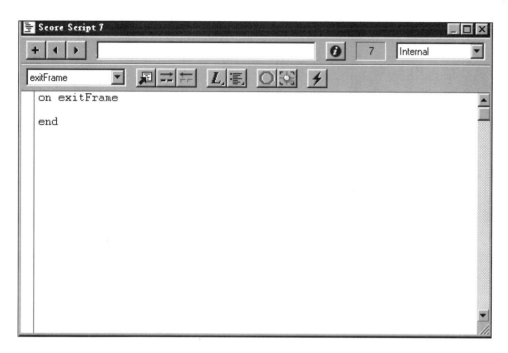

Now we finally get to use that *go to frame 1* command! Type it between *on exitFrame* and *end*. The completed script should look like this.

```
on exitFrame

  go to frame 1

end
```

Taken together, these three lines form what is called an event handler. These three lines **define** how Director should **handle** an event. Get it?

Close the Script Window. Click again in the Script Channel on frame 10. You should see a few differences in the Score. First, the Script Preview Button should show a couple of lines of our event handler. (It's showing you a preview of the Script.) Second, the cell that you clicked on, in the Script Channel on frame 10, should have a number in it. This is the number of the Cast Member that the event handler is living in. When you closed the Script Window, Director knew it had to put the Script somewhere obvious. The most obvious place for anything in Director is, of course, the Cast. So, when you type a Script into the Script Window, it gets put into the first free Cast Member.

When you're finished, the Score should look something like Figure 2.7.

Basking in Glory

Go ahead, see if it works! Close all the windows, rewind, and press Play. You should see a gloriously looping skull that is happier than you might ever expect a skull to be.

Congratulations, you have survived your first Lingo programming project! Save this masterwork to your hard drive, get a glass of milk, and figure out if you are ready to tackle the next chapter right away.

Chapter Summary

This chapter was a quick introduction to the very basics of Lingo programming.

Figure 2.7 The finished Score.

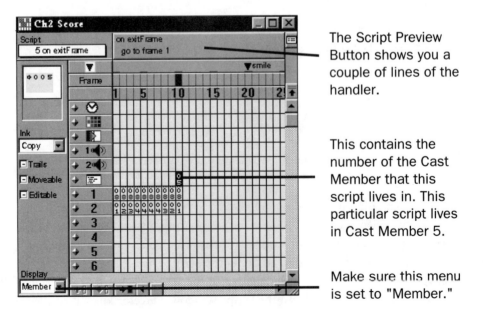

The Script Preview Button shows you a couple of lines of the handler.

This contains the number of the Cast Member that this script lives in. This particular script lives in Cast Member 5.

Make sure this menu is set to "Member."

Here are a few of the important points:

- **Scripting** is synonymous with **programming**. A **Script** is a piece of Lingo.

- To program in Lingo, you type text into appropriate places in your movie. Director translates the text into commands that it understands. It then executes the commands at the appropriate time.

- A Lingo **command** is a verb that causes Director to **do** something. Some commands need one or more **arguments**, which are extra pieces of information that modify how Director will execute the command.

- The **Message Window** is a special place in Director where you can type in Lingo commands and see their immediate results.

- The **Playback Head** determines which frame of the Director movie is displayed. The Playback Head likes to move forward.

- An **event** is something that the user does or that Director does. Examples of an event occur when the Playback Head leaves a frame, when the user presses down the mouse button, or when a user releases the mouse button.

- To attach Lingo commands to an event, you write a Script called an **event handler**. This handler takes the following form...

```
on eventName

    Lingo commands

end
```

- We covered two Lingo commands.

    beep num The beep command takes one argument, *num*, which determines the number of times it beeps.

    go to frame num The *go to frame* command takes one argument, *num*, which determines the number of the frame to which the playback head should jump.

- We covered one event.

    exitFrame This event is generated by the Playback Head when it leaves a frame. For example, if the Playback Head has already displayed frame 10 and it attempts to move forward to frame 11, frame 10 will receive an *exitFrame* event. You can attach commands to this event by typing an *on exitFrame* event handler into the Script Channel, on frame 10.

Check your toe, it should be wet with Lingo knowledge. If this stuff feels alien to you, don't blame yourself. Director is a quirky tool that arose from no solid, rational foundation. We use it because, after all is said and done, it works. Try hard to wrap your brain around these concepts, but take enough time to keep your cortex from rupturing.

In the next chapter, we'll explore some more of Lingo's simple-yet-powerful navigation commands, and play with a couple more events. It'll be fun. I hope to see you there!

3

Where to Stick Scripts

Chapter Objective

In the last chapter, we talked about how to create an event handler script. In this chapter, we examine the different pieces of a movie to which you can attach event handlers. In the process, we clearly define a few of the pieces, such as Cast Members and Sprites, and we learn a few new events and commands.

If you already have some Lingo experience, this stuff will still seem pretty simple to you. However, I know many experienced Lingo programmers who don't really understand the difference between Sprite Scripts and Movie Scripts. Read the chapter; it's short.

Introduction to Project: An Expressive Skull

Don't worry; this isn't much harder than the last project. The goal of this project is simple: to enable the user to play four separate pieces of animation by clicking on a menu. The menu looks like Figure 3.1.

Figure 3.1 First frame.

The four thumbnails on the left represent expressions that the big skull can make. When the user clicks on a thumbnail, the big skull animates into that expression and keeps looping it. The user can jump to a different expression at any point by clicking its thumbnail on the left. If the user clicks on the big face itself, it will return to its non-animating, bored expression.

If you want to play with the finished version, open the file Ch3_done.dir from the Chapter3 directory on the CD-ROM and press Play. Isn't it cute? The unprogrammed, script-it-yourself version is called Ch3.dir, also in the Chapter3 directory.

A Little More Navigation

In Chapter 2, we learned the command *go to frame x*, where *x* was the number of the frame. This works great, unless you or somebody else goes into the Score and moves some frames around. Say the animation originally started at frame 5, but you had to move the animation over a little, so now it starts on frame 10. You actually have to go back into the script and change *go to frame 5* to *go to frame 10*.

Now think about real life, where you might have 30 pieces of animation, all that loop using *go to frame x* commands. Ten minutes before your presentation, you are asked to insert a frame in the second animation, which, of course, throws the remaining 28 animations off by a frame. Are you going to fix all 28 commands correctly just before you present? Of course not. So here is a trick to help you out.

In the Score, you can label a frame with a piece of text, and the *go to frame* command will accept the label instead of a frame number. Because it is easy to move the label around when you are moving around frames, your *go to frame* commands never point to the wrong frame.

To create a label, you hold the mouse button down on the upside-down triangle, just above the word "Frame" in the Score. Then drag the mouse to the right, until you reach the frame you want to label. Release the mouse button, type the text of the label, then press Return.

To delete a label, grab its triangle and drag it out of the window. It will disappear.

The *go to frame* command will accept the label of a frame, just like it accepts the number of a frame. So, in Ch3.dir, we could use the command:

```
go to frame "mad"
```

to always go to the frame labeled "mad," regardless of where it is in the Score.

From now on, we will use frame labels instead of frame numbers in most navigation commands.

Figure 3.2 The Score.

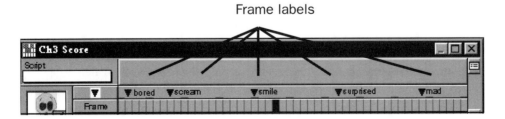

EZ Interactivity—mouseUp

This chapter's project, as you may have noticed, is a little bit interactive. It responds to the user's mouse clicks. You may be asking yourself, "Self, how do I respond to those mouse clicks?" And you respond, "I'll know as soon as Mister Know-it-all Shah tells me!"

To which I'll answer, "The holy *mouseUp* event, my friend."

Just like *exitFrame*, from Chapter 2, Lingo has another event that you can catch, called *mouseUp*. A typical *mouseUp* event handler might look like this:

```
on mouseUp

  go to frame "mad"

end
```

If you put this event handler into your movie, whenever the user presses down the mouse button, then lets go of the mouse button, this event will be triggered, and the Playback Head will jump to the frame labeled "mad." If you have a two- or three-button mouse, this refers to the left button.

The question remains, of course, to what part of a movie can you attach *mouseUp* event handlers? Well, anything you want, actually. We generally attach them to Cast Members or Sprites.

Cast Members versus Sprites

Sprite: It's not just for soft drinks anymore.

When you are creating a Director animation, you generally start by painting graphics in the Cast. Let's say you create the image of a smiling skull in Cast Member 1 (Figure 3.3). As a Cast Member, the skull does not have a specific location on the Stage, and it isn't attached to any particular frames. "Of course not," you say, "it's only a Cast Member."

Next, you would probably drag the skull onto the Stage. Seems pretty innocent, right? Wrong.

The moment you dragged the Cast Member onto the stage, you created a new Director entity called a **Sprite**. Unlike a Cast Member, a Sprite **does** have a specific location on the Stage and **is** attached to particular frame. If you open the Score Window, then click on the skull on the Stage, Director will automatically highlight the corresponding Sprite in the Score (Figure 3.4).

Figure 3.3 Cast with one skull.

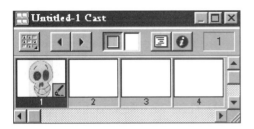

Figure 3.4 Diagram of Cast, Stage, and Score.

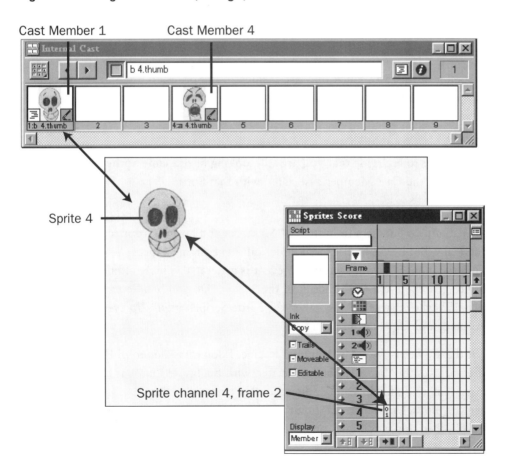

Let's say you put this Sprite into channel 4 of frame 2. This is done for you in file Sprites.dir in the Chapter3 folder on the CD-ROM which you might want to open now.

Let's say you press Play. What happens when the Playback Head reaches frame 2?

Whenever you play a movie, the Runtime Engine takes over. When the Playback Head reaches frame 2, the Runtime Engine figures out how to display the frame. First, it looks at channel 1. Is there a Sprite there? There isn't, so it looks at channels 2, 3, and 4.

Hey, look, a Sprite! Now, the Runtime Engine asks Sprite 4 which Cast Member it is associated with. This Sprite is associated with Cast Member 1, the smiling skull. The Runtime Engine then asks the Sprite where on the Stage it should draw this Cast Member. Based on this information, it goes ahead and actually paints the graphic onto the Stage. Then, it checks Sprite 5, Sprite 6, and onward until Sprite 48.

Look at it this way. Click on Cast Member 4 in Sprites.dir, the screaming skull. Now click on the Sprite in the Score Window. Finally, choose Exchange Cast Members from the Edit menu. The image on the Stage changes to the screaming skull, just as we expected.

The thing to realize is that you are still looking at **the same Sprite**. All you did was change the Cast Member associated with that Sprite.

Types of Scripts

You can attach handlers to both Cast Members and Sprites. Your script will behave identically, but it will be triggered under different circumstances. When the user clicks the mouse button, a *mouseUp* event is generated. The Runtime Engine first tries to give the event to the Script of the Sprite. "Do you handle *mouseUp*s, Mr. Sprite?" If the answer is "yes," then the Sprite Script's *mouseUp* event handler is executed, and life goes on.

If the answer is "no, Ms. Runtime Engine, I don't handle *mouseUp* events," then Director asks the Cast Member associated with the Sprite that was clicked, "Hey, Cast Member dude, do **you** handle *mouseUp* events?" If the Cast Member does, then the *mouseUp* event is captured and handled by the Cast Member Script. If it doesn't, then the search goes on.

Next, the Runtime Engine asks the Frame Script if **it** handles the *mouseUp* event. If it does, then the *mouseUp* handler of the Frame Script is executed. If the frame doesn't want the *mouseUp* event, then the Runtime Engine asks one final entity—the Movie.

Yes, the Movie has a script all its own. It is always the last stop for any event. If nobody else in Directorland has captured the *mouseUp* event, the Runtime Engine asks the Movie Script, "Um, sir, would you like the *mouseUp* event that just happened?" If the Movie Script says "no," then the event is promptly forgotten. If no Director entity wants the event, the Runtime Engine pretends it never happened.

This sequence of entities to whom Director offers a particular event is called that event's **Message Path**. The Message Path for the *mouseUp* event is **Sprite to Cast Member to Frame to Movie**. In contrast, the *exitFrame* event that we explored earlier has this Message Path: **Frame to Movie**. Sprites and Cast Members are never offered the *exitFrame* event.

This section is demonstrated in the file Messages.dir in the Chapter3 directory of the CD-ROM. Open and play this file, then follow the on-screen instructions. This file has examples of Sprite Scripts, Cast Member Scripts, Frame Scripts, and a Movie Script, all waiting to hear the *mouseUp* event.

If you're wondering why we haven't told you how to attach event handlers to Sprites, Cast Members, and Movies yet, well, we have to save **something** for the project, don't we?

Project: Understanding the Problems

The finished version of the project is file Ch3_done.dir in the Chapter3 directory of the CD-ROM. Play with it for a little while before attempting the project.

When you are ready, open the file Ch3.dir from the same directory, and read on.

The first frame of the movie looks like Figure 3.5.

When the movie is played, it should present the user with this frame. Nothing more should happen until the user clicks something.

If the user clicks on the skull thumbnails to the left, at any point during the movie, the big face in the middle should start looping a different animation. For

Figure 3.5 First frame.

instance, if the user clicks the screaming skull, the big skull should start screaming non-stop (don't worry; there is no audio in this project.) If the user then clicks the smile thumbnail, the big skull should start smiling repeatedly.

At any point in the movie, if the user clicks on the big skull, it should immediately return to this bored frame.

At any point in this movie, if the user clicks on something besides a skull, the user should get a message saying "Don't click there, bozo!"

How should we attack this problem? Well, let's look at what we know.

1. If you look at the Score of Ch3.dir, you'll see that each of the four animations are laid out normally in the Score.

2. We know that each face thumbnail always does the same thing, no matter where it may be in the movie. In other words, whenever you click on the smile thumbnail, it should always execute the same Lingo commands.

3. The big skull in the middle always jumps back to the bored frame when it is clicked. The Cast Member associated with that Sprite changes with every frame because it animates. However, all the Cast Members that make up the animation are in the same Sprite, that is, Channel 2.

4. The "Don't click there, bozo!" message should appear whenever the user clicks somewhere other than a skull.

Project: Solving the Problems

In this section, we're going to use frame labels, a couple of event handlers, a new command or two, and the *mouseUp* event we just met. We'll put these scripts into Sprite Scripts and Cast Member Scripts and Movie Scripts. It'll be like a party! (kind of...)

Label the Score

The first thing we want to do is get organized! Open the Score Window. You can see that the frames are grouped together, with white space between groups. Each group is an animation of one expression.

To make a label, drag the upside-down triangle out to the right. When you release the mouse button, there will be a blinking insertion point. Type the text for the label, then press Return.

Label the sections "bored," "scream," 'smile," "surprise," and "mad." The labeled Score should look like Figure 3.6.

Figure 3.6 The labeled Score.

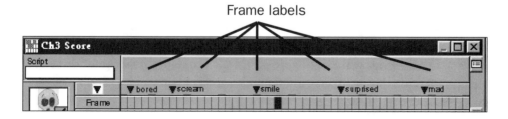

Looping on the Bored Frame

The rest of the project will look pretty silly if we can't keep the Playback Head on the bored frame until the user clicks a thumbnail. How do we do this? You might have seen Lingo's *delay* or *pause* commands. Take it from me, they are evil. They tend to do weird things to interactivity. Save yourself the agony: Don't use them.

Instead, we use a variation of the good old *go to frame* command. The command *go to the frame*, inserted into the *exitFrame* event of a Frame Script, will keep the Playback Head in that frame. Every time the Playback Head tries to leave the frame, the *exitFrame* handler will be executed, which will tell the Playback Head to go to the current frame. The overall effect is that the Playback Head stays on the same frame indefinitely. It works quite nicely, actually.

In the Script Channel on frame 2, which you have labeled "bored," put this script.

```
on exitFrame

    go to the frame

end
```

If you have forgotten how to make a Frame Script, you might want to review Chapter 2. In short, click in the Script Channel in the frame you want, then click the Script Preview button, the gray rectangle at the top of the Score Window. This will open a Script Window into which you can type a script.

Creating Cast Member Scripts

We know that a thumbnail should always do the same thing when clicked, no matter which channel or which frame it appears in, in the Score. This makes a thumbnail a good candidate for a Cast Script, because a Cast Script is attached to that Cast Member wherever and whenever it appears. To attach a script to a Cast Member, you must first find the Cast Member.

On any frame, click the screaming skull thumbnail on the Stage. Then, go to Cast Member under the Modify menu. From the resulting pop-up menu, choose Script to open a script window (Figure 3.7), which contains the script of this Cast Member. Because this is the first time we opened this Cast Member Script, an empty *mouseUp* handler awaits us.

Figure 3.7 The Script Window.

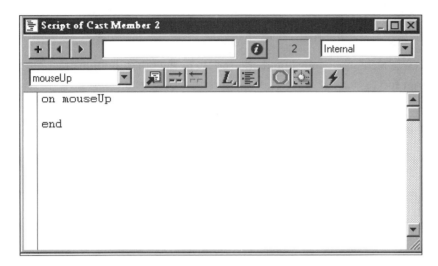

You can also get to this window by clicking on the Cast Member in the Cast Window, then clicking the Script icon at the top of the Cast Window (Figure 3.8).

Scripting the Thumbnails

The screaming skull thumbnail should play the "scream" animation when it is clicked. Using the *go to frame* command that we already know, this is a piece of cake. Here's what the final script should look like.

Figure 3.8 The Cast Window.

First, click on a Cast Member.

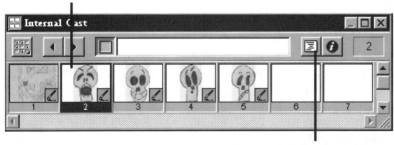

Then, click the script icon.

```
on mouseUp

   go to frame "scream"

end
```

Using the same technique, you should add scripts to the other thumbnail cast members. From top to bottom, the rest of the scripts should be as follows.

For the "smile" thumbnail, in Cast Member 3:

```
on mouseUp

   go to frame "smile"

end
```

For the "surprise" thumbnail, in Cast Member 4:

```
on mouseUp

   go to frame "surprise"

end
```

For the "mad" thumbnail, in Cast Member 5:

```
on mouseUp

   go to frame "mad"

end
```

Regrouping

Let's see how far we are, hmm? Rewind the movie and press Play. The screen should be the bored frame, with nothing happening. Now, click on the screaming skull thumbnail. The big skull should animate into a scream. Then, the screen should flash, and the smile animation should play. Another flash, then the surprise animation; a flash, and the mad animation. If this isn't the behavior that you see, you should backtrack and try to figure out where you diverged.

Why did the wrong animations play? When you clicked on the screaming skull, the Playback Head jumped to the "scream" frame. So far, so good. Then it moved forward, playing all the frames of the scream animation. When it hit the end of the scream animation frame, nobody told the Playback Head to stop moving forward.

So, it just kept moving forward, as it likes to do, playing all the frames in the Score, until it ran out of frames and stopped.

I think it is time to tell the Playback Head when to stop.

Looping an Animation

This problem is almost identical to the problem in Chapter 2. We have to use Lingo to loop an animation. "Stupidly easy," you say, "just put a *go to frame* into the *exitFrame* event at the end of each animation."

Well, you could do it that way. However, you're here to learn new stuff, aren't you?

Lingo has yet another variation on the *go to frame* command, specially created for these situations. It's called *go loop*, and it makes the Playback Head jump directly to whichever label is most directly to the left of the current frame.

Let's put the following event handler into the Frame Script for frame 17. When the Playback Head tries to leave frame 17, the *go loop* command will be executed. The Runtime Engine will start searching backward in the Score, looking for a label. The first label it finds is, of course, "scream" on frame 10. So, it moves the Playback Head directly to frame 10, then starts it playing forward again. It plays forward until frame 17, when the process starts again. Our loop is complete.

Put the following event handler into the Frame Script for frame 17, the last frame of the scream animation.

```
on exitFrame

        go loop

end
```

Try it out to make sure it works.

Reusing a Frame Script

When you create a Frame Script, as we just did, the Script itself gets saved in the Cast. If you look in the Script Window, which you can do by clicking on the Script Channel for the frame and clicking the Preview button, the title will be something like "Score Script 8," where 8 is the number of the Cast Member where you will find this Script. In fact, if you open the Cast Window and double-click on the Cast Member, you will open the same Script Window.

Another thing that happens when you create a Frame Script is that it gets registered in the Script Pop-up Menu, which is in the top left of the Score Window, under the word "Script." This exists to help you reuse already-typed scripts. Instead of typing the *go loop* event handler three more times, we can use the Script Pop-up Menu as a shortcut.

Click in the Script Channel on Frame 29, which should be the end of the smile animation. Then, select the *go loop* handler from the Script Pop-up Menu. Done. Do this for the last frames in the surprise and mad animations as well.

Watch out! Although this is a nice shortcut, it also leads to a ton of bugs in Director projects. Remember that when you reuse a script this way you are really adding a reference to the same Cast Member as the first use of the Script. You are not adding a new Cast Member for each use. If you change any use of this Script, all the uses will change.

Sprite Scripts, which we are about to discuss, also work with the Script Pop-up Menu.

Scripting the Big Skull

As we have discussed, if the user clicks on the big skull, the Playback Head should jump to the bored frame. At first glance, you might think, "Why not just add a *go to frame "bored"* to the Cast Member Script of the big skull?"

This doesn't work because the big skull is made of several Cast Members. When the skull goes from a half-smile to a full smile, it switches Cast Members. Do you put the script on the half-smile Cast Member or the full-smile Cast Member? You could do both of them, but 16 different Cast Members make up the big skull. Even if you put the script on all 16, it would be difficult to go back and change all 16 scripts if you made a mistake.

Looking at the Score suggests another approach. All the Cast Members that make up all the frames of the big skull are located in one channel, that is, channel 2. In other words, all the big skulls are in Sprite 2. This is a perfect opportunity for a Sprite Script.

Creating a Sprite Script

You create a Sprite Script much the same way you create a Frame Script. First click on the Sprite. Next, click on the Script Preview Button, the big gray rectangle at the top of the Score Window. This will open up a Script Window. The first time you do this for a Sprite, the Script Window will have an empty *mouseUp* handler waiting for you.

Our task is pretty simple: putting a *go to frame "bored"* command into the *mouseUp* event handler of Sprite 2, across all the frames of the movie.

If it was just one frame, this would be a no-brainer. All you would have to do is click Sprite 2 of, say, frame 10. Then click the Script Preview Button, and type this script:

```
on mouseUp

  go to frame "bored"

end
```

But we have to do it for every frame in the movie! Isn't this a problem? Nope.

Double-click on the number "2" in the Score. This will select Sprite 2 in every frame of the movie. Then, click the Script Preview Button, and enter the above Script. That's all there is to it (Figure 3.9).

FYI: Sprite Scripts show up in the Cast and are registered in the Script Pop-up Menu, just like Frame Scripts.

The Final Touch: Adding the Bozo Message

If the user clicks anywhere other than a Sprite or Cast Member (where we want them to click) they should get a bozo message. Because this should happen anywhere in the movie, and it isn't related to just one Frame, Cast Member, or Sprite, the event handler that does it should go into the Movie Script.

To get to the Script of the current movie, you press Ctrl-Shift-U in Windows or Command-Shift-U on the Macintosh. (Command is the key with the hollow Apple on it.) This is the easiest, most consistent way to get to the Movie Script, even though it doesn't really make sense. If you need a way to remember it, think of "u" as standing for "Über," since the Movie Script is kind of the Uber script. (For those of you who don't speak German, "uber" is a prefix that means "over" or "above.") Yes, I know it's a weak mnemonic. I just work here.

Anyway, pressing this key combination opens a Script Window for the Movie Script. This is the first Script Window that hasn't given you a default empty event

Figure 3.9 The whole Score.

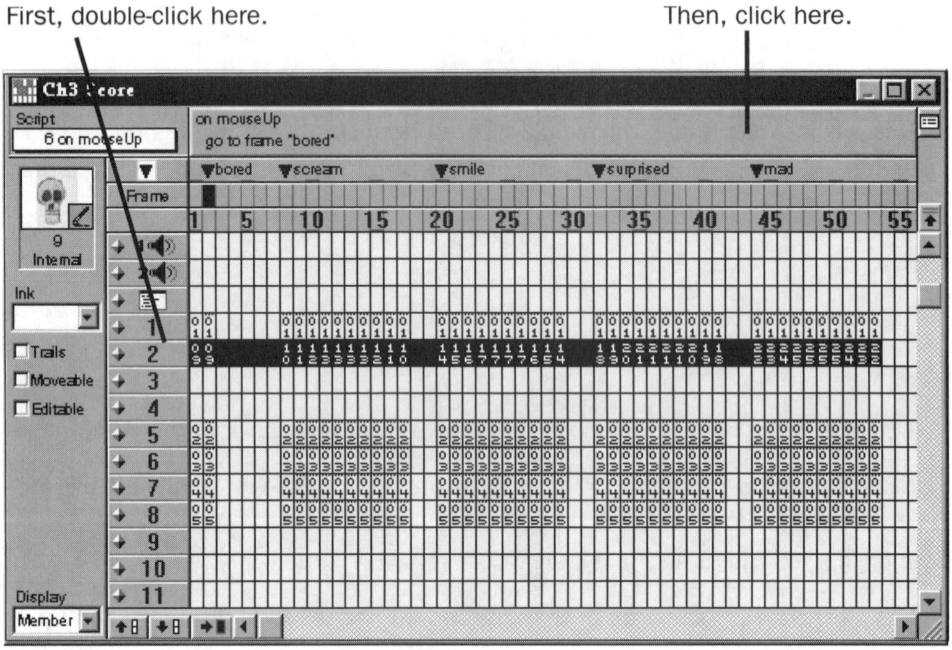

First, double-click here.   Then, click here.

handler because Director doesn't really know which event you will want to handle here. Pretty much all events end up here, unless they are captured by a Sprite, Cast Member, or Frame.

The event we are dealing with right now is the *mouseUp* event. If the user clicks the mouse, generating a *mouseUp*, and no Sprite, Cast Member, or Frame Script wanted it, then the user must have clicked in an awkward place. We don't like to let the user get away with things like that (especially when it illustrates a Lingo principle) so we put a *mouseUp* event handler into the Movie Script, the last place in the *mouseUp* Message Path where we can catch it.

To make the bozo message happen, we must also use a new command called *alert*. This command makes the computer beep and bring up a warning dialog box. *Alert* takes one argument, a string, which is the message it should display in the dialog box.

This is what you should type into the Movie Script:

```
on mouseUp

   alert "Don't click there, bozo!"

end
```

Close the Script Window, and try out your movie. Make sure it behaves the way it should.

1. It waits on the bored frame.

2. When you click an expression, it loops that animation.

3. Clicking on the big skull brings you back to the bored frame.

4. Clicking on the background brings up the bozo message.

Stick a fork in it; it's done.

Chapter Summary

We started to pick up the pace in this chapter. We explored the difference between Sprites and Cast Members, looked at the types of Scripts, learned about Message Paths, and built a slightly interactive animation.

- The *go to frame* command can take a string as an argument as easily as a number. The string should be the name of a label in the Score, and it must be enclosed in quotes. For example, *go to frame "bored"*.

- A variation of this command is *go to the frame*, which makes the Playback Head loop in the same frame.

- Another variation, *go loop*, causes the Playback Head to jump to the labeled frame that is most immediately to the left of the current frame in the Score. If there isn't a labeled frame to the left of the current frame, the Playback Head will jump to frame 1.

- A Cast Member contains media information like pictures or video, but it has no location in the Score or on the Stage.

- A Sprite contains no media information. Instead, it contains a reference to a Cast Member. However, a Sprite does have a specific location on the Stage and in the Score. The Sprite remembers all the properties necessary to display the Cast Member on the Stage.

- A Message Path is the order of Director entities that can hear an event. For the *mouseUp* event, the first entity that hears the event is a Sprite. If the clicked Sprite does not want it, the event goes on to the Cast Member, then to the Frame, and finally to the Movie.

- The *mouseUp* event is triggered when the user releases a pressed mouse button. On a multibutton mouse, this is the leftmost button. The Message Path for *mouseUp* is Sprite to Cast Member to Frame to Movie.

- The Message Path for the *exitFrame* event is Frame to Movie.

- The Movie Script is the script of the movie file itself—it is the über script. All events end up in the Movie Script unless they are captured first by a Sprite, Cast Member, or Frame Script.

- Press Ctrl-Shift-U (Windows) or Command-Shift-U (Macintosh) to open the Movie Script Window. You can also do this by finding the Movie Script in the Cast and double-clicking it.

By now, you know enough Lingo to get around and do some nice projects. Play with it a little. Enjoy your level of competence now, because in the next chapter, well...

Remember the Director-as-war metaphor from Chapter 1? In the first three chapters, you were the unsuspecting recruit, still being enticed by nice-sounding promises. In Chapter 4, you hit boot camp. Your mind will never be the same. You'll become a programmer.

4

Lingo Crash Course

Chapter Objective

Put simply, the objective of this chapter is to turn you into a capable Lingo hacker. Doing this project requires that we learn about all the basic building blocks of a Lingo program: puppet Sprites, variables, conditionals, handlers, functions, and loops. If you don't know what these terms mean, don't worry. You will soon.

Because we are covering a breadth of material, I have created a few exercises that isolate small parts of this project. With each exercise, we get closer and closer to implementing the full project, "Skull Sequencer."

Take your time with this chapter; there's a whole lot of stuff in here. Some of these concepts will take time to sink into your brain. I designed this chapter and project to help you learn most of what you need to survive in the world of Lingo programming. The rest of the book, the rest of Lingo, deals with special purposes or advanced solutions. The core of Lingo programming is all in this chapter.

Introduction to Project: Skull Sequencer

Boy, is this a great project! It seems simple on the outside, but it exercises the core of all Lingo. By the time you complete it you will be a Lingo veteran. Trust me, you'll like it. After you finish programming this project, you'll find that it is still fun to play with and you can impress all of your friends. Figure 4.1 shows the first frame of the project.

You'll notice some changes from the last project, namely the empty picture-frames and the painter. Here's how the project is supposed to work:

1. The user drags a skull thumbnail into one of the picture frames. When the user lets go of the mouse button, the skull snaps back to its resting place. If the user drags the skull on top of a picture frame and then releases the mouse button, a copy of the skull stays in the frame.

Figure 4.1 First frame of Skull Sequencer project.

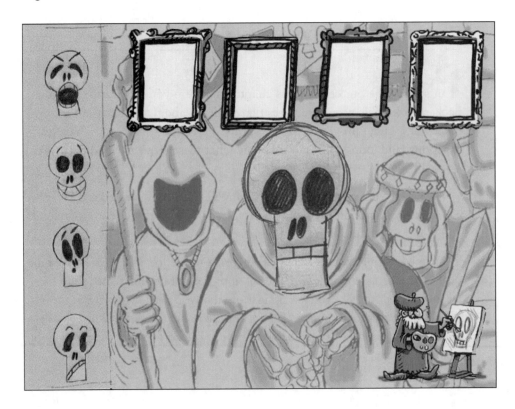

2. The user puts skull thumbnails into all the picture frames. The user is allowed to put the same skull in multiple picture frames.

3. The user clicks the painter. The program responds by animating the big skull into expressions. The first expression is what the user placed in the first picture frame, the second expression is placed in the second frame, and so on.

If the sequence that the user created was smile, smile, scream, smile, then clicking the painter would make the big skull smile twice, scream once, then smile again before returning to its bored state.

Play with the finished version a little, in file Ch4_done.dir in the Chapter4 folder on the CD-ROM. Remember how much fun it is because it's going to take us six exercises to create the finished version.

The no-Lingo-yet version is in file Ch4.dir in the same folder. You might not need this for a while, though. We have a lot of things to learn first.

Exercise 1: Puppet Master

Open the file Puppet.dir from the Chapter4 folder on the CD-ROM. It shows a lone skull on the Stage (Figure 4.2).

Figure 4.2 Frame 1 of puppet.dir, showing the lone skull.

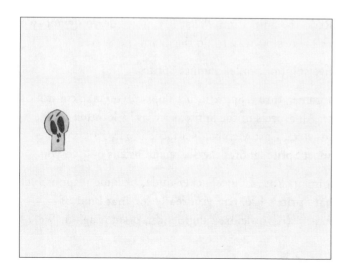

Here's the first exercise: When the user clicks on the skull, the skull should move a few pixels to the right. Can you accomplish this with what we already know? Sure. You could do a Score animation of the skull moving left to right. The *exitFrame* handler on every frame would be

```
on exitFrame

    go to the frame

end
```

The *mouseUp* handler in the Cast Member Script of the skull would be

```
on mouseUp

    go to the frame + 1

end
```

The movie starts playing on frame 1 and stays on frame 1. When the user clicks the skull, the Playback Head goes to frame 2, where it stays. On frame 2, the skull is moved a little bit to the right. No problem. This solution is done for you in file Inscore.dir in the Chapter4 folder on the CD-ROM.

This solution, however, is not the best one. The trouble is that this solution makes it very hard to change your mind later. What if you decide 10 minutes from now that you want to move the skull much farther on each click? You would have to redo the animation. What if you decide to move the skull a little bit vertically, in addition to horizontally? Redo the animation. What if you decide you want two skulls, moving independently? There's no way to do that with the Score.

Lingo provides an alternative solution, called **Puppet Sprites**.

When you, the Lingo programmer, turn a Sprite into a Puppet, you take control of the Sprite away from the Score. All aspects of the Sprite, such as its location on the Stage, its size on the Stage, and which Cast Member is attached to it, are controlled from your Lingo scripts. **A Puppet Sprite ignores the Score** and listens only to you.

Think about that for a moment. You, Lingo hacker-dude, become responsible for almost every aspect of that Sprite's life. Are you ready for that kind of responsibility? Of course you are! (If you closed Puppet.dir, open it again. We are going to use it soon.)

A Puppet Sprite begins its life as a normal, run-of-the-mill Sprite. You start the Puppet process by laying a Cast Member into the Score, using a normal Sprite Channel. This is done for you in Puppet.dir; the surprised-skull thumbnail is in Sprite Channel 1.

Also already done for you is a simple *go to the frame* Script in the Sprite Channel of frame 2. We want the Playback Head to loop on frame 2 indefinitely. Figure 4.3 shows what the Score looks like.

Making Puppets

The first step in transforming a normal Sprite into a Puppet Sprite is a simple Lingo command called *puppetSprite*. This line turns Sprite 1 into a Puppet...

```
puppetSprite 1,true
```

As soon as Director executes this line of code, it will say "No way, Mr. Score, You have no control at all over this Sprite. That Lingo hacker out there is controlling it now." When you are done with the Sprite, it is good manners to give control back to the Score. This line releases Lingo control of Sprite 1...

```
puppetSprite 1,false
```

True means "I want control of this Sprite." *False* means "I don't want control of this Sprite. I never liked it anyway."

Figure 4.3 The Score.

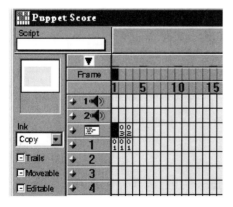

Generally, you make Puppets in the frame just previous to the frame in which you need them. In Puppet.dir, we loop the Playback Head on frame 3. So, we should probably turn on the Puppet in frame 2. Put the following handler in the frame script of frame 2.

```
on exitFrame

    puppetSprite 1,true

end
```

When this script executes (that is, when the Playback Head attempts to go to frame 3) Director will give you, Lingo-guy/gal, control over every aspect of the Sprite. Let's see what you can do with it.

Controlling Sprites

Now, as we've been saying for what seems like forever, **you** have control of a Sprite. How do you affect that Sprite? Through its properties!

Director remembers many things about a Sprite: its horizontal location on the Stage and its vertical location on the Stage, to name two. Each individual aspect of the Sprite is called a **property** of that Sprite. Think of the Sprite as a noun and each property as an adjective. Every property has a specific name. The name of the horizontal location of a Sprite is *the locH of sprite*. The name of the vertical location of a Sprite is *the locV of sprite*.

If you want to know the horizontal location of Sprite 1, you can get Director to tell you. Press Play in movie Puppet.dir. Show the Message Window, then type this into it:

```
put the locH of sprite 1
```

Director will answer with a number:

```
-- 77
```

This means that the registration point (generally the center of a bitmap Cast Member) is on the 77th pixel from the left of the Stage. The same method also works for *the locV of sprite*.

If you really want to start messing with Director's mind, you can change the location of the Sprite. Instead of using the *put* command, you can use the *set* command. Try this in the Message Window (while the movie is running!):

```
set the locH of sprite 1 to 100
```

Boom! Did you see that Sprite jump? If you didn't perhaps you haven't turned Sprite 1 into a Puppet. Make sure you typed the *exitFrame* event handler from the last section correctly. Also, make sure you Rewind the movie before you hit Play.

We're almost done with this exercise. We know how to change a property of a Sprite, using the *set* command. The general form of the *set* command is:

```
set propertyName of sprite spriteNumber to value
```

Value in this case is a specific number, such as 100. To make this exercise happen, to make the skull jump a little on every click, we have to use a relative number. We don't want to say "Move to horizontal position 97." Instead, we want to say "Move 20 pixels farther to the right than you are." We can accomplish this with the following command:

```
set the locH of sprite 1 to the locH of sprite 1 + 20
```

This statement might look confusing because it has *the locH of sprite 1* listed twice. However, Lingo readily understands this line, which means "Set the horizontal location of Sprite 1 to whatever it is right now plus 20 pixels."

When Lingo tries to understand this line, it first sees the word *set*. "OK," the Lingo elf says to itself, "I'm going to change something." Then it sees *the locH of sprite 1*, and it says to itself, "I'm going to change the horizontal location of Sprite 1." Next, it sees the word *to* and says "Oh boy, everything after this word *to* is going to be the new value!"

At this point, the Lingo elf gets tricky. It knows that it is looking for a number because **the *locH of sprite 1*** is a numeric property. However, it is faced with "*the locH of sprite 1 + 20.*" Undeterred, the elf tries to turn this into a number. It first figures out, or **evaluates**, the phrase "*the locH of sprite 1.*" It checks to see what this property is **right now**, before this line has finished executing. For sake of argument, let's say that the Sprite is at horizontal location 77. Now, the Lingo elf is faced with the phrase "77 + 20,"which it knows equals 97.

The final command that the Lingo elf tries to execute is "*set the locH of sprite 1 to 97.*" It easily understands and does this with no problem. Now let's say this line executes again. This time, when the Lingo elf checks the value of the *locH of sprite 1*, it will get 97. It will add 97 and 20, and wind up executing the command *set the locH of Sprite 1 to 117.* Every time this line executes, the right-hand value will increase by 20, causing the Sprite to move 20 pixels to the right.

This whole process, in which the Lingo elf takes apart a line of text until it understands how to execute it, is called **parsing**. When Lingo is presented with a line of text, it **parses** the text until it has a simple understanding of the command and all its arguments, which it can then execute. If the pieces of the line don't come apart correctly, then the Lingo elf gets confused and can't figure out what you are telling it to do. Generally, this causes the movie to stop playing and an Error dialog box to appear.

Finishing Exercise 1

Now we've got all the pieces, so let's put them together.

At this point, our movie Puppet.dir has two event handlers:

- An *exitframe* handler in frame 2 that makes Sprite 1 a Puppet

- An *exitFrame* handler in frame 3 that loops on frame 3

The remaining task in this exercise is to make the face move to the right when it is clicked. We can do this in a *mouseUp* event handler on the skull, either in a Sprite Script or a Cast Member Script. In this case, it doesn't really matter which type of script we use (this is a pretty simple example).

When faced with a situation like this, I usually use Sprite Scripts. The programmer part of my mind likes these more than Cast Member Scripts because they are more flexible in the long run. If I use a Cast Member Script, the script will be attached to the skull no matter where in the movie we use it, forever. If I use the skull six months from now, the Script (which I will have forgotten about) will still be there. Whenever you forget about a Script, it causes bugs. However, if I used a Sprite Script, the skull won't have any baggage attached to it, and I can use it without worry.

Let's put the *mouseUp* event handler on the Sprite Script! In the Score Window, select Sprite 1 in all the frames. Click the Script Preview Button, and type in this Script:

```
on mouseUp

    set the locH of sprite 1 to the locH of sprite 1 + 20

end
```

Close the window, and play the movie. Not bad, eh? Just for kicks, let's make the face move up 10 pixels on every click, in addition to moving right 20 pixels. To do this, we need to add only one line to our Sprite Script. The new event handler should look something like this:

```
on mouseUp

    set the locH of sprite 1 to the locH of sprite 1 + 20

    set the locV of sprite 1 to the locV of sprite 1 - 10

end
```

The finished version of this exercise is saved in Ex1_done.dir.

The next few sections still deal with Puppet Sprites in some way, so don't worry if the concept doesn't seem crystal clear yet.

Exercise 2: Skulls and Cursors

In Exercise 1, we made a skull jump when it was clicked. Our next step is to make it follow the cursor around the stage. To make this happen, we will need to use a new kind of Lingo phrase. So far, we have mostly dealt with Lingo **commands**, which are words or phrases that cause Director to take some action, and **events**, which specify when Lingo should execute specific commands. In this chapter, we have introduced Lingo **Sprite properties**, which describe and define aspects of Sprites.

However, we have also seen a different kind of Lingo phrase, called a **function**. Instead of causing Director to **do** something, a function makes Director reveal a piece of information. The function that we have used already is *the frame*, as in *go to the frame*. The phrase *the frame* doesn't cause Director to take an action; it simply replaces itself with the number of the current frame. When Lingo tries to execute the line *go to the frame*, it first parses the text. The Lingo elf sees *go to* and understands that it is going to make the Playback Head jump somewhere. In the rest of the phrase, the elf expects a frame number or a frame label. In this case, however, it finds neither. Instead, it sees the phrase "the frame" and scratches its head for a microsecond.

Then it realizes, "Hey, that might be a function!" It looks deep into the bowels of Lingo for a function called "the frame." It finds one, so it executes it. The function returns a number, for example, 10. Then the Lingo elf says, "OK, so now the phrase I am looking at is *go to 10*. Hey! I understand that! It means that I should make the Playback Head jump to the tenth frame." (See Figure 4.4.)

So why did I bring this up? (Remember, I always have a reason, even when I can't remember what it is.) We are going to use a couple of functions to keep track of the mouse.

There is a Lingo function called *the mouseH* that returns the horizontal location of the mouse pointer. A related function, *the mouseV*, returns the vertical location of the mouse pointer. If these sound to you like *the locH of sprite* and *the locV of sprite*, well, good. We are going to use these functions and Sprite properties to make the skull follow the mouse.

Implementing Exercise 2

Open the file Puppet.dir again. We are going to modify this movie to complete Exercise 2. As with the last exercise, the first step is to turn the skull Sprite into a Puppet. In the Frame Script of frame 2, put the following script:

Figure 4.4 With *Go to the frame* the Playback Head will jump to the current frame.

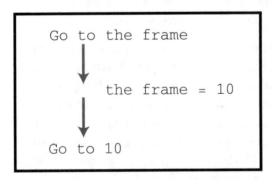

```
on exitFrame

    puppetSprite 1,true

end
```

All right, now Sprite 1 will be put under Lingo control as soon as the Playback Head leaves frame 2.

As the movie plays, the Playback Head will reach frame 3 and start to loop. The Frame Script on this frame is currently

```
on exitFrame

    go to the frame

end
```

Now, we can use *the mouseV* and *the mouseH* to set the position of the Sprite. The Script should become

```
on exitFrame

    set the locV of sprite 1 to the mouseV

    set the locH of sprite 1 to the mouseH

    go to the frame

end
```

Now rewind and play the movie. The skull should follow the mouse pointer as you drag it around.

What is going on here? The Playback Head tries to leave frame 3, triggering an *exitFrame* event. The event is offered to the Frame Script first, which wants it. Then, the Lingo elf executes *set the locV of sprite 1 to the mouseV*, which sets the vertical location of the skull to the vertical location of the mouse pointer. Then it executes *set the locH of sprite 1 to the mouseH*, which sets the horizontal location of the skull to the horizontal location of the mouse pointer. Finally, the Lingo elf executes *go to the frame*, which causes the Playback Head to reenter this frame. Then it tries to leave again, and it repeats the whole process.

Smoothing Exercise 2

Does the movement of the head seem a little choppy to you? That's because the file Puppet.dir is set to run at 15 frames per second. The Playback Head tries to leave a frame every fifteenth of a second, which triggers the *exitFrame* script every fifteenth of a second (if your computer can process that fast). Television, most peoples' default impression of smooth screen movement, runs at 30 fps, or twice the frame rate of our movie. To make the movie run more smoothly, then we'll have to raise the frame rate.

This is easier to do than you might think. You can change the frame rate in the Control Panel Window. Choose Control Panel from the Window menu to open the window. Then, click the Up Arrow in the Tempo area until it reads 30, meaning 30 frames per second (Figure 4.5). Rewind and play the movie. The skull should move much more smoothly now.

The finished version of Exercise 2 is available in the file Ex2_done.dir in the Chapter4 folder on the CD-ROM.

Stop Exercising and Relax for a Minute

When real programmers sit down at a computer to create a program, how do they start? Most people think that they look at a problem, see the solution in their eccentricly brilliant minds, and start typing immediately. This is, of course, complete and utter nonsense.

In real life, programmers proceed much the way this chapter is proceeding (at least I do, and I'm a real programmer, as far as you know). First, I sketch out what

Figure 4.5 Control Panel and the Up Arrow.

Click the Up Arrow
in the Tempo area to
raise the frame rate.

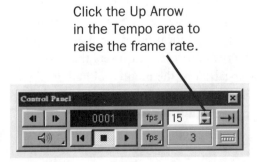

the program is going to be. I try to define the different sections that the finished program will have and get a broad sense of how each of those sections should behave. Then, I pick the sections that I don't know how to program, and I start to hack.

Hacking isn't about breaking into government defense computers. It's about trying to persuade a computer to do something, by any means necessary. Any sufficiently interesting project will require you to do something new, to figure something out. That's when you start hacking the problem.

How do I hack a problem? First, if it's a big problem, I pick just one part of it. Then, I set up a small, isolated situation, with few variables, that lets us experiment easily. Finally, I try any solution that comes to mind.

This solution pretty much never works. But, in making mistakes, I generally get a clearer idea of what I don't understand about the problem. We pull out the books and look for related situations. Then, I try to solve the small, isolated problem again.

This generally doesn't work either, but it gets us closer and helps us understand the problem even better. There are usually a few things (a lot of things) that I didn't even consider at first. Eventually, I figure it out.

Then I hack all the other little problems that make up the program. I usually have tons of little experiment movies lying around, cluttering up the hard disk, by the time I try to tackle the real project.

The process is kind of like what we're doing now, so don't get frustrated. Programming is about guessing, trying, guessing again, looking stuff up, and progressing toward a goal, in baby steps. It will take a few more steps, but we'll get there.

Exercise 3: What a Drag

Our next goal is to let the user drag a skull around. The skull should not move until the user presses down on it with the mouse button. Then, it should follow the mouse around while the button is pressed. Finally, it should stay where it was put when the mouse button is released.

We already know most of the Lingo we will need to accomplish this. To respond to a button-down event, we will use *on mouseDown*. To gain Lingo control of the Sprite, we will use the *puppetSprite* command. To change the location of the Sprite, we will set *the locH of sprite* and *the locV of sprite* properties. To keep track of the mouse pointer, we will use *the mouseH* and *the mouseV* functions.

Going back to Puppet.dir, we could put this event handler in the Sprite Script of Sprite 1, the skull.

```
on mouseDown

    puppetSprite 1,true

    set the locV of sprite 1 to the mouseV

    set the locH of sprite 1 to the mouseH

end
```

Feel free to try this Script. Can you predict what will happen? When you run the movie and click on the skull, the skull will move a little to the cursor—once. It won't follow the mouse pointer around unless you click repeatedly.

The problem? A *mouseDown* event is triggered only **once** when the mouse button is pressed. It will not be triggered again until the button is released and pressed again. When you press the button, the *mouseDown* script is executed, and the skull moves to the mouse pointer. That's it; the event handler won't execute again until you let go of the mouse button and press it again. This is a jump, not a drag.

What we're looking for is a way to execute these commands repeatedly until the mouse button is released. Can't you just feel the new Lingo phrases coming?

Lingo Looping with *repeat while*

Lingo has a couple of commands that let us execute a series of commands, like those above, over and over again while a certain condition, like the mouse button being down, is true. The commands are *repeat while* and *end repeat*. You usually see them in this form:

```
repeat while (some condition)

    -- a bunch of Lingo commands

end repeat
```

You always put the *repeat while* line **immediately before the series of commands to execute repeatedly.** You always put the *end repeat* line **immediately after this series of commands.** Think of this as **framing** the series of commands.

Consider the following example:

```
on mouseDown

    repeat while (3=3)

        beep

    end repeat

end
```

When this script executes, the Lingo elf will first see the line *repeat while (3=3).* It will think to itself, "Is 3 = 3 a true statement? Duh, yes!" Because it is true, the elf will then go inside and execute *beep,* causing your computer to beep once. Then the elf will see the *end repeat* line and realize that it has to jump back to the first line, *repeat while (3=3).*

Again it thinks to itself, "Is 3 = 3 a true statement? Duh, yes!" and starts again, creating a loop. **This will loop an infinite number of times because three will always equal three!** Don't try this at home, or your computer might crash.

The condition inside the parentheses is of paramount importance because it determines how long the loop will continue. Try to figure out this next example:

```
on mouseDown

    go to frame 1

    repeat while (the frame<3)

        go to the frame +1

    end repeat

    beep

end
```

Can you predict the elf's behavior? When this script is executed, the elf will see *go to frame 1,* which will make it move the Playback Head to frame 1. Easy enough.

The next line the elf sees is *repeat while (the frame<3)*. The elf always looks at whatever is in parentheses first, so it narrows its focus to *(the frame < 3)*. The function *the frame* returns the current frame, which was just set to 1. Now the elf sees *(1<3)*, which translates in English to "Is 1 less than 3?" Now, the Lingo elf is no genius, but it is smart enough to know that 1 is, indeed, less than 3. The statement in the parentheses is **true**. Because the condition evaluates to true, the elf executes the first line that is **inside** the loop.

The first line inside the loop is *go to the frame + 1*. *The frame* returns 1, so the elf then sees *go to 1 + 1*. It knows how to add, so the line becomes *go to 2*. The elf recognizes *go to* as slang for *go to frame*, so it moves the Playback Head to frame 2.

The next line is *end repeat,*, which, to the Lingo elf, means "go back to the last *repeat* line, and check the condition again." "Fine," thinks the elf to itself, "I'll go back to *repeat while (the frame<3)*."

This time, *the frame* returns the number 2 because the Playback Head is now on frame 2. The condition is *(2<3)*, or "Is 2 less than 3?" Of course it is, so the elf goes to the inner line again.

This time, *go to the frame + 1* moves us to frame 3. Then the elf moves on to *end repeat*, which pops us back to the *repeat while (the frame<3)*. However, **this time the condition is false.**

The current frame by this time is frame 3, so the condition becomes (3<3), or "Is 3 less than 3?" Even the silly little Lingo elf knows that the answer is **no**, so it decides the condition is now **false**. Because the condition is false, the elf skips right over the inner lines of the loop, past the *end repeat*, and directly to *beep*. The elf makes the computer beep once, and it is done with the handler!

We're Almost There

So, we have established that we need to use *the locV of sprite, the locH of sprite, repeat while,* and *end repeat* to make the skull be dragged around the stage. With what we know, we could get as far as this script, which would be in the Sprite Script of Sprite 1, the skull.

```
on mouseDown

    puppetSprite 1, true

    repeat while ( What goes in here? )
```

```
      set the locV of sprite 1 to the mouseV

      set the locH of sprite 1 to the mouseH

   end repeat

end
```

It's beginning to look useful, isn't it? Our next step is to figure out the correct condition for the repeat loop, that is, to answer the question, "What goes in here?"

To find the answer, let's recall our goal: to move the skull around as long as the mouse button is pressed. Our condition should be, "Is the mouse button pressed down?" Lingo makes this very easy by giving us another built-in function, like *the mouseV* or *the mouseH*. This one is called *the mouseDown* and returns TRUE if the mouse button is down or FALSE if the mouse button is up.

Here is the script now. Remember, it goes in the Sprite Script for Sprite 1, the skull.

```
on mouseDown

   puppetSprite 1, true

   repeat while (the mouseDown = TRUE )

      set the locV of sprite 1 to the mouseV

      set the locH of sprite 1 to the mouseH

   end repeat

end
```

When the user presses the mouse button down on the Sprite, a *mouseDown* event will be triggered, causing this script to be executed. The first thing that the Lingo elf will do is *puppetSprite 1, true*, which will turn Sprite 1 into a Puppet. From now on, you, the Lingo hacker, have total control over this Sprite.

Next, the elf figures out whether it should go inside the *repeat while* loop by checking the condition. When the Lingo elf tries to evaluate the condition *(the mouseDown = TRUE)*, it will first see the words *the mouseDown*. It will say, "Hmm, let me check the mouse button (the left mouse button on a two-button mouse). Oh, yes, it is being pressed right now. This function should return TRUE."

When the function returns, the elf takes another look at the condition, which now is *(TRUE = TRUE)*, or "Does TRUE equal TRUE?" It does, sure as shootin'. Because the condition is true, the elf will go inside the *repeat while* loop and execute the two *set* commands. These commands change the location of the Sprite to the mouse location. Eventually, it will hit the *end repeat*, go back up to the *repeat while*, and check the condition again.

Let's pretend, by this time, that the user has let go of the mouse button. The Lingo elf will see *(the mouseDown = TRUE)* and go out and check the mouse button. Because the button is up, the function will return FALSE. At this point, the elf will take another look at the condition, which has become (FALSE = TRUE) or "Does FALSE = TRUE?" The elf will say "Hell, no!" and decide not to go inside the *repeat while* loop. Instead, it will skip to the line after the *end repeat*, which is *end*. This tells the elf to finish executing the handler.

Aren't we done with Exercise 3? Doesn't it seem to do everything we have ever wanted it to do? Can't we go home now?

Almost. We still have a problem. Logically, this script seems to do everything we could want. It starts when the mouse is pressed down on the Sprite, moves the Sprite around continuously until the button is released, and, because the Sprite is a Puppet and doesn't listen to the Score anymore, the Sprite will stay just where we left it. It won't move again until it gets another Lingo command to move or a *puppetSprite 1,FALSE* command to release it from the bonds of Puppethood and put it back under the spell of the Score.

So what's the problem? Type the script into Puppet.dir and see for yourself. The logic is flawless, but the program doesn't work. When you drag the skull, it doesn't go anywhere. When you release the mouse button, it suddenly jumps to the mouse pointer. What's going on? More than you know. The Stage is not alone.

The Invisible Stage

Don't worry, I'm not going off on a transcendental, New Age discourse about the invisible universe behind the Director Stage that parallels the Stage that we know. Instead, I'll go off on a technical discourse about the invisible universe behind the Director Stage that parallels the Stage that we know.

Let's call it the **Invisible Stage**. Director actually keeps a copy of the Stage somewhere off-screen. You can't see it, but it's there. When you make changes to Puppet

Sprite properties, such as the *locV of sprite* or the *locH of sprite*, **Director only changes their locations on the Invisible Stage** (Figure 4.6a). The Normal Stage doesn't change at all (Figure 4.6b).

However, the next time the Playback Head moves, Director copies the contents of the Invisible Stage to the Normal Stage. Let me say this again.

Figure 4.6a The Invisible Stage. Notice the position of the skull.

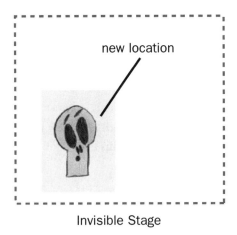

new location

Invisible Stage

Figure 4.6b The Normal Stage. Notice the position of the skull.

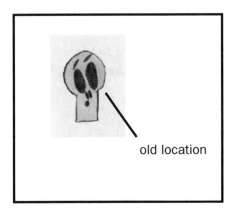

old location

Normal Stage
(will update when
Playback Head moves)

Changes to Puppet Sprites occur only on the Invisible Stage. The Normal Stage is updated only when the Playback Head moves between frames or within the same frame.

If all this is true, then why did Exercise 2 work? We didn't even know about the Invisible Stage back then, and it still worked fine. You might be thinking I'm trying to pull one over on you.

Let's take a look at the scripts from Exercise 2. The first script that gets executed is in the Frame Script of frame 2.

```
on exitFrame

    puppetSprite 1,true

end
```

From now on, Sprite 1 will be a Puppet. Then the Playback Head advances to frame 3 and tries to leave it, causing this next Script to execute. This event handler is in the Frame Script of frame 3.

```
on exitFrame

    set the locV of sprite 1 to the mouseV

    set the locH of sprite 1 to the mouseH

    go to the frame

end
```

The Lingo elf comes along and executes *set the locV of sprite 1 to the mouseV*. The elf immediately changes the vertical location of Sprite 1 **on the Invisible Stage.** Then it executes *set the locH of sprite 1 to the mouseH*. It immediately changes the horizontal location of Sprite 1 **on the Invisible Stage.**

Finally, it executes *go to the frame*. This causes the Playback Head to move within the current frame (from frame 3 to frame 3.) When this happens, Director **copies the contents of the Invisible Stage onto the normal Stage,** showing us the newly positioned Sprite 1.

If you want to force Director to copy the contents of the Invisible Stage to the Normal Stage, all it takes is one command: *updateStage.* Whenever the Lingo elf sees this command, it forces Director to update the normal Stage from the Invisible one.

Finishing Exercise 3

In Exercise 3, we want to update the Stage every time the Sprite is moved. The Sprite is moved on every pass through the *repeat while* loop, so we'll put the *updateStage* command inside the loop.

Here's the final script for Exercise 3. It goes in the Sprite Script of Sprite 1, on frame 3. A finished version of Exercise 3 is in file Ex3_done.dir in the 4Chapter4 folder on the CD-ROM.

```
on mouseDown

    puppetSprite 1, true

    repeat while (the mouseDown = TRUE )

        set the locV of sprite 1 to the mouseV

        set the locH of sprite 1 to the mouseH

        updateStage

    end repeat

end
```

Let's try a variation of this exercise. The next step: After the user drags the Sprite around and lets go of the mouse button, the skull should snap back to where it started. Instead of staying where it was put, the skull always returns to the same location it started in.

How can we do this? Well, the position that it started in is the Sprite's position in the Score. How can we release Lingo control of the Sprite, to force it to take orders from the Score? We can un-Puppet it!

To turn Sprite 1 from a nice, Lingo-controlled Puppet back to a plain old Score-controlled Sprite, we issue the command *puppetSprite 1, false*. Here's the script for the revised Exercise 3.

```
on mouseDown

    puppetSprite 1, true
```

```
repeat while (the mouseDown = TRUE )

    set the locV of sprite 1 to the mouseV

    set the locH of sprite 1 to the mouseH

    updateStage

end repeat

puppetSprite 1, false

end
```

Exercise 4: Getting the Picture

We continue in our relentless march toward the Chapter 4 project. We know that in the chapter project, the user is able to drag the skulls around and deposit them in the picture frames. We have already figured out how to drag the skulls. The next problem: How do we deposit them in a picture frame?

To solve this problem, we will set up a simple case, in which we have one skull and one picture frame. Here's how Exercise 4 is supposed to work:

- The user drags the skull around the Stage, as in Exercise 3 (Figure 4.7).

- When the user lets go of the button, the skull snaps back to its original position.

- If the skull was touching the inside of the frame when the user let go, a copy of the skull appears in the frame (Figure 4.7).

The finished version of Exercise 4 is in file Ex4_done.dir in the 4Chapter4 folder on the CD-ROM. The unfinished version is in file Ex4.dir in the 4Chapter4 folder on the CD-ROM. Open the file now, so we can work with it.

Starting with What We Already Know

The first part of this exercise is a problem that we solved back in Exercise 3. The user must be able to drag the skull around and let go of it. When the user lets go of the mouse button, the skull should snap back to its original position.

To put this functionality into Exercise 4, we can just use the script from the last exercise. Of course, we will have to adjust the Sprite numbers to reflect the Score for Ex4.dir, which is different from the Score in Exercise 3 (Figure 4.8).

Figure 4.7 The user drags the skull. If the user releases the skull, a copy stays in the picture frame.

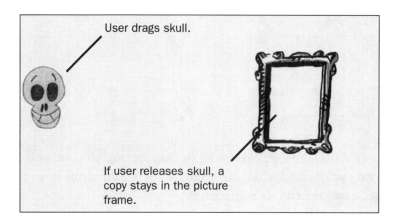

In this movie, the skull is in Sprite Channel 3. So, put this Script into the Sprite Script of Sprite 3, in frame 2.

```
on mouseDown

    puppetSprite 3,true
```

Figure 4.8 The Sprites.

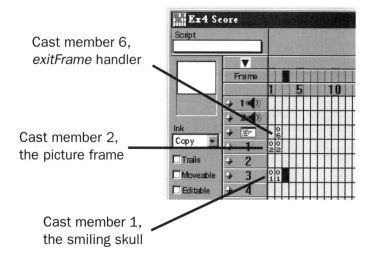

```
repeat while (the mouseDown = TRUE )

    set the locV of sprite 3 to the mouseV

    set the locH of sprite 3 to the mouseH

    updateStage

end repeat

puppetSprite 3,false

end
```

Rewind and play your movie. You should be able to drag the skull around, as in the last exercise. If it isn't working, check to make sure you typed the script correctly and that you put it into the correct Sprite Script.

Making Decisions with If .. Then

As a Lingo programmer, you won't always be there when the Lingo elf is faced with a tough decision. Lucky for you, the elf is a faithful servant and will follow the guidelines that you set up for it.

We have already seen one way to define the guidelines for a questionable situation. The *repeat while* command serves as a guideline to help the elf make a decision.

```
repeat while (the mouseDown = 1)

    beep

end repeat
```

Here's the situation: The elf has to decide whether to execute the command *beep*. How is it going to make this decision? It's going to look for the guidelines laid down by you, its master. **The guideline that you left was in the condition** "If the mouse is down, then execute *beep*. Otherwise, just skip over it." The elf, confident that it understands what you expect of it, goes ahead and makes the decision based on the current information at the time.

The problem with *repeat while* is that it is only well suited for situations that need to make the same decision repeatedly, such as loops. It is awkward to use this command if you want the decision to be made only once.

Lingo gives us another command that we can use to define guidelines for the elf, called *if .. then*. Here is the normal form:

```
if (some condition) then

    -- a bunch of Lingo commands

end if
```

That's right, *if .. then* uses the same kind of condition that *repeat while* uses. If we wanted to restate the *repeat while* example, we could do it like this:

```
if ( the mouseDown = 1 ) then

    beep

end if
```

As the Lingo elf gets to the first line, it sees *if (the mouseDown = 1) then*. When it starts to parse the line, it sees "if" and "then."

"OK," says the elf to itself, "I'm about to make a decision." Next, it tries to figure out whether the condition, inside the parentheses, is TRUE or FALSE. Let's say that it is TRUE, meaning that the mouse button is depressed at this moment. This will cause the elf to execute whatever is inside the "if.. then," which is *beep*. After making this decision, the elf keeps going forward in the script. **It does not loop back up**, as it would with *repeat while*.

Let's try another example, this time in English instead of Lingo. Let's make it a guideline for your Significant Other (or a friend, if you're single). Here's the guideline: "**If** you are late, **then** you will beg and grovel."

So your Significant Other gets to the party late and is sweating buckets. At this point, he/she/it has to decide what to do. What are the guidelines? Oh yeah, check the piece of paper in the back pocket.

```
if ( on time = false ) then

    beg

    grovel

end if
```

Because he/she/it is not on time, then he/she/it knows what to do. Your Significant Other decides to come in, begging and groveling. And then goes on with the party.

Let's say that, back when you wrote the guideline, there was another incentive: "**If** you are late, **then** you will beg and grovel, **otherwise** you will gloat and strut." Here's what that would look like.

```
if (on time = false) then

    beg

    grovel

else

    gloat

    strut

end if
```

Lingo's term for "otherwise" is *else*. So if your SigOth gets to the party on time, meaning that *(on time = false)* **is not a true statement**, then he/she/it will gloat and strut. If he/she/it is late, then he/she/it will still beg and grovel.

If .. Then and Exercise 4

What does all this have to do with Exercise 4? Well, our task was to figure out whether the skull that has been dragged around is touching the picture frame. In other words, we would like to lay down this guideline for the elf: "**If the skull Sprite touches the painting Sprite, then** put a copy of the skull into the painting." Here it is in pseudo-Lingo:

```
if ( skull sprite touches painting sprite ) then

    put a copy of the skull into the painting

end if
```

The Sprite..Intersects Function

Conveniently, Lingo supplies us with a function that will tell us if two Sprites are touching. It is called *sprite..intersects*.

This function takes two arguments. If we wanted to check if Sprite 5 was touching (intersecting) Sprite 6, then the function would look like this: *sprite 5 intersects 6*. If they intersected, the function would return TRUE, otherwise, FALSE. Which Sprite number you put first makes no difference.

Take a look at the file Ex4.dir again. If you look in the Score, you'll see that the skull is in Sprite Channel 3 and the picture frame is in Sprite Channel 1. So, our *if.. then* command is beginning to take shape.

```
if ( sprite 3 intersects 1 ) then

    - put a copy of the skull into the painting

end if
```

Regrouping

Here's what the Sprite Script for the skull looks like with the if..then.

```
on mouseDown

    puppetSprite 3,true

    repeat while (the mouseDown = true)

        set the locV of sprite 3 to the mouseV

        set the locH of sprite 3 to the mouseH

        updateStage

    end repeat

    if ( sprite 3 intersects 1 ) then

        -- put a copy of the skull into the painting

    end if

    puppetSprite 3,false

end
```

When the user presses the button on the skull, this event handler is executed. First, the skull Sprite is puppetted. Next, the skull is dragged in the *repeat while* loop. When the mouse button is released, the elf skips past the loop to the *if..then* line.

At this point, we check to see if the skull was put down on top of the painting, using sprite..intersects. If they do intersect, the elf will execute that enigmatic line, "—put a copy of the skull into the painting." Finally, we un-Puppet the skull Sprite, which causes it to snap back to its starting place.

Putting the Skull into the Painting: The memberNum property

We will finish Exercise 4 in a way that may seem weird to you but is a normal technique in programming. First, we are going to finish the exercise the easy way, which will lead to a couple of errors. Then, we will go back and fix the errors, one by one. First, though, let's go the easy route.

Back when I introduced you to Puppets, we talked about properties of Sprites. The two that we used were *the locV of sprite* and *the locH of sprite*, which determine the vertical and horizontal locations of a Sprite on the Stage. To put a copy of the skull onto the Stage, we are going to use another Sprite property called *the memberNum of sprite*.

You can think of a **Sprite** as an invisible rectangle on the Stage, having no picture information of its own. Instead, it is attached to a member of the Cast.

In Ex4.dir, the picture frame is attached to Sprite 1. The image itself lives in Cast Member 2. So, we could say that "the memberNum of Sprite 1 is 2" (Figure 4.9). In fact, if you are running the movie, you can open up the Message Window and type this:

```
put the memberNum of sprite 1
```

Director will answer immediately.

```
-- 2
```

The useful thing about this is that you can change *the memberNum of sprite* property at any time, as long as the Sprite is a Puppet. In fact, we could easily change the Cast Member attached to Sprite 1 with these two lines of Lingo...

```
puppetSprite 1, true
```

```
set the memberNum of sprite 1 to 1
```

Figure 4.9 Sprite 1 is attached to Cast Member 2.

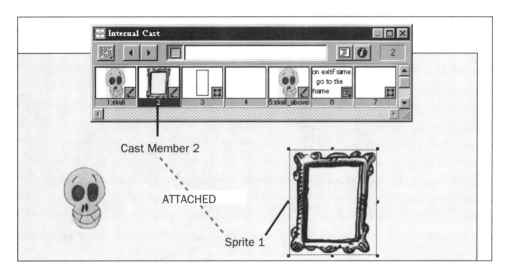

The first line turns Sprite 1 into a Puppet, if it wasn't already. The second line **sets** a Lingo property **to** a new value, just like we did earlier with *the locV of sprite* and *the locH of sprite*. This time, we are setting *the memberNum of sprite 1 to 1*, which is the Cast Member number of the skull. In effect, we are replacing the picture frame image with the smiling skull image.

In the context of Exercise 4, we want this to happen only if the skull Sprite was dragged on top of the picture frame Sprite, so we put these lines inside the *if..then*. Our latest Sprite Script reads like this:

```
on mouseDown

    puppetSprite 3,true

    repeat while (the mouseDown = true)

        set the locV of sprite 3 to the mouseV

        set the locH of sprite 3 to the mouseH

        updateStage

    end repeat
```

```
if ( sprite 3 intersects 1 ) then

    puppetSprite 1, true

    set the memberNum of sprite 1 to 1

  end if

puppetSprite 3,false

end
```

Try typing this into Ex4.dir. The above script goes on Sprite 3, in frame 3.

Let's review. The functionality we have accomplished so far is the following:

- The user drags the skull around the Stage, as in Exercise 3.

- When the user releases the button, the skull snaps back to its original position.

- If the skull was touching **any part** of the frame when the user released the mouse button, a copy of the skull **replaces** the picture frame.

This isn't quite what we wanted to do, but we're getting there. There are a couple of problems:

1. If the skull touches the picture frame anywhere, the switch happens. It should happen only when the skull touches the **inside** of the frame.

2. The copy of the skull replaces the entire picture frame, instead of just appearing inside it.

Fixing the Problems

We ran into the first problem because Lingo, for good reason, does not have a "Sprite 3 intersects **the inside of the picture frame of 1**" function. Lingo doesn't understand the contents of the image; that's up to us. What we can do, though, is add a new Sprite. This Sprite will be an invisible box, placed and sized just inside the frame. You're going to have to draw it yourself.

Show the Tool Palette. Choose Tool Palette under the Window menu, if you don't see it (Figure 4.10). Next, click its empty box and dotted line icons.

Now, draw a rectangle on the Stage, directly covering the inside area of the picture frame, as in Figure 4.11.

Figure 4.10 Click the empty box and dotted line icons in the tool palette.

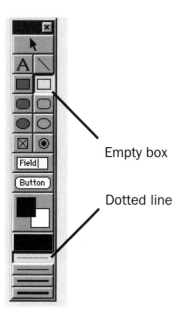

Empty box

Dotted line

Open the Score Window. You just created a Cast Member and a Sprite. The Sprite probably showed up in Sprite Channel 4. Click on it, and drag it up to Sprite Channel 2, in frame 1. Double-click on the number 2, to select all of channel 2. Finally, choose In Between from the Modify menu to fill frame 2 with the same Sprite. Your finished Score should look like Figure 4.12.

Figure 4.11 Directly cover the inside of the picture frame.

Drag from here to here

Figure 4.12 The finished Score.

Cast Member 6,
exitFrame handler

Cast Member 2,
the picture frame

Cast Member 7,
the invisible box

Cast Member 1,
the smiling skull

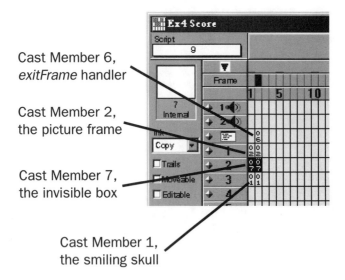

Now we can fix our Script. When we test for intersection, we have been check-ing to see if the skull Sprite (Sprite 3) intersects the picture frame Sprite (Sprite 1). The *if..then* test has looked like this:

```
if ( sprite 3 intersects 1 ) then
```

Now we can change this to what we **really** want. We really want to check if the skull Sprite (Sprite 3) is intersecting the invisible box Sprite that we just cre-ated (Sprite 2). Because the invisible box is in the correct shape and location for the inside of the picture frame, it makes a perfect test. The new *if..then* should be this:

```
if ( sprite 3 intersects 2 ) then
```

The latest version of our Sprite Script is this:

```
on mouseDown

    puppetSprite 3,true

    repeat while (the mouseDown = true)

        set the locV of sprite 3 to the mouseV
```

```
     set the locH of sprite 3 to the mouseH

     updateStage

   end repeat

   if ( sprite 3 intersects 2 ) then

     puppetSprite 1, true

     set the memberNum of sprite 1 to 1

   end if

   puppetSprite 3,false

end
```

Update your own Script, and experiment with the places of intersection. This solves the first problem.

Our new, invisible-box Sprite also solves our second problem. Instead of changing the Cast Member attached to the picture frame Sprite, we can change the Cast Member associated with the invisible box Sprite. This way, the picture frame will stay on-screen, and the copy of the skull will appear inside it!

We continue to change the *if..then* block of commands. We have already changed it to read "If the skull Sprite intersects the invisible box Sprite, then do some commands." Now we want to change these commands.

Instead of turning Sprite 1, the picture frame, into a Puppet, we want to turn Sprite 2, the invisible box Sprite, into a Puppet. So, we change *puppetSprite 1, true* to *puppetSprite 2,true*.

Now that Sprite 2 is a Puppet, we can change its attached Cast Member to the skull Cast Member. Instead of *set the memberNum of sprite 1 to 1*, we type *set the memberNum of sprite 2 to 1*. The whole *if..then* block will look like this:

```
if ( sprite 3 intersects 2 ) then

   puppetSprite 2, true

   set the memberNum of sprite 2 to 1

end if
```

Update the Sprite Script and try it out. We solved our second problem! But now we have a couple more.

Fixing the Fixes for Exercise 4

If you have kept your movie current with this discussion, Figure 4.13 is the result you should see when you drag the skull into the picture frame.

Again, there are a couple of problems with the solution:

1. The new copy of the skull is bigger than it should be.

2. The new copy of the skull does not appear in the center of the picture frame but actually appears near the top-left corner.

The first problem arises because the invisible box you drew was a different size than the skull Cast Member (Figure 4.14). When you change the *memberNum* of a Puppet Sprite, Director assumes that you want it to stretch the Cast Member to fit the width and height of the existing Sprite.

You can alter this behavior with Lingo. There is another Sprite Property called *the stretch of sprite*. The stretch of a Sprite can be TRUE, which tells Director to stretch a new Cast Member to fit, or FALSE, which tells Director to leave the Cast Member at its normal size. Because the default for this property is TRUE, and the results aren't pretty, we want to set it to FALSE. We can do that with a normal *set..to* command.

Figure 4.13 After the skull has been dragged, it appears bloated and off-center.

Figure 4.14 Because the box was a different size than the skull Cast Member, the skull appears stretched.

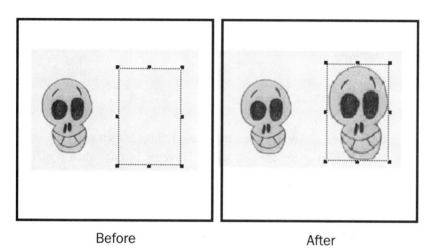

Before   After

```
set the memberNum of Sprite 2 to 1

set the stretch of sprite 2 to false
```

Because this command works only on Puppet Sprites, we have to insert it after we turn Sprite 2 into a Puppet. Here's the new *if..then* block.

```
if ( sprite 3 intersects 2 ) then

   puppetSprite 2, true

   set the stretch of sprite 2 to false

   set the memberNum of sprite 2 to 1

end if
```

Now, the skull will be the correct size when we switch it in. It still won't be in the right place, of course. One down, one to go.

Registration Points

Our second problem is also related to switching a Sprite's Cast Members on the fly. We have a conflict of **registration points**.

Every Cast Member has a point by which it is anchored. For a bitmap Cast Member, this point is, by default, the center of the image. To see a bitmap's

registration point, open the Cast Member in the Paint Window and click the
Registration Point icon. If you wanted to, you could change the registration point
for this bitmap by clicking on the image with this tool selected (Figure 4.15).

In our movie, Sprite 3 is attached to Cast Member 1, the skull. Let's say we execute the following two lines of Lingo:

```
set the locH of sprite 3 to 100

set the locV of sprite 3 to 120
```

What are we actually saying? Well, we are definitely telling Director to move the
Sprite to location 100,120. What we are also telling Director is that, when it paints

Figure 4.15 The registration point tool and the registration point.

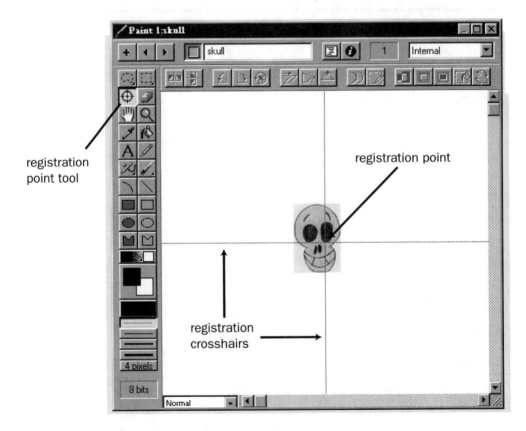

the attached Cast Member to the Stage, it should position the image so that location 100,120 matches the registration point of the Cast Member. Because the registration point is at the center of the image, the image will be centered around 100,120 on the Stage.

First, save the movie. Then try changing the registration point on Cast Member 1, then running the movie. Change it a few times until you begin to get a feel for the way the registration point affects location. Double-click on the registration tool to make it jump back to the center of the bitmap.

Our problem exists because Director's design is inherently silly, in many ways. For a bitmap Cast Member, the registration point always defaults to the center of the image. This is great except that for a **shape**, which is drawn from the toolbox, the Registration Point is always the top left (Figure 4.16).

This creates a major problem for us. When this line executes

```
set the memberNum of sprite 2 to 1
```

Director will change the Cast Member attached to Sprite 2. It will switch the box shape, with a top-left registration point, for the skull bitmap, with a center registration point. In other words, it aligns the center of the skull image with the top left of the invisible box shape. The resulting situation looks like Figure 4.17.

Figure 4.16 The registration point default is the center for an image, top left for shapes.

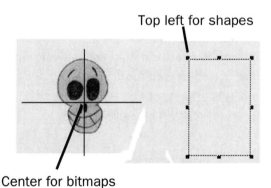

Top left for shapes

Center for bitmaps

Figure 4.17 Unstretched skull in top left of picture frame.

When I created this exercise, my first solution was to move the skull's registration point above and to the left of the skull. This way, when we switch the invisible box for the skull, their registration points would align, and the skull would be painted below and to the right of the registration point. In other words, the skull would appear in the middle of the picture frame.

Try moving the registration point for the skull Cast Member to somewhere above and to the left of the skull (Figure 4.18). Run the movie, and see what happens.

Almost! The skull gets placed more or less correctly, but it seems like it's in the wrong place when you drag it (Figure 4.19). When we drag the skull, we repeatedly set its horizontal and vertical locations to those of the mouse. Whenever Director paints the Sprite's attached Cast Member, it lines up the registration point with the Sprite location. Because the registration point is above and left of the skull, it looks like you are dragging air.

There are a dozen ways to fix this, but I chose one that seems simple. I put two copies of the skull in the Cast, one with a centered registration point and one with an above-left registration point. The centered skull is used for dragging, and the top-left skull is used to switch into the invisible box Sprite. The centered skull is called "skull" in Cast Member 1, and the above-left skull is called "skull_aboveleft" in Cast Member 5.

To finally finish Exercise 4, you should first make sure the registration point for Cast Member 1 is centered (double-click on the registration tool in the Paint

Figure 4.18 The skull is dragged when the mouse is above and to the left.

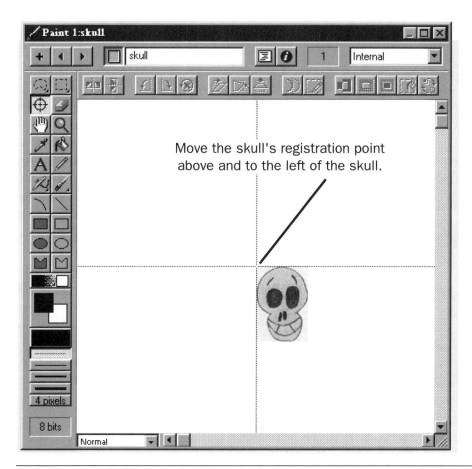

Figure 4.19 Skull with top-left registration point.

Window). This will allow dragging to work correctly. Next, modify our script so that the invisible box is switched for Cast Member 5, instead of Cast Member 1.

```
if ( sprite 3 intersects 2 ) then

    puppetSprite 2, true

    set the stretch of sprite 2 to false

    set the memberNum of sprite 2 to 5

end if
```

That's it! Exercise 4 is officially finished. If you can't get your copy working, compare it to the file Ex4_done.dir in the 4Chapter4 folder on the CD-ROM.

Here is the final Sprite Script for Sprite 3.

```
on mouseDown

    puppetSprite 3,true

    repeat while (the mouseDown = true)

        set the locV of sprite 3 to the mouseV

        set the locH of sprite 3 to the mouseH

        updateStage

    end repeat

    if ( sprite 3 intersects 2 ) then

        puppetSprite 2, true

        set the stretch of sprite 2 to false

        set the memberNum of sprite 2 to 5

    end if

    puppetSprite 3,false

end
```

Take a break; you deserve it. When you're ready, we'll move on to Exercise 5.

Exercise 5: Handling Handlers

As I mentioned before, it is quite common to start building a program by experimenting with small test cases, like the exercises in this chapter. You always reach a point, of course, when you have to apply your small test cases to your big project.

This exercise is an example of growing a small test case. Exercise 5 is based on the solution we invented in Exercise 4, that is, dragging and dropping a skull into a picture frame. This time, however, there are four picture frames and four skulls.

Figure 4.20 shows the first frame of the file Ex5.dir.

If you're keeping track, this is the same setup as the final project later in this chapter. I left out the background and the painter, though, so we can concentrate on getting the skulls and picture frames working. In Exercise 6, we'll finish the chapter project.

Figure 4.20 The first frame.

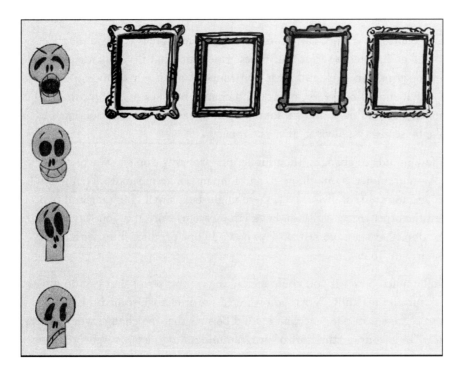

OK, here's the intended behavior for this project:

- The user can drag any of the four skulls around, but when the mouse button is released, the skull snaps back to its normal position.

- If the user drops a skull on a picture frame, a copy of the skull is left in the frame.

- The user can put the same skull in as many picture frames as he or she wants.

So What's Hard About This?

I know what you're thinking. You're thinking "I just did this. It's like Exercise 4 all over again." Well, in a way it is. Instead of one skull Sprite, there are four. You could just copy the Sprite Script for the skull from Exercise 4 and paste it into the Sprite Scripts for each skull in this chapter. You might have to adjust a few Sprite numbers, but that's not hard. You'd probably have to add a few more *if..then* statements, to check for intersection with the other three picture frames. No sweat!

Normally, our theory is "Any solution that works is a good solution." So, theoretically, I don't have a problem with this solution.

Except, of course, that I do. Duplicating a script many times is a bad idea. Let's say you copied and pasted a script four times. Fine, but what if you made a mistake in the original script? Go back and fix it four times. What if you change your mind about the way it should behave? Go back and change four scripts. Oops, that caused another bug. Go back and fix four scripts. In case you are wondering, changes like these always, always, always happen.

After a few rounds of changes, the four scripts probably don't look exactly alike anymore. A programmer is only human, and humans make mistakes. Even if skulls one, three, and four are totally correct, there might be a small glitch in skull two. But you test the other three skulls, and everything seems fine, and you forget or are too tired or don't have time to test skull two. And your product ships with a bug, just waiting to bite an end user.

It would be much better if you could create one central script that can do most of the work for all the skulls. When you want to fix or change something, you'd only have to change it in one place, and you'd be sure that the change would affect all the skulls. To encourage this sort of programming, Lingo lets us write our own custom handlers.

Script Central: Rolling Your Own Handlers in the Movie Script

So far, we have been adding our Lingo commands to event handlers: *mouseUp* handlers, *mouseDown* handlers, *exitFrame* handlers, and so on. If you've wanted the same (or almost the same) Lingo commands to execute in four different *mouseDown* handlers, you have had to make four copies of the script, leading to the problems we just talked about.

What Lingo allows you to do is to write one handler, a **custom, programmer-defined handler**, into which you can put one sequence of commands. Any other handler, such as the four *mouseDown* handlers I just mentioned, can execute your custom handler, just by calling its name. (This is the same way you invoke a demon, in case you were wondering.)

For example, if I wanted to put the *mouseDown* commands from Exercise 4 into a roll-our-own handler, I could type this:

```
on dragSprite3AroundForAwhile

    puppetSprite 3,true

    repeat while (the mouseDown = true)

        set the locV of sprite 3 to the mouseV

        set the locH of sprite 3 to the mouseH

        updateStage

    end repeat

    if ( sprite 3 intersects 2 ) then

        puppetSprite 2, true

        set the stretch of sprite 2 to false

        set the memberNum of sprite 2 to 5

    end if

    puppetSprite 3,false

end
```

My arbitrary, made-up name for the handler is *dragSprite3AroundForAwhile*. I would probably put this handler into the Movie Script.

To edit the Movie Script, hold down Control-Shift-U (or Command-Shift-U on the Macintosh). This key combination is a relic from Director's scandalous past, and it doesn't really make much sense anymore. You can create a new Movie Script for the first time by clicking the + button in any Script Window. You can also edit the Movie Script by finding the Movie Script Cast Member in the Cast and double-clicking it. Control-Shift-U is generally the easiest way to get to it.

Once you open the Movie Script, you can type the *dragSprite3AroundForAwhile* handler. Because it lives in the Movie Script, the *dragSprite3AroundForAwhile* handler will be available to any other handler in this Movie.

Say you wanted to drag a skull around using this handler. You could easily put a *mouseDown* handler in its Sprite Script. All the handler would have to do is call our custom handler.

```
on mouseDown

    dragSprite3AroundForAwhile

end
```

When the user presses on this Sprite, the Lingo elf executes the *mouseDown* handler. The first line it sees, of course, is *dragSprite3AroundForAwhile*. "Hmm," it says to itself, "what is this? It sure isn't in my normal vocabulary. Hey, what if it is a custom, programmer-defined handler? Let me check the handlers in the Movie Script. Look, there it is! I think I'll execute it."

So the elf goes ahead and executes the commands in the *dragSprite3Around-ForAwhile* handler. All the commands work as they had before, and eventually the elf reaches the end of the custom handler. When it sees the *end* statement, it says to itself, "Now which handler called this one? Oh yeah, that *mouseDown* handler. I guess I should go back up there." Finally, the Lingo elf looks at the next line in the *mouseDown* script, the one directly after the completed handler call. The next line is *end*, which is the Lingo elf's cue to take a rest until something else happens.

You can put as many custom or event handlers as you want into a Movie Script. All the custom handlers in a Movie Script are accessible to any other handler anywhere in the Movie, meaning any Sprite, Cast, Frame, or Movie Script handler. A custom handler can call another custom handler. Creating a new custom handler is like adding a new verb to Lingo's vocabulary.

We still haven't solved our problem, though. If we have four skulls that we have to drag around, each skull is going to be in a different Sprite. Unfortunately, the script in *dragSprite3AroundForAwhile* only moves around Sprite 3, so these commands apply only to one skull. We need a way to **generalize** this script so that we can use it for any Sprite. To do this, we need to use a **variable**.

Variables Are Your Friends

Computer programs often need to store a piece of information that will change from time to time. Because this factoid is not constant, it is called a **variable**.

Lingo supports two categories of variables: **global** and **local**. A **global variable** is a variable that remembers its factoid forever, until the program quits. We don't need global variables for this project, so I'll save the discussion of them until later. If you want a discussion of global variables, read Chapter 6, "A Quicktime Player."

A **local variable** remembers its factoid only for the length of the handler. Once the handler is over, the factoid is forgotten. In fact, the existence of the variable is completely forgotten, so the next time the handler executes, the variable is created again, and it is again destroyed when the handler finishes.

Understanding and Using Variables

You can think of a variable as an **invisible box** that exists in the Lingo elf's mind. If you aren't feeling so poetic, you can think of a variable as a **location** in the computer's RAM memory. (Yes, I know "Random Access Memory memory" is redundant, but I'm trying to be clear.) This location in memory, this invisible box, is always stuffed with a **value**, like a number or a string. This box also has a **name**, so you can refer to it.

You use variables to keep track of things in your program that change. To generalize *dragSprite3AroundForAwhile*, we are going to use a variable to keep track of the Sprite number. We might call this variable "spriteNum" because we want it to contain a Sprite number. We could just as easily call it "harry" or "x125" or "auntMary." You can picture a variable looking a little like Figure 4.21, in RAM.

Figure 4.21 A variable.

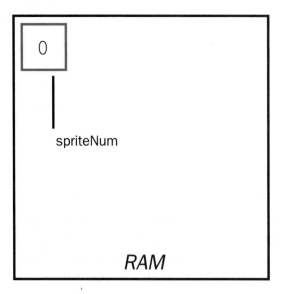

As you can see, this variable *spriteNum* is a place in the computer's RAM, and it holds the number value, zero.

You can put a different value into the variable, meaning you can stuff it with a different piece of information, with a simple Lingo command. We use the *put* command, which we have seen before. This time, though, it has an *into* clause. The following line stuffs the number 6 into the variable *spriteNum*.

```
put 6 into spriteNum
```

After executing this line, the variable in memory might look like Figure 4.22.

You can also put a different **type** of value into this variable, like a string.

```
put "Don't you just love that Lingo Elf?" into spriteNum
```

Now the variable looks something like Figure 4.23.

However, if we stuffed a string into this particular variable, we would be committing a serious programmer's faux pas. We called this variable spriteNum because we were going to use it to keep track of a sprite number. A string, especially a string like "Don't you just love that Lingo elf?" doesn't really hold true to the idea of a Sprite number.

Figure 4.22 New variable.

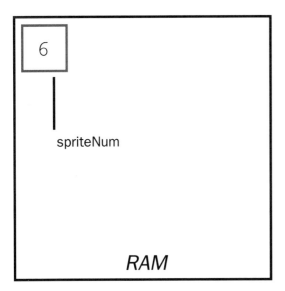

Lingo lets us do this, of course. We're only confusing ourselves. You can refer to a variable's value just by stating its name. This is similar to executing a custom handler

Figure 4.23 Variable with a string as value.

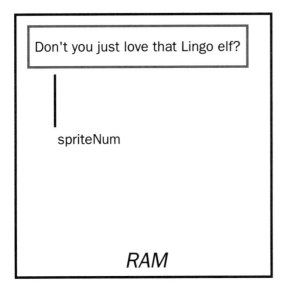

just by stating its name. This is also similar to invoking a demon just by stating its name.

This code fragment will turn Sprite 6 into a Puppet.

```
put 6 into spriteNum
```

```
puppetSprite spriteNum, TRUE
```

The first line causes the Lingo elf to create a box in its mind and give it the name *spriteNum*. When the Lingo elf sees the second line, it first reads the word *puppetSprite*. This lets it know to look for a number in the next word. Instead it encounters *spriteNum*. "This isn't a number!" the elf declares. "It's not the first word in the command, so it can't be a custom handler. Is it perhaps a variable?"

The elf then looks into its memory for a box called *spriteNum*. "There it is! The value of *spriteNum* right now is 6." It takes the value and replaces the variable name with it. The new line it tries to parse is this:

```
puppetSprite 6, TRUE
```

The elf understands readily enough and executes. Sprite 6 is now a Puppet.

What you should realize is that we could easily change the effect of these two lines of Lingo by changing just one character. This small fragment of code will turn Sprite 3 into a Puppet.

```
put 3 into spriteNum
```

```
puppetSprite spriteNum, TRUE
```

So, the first step in generalizing our custom handler is to turn all the hard-coded references to the number 3 into soft-coded, generalized references to a variable. We could call this variable *spriteNum*, as we have been. But just to mess with your mind, we're going to call it *snum*. You should remember, *snum* is short for **sprite number**, which means we want to store a **number** in this variable that represents a **sprite channel**. You should also remember that variable names are made up by the programmer and are completely arbitrary.

A rewrite of the custom handler might look like this.

```
on dragSprite3AroundForAwhile

    put 3 into snum
```

```
    puppetSprite snum,true

    repeat while (the mouseDown = true)

        set the locV of sprite snum to the mouseV

        set the locH of sprite snum to the mouseH

        updateStage

    end repeat

    if ( sprite snum intersects 2 ) then

        puppetSprite 2, true

        set the stretch of sprite 2 to false

        set the memberNum of sprite 2 to 5

    end if

    puppetSprite snum,false

end
```

When the elf executes this handler and sees the first line, *put 3 into snum*, it will create a variable in memory called *snum* and stuff it with the number 3. Then, it will execute the rest of the handler as if there were a 3 wherever it sees *snum*. When the elf hits the *end* statement, it will destroy the variable *snum* without a trace, as if it never existed.

Now the handler is nice and generalized, right? Wrong. We haven't actually changed much, except centralizing all the Sprite references in one variable.

Wouldn't it be nice if we could somehow create the variable, and put a value into it, from outside this handler? That way, we could make the handler operate on any Sprite we want, without having to change a single line of code inside it. Is there a way to do this? Of course. We need to use a **parameter**.

Lazy Like a Fox

A good programmer is a lazy programmer. You should strive to write as little code as possible to get the job done. I know I do. A little laziness lets me get my work done faster and helps my code run better. That's why I like parameters so much. They let me wring a lot of use out of each custom handler that I write.

When you write custom handlers, a parameter is a local variable that gets its initial value from the calling handler. So, where we used to call our custom handler just by stating its name

```
on mouseDown

    dragSprite3AroundForAwhile

end
```

we now supply a starting value for *snum*, too.

```
on mouseDown

    dragSprite3AroundForAwhile 10

end
```

This *mouseDown* handler calls *dragSprite3AroundForAwhile* and tells it to put the number 10 into the variable *snum*, **before** *dragSprite3AroundForAwhile* starts to execute.

We have to alter our custom handler to make it accept a parameter. In this case, we want to call our parameter *snum*. To let the Lingo elf know that we want the handler to expect a parameter, we add the name of the parameter to the *on handlerName* line.

```
on dragSprite3AroundForAwhile snum

    . . .
```

This tells the elf to create a local variable called *snum* before it starts executing the handler. It also tells the elf to accept a starting value from the calling handler. When the elf starts executing the new parameter version of *dragSprite3AroundForAwhile*, it will create the local variable *snum*, and put a 10 in it to start.

We are doing this because we want the custom handler to be able to work with any Sprite, without changing code inside the handler. We want it to be a "black box" that will work its magic on any Sprite number that we supply (Figure 4.24). In light of its new function, it might be time to change the handler's name to something more general, like *moveFace*.

Here's the parameter version of the handler, with its spiffy, new name. Go ahead and put this into the Movie Script of Ex5.dir.

Figure 4.24 Calling a custom handler (*moveFace*) with a parameter (*snum*) from an even handler (*mouseDown*).

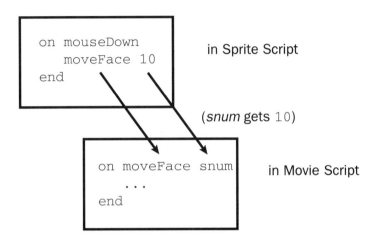

```
on mouseDown
     moveFace 10
end
```
in Sprite Script

(*snum* gets 10)

```
on moveFace snum
     ...
end
```
in Movie Script

```
on moveFace snum

   puppetSprite snum, true

   repeat while (the mouseDown = true)

      set the locV of sprite snum to the mouseV

      set the locH of sprite snum to the mouseH

      updateStage

   end repeat

   if ( sprite snum intersects 2 ) then

      puppetSprite 2, true

      set the stretch of sprite 2 to false

      set the memberNum of sprite 2 to 5

   end if

   puppetSprite snum, false

end
```

If you compare this version with the last one, you'll see that we took out the first line, *put 3 into snum*. Now that *snum* gets its value from outside the handler, we don't have to give it one.

So, let's say we want to drag around the skull in Sprite 10. We would put this event handler in the Sprite Script of sprite 10.

```
on mouseDown

    moveFace 10

end
```

Now, the user presses on Sprite 10. This handler is triggered by the event, and the elf starts to execute some Lingo. It sees *moveFace 10*. Checking its list of custom handlers, it finds *moveFace* and gets ready to execute it.

It sees from the definition line, *on moveFace snum*, that the handler is expecting a parameter. Looking back at the calling line, it sees that the number 10 is, indeed, supplied. So, the elf creates a local variable call *snum* and puts a 10 into it. Finally, it starts to execute the handler.

While the elf is executing the handler, wherever it sees *snum*, it inserts the current value of *snum*. Because we never put anything new into the variable, it always inserts the number 10.

In this exercise, we have four faces to drag around. We can make the three remaining faces draggable by putting a one-line *mouseDown* handler in the three Sprite scripts. Type these into the Sprite scripts in Ex5.dir.

```
For Sprite  11:
on mouseDown

    moveFace 11

end
```

For Sprite 12:

```
on mouseDown

    moveFace 12

end
```

For Sprite 13:

```
on mouseDown

    moveFace 13

end
```

So far, we have met the first objective for Exercise 5:

- The user can drag any of the four skulls around, but when the mouse button is released, the skull snaps back to its normal position.

However, we really haven't addressed the second and third objectives:

- If the user drops a skull on a picture frame, a copy of the skull is left in the frame.

- The user can put the same skull in as many picture frames as he or she wants.

To finish the exercise, we will have to fix *moveFace*.

Fixing Exercise 5

In the *moveFace* handler right now, we check to see if the skull intersects with a picture frame. We assume the interior of the picture frame image is covered by an invisible box shape, in Sprite Channel 2.

. . .

```
if ( sprite snum intersects 2 ) then

    puppetSprite 2, true

    set the stretch of sprite 2 to false

    set the memberNum of sprite 2 to 5

end if
```

. . .

There are two things wrong with this Lingo code:

1. It checks the skull Sprite (*snum*) against only one invisible box, the one in Sprite Channel 2. In Exercise 5, we want to check the dragged skull against all four invisible boxes, to see if it intersects one. (Also, 2 is the wrong Sprite number for Ex_5.dir. We borrowed this code from Exercise 4, where Sprite 2 was the invisible box.)

2. We hard-coded the number 5, so we always put a copy of Cast Member 5, the smile skull, into the picture frame. This was fine for Exercise 4—since there weren't any other skulls. In this exercise, however, the user might have dragged the scream, surprise, or mad skulls into the picture frame. This should leave a copy of the scream, surprise, or mad skull in the picture frame, not the smile skull.

As always, we'll tackle the first problem first.

For reference in the next few pages, Figures 4.25 and 4.26 show a dissection of the file Ex5.dir.

Counting to 10

We have already met a Lingo looping command, *repeat while*. You use *repeat while* to execute a sequence of commands repeatedly for an indefinite number of iterations,

Figure 4.25 Diagram of Ex5.dir

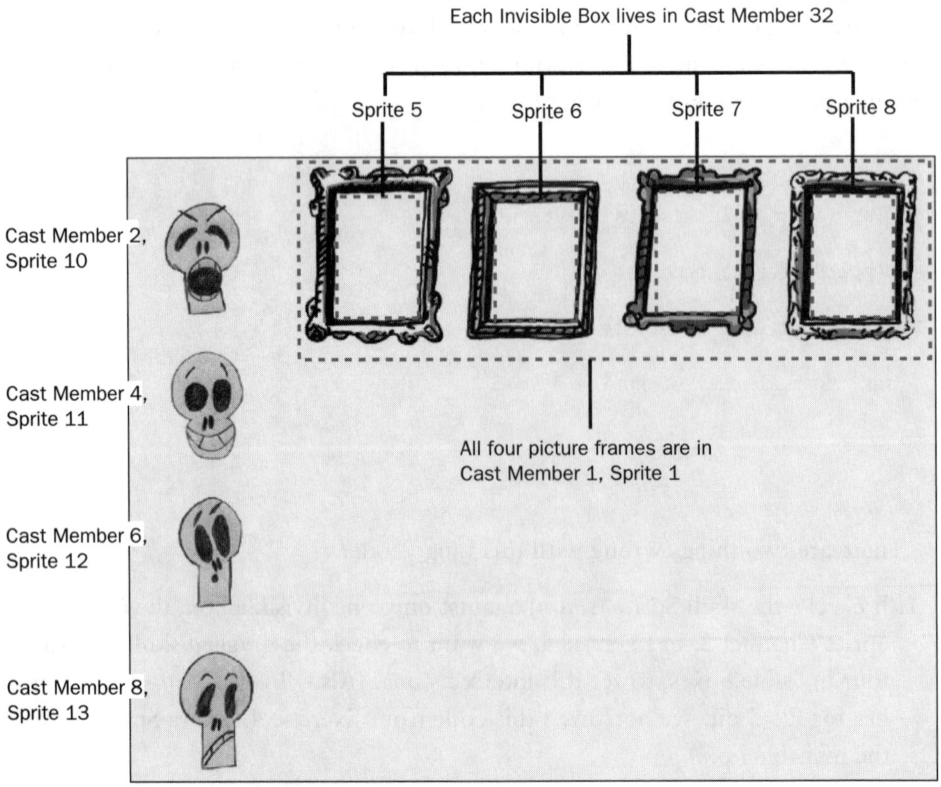

Each Invisible Box lives in Cast Member 32

Sprite 5   Sprite 6   Sprite 7   Sprite 8

Cast Member 2,
Sprite 10

Cast Member 4,
Sprite 11

Cast Member 6,
Sprite 12

Cast Member 8,
Sprite 13

All four picture frames are in
Cast Member 1, Sprite 1

Figure 4.26 Diagram of Ex5.dir score.

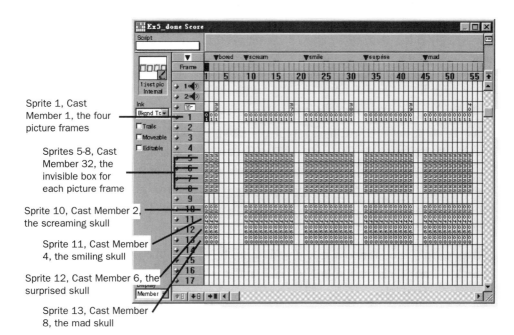

Sprite 1, Cast Member 1, the four picture frames

Sprites 5-8, Cast Member 32, the invisible box for each picture frame

Sprite 10, Cast Member 2, the screaming skull

Sprite 11, Cast Member 4, the smiling skull

Sprite 12, Cast Member 6, the surprised skull

Sprite 13, Cast Member 8, the mad skull

until the test condition changes. In other words, when you don't know quite how many times you want a loop to execute, you should use *repeat while*.

However, sometimes you know exactly how many times you want a loop to execute. Say you wanted to output the numbers 1 through 10 in the Message Window. (I know you'd never want to do this, but stay with me.) You would want the loop to repeat 10 times.

Moreover, you would want a variable to keep track of the current iteration. If this is the third time the loop is executing, you want some variable to have the value 3. If you wanted to use a *repeat while* loop, you could do it like this.

```
put 1 into loopNum

repeat while ( loopNum <= 10 )

    put loopNum

    put loopNum + 1 into loopNum

end repeat
```

When the Lingo elf executes this code, it first reads the line *put 1 into loopNum*, so it creates a local variable called *loopNum* and puts a 1 into it. Then, it sees the *repeat while* line. The elf looks at the test condition (*loopNum <= 10*) and decides that 1 really is less than or equal to 10, so it ventures inside the loop for the first time.

The first line inside the loop, *put loopNum*, prints the value of *loopNum* into the Message Window. At this point, it prints *1*.

As the elf parses the next line, it replaces *loopNum* with its value, 1, as soon as it sees it. The elf sees the line *put 1 + 1 into ...* and then changes how it thinks about loopNum. The elf, which knows Lingo like the back of its little, elfen hand, knows that it needs a variable to put the value of 1 + 1 **into**. When it sees the word *loopNum* a second time, it fills it with a 2. The elf is always looking for a **value** after *put* and a **variable** after *into*.

Afterward, the elf hits *end repeat* and jumps back up to the *repeat while* line, to recheck the test. This time, *loopNum* is 2, and 2 is still less than or equal to 10. It ventures inside the loop again and executes the code as we have just discussed.

This loop will keep iterating until the numbers 1 through 10 have been printed in the Message Window. No, it's not very impressive. It is a lot of code for not very much function. Remember, less code is better. A good programmer is a lazy programmer.

There's a lazier way.

Lingo Looping with Repeat With

This code fragment also counts to 10.

```
repeat with loopNum = 1 to 10

    put loopNum

end repeat
```

It's shorter, more readable, and just what the lazy programmer asked for.

It uses another kind of loop, *repeat with*. Sometimes, you know how many times you want the loop to execute, **and** you want a variable to keep track of the iteration. Because this is such a common task, Lingo gives us *repeat with* to make it easy to program.

Repeat with has a more complicated structure than *repeat while*. It looks like this.

```
repeat with variableName = firstValue to lastValue

    -- stuff inside loop

end repeat
```

The first time the Lingo elf executes a *repeat with* loop, it looks in its memory for a variable called *variableName*. If it doesn't exist, the elf will create one. Before it goes inside the loop, the elf puts value *firstValue* into the variable, to keep track of the current iteration.

The elf goes inside the loop, executing each inner line of code. When it hits the *end repeat*, it **adds 1 to the variable *variableName***, then jumps to the *repeat with* line. If the variable is **less than or equal to the value *lastValue***, it will go inside the loop. If the variable is greater than *lastValue*, the elf skips past the loop.

Let's step through the counting loop.

```
repeat with loopNum = 1 to 10

    put loopNum

end repeat
```

The elf comes to the first line and creates a local variable called *loopNum*. Before going on, the elf puts a 1 into *loopNum*. After this is done, it goes inside the loop.

The command *put loopNum* outputs the current value of *loopNum*, which is 1.

The elf hits *end repeat*, adds 1 to *loopNum*, making it equal 2, and jumps back up to the *repeat with* line. Because 2 is between 1 and 10, it goes into the loop again. It outputs the number 2, hits *end repeat*, increases *loopNum* to 3, and jumps back up.

And so on, and so on.

Eventually, the elf hits *end repeat* and increases *loopNum* to 10. It goes back up to the *repeat with* line, and decides that 10 is less than or equal to 10, so it goes inside the loop. It outputs the number 10, hits *end repeat*, increases *loopNum* to 11, and jumps back up to the *repeat with* line.

Bam! The value of *loopNum*, 11, is greater than 10, so the elf decides it is done with the loop and skips past *end repeat*.

Fixing the First Problem with Repeat With

Because the intersect-checking code has to check if the skull Sprite intersects with four different invisible boxes, one for each picture frame, it makes sense to use a *repeat with* loop. We want the *if..then* statement to be executed four times, for each of the four invisible box Sprites. If you look in the Score for Ex5.dir you'll see that the invisible boxes are in Sprites 5, 6, 7, and 8.

The first step is to envelop the *if..then* statements inside a *repeat with* loop:

```
. . .

if ( sprite  snum intersects 2 ) then

    puppetSprite 2, true

    set the stretch of sprite 2 to false

    set the memberNum of sprite 2 to 5

end if

. . .
```

This code becomes the following:

```
. . .

repeat with loopNum=5 to 8

    if ( sprite snum intersects 2 ) then

        puppetSprite 2, true

        set the stretch of sprite 2 to false

        set the memberNum of sprite 2 to 5

    end if

end repeat

. . .
```

Now, this doesn't do us much good. We are repeating exactly the same intersect-check four times. Instead of checking if *snum* intersects with Sprite 2, we want to check if *snum* intersects with the current value of *loopNum*.

. . .

```
repeat with loopNum=5 to 8

    if ( sprite snum intersects loopNum ) then

        puppetSprite loopNum, true

        set the stretch of sprite loopNum to false

        set the memberNum of sprite loopNum to 5

    end if

end repeat
```

. . .

The first time this loop is executed, *loopNum* is 5. The *if..then* will check if Sprite *snum* (the dragged skull) intersects with Sprite 5. If it doesn't, *loopNum* will be increased to 6, and the loop will execute again. This will happen again and again, with *loopNum* equaling 7 and 8.

Let's step through the code again, this time assuming an intersection. Let's say that the dragged skull in Sprite *snum* intersects with Sprite 6, the invisible box in the second picture frame (Figure 4.27). Let's additionally say that the dragged face is the scream skull, in Cast Member 3.

The second time through the loop, *loopNum* will equal 6, and the *if..then* test will be true. As the Lingo elf goes inside the *if..then*, it will turn Sprite 6 into a Puppet and set *the stretch of Sprite* 6 to FALSE. So far, so good. Now we have to set *the memberNum of sprite* 6 to the correct face.

Fixing the Second Problem with a Director Trick

If we have intersection between the dragged skull and an invisible box, we have to figure out how to put the correct face into the box. In simpler terms, what do we put inside the *if..then*?

Figure 4.27 Scream skull intersecting the second picture frame.

Sprite 6, the Invisible Box for
the second picture frame

Sprite *snum*, in this case, Cast Member 3,
the screaming skull

The first thing that might pop into your head could be, "Well, I know which skull expression is in each Sprite, just by looking at the Score (Figure 4.28). I guess I could use an *if..then* to match *snum* to the correct Cast Member number." This solution would look like this.

. . .

```
repeat with loopNum=5 to 8

   if ( sprite snum intersects loopNum ) then

      puppetSprite loopNum, true

      set the stretch of sprite loopNum to false

      if ( snum = 10 ) then -- scream

        set the memberNum of sprite loopNum to 2

      else if ( snum = 11 ) then -- smile

         set the memberNum of sprite loopNum to 4

      else if ( snum = 12 ) then -- surprise

         set the memberNum of sprite loopNum to 6
```

```
    else if ( snum = 13 ) then -- mad

        set the memberNum of sprite loopNum to 8

    end if

  end if

end repeat
```

. . .

The *repeat with* and outer *if..then* work as they did before. When the inner *if..then* executes, the first test is (*snum = 10*). We know that if Sprite 10 was dragged, the user is dragging the scream skull. By looking in the Cast, we can see that the scream skull lives in Cast Member 2. We set the *memberNum* of the invisible box to 2 to put a copy of the scream skull in the picture frame.

After I thought this out, I came up with a better, lazier solution. I realized that the Sprite *snum* knows what its attached Cast Member number is. I could just ask it! This makes the code much more compact. All I have to do is set the *memberNum* of the invisible box Sprite to the *memberNum* of the dragged skull Sprite.

Figure 4.28 Determining which skull expression is in each Sprite by looking at the Score.

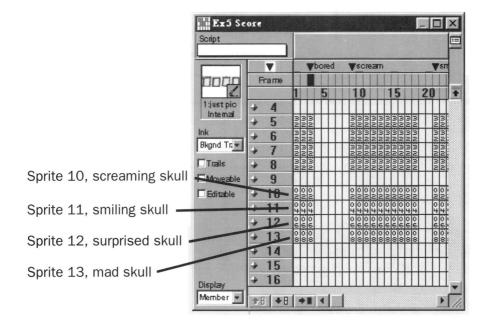

. . .

```
repeat with loopNum=5 to 8

    if ( sprite snum intersects loopNum ) then

        puppetSprite loopNum, true

        set the stretch of sprite loopNum to false

        put the memberNum of sprite snum into skullCast

        set the memberNum of sprite loopNum to skullCast

    end if

end repeat
```

. . .

Going back to our example, the user has just dragged the scream skull onto the second picture frame. The skull Sprite, *snum*, is 10. The picture frame Sprite, *loopNum*, is 6. The elf has just entered into the *if..then* and turned Sprite 6 into a Puppet. Now what happens?

The elf sees *put the memberNum of sprite snum into skullCast*. This causes the elf to create a local variable called *skullCast* and to put *the memberNum of sprite 10* into it. The scream skull lives in member 2 in the Cast so the value in variable *skullCast* is 2.

The next line, *set the memberNum of sprite loopNum to skullCast*, changes the attached Cast Member of the invisible box Sprite to 2, the scream skull. Hooray!

There's one last wrinkle. (Isn't there always one last wrinkle?) The code, as it is, will cause a registration problem, just like the problem we had in Exercise 4 (Figure 4.29).

We can fix this the same way we fixed Exercise 4: Keep another copy of the Cast Member with an above-left registration point. If you look at the Cast, you'll see I have two copies of each skull. The first is registered to the center of the skull; the second is registered above and left of the skull, so it will line up correctly against a picture frame (Figure 4.30).

The skulls that get dragged around are in Cast Members 2, 4, 6, and 8. The ones we want to switch into the picture frame/invisible box Sprites are 3, 5, 7, and 9. Do

Figure 4.29 Scream skull misregistered on the picture frame.

you see a pattern? I set up the Cast so that the picture frame skull will always be the draggable skull plus 1. This makes our coding easy!

We can change the code fragment to:

. . .

```
repeat with loopNum=5 to 8

    if ( sprite snum intersects loopNum ) then

        puppetSprite loopNum, true

        set the stretch of sprite loopNum to false

        put the memberNum of sprite snum + 1 into skullCast

        set the memberNum of sprite loopNum to skullCast

    end if

end repeat
```

. . .

Figure 4.30 The Cast with two Cast Members per expression.

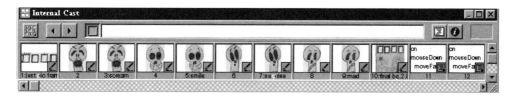

Just by inserting the + *1* into the line *put the memberNum of sprite snum into skullCast*, we have solved our registration problem!

Here's the final code listing for the *moveFace* handler.

```
on moveFace snum

    puppetSprite snum,true

    repeat while (the mouseDown = true)

        set the locV of sprite snum to the mouseV

        set the locH of sprite snum to the mouseH

        updateStage

    end repeat

    repeat with loopNum=5 to 8

        if ( sprite snum intersects loopNum ) then

            puppetSprite loopNum, true

            set the stretch of sprite loopNum to false

            put the memberNum of sprite snum + 1 into skullCast

            set the memberNum of sprite loopNum to skullCast

        end if

    end repeat

    puppetSprite snum,false

end
```

This finishes Exercise 5. In the next exercise, we finish the entire project for Chapter 4.

Exercise 6: Skull Sequencer

At long last, we are ready to finish the Chapter 4 project!

The unprogrammed version of the chapter project is in file Ch4.dir in the Chapter4 folder on the CD-ROM. The first frame looks like Figure 4.31.

If you've forgotten, here's how the program is supposed to work:

1. The user drags a skull thumbnail into one of the picture frames. When the user lets go of the mouse button, the skull snaps back to its resting place. If the user had dragged the skull on top of a picture frame, when the mouse button is released, a copy of the skull stays in the frame.

2. The user puts skull thumbnails into all the picture frames. The user is allowed to put the same skull in multiple picture frames.

3. The user clicks the painter. The program responds by animating the big skull into expressions. The first expression is what the user placed in the first picture frame, the second expression is the contents of the second frame, and so on.

Figure 4.31 First frame.

Lazy and Loving It

As you've probably noticed, we already know how to implement behaviors 1 and 2. That's what we did in Exercise 5.

So, go ahead, get lazy. If you can't steal from yourself, who can you steal from?

Go back and copy the *moveFace* handler from Exercise 5. Come back to this movie, hold down Control-Shift-U (or Command-Shift-U on the Macintosh), and Paste into the Movie Script. You're almost there.

Make the Sprite Scripts for the skull Sprites, so that they will call *moveFace*. The skulls are in Sprite Channels 10 through 13. The call to *moveFace* must include, as a parameter, the number of the Sprite to drag. So, for Sprite 10, the script should be as follows:

```
on mouseDown

    moveFace 10

end
```

You'll have to put similar scripts in Sprites 11, 12, and 13 (Figure 4.32). This is the same as it was in Exercise 5.

Figure 4.32 Attach *mouseDown* scripts to Sprites 10, 11, 12, 13.

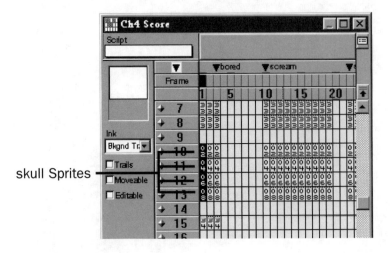

Rewind and play the movie. If all has gone well, the skulls will move around and stick to the picture frames, just as they did in Exercise 5.

The unique problem in Exercise 6 is how to make the painter work.

The Painter Problem

Here's the situation: We have four skulls that have been put into picture frames. When the painter is clicked, we have to figure out which skull is in each picture frame, and which animation corresponds to it.

Let's say the user set up the sequence smile, scream, surprise, mad, as in Figure 4.33.

The painter must play the smile, scream, surprise, and mad animations, in that order. The animations are set up in the Score, in frames 10 through 55, shown in Figure 4.34.

The animation for each expression is labeled in the Score: **scream**, **smile**, **surprise**, and **mad**. Our Lingo code has to figure out that the **smile** skull is in the first picture frame and play the **smile** animation. Then it has to do the same for the second, third, and fourth picture frames.

Kind of an interesting problem, isn't it? Take a few minutes to think about it before continuing.

My Solution to the Painter Problem

There are dozens of ways to solve this problem with Lingo code. The one I chose is cool because it ties together Lingo, the Cast, and the Score. I mentioned that the

Figure 4.33 The sequence.

Figure 4.34 Frames 10 through 55 of Score.

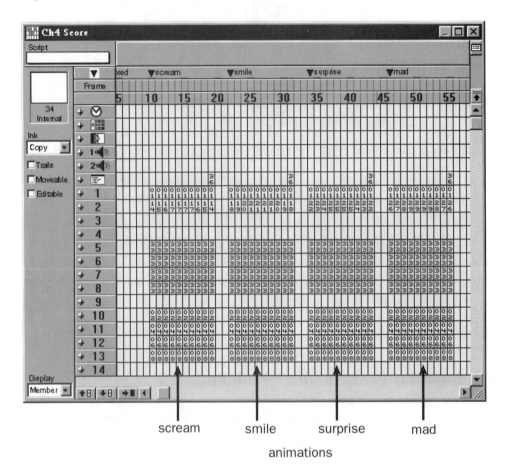

scream   smile   surprise   mad

animations

animation's frame labels in the Score are **scream, smile, surprise,** and **mad.** Now
take a look at how I set up the Cast in Figure 4.35.

Figure 4.35 The Cast.

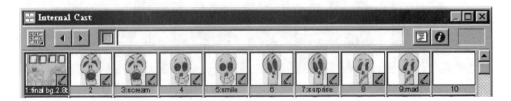

The Cast Members that get attached into the invisible boxes that represent the picture frames are 3, 5, 7, and 9. The names of the Cast Members are scream, smile, surprise, and mad.

Notice a pattern?

All we need to do is get the name of the Cast Member that is attached to a picture frame. Then, we call *play frame* with that name, which also happens to be a frame label.

Implementing My Solution

This, of course, brings up the question: "How do you get the **name of a Cast Member,** when all you know is the **number of a Sprite?**" As always, we start with what we know and a small test case.

Here's the test case: We are looking at the first picture frame, in Sprite 10. The Cast Member attached to Sprite 10 is the smile skull, Cast Member 5. We want to figure out which animation to play.

Q: What can we get Director to tell us about the Cast Member attached to Sprite 10?

A: It will tell us the **number** of the attached Cast Member, via the *memberNum* property.

That's a good start. We can ask for the *memberNum* of Sprite 10, and remember it in a variable, with the following line of code:

```
put the memberNum of Sprite  10 into mnum
```

We are using a local variable called *mnum*, which we will pretend stands for **memberNum.** The value of *mnum* after this line will be 5 because the smile skull is in Cast Member 5.

Now that we have the number of the Cast Member, we have to get its name. Lucky for us, there is a **Cast Member property** that we can use, called *name of member.* When you give this property a number, it returns the name of the Cast Member with that number. To find out the name of the Cast Member, we would use a line like this:

```
put the name of member mnum into animName
```

In our example, this would put the string "smile" into a variable called *animName.*

Now we know the name of the Cast Member, which is also the label for the animation in the Score. All we have to do is supply the name to the *play frame* command.

```
play frame animName
```

Here's the code to solve our test case.

```
put the memberNum of sprite 10 into mnum

put the name of member mnum into animName

play frame animName
```

OK, we're getting somewhere. Next, we want to generalize the Script to work on all four picture frame Sprites. We could simply copy and paste, resulting in the following.

```
put the memberNum of sprite 10 into mnum

put the name of member mnum into animName

play frame animName

put the memberNum of sprite 11 into mnum

put the name of member mnum into animName

play frame animName

put the memberNum of sprite 12 into mnum

put the name of member mnum into animName

play frame animName

put the memberNum of sprite 13 into mnum

put the name of member mnum into animName

play frame animName
```

As we discussed before, duplicating code isn't pretty, and it generally isn't a good idea. In this test case, we can use a *repeat with* loop to make the script prettier. While we're at it, why not put this script into the *mouseDown* handler, in the Sprite script of the painter? The image of the painter is actually part of the background, but I drew an invisible box around him in Sprite 15. Put this handler into the Sprite script of Sprite 15, the painter.

```
on mouseDown

   repeat with loopNum = 5 to 8

      put the memberNum of sprite loopNum into mnum

      put the name of member mnum into animName

      play frame animName

   end repeat

end
```

This should finish the chapter project, don't you think? I thought so too, when I wrote this program. But when I ran it, I found a bug—a big, bad, bizarre bug.

The Last Bug

After setting up the sequence in the picture frames, you click the painter. The animations play out in the correct sequence. Everything is great.

After the last animation, though, the Stage flashes white. The scream animation plays again. The face takes a little too long to get back to its normal, bored state. Finally, you're back at the bored state, and the horrifying bug seems like some dream. Then you click the painter again, and it happens again. Help!

What is going wrong? You have entered Director's Twilight Zone. **Director has weird, obscure, buggy, mysterious ways.** This insight has given me strength in my years of Director development.

The problem is that Director starts to act weird when you put multiple *play* statements in one handler. If you want a discussion of this bizarre Director behavior, see "What I didn't tell you about Navigation" in Chapter 5.

Q: What do you do when you find a problem you can't fix?

A: Work around it.

So here's the problem in a nutshell. When calling more than one *play frame/play done* pair from a script, the Playback Head returns to the wrong frame.

In the case of this movie, the Playback Head ends up on frame 8 after the above *mouseDown* handler is finished. Why frame 8? I'll give you a lollipop if you can justify this behavior of Director. From frame 8, it continues forward, playing the scream animation that starts at frame 10. Finally, it triggers the *exitFrame* handler on frame 19...

```
on exitFrame

    play done

end
```

When *play done* executes, Director does not know where to put the Playback Head because it is unmatched by any *play frame* command. By default, it sends the Playback Head to frame 1; from there it continues forward until it is caught by the *go the frame* in the *exitFrame* handler on frame 3.

I can't tell you why this happens, but I can tell you how I worked around the problem. I decided that because the Playback Head would return to the wrong place on its own, I could force it to go where I wanted. Before I start calling *play frame*, I save the number of the current frame into a variable called *originalFrame*. After I am finished calling *play frame*, I use *go to frame* to force the Playback Head to the original frame, back where we started.

Here's my final handler for the painter. It goes in the Sprite Script for Sprite 15.

```
on mouseDown

    put the frame into originalFrame

    repeat with loopNum = 5 to 8

        put the memberNum of sprite loopNum into mnum

        put the name of member mnum into animName

        play frame animName

    end repeat

    go to frame originalFrame

end
```

And, so help me, this works. I'm annoyed that it is necessary, but it works.

In the end, that's all that really matters.

Chapter Summary

The following is a summary of the key concepts and terms I have discussed throughout this chapter. Having a good grasp on what they mean will make it easier to do the exercises throughout the rest of the book.

- A Puppet Sprite is a Sprite channel that has been taken over by the Lingo programmer, and no longer listens to the Score.

    To turn Sprite 1 into a Puppet, use *puppetSprite 1,true*. To make it leave puppethood, use *puppetSprite 1,false*.

    Whenever you use the *puppetSprite* command, the Sprite channel of the current frame in the score must have something in it, or you will get Director really confused.

    You affect Puppet Sprites by changing their properties. The horizontal location of a Sprite is held in *the locH of sprite* property, and the vertical location is held in *the locV of sprite* property.

- There is a shadow version of the Stage that I call **The Invisible Stage**. Everything appearing on the real Stage first appears on the invisible one.

    Changing a Sprite Property from Lingo only changes the Invisible Stage. To show the change on the real Stage, issue the *updateStage* command. The real Stage is also updated when the Playback Head moves.

- A **function** is a lingo phrase that returns a value, but isn't a property of some object. A function that returns the current frame number is *the frame*. Another function, *the mouseDown*, returns the state of the mouse button, TRUE or FALSE.

- You can execute a bunch of Lingo statements repeatedly by putting them into a *repeat while* loop. A *repeat while* uses a test condition to determine whether to go inside the loop. If the condition is true, the Lingo elf will go inside the loop. The following loop will keep spending money until there is no money left. (It isn't real Lingo.)

```
repeat while (I still have money)

    spend money

end repeat
```

You can check if two sprites overlap on the Stage by using the *sprite intersects* function. The following code fragment beeps if sprite 3 and sprite 4 are touching:

```
if sprite 3 intersects 4 then

    beep

end if
```

The sprite property *the memberNum of sprite* is the number of the Cast Member attached to the sprite. You can read this property from the sprite and change it. The following *exitFrame* event handler would change the Cast Member attached to sprite 4 from member 1, to member 2, to member 3, then back to member 1. This is useful for animating a dragged sprite, if you wanted to do such a thing. The sprite must already be puppetted.

```
on exitFrame

    if (the memberNum of sprite 4 = 3) then

        set the memberNum of sprite 4 to 1

    else

        set the memberNum of sprite 4 to the memberNum of sprite 4 + 1

    end if

end
```

When a Cast Member is drawn to the Stage, the sprite location is aligned with the registration point of the Cast Member. By default, bitmap Cast Members have a centered registration point, but most other types default to a top left registration point.

You can create your own handler by giving it a name and putting it into a script. Custom handlers usually are put into the Movie Script. The following handler beeps five times.

```
on mySillyHandler

    beep 5

end
```

You can get to the Movie Script by pressing Control-Shift-U (Windows) or Command-Shift-U (Macintosh).

A **variable** is a place in memory that holds a value. A **local variable** holds its value as long as the handler it is in still executes. When the handler finishes, the local variable is zapped into oblivion. A **global variable** lasts longer, but we'll talk about that in Chapter 6.

You can create a parameterized custom handler by specifying a local variable to hold the passed value. The following custom handler beeps however many times the caller specifies.

```
on mySillyHandler num

    beep num

end
```

When calling a parameterized handler, specify a value to the right of the handler call. To make the above handler beep three times, use the command *mySillyHandler 3*.

A *repeat with* command will loop a certain number of times. The following is an alternate version of *mySillyHandler*.

```
on mySillyHandler num

    repeat with i=1 to 3

        beep I

    end repeat

end
```

I don't believe how much you have accomplished in the last few dozen pages! Play with what you've learned for a while, and get really comfortable with the basics. When you feel comfortable, read Chapter 5, which will fill in many of the details I intentionally left out of this chapter.

Congratulations. You are now a Lingo programmer.

5

What I Didn't Tell You

Chapter Objective

I have tried to avoid a common pitfall that many programming books fall into—telling you too much too soon. As I have introduced new concepts, I deliberately hid details, pitfalls, and options from you. I did this to keep you from being overwhelmed with minutia while you were trying to understand a new idea. By now, though, you've met the concepts; you've gotten your hands dirty. I think you are ready for the details.

I'm still not going to tell you everything, though. Some of the options for these commands won't make sense until you work through the rest of the book (that's why there is a rest of the book). I'll tell you about these as we come to them.

What I Didn't Tell You About *Navigation*

The navigation commands, *go* and *play*, seem simple and easy to use. Wrong. Each has a zillion options, variations, and subtleties. These will drive you crazy throughout your Lingo career.

You Can Slang the Navigation Commands

We have used the *go to frame* and *play frame* commands a lot already. We have used their more-or-less "official" Lingo versions. Lingo actually accepts many slang versions of these commands. For example, all of the following do exactly the same thing. Let's say frame 5 is labeled "scream."

```
go to frame "scream"

go to "scream"

go "scream"

go to frame 5

go to 5

go 5
```

The *play frame* command is also slangy.

```
play frame "scream"

play "scream"

play frame 5

play 5
```

You might see any of these forms in other people's Lingo code. In fact, you might even see them in this book. Don't let them confuse you.

Don't Loop on a Transition

Whenever we have had to keep the Playback Head on a frame, we have used a simple frame script.

```
on exitFrame

   go to the frame

end
```

This is a great script, except when there is a transition on this frame in the Score, like a dissolve or wipe. When you do this, Director seems to stop reacting to the user, things stop working, and you end up scratching your head. See, Director spends a lot of effort making a transition happen. It ends up repeating the transition after every *exitFrame*, taking up all of the computer's processing power, leaving none to accept user input. Put the transition **before** the frame you want to loop on.

You Can Navigate to Other Movies

In a large project, it is common to use multiple movie files. In one recent project, I used a movie called Main.dir as the main menu file, which lead to different sections. Each section was contained in a separate movie, called Section1.dir, Section2.dir, and so on. All of the movies were in the same folder. You can use the *go* and *play* commands to navigate between actual movie files. To get from Main.dir to Section1.dir, you could use

```
go to movie "Section1.dir"
```

In fact, you could decide to go to frame 5 of the new movie, labeled "scream." Both of these commands do the same thing:

```
go to frame 5 of movie "Section1.dir"

go to frame "scream" of movie "Section1.dir"
```

These variations also work for *play*:

```
play movie "Section1.dir"

play frame 5 of movie "Section1.dir"

play frame "scream" of movie "Section1.dir"
```

Any of these commands will replace the onstage movie with Section1.dir, the latter two going immediately to frame 5. When the Lingo elf eventually hits a *play done*, the Stage will go back to showing Main.dir.

When your movies are in different folders on the disk, you have to supply a full pathname to these commands. For a discussion of pathnames, see Chapter 8.

Play done Doesn't Always Bring You Back to Where You Started

The basic concept behind the *play* command is simple: You issue a *play frame* command to jump to a certain frame, and when a *play done* command executes, the Playback Head jumps back to the original frame. Simple, right?

Wrong. As it turns out, there are a lot of peculiarities in the way this pair of commands works. First off, if the Lingo elf stumbles across a *play done* command without having first seen a matching *play frame* command, it gets confused and jumps the Playback Head to frame 1. Fair enough.

Next, if you issue the *play frame* command from a **Sprite or Cast Member Script**, the Playback Head will, indeed, return to the frame from which you issued the *play frame* command.

However, if you issue the *play frame* command from a **Frame Script**, the Playback Head will return to the frame **after** the one you called it from. If you put a *play frame 30* command into the *exitFrame* script on frame 10, after a *play done*, the Playback Head will return to frame 11. I'm not kidding.

Oh, it gets worse. What if, from a **Frame Script**, you issue **multiple play frame** commands? Say this *exitFrame* handler is in the Frame Script of frame 10.

```
on exitFrame

    play frame 30

    play frame 40

    play frame 50

end
```

After the third *play done* is executed, the Playback Head will end up **on frame 13!** I guess the reasoning is, after one *play frame/play done* pair, the return-frame would be frame 11. After two pairs, it would be frame 12. After three pairs, it would be frame 13. The formula turns out to be as follows:

```
returnFrame =  starting frame + number of play frame/play done pairs
```

I'm not even done yet. What if, as we did in the Painter Script in Chapter 4, you issue multiple play frame commands from a **Sprite Script** or **Cast Member Script**? Let's say we put this Script into a Sprite in frame 10

```
on mouseDown

    play frame 30

    play frame 40

    play frame 50

end
```

After the third *play done* executes, the Playback Head winds up **on frame 12!** It's enough to start a hair-loss trend. The formula for the return frame turns out to be as follows:

```
returnFrame = starting frame + number of play frame/play done pairs -1
```

I'm not going to try to justify this behavior of Director. I guess it all makes sense to somebody at Macromedia. (Do you see why I didn't bring this up in Chapter 2?) All you can really do is work around this behavior, the way we did in Chapter 4. Before you issue a *play frame*, save the current frame into a variable. When you are finished calling play frame, force the Playback Head to jump to the saved frame. For example:

```
on mouseDown

    put the frame into originalFrame --save frame num into a var

    play frame 30

    play frame 40

    play frame 50

    go to frame originalFrame -- go back to the saved frame

end
```

The Lingo Elf and the Playback Head Do an Intricate Dance

Two entities can be seen as "controllers" of a Director movie: the Playback Head and the Lingo elf. Understanding how they relate to each other is often very useful. The Playback Head represents the frame currently displayed onstage. It goes forward, frame by frame, unless it is moved by Lingo. The Lingo elf represents the **Lingo execution point**. It determines the current line of Lingo being executed.

In general, first the Playback Head moves to a new frame. It triggers *enterFrame* and *exitFrame* events in that frame. If this triggers an event handler, the elf starts executing the Lingo in that handler. When it is finished, meaning it has reached the final *end* statement, it releases control of the movie to the Playback Head. The elf goes into hibernation until the next time it is needed. As soon as this happens, the Playback Head goes to the next frame, and the cycle starts again. Their interaction gets a little more complicated when there are navigation commands in the Script being executed.

When you use a *go* command, the sequence looks like this:

1. The elf immediately moves the Playback Head to the new frame.

2. The Playback Head triggers an *enterFrame* event in the new frame.

3. If there is an *enterFrame* event handler, the elf executes it.

4. The elf finishes executing the original handler and goes into hibernation.

5. The Playback Head triggers an *exitFrame* event in the new frame.

6. If there is an *exitFrame* event handler, the elf executes it.

7. The Playback Head moves to the next frame.

When you use a *play* command, from within a Sprite Script or Cast Member Script, the sequence goes like this:

1. The elf immediately moves the Playback Head to the new frame.

2. The Playback Head triggers *enterFrame* and *exitFrame* events in the new frame, which get executed by the elf.

3. The Playback Head continues to march along the Score, frame by frame. Eventually, it hits a *play done* command, for example, in frame 30.

4. The Lingo elf finishes executing the calling handler, **but the Playback Head stays on frame 30.**

5. **After** the elf finishes executing the calling handler, the Playback Head returns to the calling frame, triggering an *enterFrame* and *exitFrame* event in the calling frame.

And finally, when you use a *play* command from within a Frame Script, the sequence goes like this:

1. The elf immediately moves the Playback Head to the new frame.

2. The Playback Head triggers *enterFrame* and *exitFrame* events in the new frame, which get executed by the elf.

3. The Playback Head continues to march along the Score, frame by frame. Eventually, it hits a *play done* command, for example, in frame 30.

4. The Lingo elf finishes executing the calling handler, **but the Playback Head stays on frame 30.**

5. **After** the elf finishes executing the calling handler, the Playback Head returns to the frame **directly after the calling frame,** triggering an *enterFrame* and *exitFrame* event in the new frame.

Didn't they seem like simple, innocent commands?

What I Didn't Tell You About *Puppets*

New Lingo programmers often find Puppets the most difficult-to-get-right part of programming. Generally, it's because they haven't read this section.

When You Turn a Puppet Sprite On, There Must Be Something in the Sprite Channel

When Lingo executes *puppetSprite 3,true*, there has to be some Sprite in channel 3 in the current frame (Figure 5.1). If the channel is empty in the current frame, Director gets confused. The Puppet won't respond to your Lingo commands, but Director will kind of treat it like a Puppet anyway (Figure 5.2). This situation leads

Figure 5.1 Good puppet situation.

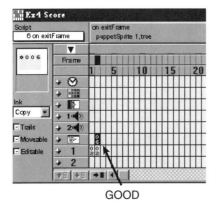

GOOD

Figure 5.2 Bad puppet situation.

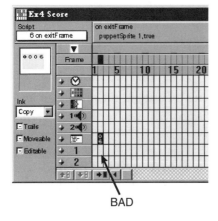

BAD

to unpredictable behavior, so avoid it at all costs. If your puppets don't seem to be working, this is often the cause.

What Lingo programmers generally do is put an invisible box into the Sprite Channel in the frame where the Sprite becomes a Puppet. Another popular solution is to create a bitmap that has only one pixel and put that into the Sprite Channel. These are "placeholder" Sprites, whose only purpose is to be in the Sprite Channel so you can turn them into Puppets.

When You Turn a Puppet Sprite *Off,* There Must Be Something in the Sprite Channel

Just as above, there must be something in the Sprite Channel when you turn off a Puppet, that is, *puppetSprite 3,false.* If this statement executes when sprite 3 is empty in the current frame, unpredictable behavior may occur.

The *puppet of sprite* Property Will Tell You If a Sprite Is Puppetted

If you are having trouble with a certain Puppet Sprite, you can find out if Director thinks it is a Puppet. The *puppet of sprite* property will return TRUE if it **is** currently a Puppet or FALSE if it isn't. For example, *put the puppet of sprite 1* will return TRUE if sprite 1 has been puppetted. This property is not accurate if you haven't followed the last two tips. (Actually, this property returns 1 for TRUE or 0 for FALSE. See "Conditions"later in this chapter for further explanation.)

If You Set *the membernum of sprite* Property Without Turning the Sprite into a Puppet, the Sprite Will Flash

Another common mistake is to set a Sprite property without turning the Sprite into a Puppet. For example, look at this script...

```
set the memberNum of sprite 3 to 10

updateStage
```

It will make the sprite flash to cast member 10 for an instant, then return to its normally attached Cast Member, as recorded in the Score. If you see this, the sprite was not puppetted properly.

Turn Off the Puppets When You Are Done with Them

Let's say you have turned sprite 3 into a Puppet, on frame 4. Let's say further that you have *set the memberNum of sprite 3 to 5,* the smile skull. Then, the user goes to a completely different part of your movie, where there is a surprise skull in channel 3 in the Score. However, the user doesn't see it on Stage. Instead, she sees a skull. What happened?

You forgot to turn off Puppet Sprite 3! The Sprite is still under Lingo control. Fix this by adding *puppetSprite 3, false* before you go to the next section.

Puppets Go Away When You Rewind the Movie

If you have set the *memberNum* or location of a Puppet Sprite with Lingo, the Sprite will stay in that location when you stop the movie. When you rewind, however, the Sprites are reset to reflect the Score, and all Puppets are forgotten. In a projector, the Puppets are forgotten as soon as the user quits.

Puppets Don't Last Between Movies

Let's say the you turned sprite 3 into a Puppet with *puppetSprite 3,true*. Then, you use the *go to movie* or *play movie* command to load a different movie file. When the new movie appears on screen, sprite 3 is no longer a Puppet. Control of sprite 3 has reverted back to the Score. In fact, even if you go back to the first movie, sprite 3 is not a Puppet anymore.

updateStage Doesn't Always Work

Sometimes, when you least expect it, the *updateStage* command fails to do anything. By all conceivable logic, it should be copying the Invisible Stage to the normal Stage, but it isn't.

When this happens, I usually add a *go to the frame* command, just after the *updateStage*. It seems weird and redundant, but it often helps. It might look like this:

```
puppetSprite 3,true

set the memberNum of sprite 3 to 1

updateStage

go the frame
```

When You Turn Off a Puppet, the Score Won't Reassert Itself Until the Playback Head Moves

When you issue a *puppetSprite 3,false* command, don't expect to see the result immediately, or even after an *updateStage*. You won't see a result until the Playback

Head moves, either to the current frame or a different one. To show the result immediately, use a *go to the frame* command, like this one:

```
puppetSprite 3, false

go the frame
```

updateStage Doesn't Apply to All Kinds of Sprites Equally

We'll explore this one more when we start using different types of Sprites, but *updateStage* becomes less and less logical the more types of Sprites you use. For example, if you change the contents of a field that is onstage, the Stage will update immediately, without waiting for an *updateStage*. Quicktime (Digital Video) Sprites also update themselves as soon as you change one of their properties, usually. Sound Sprites wait for the *updateStage* command to start, except when they don't.

It's a wild and woolly Director world out there, and we're just starting to explore it.

What I Didn't Tell You About *Conditions*

There are a few things I didn't tell you before about the test conditions used in *repeat while* and *if..then* statements. The conditions work the same way in *repeat while* and *if..then*.

The Parentheses Around the Condition Are Optional

Yes, that's right, I've been making you type more characters than you have to. There is no difference between

```
repeat while (the mouseDown = TRUE)

    beep

end repeat
```

and...

```
repeat while the mouseDown = TRUE

    beep

end repeat
```

This is also true for *if..then*.

```
if (the mouseDown = TRUE) then

    beep

end if
```

is completely equivalent to

```
if the mouseDown = TRUE then

    beep

end if
```

I didn't tell you this because I wanted you to be really clear that the condition was separate from the rest of the command. For the rest of the book, I won't use parentheses.

TRUE Means 1, and FALSE Means 0

The designers of Lingo decided that TRUE would be synonymous with the number 1, and FALSE would be synonymous with the number 0. In fact, all Lingo functions and properties that return TRUE or FALSE actually return 1 or 0. So,

```
repeat while the mouseDown = TRUE
```

is the same as

```
repeat while the mouseDown = 1
```

And don't forget that

```
if the mouseDown = TRUE then
```

is the same as

```
if the mouseDown = 1 then
```

If you open the Message Window and type

```
put the mouseDown
```

it will display

```
-- 0
```

which means FALSE, the mouse is not down.

You Can Drop the "equals true" From the Condition Because It Is Implied

In the line

```
repeat while the mouseDown = 1
```

the conditional question is "Is the *mouseDown* equals true a TRUE statement?" This is actually the same question as "Is the *mouseDown* a TRUE statement?" This line has the same effect as the last one:

```
repeat while the mouseDown
```

Similarly, the following lines are the same:

```
if the mouseDown = TRUE then
```

```
if the mouseDown = 1 then
```

```
if the mouseDown then
```

All Conditions Are Not Created =

In a condition, the bottom line is always "Is the condition TRUE or FALSE?" Most of the conditions we have seen always test if two values are equal, like *the mouseDown = 1*. However, sometimes you want to know if one value is bigger, smaller, or not equal to the other. That's when you need the other logical operators.

The following operators work on **numbers**. The columns on the right are examples of a TRUE condition and a FALSE condition using the specified operator.

Operator		TRUE	FALSE
=	Equals	5 = 5	5 = 3
<>	Does not equal	5 <> 3	5 <> 5

Operator		TRUE	FALSE
<	Less than	3 < 5	5 < 3
>	Greater than	5 > 3	3 > 5
<=	Less than or equals	3 <= 3 3 <= 5	5 <= 3 3 <=2
>=	Greater than or equals	3 >= 3 5 >= 3	3 >= 5

These operators work on strings. The <, >, <=, >= operators work alphabetically.

Operator		TRUE	FALSE
=	Equals	"abc" = "abc"	"abc" = "hij"
<>	Does not equal	"abc" <> "efg"	"abc" <> "abc"
<	Less than	"abc" < "efg"	"efg" < "abc"
>	Greater than	"efg" > "abc"	"abc" > "efg"
<=	Less than or equals	"abc" <= "abc" "abc" <= "efg"	"efg" <= "abc"
>=	Greater than or equals	"abc" >= "abc" "efg" >= "abc"	"abc" >= "efg"
contains	Does a contain b?	"abc" contains "bc"	"abc" contains "def"

What I Didn't Tell You About *Repeat loops*

Are you beginning to understand just how wacky Lingo can be? As you begin to mature as a Lingo programmer, these options and quirks will become second nature. They still seem screwed up at first for everybody. It's not just you.

As you may have guessed, repeat loops aren't as straightforward as I may have lead you to believe. Nothing is or will be.

You Don't Have to Finish a Loop If You Don't Want To

Often, you want to hop out of a *repeat* loop before it would normally be over. To allow this, Lingo supplies a command called *exit repeat*. Whenever the Lingo elf sees this command, it jumps out of the current loop and executes the line after the *end repeat*.

This example outputs increasing integers forever, until the mouse button is pressed. Then, it beeps.

```
put 1 into num

repeat while TRUE

    put num

    put num+1 into num

    if the mouseDown = TRUE then

        exit repeat

    end if

end repeat

beep
```

This next example is taken from the final *moveFace* handler in the Chapter 4 project. As soon as an intersection is found, we kick out of the loop because we already have what we want.

```
. . .repeat with loopNum=5 to 8

    if ( sprite snum intersects loopNum ) then

        puppetSprite loopNum, true

        set the stretch of sprite loopNum to false

        put the memberNum of sprite snum + 1 into skullCast

        set the memberNum of sprite loopNum to skullCast

        exit repeat

    end if

end repeat. . .
```

Don't confuse *exit repeat* with *exit*. The *exit* command jumps out of the current handler, and the *exit repeat* command jumps out of the current repeat loop.

You Can Count *down* with *repeat with*

It's easy to use *repeat with* to count to 10.

```
repeat with i = 1 to 10

    put i

end repeat
```

But can we count from 10 to 1? It turns out that we can, using the **down** keyword.

```
repeat with i = 10 down to 1

    put i

end repeat
```

Sometimes the Lingo Elf Will Skip the Whole Repeat Loop

The elf will never venture inside a *repeat while* loop if the condition is false. For example,

```
repeat while (the mouseDown = FALSE)

    beep

end repeat
```

If the mouse is pressed when the elf gets to the *repeat while* line, it will skip right past this loop.

It's quite common to use a variable in a *repeat with* test condition. This next code fragment moves all the Sprites between 1 and the variable *numSprites* to location 320,240.

```
repeat with i = 1 to numSprites

    puppetSprite i, true

    set the locH of sprite i to 320
```

```
    set the locV of sprite i to 240

    updateStage

end repeat
```

This loop will never execute, though, if the value of *numSprites* is less than 1. However, if *numSprites* is 1, the loop will execute once.

The *repeat with* Variable Hangs Around Until the End of the Handler

The counter variable you use in a *repeat with* loop gets created like any other local variable. It keeps together and holds its value until the end of the handler. In this next example, the final value that gets output to the Message Window is 11.

```
repeat with i= 1 to 10

    put i

end repeat

put i
```

What We Didn't Tell You About *If..then*

There are many ways to use slang and shorten if..then statements. Most of them will leave you confused when you try to edit your code two weeks later. Remember, writing clear and readable code is more important than saving on typing a few characters. The number of characters rarely makes a difference in performance.

For Short *if..then* Statements, You Can Fit Everything on One Line

When you want to use an *if..then* statement, and you want to execute only one command, you can fit the whole statement on one line.

```
if the mouseDown = TRUE then

    beep

end if
```

This construct can be shortened to

```
if the mouseDown = TRUE then beep
```

For this version, you don't need an *end if*.

This version of *if..then* isn't for lazy programmers; it's for sloppy programmers. You can't add an *else* clause; you can't add another command; it's hard to read; and it's hard to debug. I mention it only because you might see it in other people's code. You shouldn't use it because you know better.

You Can Chain *if..then* Statements with *else if*

Say you have an interface in which a user has to drag a running man into one of three doors. Perhaps you have saved which door the user chose in a local variable, *door*. Now your program has to figure out what to do, based on the value of door. The code might look like this:

```
if door = 1 then

    go to movie "livingRoom.dir"

else

    if door = 2 then

        go to movie "diningRoom.dir"

    else

        if door = 3 then

            go to movie "familyRoom.dir"

        else

            alert "please choose door 1, 2, or 3"

        end if

    end if

end if
```

Can you imagine if you had 5 or 10 rooms? The nested *if..then* structures get unwieldy pretty quickly.

For situations like this, Lingo provides a variation of the *else* statement, called *else if*. By combining an *else* and an *if*, you are extending the first *if..then*, instead of embedding one within another. You need only one *end if* to bookend the construct. The code would look like this:

```
if door  = 1 then

    go to movie "livingRoom.dir"

else if door = 2 then

    go to movie "diningRoom.dir"

else if door = 3 then

    go to movie "familyRoom.dir"

else

    alert "please choose door 1, 2, or 3"

end if
```

You Can Replace *if..then* Chains with a *case* Statement

Lingo gives us a cousin of *if..then* for special situations, called *case*. When you want to compare a single variable or expression, like *door* in the above example, against a series of values, it is more efficient to use a *case* statement than chained *if..then* statements.

The same example would look like this in a *case* statement.

```
case door of

    1:  go to movie "livingRoom.dir"

    2:  go to movie "diningRoom.dir"

    3:  go to movie "familyRoom.dir"


    otherwise alert "please choose door 1, 2, or 3"

end case
```

We will be using *case* again in future chapters, and we'll examine it more closely.

What I Didn't Tell You About *Variables*

Well I didn't tell you anything about global variables, but I'm still saving that for Chapter 6. The following tips, however, apply to both local and global variables.

Put into, set to, and *set* = All Do the Same Thing

There are actually several ways to put a value into a variable. You will see all of them in other people's movies. I tend to use *put into* with variables, *set to* with properties, and *set* = with xtras.

The following lines are all the same:

```
put 2 into door

set door to 2

set door = 2
```

Avoid Keywords When Naming Variables

You can name a variable anything you want, almost. You can't use a Lingo **keyword**, meaning a command, function, or any other word that Lingo considers part of its vocabulary. For example, *door* is a legal variable name, but *repeat* is not.

You Can Use the Same Local Variable Name in Different Handlers

We have already established that a local variable exists only as long as its handler is executing. What I didn't mention was that **a local variable is visible only to the handler that created it**. This means that it is OK to use the same variable name in two different handlers because each handler can only see its own variable.

Let's say we have two handlers, *dragFace* and *switchFace*:

```
on switchFace spriteNum

   put 3 into castNum

   -- blah, blah, blah
```

```
end


on moveFace spriteNum

   -- move face around blah, blah, blah

   put 5 into castNum

   switchFace spriteNum

end
```

Let's say *moveFace* is called with an initial value of 5 for *spriteNum*. Some hypothetical code for dragging the Sprite around is executed, then the line *put 5 into castNum* is executed. This causes the elf to create a local variable called *castNum* and put a 5 into it. Simple enough.

Next, *switchFace* is called, with *spriteNum* as a parameter. Because the current value of *spriteNum* is 5, 5 is supplied to *switchFace* as an initial value.

The Lingo elf prepares to execute *switchFace* by creating a new local variable called *spriteNum* and sticks a 5 into it. It continues executing, creating a new local variable called *castNum* and putting a 3 into it.

At this point, there are two variables named *spriteNum* and two variables called *castNum*. The handler *moveFace* owns one variable of each name. The handler *switchFace*, also owns one variable of each name. Each handler can see only the local variables that it owns. The situation looks like Figure 5.3.

Eventually, *switchFace* finishes executing. The variables that it owns are killed, and the Lingo elf returns to *moveFace*. It hits the end of this handler and kills the remaining local variables called *spriteNum* and *castNum*.

Use Quotes to Surround Strings, But Not Variables

Whenever you want Lingo to accept a string of characters, you have to surround it in quotes.

```
put "abcdef" into myStringVariable
```

is legal, but

```
put abcdef into myStringVariable
```

Figure 5.3 Four distinct local variables in two distinct handlers.

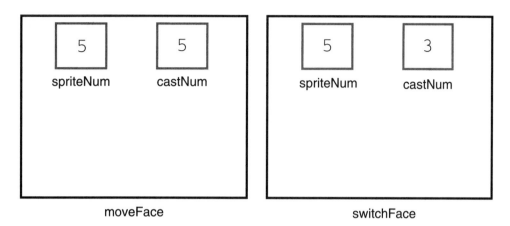

is not. This works for Cast Member names and frame labels, too.

```
go to frame "smile"
```

is legal, but

```
go to frame smile
```

is not.

However, when you specify a variable name, you can't use quotes.

```
put "abcdef" into myStringVariable
```

is legal, but

```
put "abcdef" into "myStringVariable"
```

is not.

What We Didn't Tell You About *Custom Handlers*

Many novice programmers are scared of Custom Handlers or wonder why they should bother with them. The Custom Handlers is the most useful concept for organizing your thoughts, intentions, and code. The larger your project, the more you need them.

You Can Make a Custom Function

Adding a custom handler is like adding a command to Lingo. By including one statement, you can turn the handler into a custom *function*. A function is simply a handler that returns a value to its caller.

The magic command is *return*. If you want to your function to return an 8, for example, you would place the command somewhere in the handler:

```
on blah

    .  .  .

    return 8

    .  .  .

end
```

The handler must call the function with parentheses around any parameters that it sends to the function. If the function does not expect parameters, like *blah*, the caller must use empty parentheses.

The important thing to remember is that, as soon as the Lingo elf executes a *return* command, it immediately returns to the caller, forgetting that the rest of the handler exists. Here is a simple handler that outputs the return value of the function *blah*.

```
on mouseDown

    put blah()

end
```

We could split the *moveFace* handler from Chapter 4 into a handler and a function to see how these functions work. We would probably want to put the intersect-checking code into its own function. This function would return the number of the sprite that was intersected by *snum* or zero if none of the sprites was intersected.

```
on checkIntersections snum

    repeat with loopNum=5 to 8
```

```
    if ( sprite snum intersects loopNum ) then

        return loopNum

    end if

  end repeat



    return 0

end
```

This function *checkIntersections* takes one parameter, *snum*. Remember, *snum* is local to *checkIntersections* and is different from any other handler that has a local variable that happens to be called *snum*. It loops through sprites 5, 6, 7, and 8, checking to see if any of them intersect with sprite *snum*. As soon as an intersection is found, the inside of the *if..then* is executed, and the current value of *loopNum* is returned to the caller. None of the rest of the handler is executed.

If there are no intersections, the *repeat with* loop will finish without executing the inside of the *if..then*. The Lingo elf will reach *return 0*, which will return a 0 to the caller.

We could modify *moveFace* to take advantage of our new handler. Here's a version of what that might look like.

```
on moveFace snum

  puppetSprite snum,true

  repeat while (the mouseDown = true)

    set the locV of sprite snum to the mouseV

    set the locH of sprite snum to the mouseH

    updateStage

  end repeat



  put checkIntersections(snum) into intersected
```

```
if intersected > 0 then

    puppetSprite intersected, true

    set the stretch of sprite intersected loopNum to false

    put the memberNum of sprite intersected + 1 into skullCast

    set the memberNum of sprite intersected to skullCast

end if



    puppetSprite snum,false

end
```

One movie Can Have Multiple Movie Scripts

Often, you will have to create many handlers to handle a specific screen or a specific task. In a typical large movie, you will have two or three "sets" of custom handlers and functions. Putting them all into one Movie Script can become an organizational and scrolling nightmare.

Director can actually handle multiple Movie Scripts in the same movie. To you, they seem like two different Scripts because they will live in separate Cast Members. Lingo behaves as though all the Movie Scripts in the movie were appended together, in one huge script. The separation is to help humans organize things (and to get around a size limit).

To create a new Movie Script, go to the first one by pressing Control-Shift-U, (or Command-Shift-U on the Mac). Then, click the + button in the upper left of the Script Window (Figure 5.4).

You should probably name both Movie Script Cast Members so that you can tell them apart. When you press Control-Shift-U, whichever Movie Script is first in the Cast will be opened. You can move them around in the Cast as much as you like.

One Handler Can Take Multiple Parameters

In Chapter 4, the *moveFace* handler took one parameter, *snum*. The idea of using a parameter was to generalize the handler. Instead of hard-coding a Sprite number in

Figure 5.4 The Script Window.

New Movie Script

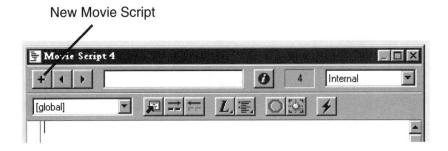

the handler, we wanted it to be able to work on any Sprite number. Here is the final version of that handler.

```
on moveFace snum

    puppetSprite snum,true

    repeat while (the mouseDown = true)

        set the locV of sprite snum to the mouseV

        set the locH of sprite snum to the mouseH

        updateStage

    end repeat


    repeat with loopNum=5 to 8

        if ( sprite snum intersects loopNum ) then

            puppetSprite loopNum, true

            set the stretch of sprite loopNum to false

            put the memberNum of sprite snum + 1 into skullCast

            set the memberNum of sprite loopNum to skullCast

        end if
```

```
    end repeat


    puppetSprite snum,false

end
```

This was invoked from an event handler like this one:

```
on mouseDown

    moveFace 10

end
```

If we were to generalize this handler even further, we would want to change it to check for intersection against any range of Sprite numbers, instead of just 5 to 8. It would make a lot of sense for the handler to accept both numbers, a first and last sprite in the range, as parameters.

When you define a handler with multiple parameters, you separate each parameter with a comma in the definition line. The more generalized *moveFace* would look like this.

```
on moveFace snum, firstSprite, lastSprite

    puppetSprite snum,true

    repeat while (the mouseDown = true)

        set the locV of sprite snum to the mouseV

        set the locH of sprite snum to the mouseH

        updateStage

    end repeat


    repeat with loopNum=firstSprite to lastSprite

        if ( sprite snum intersects loopNum ) then

            puppetSprite loopNum, true

            set the stretch of sprite loopNum to false
```

```
        put the memberNum of sprite snum + 1 into skullCast

        set the memberNum of sprite loopNum to skullCast

      end if

    end repeat


    puppetSprite snum, false

end
```

When you call this handler, you supply values for each parameter, in the order they are specified in the handler. This example supplies a value of 10 for *snum*, 15 for *firstSprite*, and 25 for *lastSprite*.

```
on mouseDown

  moveFace 10, 15, 25

end
```

Parameters That Aren't Sent Values Are Void

Sometimes you write a handler that a different programmer has to use. Because you can't be sure that the other programmer is going to know how to use your handlers, you can help him or her along a little. One of the more common mistakes is for the other programmer not to supply all the required parameters. You can write your handler to make sure all the required parameters are given.

If a parameter is not supplied, it is **void**. Lingo supplies a function called *voidP* that returns TRUE if a parameter or variable is **void**, and FALSE if it has a good value. The following code fragment is what you might add to the *moveFace* handler that we just wrote.

```
on moveFace snum, firstSprite, lastSprite

  if voidP(lastSprite) or voidP(firstSprite) or voidP(snum) then

    alert "You supplied the wrong number of parameters, bozo!"

  end if

      . . .
```

You would get the alert message if you called *moveFace* with fewer than three parameters; for example:

```
on mouseDown

    moveFace 3, 5

end
```

You Can Jump Out of a Handler at Any Time

There are three commands, used in different situations, that allow you to jump out of the current handler. There are three probable situations:

Situation 1: You are in handler, and you want to jump out of it.

Use the *exit* keyword. If this handler was called by another handler, the Lingo elf returns to the caller to finish executing it.

The following handler, which is meant to do some hypothetical Windows-specific stuff, stops executing if it is running on a Macintosh.

(The function **the platform** returns a "Macintosh, 68k," "Macintosh, PowerPC," "Windows, 16," or "Windows, 32" depending on the running platform.)

```
on doWindowsStuff

    if the platform contains "Macintosh" then

        exit

    end if


    -- do Windows specific calls

end
```

Situation 2: You are in a custom **function,** meaning a custom handler that returns a value. You want to jump out of it, but the calling code is expecting a value.

Take a look at the section earlier in this chapter that explains custom functions.

Situation 3: You are in a handler, but something major goes wrong, and you want to stop all active handlers from executing, meaning the current one, and the handler that called it, and the handler that called that, and so on. Perhaps you are executing a series of commands that absolutely, positively has to abort if the user presses the mouse button.

The name of this command is *abort*. Avoid using this if you can; it tends to lead to all sorts of nasty bugs because it affects more handlers than just the one that it is in.

```
on doSmallPieceOfBigSequence

    if the mouseDown = 1 then

        abort        -- stop executing any current Lingo!

    end if

end
```

You Shouldn't Put More Than 32,000 Characters in One Movie Script

In a large project, you might easily create more and more handlers in the Movie Script. Everything will seem to work normally, but when you make a projector, none of the custom handlers works anymore. No matter how hard you look at the code, none of the errors makes sense.

This might be because your Movie Script is too darned big. The reasonable limit for a Movie Script is around 32,000 characters. Any more characters, and you're asking for trouble.

You can find out just how big it is by clicking on the Movie Script in the Cast Window and choosing Cast Member: Properties from the Modify menu. In the lower left, Director will tell you how big the Cast Member is. If it is more than 32,000 bytes, you should probably split it into two Movie Scripts. Sometimes you won't see random happenings until you make a projector, and sometimes you won't run into any trouble at all. Some think this problem is mythical, but I thought I should warn you anyway.

You Don't Have to Put a Custom Handler into the Movie Script

I have told you that if you put a custom handler into the Movie Script, any handler, anywhere in the movie, can access it. This is almost always where you should put a custom handler.

However, there are other places to put a custom handler. When the Lingo elf tries to invoke a custom handler, it first looks in the current Script for the handler. If it doesn't find it there, it goes and looks for it in the Movie Script.

So, when you want to use a custom handler but you don't want it to be visible to the whole movie, place it in the same Script as its caller. As we said, there is rarely a reason to do this.

Part Two
Tricks of The Trade

6

A Quicktime Player

Chapter Objective

Quicktime is a technology from Apple Computer that lets you play **digital video,** that is, video that you watch on your computer screen. We will discuss what Quicktime is, how to use it in Director, and how to play a few common CD-ROM tricks with it.

While building the project we will find a need for **global variables.** We will also do a simple **rollover** and create two clever user interface widgets: a **slider-bar** and a **rotating dial** for the Quicktime movie.

This chapter is **not** about how to make a playable Quicktime movie—that could be a book in itself. If you are in a position where you have to make the movies yourself, you should pick up a book on Quicktime or Adobe Premiere. However, I have included a quick primer on Quicktime to explain the necessary concepts.

Introduction to Project: A Quicktime Player

This project is a Quicktime Player inset into a graphic screen, much the way you might see it in a multimedia CD-ROM. Figure 6.1 shows the first frame of the project.

Figure 6.1 The first frame of the project.

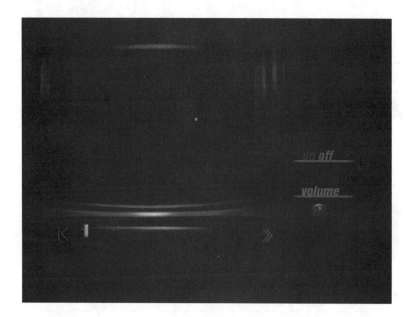

The Quicktime movie is positioned in the screen of the television set. Below it is a slider-bar, which shows the current position in the video and lets the user jump to any point in the movie. On the television control panel are the power switch, Rewind and Fast Forward buttons, and the volume knob.

Here's how the project is supposed to work:

1. When the user gets to the screen, the video is paused.

2. If the user clicks the power switch, the video plays and the switch moves to the ON position. If the user clicks it again, the video pauses and the switch moves to the OFF position.

3. If the user clicks the Rewind button, the video skips to the beginning.

4. If the user presses the Fast Forward button, the video jumps ahead a couple of seconds. This keeps happening until the user releases the mouse button.

5. If the user rolls the cursor over the video, the cursor changes to an Up Arrow. If the user clicks on the video, it grows to full-screen video mode, and the cursor changes to a Down Arrow. Clicking again returns to normal mode.

6. The slider on the bar always represents the current position in the video. If the video has played about halfway through, the slider should be about halfway across the bar. As the video plays, the slider should move across the bar.

7. If the user presses down on the bar, the slider should be dragged along with the cursor. As this happens, the current time of the video follows the slider.

8. If the user presses the mouse button down on the volume knob, he or she is able to spin the knob around until the button is released. The Quicktime volume reflects the current position of the volume knob.

Check out the finished version of this project in Ch6_done.dir in the Chapter6 folder on the CD-ROM. In case you are wondering, that is me, Vineel, jumping out of an airplane with a guy strapped to my back who holds the Guinness Book World Record for most jumps (something more than 22,000). It was a comforting thought as we fell free of the plane.

The unprogrammed version of the movie is in Ch6.dir in the same folder. You won't need it for a few pages, though, because we're going to talk about Quicktime.

If you already know a lot about Quicktime, you can skip the next couple of sections. What follows is a small primer on Quicktime.

A Quick Quicktime Primer

You could write a whole book about Quicktime. People have. I'm not.

In the following few sections I give you information that will fill your brain with the basic technical understanding of digital video that every multimedia programmer needs. I don't talk about how to create stunning Quicktime, just how to play it. Believe you me, that's enough for now.

Digital Video Is Hard on a Computer

We all know video (it's that stuff on your TV screen). The technology of television playback is pretty simple. You read an electromagnetic wave, scanline by scanline, and shoot an interpretation at the screen, scanline by scanline. You shoot audio out of a speaker in a similar way. We've gotten pretty good at making TV work.

Trying to make video play back from a computer with a CD-ROM drive has proven much more difficult. Consider what the computer has to do:

1. Come up with some digital interpretation of the analog video, and store it on a CD-ROM.

2. Read a little of the video and audio from the CD-ROM into RAM.

3. Assemble an image of the frame somewhere off-screen because the whole frame is supposed to show up, on-screen, at once.

4. Put the image into a window on the screen.

5. Play a little piece of the sound, but only enough to stay in synch with the image.

6. Repeat from step 2. Do this sequence about 30 times per second.

The first problem is that CD-ROM drives are slow. A computer can read about 150k per second from a single-speed drive. A double-speed drive gives about twice that, or 300k per second. A quad-speed drive gives 600k per second, and so on. Given the overhead in a normal computer and operating system, you can count on getting much lower data rates, by 20-30 percent. A good rule of thumb for a double-speed drive, for example, is 225k-250k per second. In normal, uncompressed form, a single frame, at 24-bit color, is a little over 900k. You couldn't read just one of these frames from a double-speed CD-ROM drive in one second, never mind 30!

The second problem is that many computers are really bad at moving data through the system. Even if the CD-ROM was lightning fast, the system still has to move the data into RAM, and then to a different piece of RAM that represents the window on the screen. Many older computers are incapable of moving and processing this much data at 30 frames per second, at full frame.

The third problem is that the digital data that represents the **sound** also has to be read into RAM from the CD-ROM, then handed to the computer's sound managing software, which then hands it off to the sound hardware. One second of uncompressed, 16-bit stereo sound (CD quality) is about 176k. That comes out of the 250k per second that you can physically read from a double-speed CD-ROM, leaving about 74k per second for the images.

The fourth problem is that every computer in the world is different from every other computer in the world. It is impossible for you, as a multimedia author, to know exactly what software and hardware configurations on which your video will be playing back.

With all these problems, it's a wonder that digital video ever works. Creating playable digital video is a process of figuring out which trade-offs to make, in terms of image size and image and sound quality, for the specific movie. Apple Computer invented Quicktime, to work within these limitations and put video into your computer.

Quicktime Files and Compression

A Quicktime movie (usually with the extension .MOV) sits in a file on your hard disk or CD-ROM. The movie file has, within it, **tracks** of different types. A movie usually has one video track and one audio track, but it may have more than one of each. There are also other types, such as a text track or a Sprite track. Director can manipulate text tracks, but not many people have a use for them.

The tracks in a Quicktime movie are laid out along a fixed timeline. This means that, if frame 10 of video track 1 is supposed to play one-half second from the start of the movie, it will always play at one-half second from the start of the movie. If the word "hello" is spoken at three-quarters second from the start of the movie, then "hello" will always be spoken three-quarters second into the movie. The data for the audio and video are laid out in the file in more or less sequential chunks, to help Quicktime read just enough from the disk to keep the audio and video in synch, along the timeline (Figure 6.2).

Since there is no way read 30 full-sized images from the CD-ROM in one second, a video track is generally **compressed**. A particular type of compression is called a **codec**, for compressor-decompressor. Quicktime has a codec that is good at compressing still images, called the **Graphics** codec. Another codec is good at crunching computer-generated (cleanly-colored) animation sequences, called the **Animation** codec. The most useful codec, which is used for almost all CD-ROM real-world video, is called **Cinepak**.

Figure 6.2 The video track and the audio track.

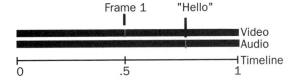

The Cinepak compressor goes through a movie, looking for similarities between frames. If the top-left corner of the movie is the same color for the first 15 frames, Cinepak just records "top left is the same for 15 frames," instead of actually recording the top left 15 times. In most frames of a Cinepak track, **all that gets written to the file are the differences between frames.** These are called, of course, **difference frames.**

However, sometimes the image in a frame is completely different from the one before it. In a case like this, Cinepak shrugs its shoulders and records the entire frame image to the disk. Because this kind of frame is the key to which differences are added, it is called a **key frame.**

Cinepak records images in 24-bit color (a.k.a. millions of colors). If the playback monitor is set to 24-bit color, then the image can play back at that quality. If the playback monitor is set to 16-bit color (a.k.a thousands of colors), the video images will be reduced to 16-bit in real time, still looking great. If the playback monitor is set to 8-bit color (a.k.a. 256 colors), the video image will be dithered to 8-bit in realtime.

Cinepak also has a 256-color mode, which you should use if you are sure your movie will be played only on 8-bit monitors. However, 16-bit displays are pretty common as of late 1996, and 256-color Cinepak won't be as good as normal Cinepak on these monitors.

We always make other concessions to data rate in Cinepak movies, too. Instead of trying for 30 fps, we usually stick to 15 fps or 10 fps. Instead of recording 640 × 480 video, we record 320 × 240 video (this is full-screen versus quarter-screen image size). With Cinepak, it is possible to compress a quarter-screen video track to play back with decent image quality at 180k–200k per second, leaving 25k–50k per second for audio.

CD-quality audio is 16-bit, 44.1 khz stereo. This means that there are 44,100 samples per second taken of the sound, each sample is recorded in a 16-bit number (2 bytes,) and there are two streams of data (one each for the left and right speakers). This comes out to about 176k per second for audio. Because we have only 25k–50k to work with, we have to make a trade-off.

Our first concession is generally to make the audio track mono. This cuts the required data rate for the soundtrack in half, to 88k per second. Next, we usually cut the sample rate in half, from 44.1 khz to 22.05 khz, which cuts the data rate by another half, to 44k per second. Sixteen-bit 22khz mono is usually as low as we have to go.

You could also compress the audio, using Quicktime's IMA compression, which will cut the data rate for 16-bit 44khz stereo soundtrack down to 44k per second. However, as of late 1996, most multimedia products have to work on 486 machines running Windows 3.1, which aren't fast enough to **decompress** compressed audio for smooth playback. If you feel you can rely on, at least, mid-level Macintosh or Pentium Windows machines, you should definitely explore IMA compression.

Quicktime Playback

If a Quicktime movie file is laid out at 15 frames per second, with audio, Quicktime will do its best to show all 15 frames and play one second of audio, every second. Unfortunately, this isn't always possible. Sometimes, the computer that Quicktime is running on isn't fast enough to display all 15 frames **and** play the audio. Something's got to go. And when something's got to go, Quicktime generally drops some video.

Quicktime's first priority is to keep up with the timeline of the movie file. If it has been 10 seconds since the movie started playing, Quicktime does not want to be displaying second 8 of the movie. It wants to display second 10.

Quicktime's second priority is to keep the audio constant and smooth. Interruptions in audio are painfully obvious to the human ear, so Quicktime tries to avoid this if at all possible.

Its last priority is to make the video play back smoothly. If Quicktime can't accomplish this, it will "drop" or "skip" a few frames. Say Quicktime can play only 13 frames per second on a given computer while maintaining smooth sound. This means that twice a second, Quicktime will skip a frame, causing a slight jerk in the on-screen video. However, this jerking is less noticeable than audio dropouts or a movie that is way behind schedule.

Quicktime: Macintosh versus Windows

As you might imagine, Quicktime generally works better on Apple Macintosh computers than it does on Microsoft Windows-based computers, since Apple wrote the software. Microsoft has a competing technology called **Video for Windows** (which has also been called DirectMovie, or ActiveMovie, or AVI, depending on what you read).

Director supports both types of digital video in Windows. However, Quicktime is the only one that is available on the Macintosh **and** in Windows. **Quicktime for Windows** also seems to perform better than Video for Windows on MS Windows machines. Everybody I have talked to in the commercial multimedia industry uses Quicktime. You probably should, too. (Brainwash alert.)

If you really want to use Video for Windows, most of this chapter will apply to you, too. Director uses pretty much the same commands to control Quicktime and VFW.

As of late 1996, you need a Macintosh to create Quicktime movies (but this might have changed by the time you read this). Adobe Premier for Windows has a special feature that makes Quicktime, but that's a special trick. As of this writing, a Macintosh-made Quicktime file can be played in Windows only after it has been "flattened." This is a process in which the Macintosh-only resource fork is copied into the cross-platform data fork of the movie file. This too might change in the future.

Quicktime versus Director

Quicktime is a piece of software that sits on your hard disk, waiting to exercise the computer's resources to play a piece of video on your screen. Director (or a projector) is a piece of software that sits on your hard disk, waiting to exercise the computer's resources to play back a piece of multimedia on your screen.

Quicktime and Director are like two siblings competing for their parents' attention.

A normal multimedia computer has only one processor, one hard disk, one CD-ROM drive, one video card, and one pool of RAM. When you play a Quicktime movie from within a Director movie, both pieces of software have to share these resources, since they are playing in the same sandbox. As you can imagine, this leads to a whole bunch of problems.

As an example: one of the least known stupid things about Microsoft Windows is that it has only one sound channel. This means that **only** Quicktime or **only** Director can be playing sound at the same time. Generally, whichever one starts playing sound first gets the sound channel, and the other is silent. The Macintosh lets you play multiple sounds at once.

The reason Director for Windows can play multiple sounds at once **without** Quicktime is that Director mixes the sounds together into one sound by itself,

before handing it off to Windows. However, Quicktime and Director are separate software entities, and they can't mix their audio together.

We will visit more problems as this chapter progresses. For now, just keep in mind that dealing with Quicktime in Director is always an adventure.

Starting the Project: Setting Up the Quicktime Movie

Unfortunately, both Quicktime and Director call their files "movies." I'll try to be as clear as possible as to which kind I'm talking about.

Open the Director movie Ch6.dir, from the Chapter6 folder on the CD-ROM. The first frame looks like Figure 6.3.

The Quicktime movie has not been placed onto the Stage yet. We'll have to prepare it for use.

Find the Quicktime movie skydive.mov in the Cast. Click the i button to get information on it. The dialog should look something like Figure 6.4.

Figure 6.3 The first frame of the Director Movie.

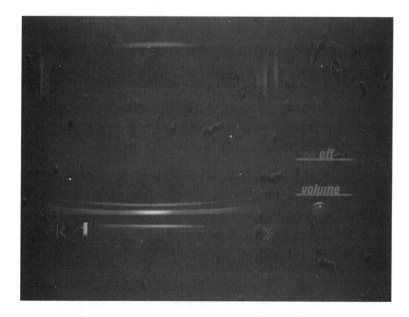

Figure 6.4 Quicktime dialog box.

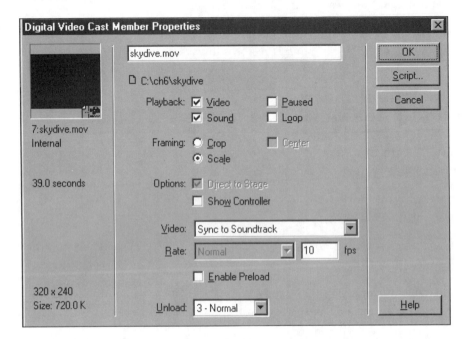

There are four **Playback** checkboxes: **Video, Sound, Paused,** and **Loop.** If **Video** is checked, Director will display the video image of the Quicktime movie when it plays. If Audio is checked, Director will attempt to play the audio while it is playing the movie. If Pause is checked, Director will **not** start playing the Quicktime movie as soon as it appears on stage. If **Loop** is checked, Director will restart the Quicktime movie from the beginning when it ends.

As a general rule of thumb, **Video, Audio,** and **Paused** should be checked when you import a movie, and **Loop** should not.

The next group, **Framing,** has two radio buttons: **Crop** and **Scale.** These buttons determine how the Quicktime movie is framed by any Sprite that is attached to it. If **Scale** is chosen, the rectangle of the Sprite is used to scale the movie to larger, smaller, or a different proportion than it normally wants to be. So, if the Sprite is twice as big as the Quicktime movie attached to it, the movie will play back at double size. This is how we'll do full-screen video soon.

If Crop is chosen, the rectangle of the Sprite will crop the Quicktime movie to its borders. Normally the image area toward the bottom and right get cropped. If you check the **Centered** option, the movie will be centered inside the crop rectangle. This is a feature of questionable value.

Put the radio button on **Scale.**

The next group, **Options,** has two checkboxes: **Direct to Stage** and **Show Controller**. (If you are using a Windows machine, **Direct to Stage** is grayed out because Quicktime for Windows is **always Direct to Stage**.) **Direct to Stage** means that Quicktime will draw each frame directly to the screen, without going through Director's normal imaging system. This means that Quicktime draws the image **on top** of anything Director tries to put into the same area, on-screen. This prevents you from putting any Sprites of any sort on top of the Quicktime movie, onstage.

Direct to Stage pretty much always should be checked, though, or the Quicktime movie won't play back smoothly. Director and Quicktime are squabbling siblings, remember?

If **Show Controller** is checked, the Quicktime controller will appear, which lets the user pause, play, speed up, slow down, change the volume, and jump around a Quicktime movie. It looks like Figure 6.5.

Pretty ugly, isn't it? It's actually too ugly to use in a professional CD-ROM, so we generally end up writing one with Lingo. That's what most of this chapter is about.

So, **Direct to Stage** should be checked, and **Show Controller** should not be.

The next section is a pop-up menu labeled **Video**. This should pretty much always be on **Sync to Soundtrack,** which means that Quicktime should do its best to sync the soundtrack to the video. The other option in the menu, **Play Every Frame (No Sound),** will display every single frame of video, regardless of how long it takes. There isn't often a reason to use this option. The **Rate** option, which should be grayed out, determines at what framerate the video is played back under the **Play Every Frame** option. Again, there isn't much call for this feature.

Figure 6.5 Quicktime controller.

Leave the pop-up menu on **Sync to Soundtrack.**

The next checkbox, **Enable Preload,** is a little weird. Checking this means that Director will try to "preload" the Quicktime movie. It is really rare, however, that a Quicktime movie is so small as to fit into RAM. In theory, Director must preload the first few frames of the movie to help it play smoothly. However, this doesn't always seem to work.

For now, leave **Enable Preload** unchecked. If you run into less-than-smooth Quicktime playback later, try checking it. Sometimes it helps.

Finally, the **Unload** menu, which determines which method Director uses to purge the Cast Member from RAM, should be left at **Normal.**

The fully configured dialog box should look like Figure 6.6. (On the Mac, **Direct to Stage** will not be grayed out.)

If you are following along, click **OK** now. The Quicktime movie is ready to be used!

Figure 6.6 Completed Quicktime Information dialog box.

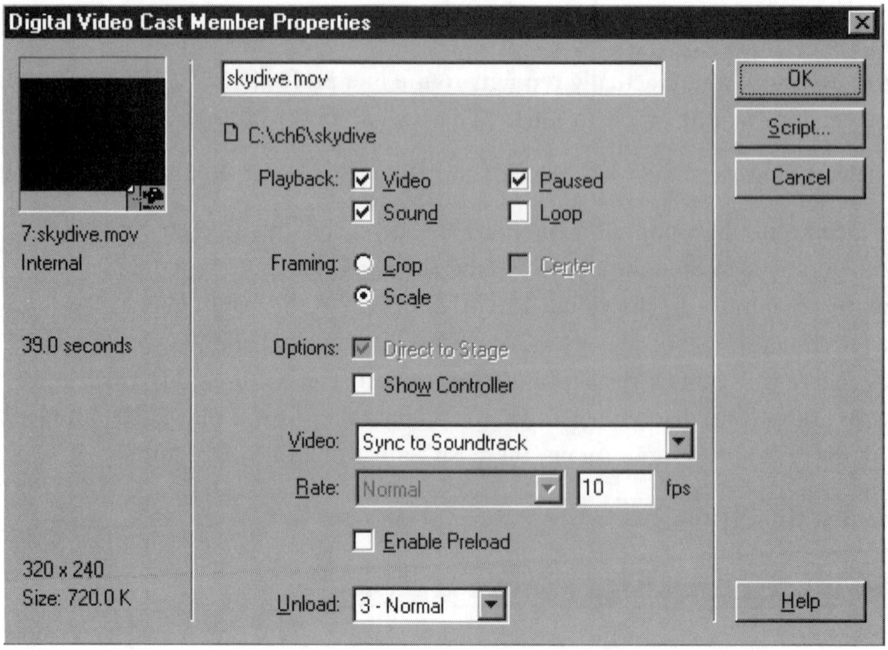

Setting Up the Director Movie

Now that the Quicktime Cast Member is properly configured, it is time to put it onto the Stage.

Open the Cast Window, and drag the Quicktime Cast Member onto the Stage, just as you would with any other Cast Member. Position it inside the screen area of the TV set graphic. Once you have done that, make sure that the Quicktime Sprite is selected and open the Sprite Properties dialog box (choose **Properties** from the **Sprite** pop-up in the **Modify** menu). Take note of the number in the field labeled "Left."

Here's a piece of Quicktime voodoo trivia. For best performance, the left coordinate of a Quicktime Sprite should be a multiple of 4. This makes a more pronounced difference on lower-end machines, but it is good practice. So, a left coordinate of 159 is bad, but 160 is good. The top coordinate doesn't matter.

Open the Score Window and make sure that the Quicktime Sprite is in channel 3, and it is in frames 1, 2, and 3. The finished Score should look something like Figure 6.7.

The last thing we need to do, before we start the cool stuff, is to put a loop on frame 3. So, as we have done before, put this Script in the Frame Script of frame 3.

Figure 6.7 Completed score with Quicktime Sprite in channel 3.

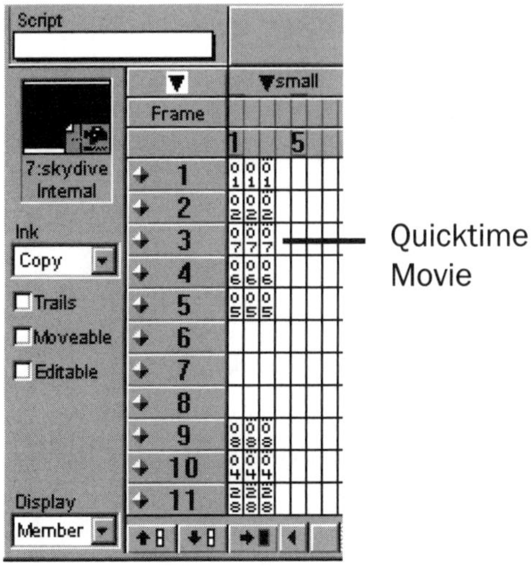

Quicktime Movie

```
on exitFrame

   go to the frame

end
```

Now let's have some fun!

Scripting the Power Switch Using *the movieRate of Sprite*

The next point on the agenda is the on/off switch, which toggles the movie between play and pause modes.

This switch has the following behavior, which we have to implement in Lingo:

1. When the user clicks the switch, it has to figure out whether the Quicktime movie is playing or paused.

2. If the movie is paused, it should be set to playing. If it is playing, it should be set to paused.

3. The switch graphic should change to on or off, to reflect the state of the movie.

To manipulate a Quicktime movie in Director, you work with its **Sprite** and **Cast Member properties**. A Quicktime Sprite has the same *locH* and *locV* properties as other Sprites, but it has a few all its own. The first unique one we will deal with is a Sprite property called *the movieRate of sprite*.

The *movieRate of sprite* property determines how fast the Quicktime movie is playing and in what direction. Assuming you have already put the Quicktime movie into sprite 3, try typing this into the Message Window:

```
put the movieRate of sprite 3
```

Director will return

```
-- 0
```

meaning that the movie is paused. If the *movieRate* is 1, the Quicktime movie is playing forward at the normal speed. If the *movieRate* is .5, the movie is playing forward at half speed. If the *movieRate* is 2, the movie is playing forward at twice its normal speed.

Similarly, if the *movieRate* is −1, the movie is playing backward at normal speed. If the *movieRate* is −2, the movie is playing backward at twice the normal speed.

A word to the wise: Compressed video hates to play too fast or backward, especially from a slow CD-ROM. Have pity on your user.

You can check the *movieRate* of a Sprite at any time, as we just did. However, if the Director movie is playing, we can also **set** the *movieRate*. Make sure the Message Window is showing, then press Rewind and Play. The Director movie should be looping on frame 3. Now type this into the Message Window:

```
set the movieRate of sprite 3 to 1
```

The Quicktime movie should start playing. When you get tired of it, type:

```
set the movieRate of sprite 3 to 0
```

This should pause the Quicktime movie immediately.

Now we know enough to script the first and second behaviors of the power switch! First, we know that the switch has to figure out if the movie is playing or paused. For this, we can use the *movieRate of sprite*. Second, we know that the script has to make a decision, based on the *movieRate* of the Quicktime Movie. Whenever we need to make a decision, an *if..then* is a safe bet. Since the behavior should be triggered when the user clicks the button, we'll put the Script in the Sprite Script of sprite 2, the power switch Sprite. Here's what we've got so far:

```
on mouseDown

    if the movieRate of sprite 3 = 1 then

        -- pause the movie because it was playing

    else

        -- play the movie because it was paused

    end if

end
```

Next, we have to make the Quicktime Movie actually pause or start playing. We have already looked at the code to do this, so all that's left is to put it into our Script.

```
on mouseDown

    if the movieRate of sprite 3 = 1 then

        set the movieRate of sprite 3 to 0

    else

        set the movieRate of sprite 3 to 1

    end if

end
```

We now have a Script that will fulfill the first two behaviors of this switch. Go ahead and try it out.

Finally, the third behavior involves making the switch graphic reflect the on or off state of the movie. There are two bitmap Cast Members for this: One is the switch in the ON position, and the other is the switch in the OFF position (Figure 6.8).

How do you switch one bitmap for another? With the same technique we used in Chapter 4, of course. We will turn sprite 2, the power switch, into a Puppet. Then, we will change its attached Cast Member. We'll throw in an *updateStage* for good measure because we want the changes to show up on the Stage immediately. We could do this with a couple of lines of code:

Figure 6.8 Two bitmap Cast Members, one in the ON position and one in the OFF position.

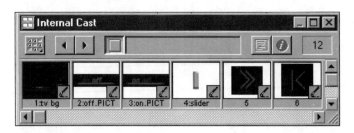

```
puppetSprite 2,true
```

```
set the memberNum of sprite 2 to the number of member "powerOff"
```

```
updateStage
```

This code fragment would set the graphic of the power switch to the OFF position, implying that the movie is paused.

We can easily combine this code with our existing *if..then* structure. For good style, we'll keep the commands that should happen regardless of the *if..then* decision, *puppetSprite 2, true* and *updateStage*, outside the *if..then* decision structure.

Here is the fully functional script.

```
on mouseDown

    puppetSprite 2,true -- the switch sprite

    if the movieRate of sprite 3 = 1 then

        set the movieRate of sprite 3 to 0

        set the memberNum of sprite 2 to the number of member "powerOff"

    else

        set the movieRate of sprite 3 to 1

        set the memberNum of sprite 2 to the number of member "powerOn"

    end if

    updateStage

end
```

Go ahead and put this handler into the Sprite Script of sprite 2. You now have a fully functional power switch!

Scripting the Rewind Button Using *the movieTime of Sprite*

The behavior of the Rewind button is pretty straightforward.

1. When clicked, it should rewind the video to the beginning.

2. If the video was playing, it should start playing again. If it was paused, it should stay paused.

Any Quicktime Sprite that is showing onstage has a current time. If a movie is 10 seconds long, and 1 second has played, then the current time of the movie is 1 second.

One second can be a very long time in multimedia, so Director gets even more specific. When we ask for the current time of a Quicktime movie, Director gives it to us in sixtieths of a second. In Lingoland, **one-sixtieth of a second is called a tick**, as in the tick-ticking of a pretty fast clock.

When we want to ask for the current time of a movie, we use a Sprite property called *the movieTime of sprite*. Let's say that our 10-second Quicktime movie was in sprite 3. If you typed this into the Message Window

```
put the movieTime of sprite 3
```

Director would return

```
-- 60
```

meaning 60 ticks, or 1 second. To get an answer in seconds, just divide the *movieTime of sprite* by 60.

You can **set** this property also. To change the current time of the Quicktime movie to the sixth second, you could use this command in the Message Window:

```
set the movieTime of sprite 3 to 360
```

This will set the current time of the movie to its 360th tick, a number we get from 60 (ticks) times 6 (seconds).

To rewind the movie, meaning to set the *movieTime* of the sprite to its beginning, we would do this:

```
set the movieTime of sprite 3 to 0
```

Zero represents the very beginning of a Quicktime movie.

Trouble is, Quicktime hates to be bothered while it is playing a movie. If a Quicktime movie was playing from a double-speed CD-ROM player, and we, all of a sudden, set the *movieTime* of that movie to 0, the playback would start to stutter or get jerky. The audio might drop out, or some frames might get dropped.

Have you ever seen Quicktime play badly? It's not a pretty sight. What you, as a Lingo programmer, have to do is treat Quicktime with kid gloves. That's right, accept its grouchiness, and work around it. (Or just plug along and hope for the best. Even if you get it to work well on your machine, it's unlikely that it will work well on your customers' machines.)

One way to work around it is to **pause the movie before doing anything radical to it**. You know, radical things like changing its *movieTime*. When the movie is paused, Quicktime isn't quite so busy, and it is much more friendly to operations like setting the *movieTime* of a movie. Once you have finished changing the *movieTime*, you can start up the movie again! Here's what the code would look like:

```
set the movieRate of sprite 3 to 0

set the movieTime of sprite 3 to 0

set the movieRate of sprite 3 to 1
```

It never hurts to get a little more paranoid, especially when Quicktime is involved. It turns out that Director doesn't always actually execute your Quicktime Sprite Lingo commands immediately. Sometimes, it waits to do a bunch at once, or it waits for a movement of the Playback Head. Either way, you lose because your Quicktime movie might stutter.

To force Director to change the Quicktime Sprite properties that you want it to, you can use *updateStage*. Yes, this is the same *updateStage* you use to copy the contents of the Invisible Stage to the normal Stage. It seems to be a multitalented command. Here's what the more-paranoid code would look like:

```
set the movieRate of sprite 3 to 0

updateStage

set the movieTime of sprite 3 to 0

updateStage

set the movieRate of sprite 3 to 1

updateStage
```

If you are wondering, yes, I **would** get this paranoid in a real project. I have learned, the hard way, never to assume that Director will do the right thing. This is especially true when dealing with Director and Quicktime.

So far, we have figured out how to implement the first behavior of the Rewind button.

1. When clicked, it should rewind the video.

How could we accomplish the second behavior?

2. If the video was playing, it should start playing again. If it was paused, it should stay paused.

Here's our situation: based on the *movieRate* of the movie, the code might have to pause the movie, change the movie's time, then set the *movieRate* back to what it used to be. There are several ways to do this. We could use the same logic we used in the power switch and solve the problem with an *if..then* decision.

```
if the movieTime of sprite 3 = 1 then

        -- Quicktime movie is playing

        set the movieRate of sprite 3 to 0

        updateStage

        set the movieTime of sprite 3 to 0

        updateStage

        set the movieRate of sprite 3 to 1 — start it playing again

        updateStage

else

        -- Quicktime movie is paused

        set the movieTime of sprite 3 to 0

        updateStage

        -- leave the movie paused

end if
```

This is not a bad solution. It addresses the situation and gets the job done. However, it is bulky and inelegant. There's a cleaner way.

We could restate the situation this way: The code has to **remember** the *movieRate* of the Quicktime Sprite, pause it, change its *movieTime*, then set the *movieRate* back to what it had been. Whenever we want the Lingo elf to remember something, we can use a **variable**.

If we were going to remember the *movieRate* of sprite 3, we might want to use a variable called *originalRate*. Here's what the code would look like.

```
put the movieRate of sprite 3 into originalRate

set the movieRate of sprite 3 to 0

updateStage

set the movieTime of sprite 3 to 0

updateStage

set the movieRate of sprite 3 to originalRate

updateStage
```

To my taste, this second code fragment is cleaner, more elegant, and more straightforward. However, there is nothing at all wrong with the *if..then* solution. Programming is an art form, as subjective as any other.

To make the Rewind button work, all we have to do is put the above code into a *mouseDown* handler and put it on the Sprite Script of sprite 5, the Rewind button Sprite.

```
on mouseDown

    put the movieRate of sprite 3 into originalRate

    set the movieRate of sprite 3 to 0

    updateStage

    set the movieTime of sprite 3 to 0

    updateStage
```

```
set the movieRate of sprite 3 to originalRate

updateStage
```

end

Scripting the Fast Forward Button

The behavior of the Fast Forward button is a bit vague: If the user presses the Fast Forward button, the video jumps ahead a couple of seconds. This keeps happening until the user releases the mouse button.

Let's start with the easy stuff. Implementing this behavior will obviously require a *mouseDown* event handler because it is triggered when the user presses down the mouse button. It should go in the Sprite Script of the Fast Forward button, which is sprite 5. To make something happen repeatedly while the mouse button is pressed, we can use a *repeat* loop similar to the skull-dragging loop from Chapter 4. Here's the bare structure of the handler.

```
on mouseDown

    repeat while the mouseDown = TRUE

        -- do fast forward stuff to Quicktime movie

    end repeat

end
```

Next, we know from the Rewind button that Quicktime hates to do anything to a movie while it is playing. It's a safe bet that we should pause the Quicktime movie before doing anything, then start playing it again, if it was playing before. We could use the same trick that we used in the Rewind button. It might look like this.

```
on mouseDown

    put the movieRate of sprite 3 into originalRate

    set the movieRate of sprite 3 to 0

    updateStage


    repeat while the mouseDown = TRUE
```

```
      -- do fast forward stuff to Quicktime movie

  end repeat


    set the movieRate of sprite 3 to originalRate

    updateStage

end
```

Now we have to face the question, "What do we put inside the *repeat* loop?"

Fast Forward Techniques

There are three techniques I thought of to make the Quicktime movie fast forward. As always, I'll present my favorite last.

Increase the movieRate

As I mentioned before, setting *the movieRate of sprite* to 2 will play the Quicktime movie at twice its normal speed. Isn't this the simplest way to fast forward?

As it turns out, this is a horrible way to fast forward a normal Quicktime movie. Playing the movie at twice its normal speed requires reading the video and sound information from the CD-ROM at twice the normal speed. If your movie was built to be read at 250k/sec, you will be asking the computer to read 500k/sec from the CD-ROM drive. If the user has a double-speed drive, the computer physically cannot read more than about 280k/sec. By pushing the computer to do more than it can, you are begging for pathetic performance.

However, sometimes you use a low-data-rate movie, like an audio-only movie. In this case, it is perfectly reasonable to double the *movieRate*. If a 16-bit, 22.050kHz, mono audio movie requires 44k/sec, asking it to play at double speed requires reading the CD-ROM at 88k/sec, which isn't a problem on any realistic system.

Because you might want to use this with a different project, or because you might specify an 8x CD-ROM drive on your target system, we should look at the code for this solution. It involves modifying what we already have a little bit.

```
on mouseDown

  put the movieRate of sprite 3 into originalRate
```

```
set the movieRate of sprite 3 to 2

updateStage


repeat while the mouseDown = TRUE

    updateStage -- keep the Quicktime movie updating

end repeat


set the movieRate of sprite 3 to originalRate

updateStage
end
```

The first new line sets the *movieRate* of the Quicktime movie to 2, doubling its playback speed.

The second new line is for the *repeat* loop, *updateStage*. Why do we need anything inside the loop? It would seem, logically, that all we need is this:

. . .

```
repeat while the mouseDown = TRUE

end repeat
```

. . .

The Lingo elf would keep repeating this loop, which does nothing, until the mouse button was released. After that, the script would continue. The problem is the way in which Director and Quicktime interact. Quicktime, the video playback software that sits on your hard disk, doesn't get to process anything unless Director lets it. So, as the Lingo elf runs in this tight little nothing of a loop, it keeps Director so busy that Quicktime never gets a chance to play the movie. As this loop iterates, the Quicktime movie just freezes. (It's not so bad under Windows 95, but it's still risky.)

There are three situations in which Director gives Quicktime a chance to process and play back a movie.

1. The Playback Head is moving, with no Lingo executing anywhere.

2. The Lingo *go the frame* loop is executed, moving the Playback Head.

3. The *updateStage* command is executed.

We have to put the *updateStage* into the loop to force Director to give Quicktime a chance.

Manually Set the movieTime

The second technique I have used is to increase the *movieTime* of the movie manually.

Let's say you want the movie to skip ahead by two seconds. You can ask Director what the current *movieTime* of the movie is, add two seconds to it, then set the *movieTime* of the movie to the new value. The code might look something like this:

```
put the movieTime of sprite 3 into mtime

put mtime + 120 into mtime

set the movieTime of sprite 3 to mtime

updateStage
```

The first line puts the current time of the Movie into a local variable called *mtime*. The second line adds two seconds' worth of ticks to the variable *mtime*. The third line actually sets the current time of the movie to the newly increased value. The fourth line makes sure that Quicktime processes the change immediately.

The net effect, of course, is that the movie skips ahead two seconds. We can add this technique to our skeleton handler pretty easily.

```
on mouseDown

    put the movieRate of sprite 3 into originalRate

    set the movieRate of sprite 3 to 0

    updateStage


    repeat while the mouseDown = TRUE
```

```
        put the movieTime of sprite 3 into mtime

        put mtime + 120 into mtime

        set the movieTime of sprite 3 to mtime

        updateStage

    end repeat


    set the movieRate of sprite 3 to originalRate

    updateStage

end
```

This is a good solution. It works for pretty much any Quicktime movie, and it works acceptably well on a CD-ROM. It's not wonderful, though. If you try it with a Quicktime movie, especially one read from a CD-ROM, you will probably notice that the images don't seem to appear as quickly or responsively as we might hope. It feels as if the computer is struggling to fast forward the movie.

Why is this happening? The explanation goes back to the **key frames** and **difference frames** that we discussed in the Quicktime primer. A Cinepak-compressed video track in a Quicktime movie is made up of **key frames** and **difference frames.** A key frame holds an entire image of the frame. A difference frame holds only the part of the image that is different from the previous frame. This is done for the sake of compression because a partial image is smaller than a full one.

The problem is, our fast-forward technique accesses the Quicktime movie at arbitrary points. If we set the *movieTime* to 140, Quicktime reads the frame at time 140. If this is a difference frame, Quicktime has to check the previous frame. This might also be a partial image. Quicktime would have to go backward, frame by frame, trying to put together all the partial images that it finds. It is easier for Quicktime to go back to the nearest key frame and move forward through the partial frames until it reaches the frame at time 140. Finally, it has a complete image to display on the Stage.

If this sounds slow, it is. Quicktime has to do this every time the *repeat* loop executes, unless we happen to land on a key frame. There's a better way.

Jump to the Next Key Frame

This particular Quicktime movie has at least 1 key frame every 15 frames. At 15 frames per second, this is about 1 key frame per second.

> **NOTE** As of Director version 5.0.1, this method works on the Macintosh, but not in Windows. Director's *trackNextKeyTime* function doesn't work in Windows. We are hoping Macromedia will fix this by the time you read this book.

Lingo has a function that will find the next key frame in a video track. The function is called *trackNextKeyTime*. You supply this function with the number of the Quicktime Sprite and a track number, and it returns the *movieTime* of the next key frame. This code fragment advances the movie to the next key frame.

```
put trackNextKeyTime( sprite 3, 1 ) into mtime

set the movieTime of sprite 3 to mtime

updateStage
```

In the first line, we call the function *trackNextKeyTime(sprite 3,1)*. The Quicktime movie is in sprite 3, and the video track is Quicktime track number 1. The video track in a Quicktime movie is generally track 1, and the audio is in track 2, but this arrangement can be changed by the movie's creator.

The function returns the *movieTime* of the next key frame in the video track and puts that value into a local variable called *mtime*. The next line sets the *movieTime* of the Quicktime movie to that value, and the third line makes sure it happens immediately.

Because we are asking Quicktime to display a key frame, it can read the entire image of the frame immediately. The display updates very quickly. It isn't hard to put this code into the skeleton handler we had before.

```
on mouseDown

    put the movieRate of sprite 3 into originalRate

    set the movieRate of sprite 3 to 0

    updateStage
```

```
repeat while the mouseDown = TRUE

    put trackNextKeyTime( sprite 3, 1 ) into mtime

    set the movieTime of sprite 3 to mtime

    updateStage

end repeat


set the movieRate of sprite 3 to originalRate

updateStage

end
```

In the rest of the chapter, we will assume that you used this option to make the Fast Forward button work. (If you are using Director for Windows 5.0.1, you should be using the "Manually Set The MovieTime option.")

Global Variables: What They Are and Why You Should Like Them

In Chapter 4, we talked about **local variables**. A local variable is a piece of memory that has a name, which is attached to a specific handler. A local variable is **local** to a specific handler. This type of variable is useful for remembering things for a little while, as with *originalRate* in the handler above, or in *repeat* loops. Local variables are the Lingo elf's short-term memory.

However, the Lingo elf also has long-term memory, in the form of **global variables**. Like the other kind, a global variable is a piece of memory that has a name. However, global variables are **not** attached to any specific handler. Once the Lingo elf creates a global variable, it continues to exist and hold its value, until the user quits Director or the projector.

Global variables live in a different place in RAM than local variables do. This **global space** is protected from the ravages of Lingo handlers that execute and die all the time (Figure 6.9). Once a variable is created in global space, it stays there for all time (until the user quits the program).

Figure 6.9 Global variables.

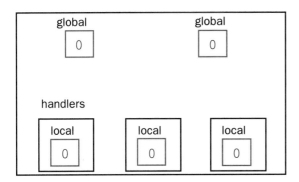

Global variables help us solve many common problems in programming. For example, it helps us avoid **hard-coding. Hard-coding** means using a literal string or number directly in your code. If we used this command in a handler

```
puppetSprite 2,TRUE
```

then the number *2* is hard-coded. This isn't a problem, until for whatever reason, you have to move the Sprite from sprite 2 into sprite 7. You would have to go back into the code and manually change the number 2 to 7.

This also is not a problem if your program is small. But consider the code we have written for this project, which is only half-done. We have used the number **3** more than a dozen times already, since the Quicktime movie is in Sprite Channel 3. By the time we are done, we will probably refer to sprite 3 a dozen more times.

What happens if we need to move the Quicktime movie to sprite 7? Are you going to go back and change two dozen appearances of the number 3? What if you miss one? Every appearance you miss creates a bug in the program.

To get around this, we can **soft-code** the Sprite number. **Soft-coding** means using a value in Lingo code that isn't literal and can be easily changed, like the parameter we used in Chapter 4's *moveFace* handler, or a **global variable**, which we will use here.

Global Variables: How to Use Them

When you use a local variable in a handler, you simply put a value into it.

```
on mouseDown

  put 2 into spriteNum
```

```
puppetSprite spriteNum, TRUE

   . . .

end
```

The local variable that this code creates, *spriteNum*, will be eradicated when the *mouseDown* handler finishes executing.

We want the variable to hang around for the whole life of the program, though. To make this handler see **global space,** we need to **declare** that the variable *spriteNum* is a global. We do that with the Lingo term **global,** like this.

```
on mouseDown

   global spriteNum

   put 2 into spriteNum

   puppetSprite spriteNum,TRUE

   . . .

end
```

The *global* line must always be the first line in the handler (only comment lines can go before it). When the Lingo elf starts to execute this handler, it will read the global *spriteNum* line. The elf knows, now, that whenever it sees the word *spriteNum* **in this handler only,** it will look in the global space for the variable *spriteNum* instead of the local space of the handler. If it doesn't find a global variable called *spriteNum,* it will create one.

Let's extend this example to use two handlers, a *mouseDown* and a *mouseUp*. Let's say that both handlers are in the Sprite Script of the same Sprite.

```
on mouseDown

   global spriteNum

   put 2 into spriteNum

   puppetSprite spriteNum,TRUE

   . . .

end
```

```
on mouseUp

    global spriteNum

    puppetSprite spriteNum, FALSE

end
```

The user presses down on the Sprite, and the *mouseDown* event is triggered. A global variable called *spriteNum* is created, and the number 2 is put into it. Sprite 2 is turned into a Puppet. Then, the elf presumably goes on to execute code that isn't relevant to this discussion.

The user lets go of the mouse button, which triggers the *mouseUp* event. The Lingo elf starts to execute the *mouseUp* handler. After the first line, it knows to look in global space for any references to *spriteNum*. When it parses the second line, it sees *spriteNum* and checks global space for the variable. The elf finds it and sees that it contains the value 2, so it substitutes the value 2 for the variable name and executes the line *puppetSprite 2, FALSE*. Sprite 2 is no longer a Puppet.

What you should realize is that both handlers, which are invisible to each other, can both see the **same variable** in global space. In fact, any handler anywhere in this movie, and any handler in any other movie that is loaded in this session, can see the same global variable if it wants to.

In the *mouseUp* handler, the Sprite number is soft-coded since it is accessed by a global variable instead of a hard number. However, the *mouseDown* handler is still hard-coded since the variable is loaded within the handler. Of course, this has to happen at some point in the code because you have to tell Lingo which Sprite to puppet.

If we end up using 10 global variables for various things, looking through all the code for the one place where a hard-coded value is put into a global variable can get awkward and tedious. That's why we usually load all the global variables in just one place, the *startMovie* handler.

Initializing Global Variables

The process of putting a value into a global variable for the first time is called **initializing** the variable. When you initialize a Lingo variable, you are also creating it. It makes sense, as we just discussed, to do all this initializing in one place, where we are sure the code will execute before any other code does. Lingo has a great event handler made just for this purpose, called *startMovie*.

The *startMovie* event handler, which must be put into the Movie Script, is triggered whenever the movie starts to play. *StartMovie* is the first thing that happens when you hit Play or when your projector starts to run. To complete our little soft-coding example, we could use these three handlers.

The *startMovie* handler would go into the Movie Script.

```
on startMovie

    global spriteNum

    put 2 into spriteNum

end
```

The *mouseDown* and *mouseUp* handlers would go into the Sprite Script.

```
on mouseDown

    global spriteNum

    puppetSprite spriteNum,TRUE

    . . .

end
```

```
on mouseUp

    global spriteNum

    puppetSprite spriteNum, FALSE

end
```

And now, both the *mouseDown* and the *mouseUp* event handlers are soft-coded, and the hard-coding is done in the central *startMovie* handler. If we moved the Sprite to channel 7, all we would have to do is change the one appearance of the number 2, in the *startMovie* handler.

Programmers use techniques like soft-coding to save themselves hassles, bugs, and headaches.

Applying Globals to Our Already-Written Code

In this chapter, we have already written three handlers that have hard-coded Quicktime Sprite numbers. I think it would be useful to go back and soft-code them, before going on with the project.

Since the value that we want to soft-code is the Sprite number of the Quicktime movie, perhaps we should call it **qtSprite**. Because I like to tell at a glance whether a variable is supposed to be local or global, I usually use a **naming convention**. A naming convention is an arbitrary rule of thumb that the programmer establishes at the outset of a project. I don't use elaborate conventions, but I do use a couple. First, I always start a variable name or handler name with a lowercase letter, then capitalize every other word in the name. *spriteNum* is an example of this.

The other convention I follow is to start a global variable name with a lowercase "g." Following this rule of thumb, the name *qtSprite* should really be *gQtSprite*.

The first thing we have to do to the chapter project is add a *startMovie* handler that initializes *gQtSprite*. Put this in the Movie Script of your movie.

```
on startMovie

    global gQtSprite

    put 3 into gQtSprite

end
```

Now, the first thing that happens when you hit Play, before any of the other handlers execute, is that the global variable **gQtSprite** will be created and initialized with the number 3. The next step is to go back to the power switch *mouseDown* handler and replace the number 3 with *gQtSprite* in the Sprite references.

```
on mouseDown

    global gQtSprite

    puppetSprite 2,true -- the switch sprite

    if the movieRate of sprite gQtSprite = 1 then
```

```
        set the movieRate of sprite gQtSprite to 0

        set the memberNum of sprite 2 to the number of member "powerOff"

    else

        set the movieRate of sprite gQtSprite to 1

        set the memberNum of sprite 2 to the number of member "powerOn"

    end if

    updateStage

end
```

I thought about soft-coding the number of the power switch Sprite because the number 2 is hard-coded in the code. However, this is the only handler that references it, so I didn't think it would be useful. This is a short-term laziness versus long-term hassle trade-off that I think is safe to make. If you feel like soft-coding this value, go for it. This is a matter of personal programming style.

The next step is to modify the Rewind button to soft-code the Quicktime Sprite number. Your finished handler should look like this.

```
on mouseDown

    global gQtSprite

    put the movieRate of sprite gQtSprite into originalRate

    set the movieRate of sprite gQtSprite to 0

    updateStage

    set the movieTime of sprite gQtSprite to 0

    updateStage

    set the movieRate of sprite gQtSprite to originalRate

    updateStage

end
```

The final step is to modify the fast-forward handler. This is what the handler from the "Jump to the Next Keyframe" option should look like.

```
on mouseDown

    global gQtSprite

    put the movieRate of sprite gQtSprite into originalRate

    set the movieRate of sprite gQtSprite to 0

    updateStage


    repeat while the mouseDown = TRUE

        put trackNextKeyTime( sprite gQtSprite, 1) into mtime

        set the movieTime of sprite gQtSprite to mtime

        updateStage

    end repeat


    set the movieRate of sprite gQtSprite to originalRate

    updateStage

end
```

Now that that's taken care of, we're ready to move on.

Pixel Doubling: Playing Full-Screen Quicktime

The next piece of functionality that we will implement is full-screen playback of the video. Many multimedia CD-ROMs play back video full-screen, meaning at 640 × 480 pixels. However, Quicktime generally can't handle playing back a video that is actually stored at 640 pixels wide by 480 pixels tall from a CD-ROM.

So, multimedia programmers use a trick. We take a quarter-screen video, which is 320 × 240 pixels, and we **stretch** it to 640 × 480. This is called **pixel-doubling**, since the full-screen frame is twice the size in each direction as the quarter-screen video. Remember, when you stretch Quicktime, you should **only** double it. Trying to stretch it to any other size or proportion will result in horrible playback problems.

As we implement this feature, we will examine how to pull off this trick. In the process, we will figure out how to do a simple rollover.

Let's break this feature down into single behaviors:

1. If the user rolls over the video, the cursor changes to an Up Arrow.

2. If the user clicks on the video, it grows to full-screen mode.

3. In full-screen mode, the cursor changes to a Down Arrow.

4. Clicking in full-screen mode switches back to normal mode.

Implementing Behavior A: Rollovers

A **rollover** is a behavior that occurs because the user drags the mouse pointer onto something. The most common rollover behavior is a change in the shape of the mouse pointer. There are several ways to do rollovers in Director. In this section, we'll concentrate on the simplest technique, using another Sprite property called *the cursor of sprite*. We'll explore more sophisticated rollover techniques in Chapter 7.

We can create a bitmap Cast Member to be our new cursor. There are restrictions on this Cast Member: It must be 1-bit color (black and white) and only the upper left 16 × 16 pixel area will be used for the cursor. This project includes two cursors, called uparrow and downarrow, as shown in Figure 6.10.

You can set the cursor of a particular Sprite like this:

```
put the number of member "uparrow" into mnum

set the cursor of sprite 3 to [mnum]
```

Figure 6.10 The uparrow and downarrow

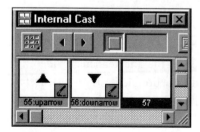

The first line puts the Cast Member number of the uparrow bitmap into the local variable *mnum*. The second line sets *the cursor of sprite 3* to the uparrow. After this, whenever the mouse pointer is rolled over sprite 3, it will become an Up Arrow. When it is rolled off, it will revert to the normal pointer.

Notice the brackets around *[mnum]*. They are necessary for this function to work correctly; this function expects a linear list as a parameter, which we will cover in Chapter 9. For now, just remember to put the number in brackets.

The only remaining question is where to put this command. We are looping on frame 4, and we want this Sprite property already set up before frame 4. So, let's put it into the *exitFrame* handler of frame 3.

```
on exitFrame

    global gQtSprite


    put the number of member "uparrow" into mnum

    set the cursor of sprite gQtSprite to [mnum]

end
```

Rewind and play the movie. The mouse pointer should change to the Up Arrow when it is over the Quicktime movie.

Implementing Behavior B and C: Pixel Doubling

Playing full-screen Quicktime implies a couple of things. First, it implies that all the other graphics on the Stage are hidden while the video is full-screen. Second, it implies that the full-screen video will be playing or paused, according to the state of the video in its normal mode.

The easiest way to get rid of all the other Sprites on the Stage is to zap them from the Score. Because we need them in frames 1-4, we can create another frame somewhere else, say frame 10. Let's put a frame label on frame 10 and name it **big**, since this is where the big Quicktime movie will be. It's only fair that we put a label on frame 4 named **small**.

Now we have to put the Quicktime Sprite into the Score, in frame **big**. Drag the Quicktime Cast Member onto the Stage and into channel 3 in frame 10. The Score should look like Figure 6.11.

Figure 6.11 Quicktime Sprite in the Score.

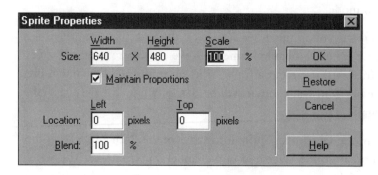

Now, click on the Quicktime Sprite in frame 10. Choose the Modify: Sprite: Properties menu item. Make sure **Maintain Proportions** is not checked, then change the numbers to width: 640, height: 480, left: 0, top: 0. The completed dialog should look like Figure 6.12.

Always keep the Quicktime movie in a the same Sprite Channel throughout your Director movie. If the Playback Head ever plays a frame that doesn't have a Quicktime movie in that channel, the movie will get "forgotten," meaning that it will be paused and rewound. As long as the same Quicktime movie is in the same

Figure 6.12 Sprite Properties dialog box.

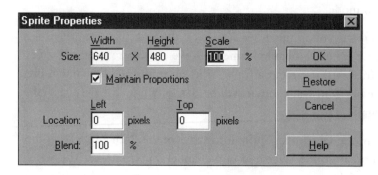

channel in every frame the Playback Head visits, the current *movieTime* and *movieRate* of the movie will stay constant.

Now that we have the Score set up properly, we can start programming. First, let's put a *go the frame* loop in the frame script of frame 10.

```
on exitFrame

    go the frame

end
```

Next, we can put a *mouseDown* script on the video in frame 4. This script mostly just has to go to frame **big**. The Quicktime movie will automatically stretch because the Sprite is stretched in the Score.

```
on mouseDown

    go to frame "big"

end
```

We also have to change the rollover cursor of the Quicktime Sprite, from the Up Arrow to the Down Arrow.

```
on mouseDown

    global gQtSprite


    go to frame "big"

    put the number of member "downarrow" into mnum

    set the cursor of sprite gQtSprite to [mnum]

end
```

Finally, we have to take reality into account. Stretching the Quicktime Sprite counts as a radical Quicktime operation. If we try to do it while the Quicktime movie is playing, the movie will stutter and hitch. We can use the same trick we used with the Fast Forward and Rewind buttons to work around this problem.

Here is the final Sprite Script for sprite 3, in frame 4.

```
on mouseDown

   global gQtSprite


   put the movieRate of sprite gQtSprite into originalRate

   set the movieRate of sprite gQtSprite to 0


   go to frame "big"

   put the number of member "downarrow" into mnum

   set the cursor of sprite gQtSprite to [mnum]


   set the movieRate of sprite gQtSprite to originalRate

end
```

Up to this point, we have implemented behaviors A, B, and C. The user rolls over the Quicktime Sprite, and the cursor changes to an Up Arrow. If the user clicks, we go to frame **big,** the Quicktime movie plays full-screen, and the cursor changes to the Down Arrow.

Now all we have to do is shrink the movie back to its normal size.

Implementing Behavior D: Shrinking

This is the easiest behavior to implement, since we've already done most of the work. The user shrinks the movie by clicking on it while in full-screen mode. The best place to put the shrink Script is in the Sprite Script of the Quicktime Sprite, in frame 10. To shrink the movie, all we have to do is go back to frame **small.** We also have to set the rollover cursor back to the Up Arrow and work around the Quicktime stutter potential.

This script does everything needed to shrink the movie. It goes in the Sprite Script of sprite 3, in frame 10.

```
on mouseDown

   global gQtSprite
```

```
put the movieRate of sprite gQtSprite into originalRate

set the movieRate of sprite gQtSprite to 0


go to frame "small"

put the number of member "uparrow" into mnum

set the cursor of sprite gQtSprite to [mnum]


set the movierate of sprite gQtSprite to originalRate
```
end

There you go. Now you know how to play back a Quicktime movie full-screen.

Implementing the Slider-Bar

The slider-bar has two distinct behaviors:

1. The slider on the bar always represents the current position in the video. If the video has played about halfway through, the slider should be about halfway across the bar. As the video plays, the slider should move across the bar.

2. If the user presses down on the bar, the slider should be dragged along with the cursor. As this happens, the current time of the movie follows the slider.

Before we start implementing the behaviors, we should examine the relationship between the Quicktime movie and the slider-bar.

The width of the bar represents the length of the Quicktime movie. The left edge of the bar is the beginning of the movie, and the right edge is the end (Figure 6.13). The slider, as it travels along the bar, represents the current *movieTime* of the movie.

The slider's location on the bar must be **proportional** to the *movieTime* of the movie. If the movie is one-third done, the slider should be one-third of the way

Figure 6.13 The slider-bar.

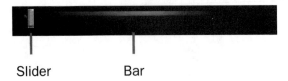

Slider   Bar

across the bar. If the movie is halfway done, the slider should be halfway across the bar. The central problem with the slider-bar behaviors is figuring out the **ratio** of the *movieTime* to the total length of the movie.

The equation that governs this relationship is as follows:

$$\frac{\text{slider position}}{\text{width of bar}} = \frac{\text{movieTime}}{\text{length of Quicktime movie}}$$

Understanding the First Behavior

Here's the situation: The Quicktime movie is playing, and we must figure out the correct position of the slider on the bar. Using this position, we have to move the slider on the Stage.

Which of the variables do we know? First, we know the width of the bar. The bar is actually part of the background graphic in Ch6.dir, but there is an invisible box Sprite that covers the entire bar. There is a Lingo Sprite property called *the width of sprite*, which will give us the width, in pixels, of the Sprite that represents the bar. The invisible box is in Sprite Channel 9.

Second, we know the length of the Quicktime movie in ticks. There is a Lingo cast member property, called *the duration of member*, which will give us the number of ticks in the total Quicktime Cast Member. The Quicktime Cast Member is called *skydive.mov*.

Third, we know the *movieTime* of the Sprite, using *the movieTime of sprite* property we have already seen. The Quicktime Sprite Channel is *gQtSprite*.

We can plug the values that we know into the equation.

$$\frac{\text{slider position}}{\textit{the width of sprite}} = \frac{\textit{the movieTime of Sprite gQtSprite}}{\textit{the duration of member skydive.mov}}$$

Using a little middle-school math, we can solve for the slider position.

$$\text{slider position} = \frac{\textit{the movieTime of sprite gQtSprite}}{\textit{the duration of member skydive.mov}} \times \textit{the width of sprite 9}$$

In English, this means that we need to divide the *movieTime* of Sprite *gQtSprite* by the duration of member *skydive.mov*, which will give us a ratio. Then we multiply the width of sprite 9 by the ratio. This result will be the new position of the slider along the bar.

The code that we write to implement this behavior will obviously have to do these simple calculations. However, doing math with Lingo isn't quite as easy as you might think.

Doing Math with Lingo

Programming a computer to do arithmetic isn't as easy as it was scratching with graphite on papyrus in Mrs. Ananian's seventh grade math class. Lingo follows its own arithmetic rules very strictly, and if you don't know them, you'll probably get wrong answers for simple equations. Don't worry, though, all the things you need to know are right here.

Arithmetic and Order of Operations

There are a few things to remember when you are doing math with Lingo. Firstly, here are Lingo's arithmetic operators...

Name	Lingo	Example
modulus	mod	5 mod 2 = 1 (returns the remainder of integer divide)
multiply	*	5 * 2 = 10
divide	/	5/2 = 2 or 5.0/2.0 = 2.5 (see below)
add	+	5 + 2 = 7
subtract	–	5 – 2 = 3

Consider the following line:

2 + 3 – 4

How would you do this? You would add 2 plus 3, which is 5, then subtract 4, which gives 1. The Lingo elf would agree. How would you do this one?

2 + 3 – 4 * 10

Try this line in the Message Window, *put 2 + 3 − 4 * 10*. The answer *−35* is returned. Does this surprise you?

When Lingo sees a multiple-operator equation, it doesn't necessarily execute it from left to right. First, the Lingo elf runs through all the operators, looking for any *mod* operations. These get done first, in the order that they occur, left to right. Next, the elf runs through the equation again, looking for multiplies or divides. It executes these in the order that they are found. Finally, the elf goes through the equation again, executing any additions or subtractions. What is left is the answer.

So in the equation *2 + 3 − 4 * 10*, the first operation that executes is *4 * 10*, which is 40. Now the line reads *2 + 3 − 40*. The elf executes the first addition, *2 + 3*, which is 5. Now the lines reads *5 − 40*. The elf does this last operation, which leaves *−35*, the answer.

This is the normal order of operations for the Lingo elf. If you want more control over the way your equation works, you can use parentheses. When you enclose one or more operations in parentheses, you are telling the Lingo elf to execute this operation first, regardless of the order of operations. Type this line into the Message Window:

```
put 2 + (3 − 4 ) * 10
```

The answer it returns is −8. First, the elf does 3 − 4, which is −1. Now the equation reads 2 + −1 * 10. Next comes the multiplication −1 * 10, which is −10. Finally comes the addition, 2+ −10, which yields the final answer, −8. If you embed one set of parentheses within another, the innermost pair will be executed first.

Dealing with Division

Your computer doesn't divide the same way you do. Look at this line:

```
put 5 / 2
```

If you were doing this on paper, your answer would be 2.5, right? Five divided by two is two and a half. Seems simple enough. Try typing that line into the Message Window.

The computer thinks that 5/2 is 2. You know this is wrong and I know this is wrong, but who's going to tell the computer?

The problem is that all modern microprocessors can do two different kinds of divide operations. The first is an integer divide, in which the processor doesn't deal with decimal points, so the division can be done unbelievably fast. The second kind of divide, which deals with decimal points, is slower.

This schizoid math is reflected in most computer software, including Director and Lingo. Lingo has two different ways to represent numbers in memory, **integer** numbers and **float** numbers. An **integer** is number that isn't allowed to have a decimal point; it is limited to whole numbers. The numbers 0, 1, 2, 3, 4, 5, 16000, are all integers. A **float** is a number that has a decimal point. The numbers 2.5, 8.333, –0.543, are all floats. (The name **float** comes from "floating point," which is the name of the programming technique that is used to compute with these numbers. We could go into that, but nobody cares.)

Lingo tries to figure out which kind of division you want to do, with decimals or without, by the kind of numbers you give it. In our previous example, 5/2, the Lingo elf looks at the 5 and the 2 and sees that they are both integers. The elf takes the hint and decides to do an integer divide. Because an integer divide doesn't deal with decimals, the .5 is dropped.

This, of course, is not acceptable because we want an accurate answer when we do math. The easiest way to improve the situation is to change one of our numbers to a decimal, as in the following line.

```
put 5 / 2.0
```

The answer in the Message Window is 2.5, which is right. What happened? The Lingo elf looked at both numbers, 5 and 2.0, and saw that at least one of these numbers had a decimal in it. If at least one number has a decimal, the elf will use the decimal divide.

Changing the number works only when we hard-code a number, as we did above. We will, much more frequently, have need to divide two soft-coded numbers, as we have to do with the slider-bar. Remember the equation?

$$\text{slider position} = \frac{\textit{the movieTime of sprite gQtSprite}}{\textit{the duration of member skydive.mov}} \times \textit{the width of sprite 9}$$

Both *the movieTime of Sprite gQtSprite* and *the duration of member skydive.mov* will return integer numbers. When we divide them, though, we need to get a very accurate, decimal value. As it turns out, Lingo provides a way.

You can change the type of a value by using a function. For example:

```
put the movieTime of sprite gQtSprite
```

might return *400*, but this line

```
put float(the movieTime of sprite gQtSprite)
```

will return *400.0*.

Float() is a built-in Lingo function that takes an integer number as a parameter. It returns the integer as a floating point, decimal number. We could use this to do our divide in Lingo code.

```
put float(the movieTime of sprite gQtSprite) into mtime

put mtime / the duration of member "skydive.mov" into ratio
```

In the first line, we put a decimal version of the *movieTime* of the Quicktime movie into the local variable *mtime*. In the second line, we divide the decimal *mtime* by the length of the Quicktime movie and put the value into the local variable *ratio*. Because at least one of the numbers in the divide is a float, the Lingo elf will use a decimal divide, and the ratio will be an accurate, decimal number.

To finish coding the equation, we have to multiply *the width of sprite 9* by *ratio*. No problem.

```
put ratio * the width of sprite 9 into sliderLoc
```

Here, we multiply the two values, one decimal and one integer, and put them into the variable *sliderLoc*, which is going to hold a decimal number. The Sprite location has to represent a pixel location onstage. Unfortunately, pixel locations must be integers or the Lingo elf can't deal with them.

What can we do? Use another built-in Lingo function, of course! Just as we can get a float value from an integer, we can get an integer value from a float. The following line takes the decimal result of the multiplication, makes it into an integer, and puts the final integer into *sliderLoc*.

```
put integer (ratio * the width of sprite 9) into sliderLoc
```

All right, you don't need any more math to implement the slider-bar. Roll up your sleeves, and let's go!

Implementing the First Behavior

We are going to be dealing with two Sprites, the slider Sprite, in channel 10, and the invisible-box Sprite that covers the bar, in channel 9. Because we are starting a new part of the project, it would be nice to soft-code these values from the start.

Let's use two global variables, *gSliderSprite* and *gBarSprite*, to hold the 10 and 9. We should initialize the variables in the *startMovie* handler, in the Movie Script. Here's what the modified handler should look like.

```
on startMovie

    global gBarSprite, gSliderSprite, gQtSprite


    put 6 into gQtSprite

    put 9 into gBarSprite

    put 10 into gSliderSprite

end
```

Notice, since I want this handler to see more than one global variable, I use one *global* command followed by multiple variables, separated by commas. If I wanted to, I could also separate them out onto different lines, like this:

```
on startMovie

    global gBarSprite

    global gSliderSprite

    global gQtSprite


    put 6 into gVideoSprite

    put 9 into gBarSprite

    put 10 into gSliderSprite

end
```

You can mix and match the way you declare globals; Lingo doesn't mind.

Next, we have to puppet the slider Sprite. Because we know we will be moving the slider around with Lingo, it makes sense to turn it into a Puppet right away and leave it puppetted for the rest of the movie. Put this Script into the Frame Script of frame 3.

```
on exitFrame

   global gSliderSprite


   puppetSprite gSliderSprite, TRUE

end
```

Finally, we have to implement the behavior of the slider. Let's create a new handler in the Movie Script to do this. Because it is supposed to set the slider position according to the *movieTime* of the Quicktime movie, let's call it *setSliderByMovieTime*.

```
on setSliderByMovieTime

   -- do stuff

end
```

The first task of this handler will be to figure out the ratio of the *movieTime* to the *duration* of the Quicktime Movie. We figured out how to do this in the last couple of sections.

```
on setSliderByMovieTime

   global gQtSprite

   put float(the movieTime of sprite gQtSprite) into mtime

   put mtime / the duration of member "skydive.mov" into ratio


   -- do stuff

end
```

After these two lines, the local variable *ratio* contains a decimal number. The next step is to multiply *ratio* by the length of the bar Sprite. Because we want the result to be an integer, we envelop the operation in an *integer()* function.

```
on setSliderByMovieTime

    global gQtSprite, gBarSprite


    put float(the movieTime of sprite gQtSprite) into mtime

    put mtime / the duration of member "skydive.mov" into ratio


    put integer(ratio*the width of sprite gBarSprite) into sliderLoc


    -- do stuff

end
```

After this line, the variable *sliderLoc* holds an integer number that represents how far across the bar the slider should be. We have discussed these three lines in the last couple of sections.

But what do we do now? We know that we have to move the slider Sprite to a new horizontal location on the Stage. As always, setting the location of the Sprite involves setting its *locH* property. Can we just set the *locH* of the Sprite to *sliderLoc*? It could look like this:

```
set the locH of sprite gSliderSprite to sliderLoc
```

Wouldn't that be nice? Unfortunately, this doesn't work. The value in *sliderLoc* represents how far across the bar the slider should be, but this isn't a Stage location.

Let's say the *sliderLoc* contains the number 50. This means that the slider should be 50 pixels from the left edge of the bar. The real question is, how many pixels should the slider be from the left edge **of the Stage?**

This answer is surprisingly straightforward to compute. The Stage location is the number of pixels from the left edge of the bar **plus** the horizontal location, in pixels, of the left edge of the bar Sprite. If the bar was 160 pixels from the left of the Stage, the situation would look like Figure 6.14.

We can translate this into Lingo using a new Lingo Sprite property, *the left of sprite*. This function always returns the horizontal location of the left edge of the Sprite. The following line puts the correct Stage location of the slider Sprite into *sliderLoc*.

```
put sliderLoc + the left of sprite gBarSprite into sliderLoc
```

Now, sliderLoc is the proper Stage location for the slider Sprite. The finished handler, which you should put into your Movie Script, looks like this.

```
on setSliderByMovieTime

    global gQtSprite, gBarSprite, gSliderSprite


    put float(the movieTime of sprite gQtSprite) into mtime

    put mtime / the duration of member "skydive.mov" into ratio


    put integer(ratio*the width of sprite gBarSprite) into sliderLoc


    put sliderLoc + the left of sprite gBarSprite into sliderLoc

    set the locH of sprite gSliderSprite to sliderLoc

end
```

Figure 6.14 Bar with slider.

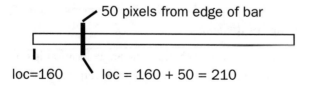

50 pixels from edge of bar

loc=160   loc = 160 + 50 = 210

We're not quite done yet, though. This handler that we have just created is wonderful, but it never gets executed because nobody ever calls it! We have to figure out from where to call it.

Well, when do we want it to be executed? Pretty much all the time. We want the slider to be constantly updated while the Quicktime movie is playing. Because the Playback Head is in constant motion while the Quicktime movie is running, it makes sense to put the call into the *exitFrame* handler of the frame.

So, go into the Frame Script of frame 4, and modify the Script to look like this:

```
on exitFrame

    setSliderByMovieTime

    go the frame

end
```

Try playing around with the project after you have brought it to this point. The slider should move of its own accord as the Quicktime movie plays. Everything should look just hunky-dory.

Except, there's still a bug. If you hold down the Fast Forward button, the movie advances but the slider doesn't. To rectify this situation, you have to put a call to *setSliderByMovieTime* into the Fast Forward Script. The Fast Forward Script is in sprite 4. You should add the handler call near the bottom of the *repeat* loop, like this:

```
on mouseDown

    global gQtSprite

    put the movieRate of sprite gQtSprite into originalRate

    set the movieRate of sprite gQtSprite to 0

    updateStage

    repeat while the mouseDown = TRUE

        put trackNextKeyTime( sprite gQtSprite, 1) into mtime

        set the movieTime of sprite gQtSprite to mtime

        setSliderToMovieTime
```

```
    updateStage

  end repeat



  set the movieRate of sprite gQtSprite to originalRate

  updateStage

end
```

Understanding the Second Slider-Bar Behavior

Remember the second behavior of the slider-bar? If the user presses down on the bar, the slider should be dragged along with the cursor. As this happens, the current time of the movie follows the slider.

This behavior is actually made of two separate but related behaviors:

1. The slider can be dragged by the mouse pointer, to the left and right limits of the bar.

2. The *movieTime* of the movie changes to reflect the position of the slider.

Behavior A is pretty straightforward; the slider can be dragged much like the skulls in Chapter 4. The only difference is that we'll have to set up some limits, such as the slider can't move vertically, and it can't leave the area of the bar.

Behavior B is a more sophisticated problem. The situation is the reverse of what we solved in the last section. Instead of figuring out the correct placement of the slider Sprite according to the *movieTime*, we have to figure out the correct *movieTime* by the placement of the slider Sprite.

This isn't too hard because we've already covered ratios and Lingo math. Our general ratio for this relationship is still as follows:

$$\frac{\text{slider position}}{\text{width of bar}} = \frac{movieTime}{\text{length of Quicktime movie}}$$

We are trying to figure out *movieTime* now, so we should solve for it. Here's our new equation:

$$movieTime = \frac{\text{slider position}}{\text{width of bar}} \times \text{length of Quicktime movie}$$

We have to get a ratio of the slider to the bar, so we divide *slider position* by the *width of bar*. We multiply this ratio with the *length of Quicktime movie* to get our new *movieTime*. Remember, it is only useful to solve this equation **after** the slider has been dragged to a new position.

Implementing Slider-Bar Behavior 2A: Dragging

The slider has to be horizontally draggable. Because this drag-problem came up in Chapter 4, it shouldn't be too hard to solve it again now.

Here's an off-the-top-of-the-head solution. Let's implement this solution in a custom handler called, for obvious reasons, *dragSlider*. (We'll connect it to a *mouseDown* handler after we're done, in "Connecting the Drag Handlers.")

```
on dragSlider

    global gSliderSprite


    repeat while the mouseDown = TRUE

        set the locH of sprite gSliderSprite to the mouseH

        updateStage

    end repeat

end
```

This handler uses a simple *repeat while* loop and constantly sets the horizontal position of the slider to the horizontal position of the mouse. Simple enough, right?

Too simple. The problem is that the slider can be dragged anywhere on the Stage (Figure 6.15). We need to keep it from being dragged off the bar (Figure 6.16).

We can restrict it with a simple *if..then* decision. If the mouse location is too far to the left, we can set it to the left edge of the bar. If the mouse location is too far to the right, we can set the slider to the right edge of the bar.

In writing the script, the first things we want to figure out are the horizontal locations of the left and right edges of the bar, using the Sprite properties *the left of sprite* and *the right of sprite*. We could save them into two variables, *barLeft* and *barRight*, like so:

Figure 6.15 The slider can be dragged off the bar.

Bad (Past Right Edge)

Figure 6.16 The proper boundaries for the slider.

Good (Right Edge)

```
put the left of sprite gBarSprite into barLeft

put the right of sprite gBarSprite into barRight
```

We'd also have to add *gBarSprite* to our globals list. Here's what we've got so far:

```
on dragSlider

    global gSliderSprite, gBarSprite


    put the left of sprite gBarSprite into barLeft

    put the right of sprite gBarSprite into barRight

    repeat while the mouseDown = TRUE

        set the locH of sprite gSliderSprite to the mouseH

        updateStage

    end repeat

end
```

Next, we have to modify the inside of the *repeat* loop to check for our **boundary conditions,** meaning the left and right of the bar. The first thing we want to ascertain, inside the loop, is the horizontal position of the mouse pointer. We can save it in a local variable, perhaps called *mh*.

```
put the mouseH into mh
```

Using *mh*, we can check to see if the mouse is too far to the left and set the *locH* of the slider Sprite appropriately.

```
if mh <= barLeft then

    set the locH of sprite gSliderSprite to barLeft

else

    set the locH of sprite gSliderSprite to mh

end if
```

If the condition *mh <= barLeft* is true, then the mouse is too far left and the Lingo elf will set the slider to the left edge of the bar. Otherwise, the Lingo elf will set the slider to the current mouse position, stored in *mh*.

Now we want to extend the *if..then* decision to include a check for the right edge, like so:

```
if mh <= barLeft then

    set the locH of sprite gSliderSprite to barLeft

else if mh >= barRight then

    set the locH of sprite gSliderSprite to barRight

else

    set the locH of sprite gSliderSprite to mh

end if
```

When the Lingo elf comes to this *if..then*, it first checks to see if *mh <= barLeft* is true. If it isn't, meaning that the mouse isn't too far left, it will execute the second *if..then* and check if *mh >= barRight* is true. If it is, meaning the mouse is too far right, then it will set the slider on the right edge of the bar. If neither of these is true, it will go ahead and set the slider to the mouse position.

Here's how the code would look in the *dragSlider* handler.

```
on dragSlider

    global gSliderSprite, gBarSprite

    put the left of sprite gBarSprite into barLeft

    put the right of sprite gBarSprite into barRight


    repeat while the mouseDown = TRUE

        put the mouseH into mh

        if mh <= barLeft then

            set the locH of sprite gSliderSprite to barLeft

        else if mh >= barRight then

            set the locH of sprite gSliderSprite to barRight

        else

            set the locH of sprite gSliderSprite to mh

        end if

        updateStage

    end repeat

end
```

Implementing Slider-Bar Behavior 2B: Setting the movieTime

Now we have to figure out how to set the *movieTime* of the movie, according to the position of the slider. The equation we came up with to solve this is the following:

$$movieTime = \frac{\text{slider position}}{\text{width of bar}} \times \text{length of Quicktime movie}$$

All we have to do is translate this equation into Lingo, adjust a few things, and get it working.

Because this task stands on its own, we can easily envelop it all in one custom handler. Let's call it *setMovieTimeBySlider*. We'll start with an empty handler.

```
on setMovieTimeBySlider

  -- do stuff

end
```

The first thing this handler will have to determine is the position of the slider. We can save the position, as we did before, into a local variable called *sliderLoc*.

```
put the locH of sprite gSliderSprite into sliderLoc
```

Remember, the *locH of sprite* function gives us a Stage location. We are really looking for a position from the left edge of the bar. This is the reverse of the problem we had with *setSliderByMovieTime*, where we had to get a Stage location from a bar location. To solve it, we can use the opposite of the technique we used in *setSliderByMovieTime*. Instead of adding the left of the bar Sprite to the slider position, we will **subtract** the left of the bar from the slider position.

```
put the locH of sprite gSliderSprite into sliderLoc

put sliderLoc - the left of sprite gBarSprite into sliderLoc
```

After the first line, *sliderLoc* may hold the number 210. This means that the slider Sprite is 210 pixels from the left edge of the stage. If the left of the bar is 160 pixels from the left edge of the Stage, then *sliderLoc* will be 210 – 160, which is 50 pixels from the left edge of the bar.

Now that *sliderLoc* is a bar location, we can divide it by the width of the bar to get a ratio. We'll turn *sliderLoc* into a float **before** we divide with it to make sure we do a decimal divide.

```
put float(sliderLoc) into sliderLoc

put sliderLoc / the width of sprite gBarSprite into ratio
```

Here's our handler so far.

```
on setMovieTimeBySlider

  global gSliderSprite, gBarSprite
```

```
    put the locH of sprite gSliderSprite into sliderLoc

    put sliderLoc - the left of sprite gBarSprite into sliderLoc


    put float(sliderLoc) into sliderLoc

    put sliderLoc / the width of sprite gBarSprite into ratio


    -- do stuff

end
```

Now that we have a (decimal point) ratio, we can multiply it by the duration of the Quicktime movie to get the new *movieTime*.

```
put ratio * the duration of member "skydive.mov" into mtime
```

Unfortunately, because one of the numbers in this multiply operation is a decimal number, the value of *mtime* is going to be a decimal number. The variable *mtime* represents the new *movieTime* of the Quicktime movie, and any *movieTime* value must be an integer. So, we have to convert the value to an integer.

```
put integer(mtime) into mtime
```

Finally, we can change the *movieTime* of the actual Quicktime Sprite.

```
set the movieTime of sprite  gQtSprite to mtime
```

Here's the final handler.

```
on setMovieTimeBySlider

    global gSliderSprite, gBarSprite

    put the locH of sprite gSliderSprite into sliderLoc

    put sliderLoc - the left of sprite gBarSprite into sliderLoc


    put float(sliderLoc) into sliderLoc

    put sliderLoc / the width of sprite gBarSprite into ratio
```

```
    put ratio * the duration of member "skydive.mov" into mtime

    put integer(mtime) into mtime


    set the movieTime of sprite  gQtSprite to mtime
```

end

Connecting the Drag Handlers

Now that we have these nice handlers for dragging the slider, we really should connect them to the rest of the Director movie.

The first connection we have to make is between the two drag handlers. In the *repeat* loop of *dragSlider*, *setMovieTimeBySlider* must be called, so the *movieTime* will change continuously during the drag. Also, because we are changing something as radical as the *movieTime* of a Quicktime movie, we have to pause the movie before we start, and perhaps start it playing again when we're done. Here is the final *dragSlider* handler.

```
on dragSlider

    global gSliderSprite, gBarSprite, gQtSprite


    put the left of sprite gBarSprite into barLeft

    put the right of sprite gBarSprite into barRight


    put the movieRate of sprite gQtSprite into originalRate

    set the movieRate of sprite gQtSprite to 0

    updateStage


    repeat while the mouseDown = TRUE

        put the mouseH into mh

        if mh <= barLeft then
```

```
            set the locH of sprite gSliderSprite to barLeft

        else if mh >= barRight then

            set the locH of sprite gSliderSprite to barRight

        else

            set the locH of sprite gSliderSprite to mh

        end if



        setMovieTimeBySlider

        updateStage

    end repeat



    set the movieRate of sprite gQtSprite to originalRate

end
```

Next, we connect *dragSlider* to a *mouseDown* handler on the slider Sprite, or nothing will ever get dragged. In the Sprite Script of the slider Sprite, sprite 10, put this handler.

```
on mouseDown

    dragSlider

end
```

If you think about it, the slider should be dragged even if the user doesn't click on the **slider** but does click on the **bar**. The behavior should be the same. So, put this handler into the Sprite Script of the bar Sprite, sprite 9.

```
on mouseDown

    dragSlider

end
```

That's it, we're done with the slider-bar! Play with it for awhile. Enjoy it. Love it. It took a lot of work, but, boy, was it worth it! (Fine, **you** try to give a programming pep-talk. It's harder than actually programming.)

Implementing the Volume Knob

The volume knob in this project rotates, just like any real-world dial. The dial is one of the most asked-for interface widgets in multimedia, and one of the least frequently used. Rotating dials are hard to implement because you have to do some trigonometric calculations.

Until now. This volume knob uses a generic handler to do the trig. You can just copy and paste it into your own rotating projects.

Let's go ahead and implement the rotating dial. We'll deal with volume-adjusting code **after** we get the dial working.

Implementing the Dial

A rotating dial can be dragged by the mouse pointer all the way around the circle. Because a dial is a circle, we have to figure out **how far around the circle** the mouse is. Distances around a circle are measured in degrees, from 0 to 360 degrees (Figure 6.17).

Figure 6.17 Degrees of a circle.

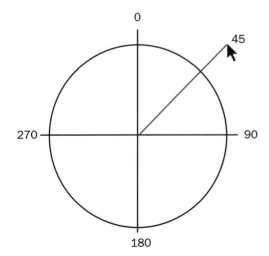

Once we figure out how many degrees around the circle the pointer is, we can figure out which dial bitmap to display. In the file Ch6.dir, there are 24 different dial bitmaps. Each one shows the dial pointing at a different angle (Figure 6.18). In this project, there is one bitmap at 15 degrees, 30 degrees, 45 degrees, and so on, until 360 degrees.

The first thing to do is establish a global variable to hold the number of the volume knob Sprite, since we are probably going to be using it a lot. The volume knob is in sprite 11. We can add it to the now-familiar *startMovie* handler in the Movie Script.

```
on startMovie

    global gBarSprite, gSliderSprite, gQtSprite, gVolumeSprite


    put 6 into gQtSprite

    put 9 into gBarSprite

    put 10 into gSliderSprite

    put 11 into gVolumeSprite

end
```

Figure 6.18 Dials.

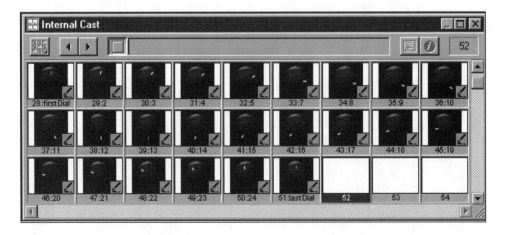

Next, we have to puppet the volume Sprite so we can eventually change its *memberNum*. We might as well do this in the same Script we puppetted the slider Sprite, the *exitFrame* handler in the Frame Script of frame 3.

```
on exitFrame

    global gSliderSprite, gVolumeSprite


    puppetSprite gSliderSprite, TRUE

    puppetSprite gVolumeSprite, TRUE

end
```

Now that we are set up, we can program the actual dial.

Whatever we do to the dial, it must be triggered when the user presses on the dial. This leads us to use a *mouseDown* handler. Also, because we are dragging something around, we know that we'll need a *repeat while* loop. This handler goes in the Sprite Script of the volume knob Sprite, sprite 11.

```
on mouseDown

    repeat while the mouseDown = TRUE

        -- do stuff

    end repeat

end
```

The big question is "How do we compute the angle of the mouse pointer on the dial?" The answer is this: Use the custom handler *getAngleDegrees* that I have already included in the Movie Script of Ch6.dir. If you are interested in the trigonometry, feel free to go over the code. Here's the code listing. (If you're not curious, skip to the end of the listing.)

```
on getAngleInDegrees ctrH,ctrV,ptH,ptV

    -- does trigonometric calculations for degrees
```

```
put empty into degrees


put (ptH -ctrH)/2 into ptH

put (ptV -ctrV)/2 into ptV


if ptV = 0 then

    if ptH >= 0 then

        put 90 into degrees

    else

        put 270 into degrees

    end if

end if


if degrees<>empty then

    return degrees

end if


put float(ptH) into ptH

put float(ptV) into ptV


if ptV > 0 then

    if ptH >0 then

        put Atan(ptH /ptV) into angle

        put integer(180 -angle *180/pi()) into Degrees
```

```
    else

        put Atan(ptH /ptV) into angle

        put integer(180 -angle *180/pi()) into Degrees

    end if

  end if

  if ptV < 0 then

    if ptH >0 then

        put Atan(ptH /ptV) into angle

        put integer(-angle *180/pi()) into Degrees

    else

        put Atan(ptH /ptV) into angle

        put integer( 360 -angle *180/pi()) into Degrees

    end if

  end if

  return degrees

end
```

Do you see why most programmers don't try to figure this out? Anyway, it's there if you need it.

As cryptic as *getAngleInDegrees* is, it is simple to use. You supply it with the coordinates of the center of the circle, and the mouse coordinates, as parameters. It returns the number of degrees around the circle that the mouse pointer is. For example:

```
put the locH of sprite gVolumeSprite into ctrH

put the locV of sprite gVolumeSprite into ctrV

put the mouseH into mH
```

```
put the mouseV into mV
```

```
put getAngleInDegrees(ctrH, ctrV, mH, mV) into deg
```

These first four lines save the center of the volume knob and the mouse coordinates into the local variables *ctrH*, *ctrV*, *mH*, and *mV*. The fifth line calls the *getAngleInDegrees* function, passing the local variables' values to the *ctrH*, *ctrV*, *ptH*, and *ptV* parameters. The result, the angle in degrees, is put into the local variable *deg*.

This process has to happen inside the *mouseDown* handler of the volume knob Sprite.

```
on mouseDown

  global gVolumeSprite


  put the locH of sprite gVolumeSprite into ctrH

  put the locV of sprite gVolumeSprite into ctrV


  repeat while the mouseDown = TRUE

    put the mouseH into mH

    put the mouseV into mV

    put getAngleInDegrees(ctrH, ctrV, mH, mV) into deg


    -- do more stuff

  end repeat

end
```

The commands that load *ctrH* and *ctrV* go **before** the loop because they need to be looked up only once. The center of the knob is not going to change.

Inside the loop, we record the mouse coordinates. Then, we call *getAngleInDegrees* to figure out the angle. Because this happens repeatedly, the variable *deg* will constantly be updated as the mouse is moved around and the user drags the dial.

The next step is to figure out which dial bitmap to display, based on the value of *deg*. Here, we use another trick. As I mentioned before, there is a separate dial bitmap for every 15 degrees of the dial. The first one in the cast corresponds to degree zero. The next one corresponds to degree 15, the next to degree 30, and so on, until the last dial bitmap corresponds to degree 345. (The 360 and 0 bitmaps are identical.)

Now that we know the degree, we have to figure out which 15 degree increment it falls into. Mathematically, we can divide the degrees by 15, without worrying about decimals, because we have bitmaps only for whole increments. We can figure out which dial bitmap we want with this line:

```
put deg / 15 into dialNum
```

Because *deg* holds an integer value, and 15 is an integer, *deg/15* is an integer divide. That means the result of the division will also be an integer. Because the largest number *deg* will hold is 360, *dialNum* will hold a value between 0 and 360/15 = 24.

This value of *dialNum* tells us which of the dial bitmaps to use. However, it is not a *memberNum*. To get the *memberNum*, we have to add *dialNum* to the number of the first dial Cast Member, called *firstDial*.

```
put dialNum + the number of member "firstDial" into mnum
```

Now all we have to do is set change the *memberNum* of the volume knob Sprite.

```
set the memberNum of sprite gVolumeSprite to mnum

updateStage
```

Here's the *mouseDown* handler so far, for sprite 11 of frame 4.

```
on mouseDown

  global gVolumeSprite


  put the locH of sprite gVolumeSprite into ctrH

  put the locV of sprite gVolumeSprite into ctrV


  repeat while the mouseDown = TRUE

    put the mouseH into mH
```

```
put the mouseV into mV

put getAngleInDegrees(ctrH, ctrV, mH, mV) into deg


put deg / 15 into dialNum

put dialNum + the number of member "firstDial" into mnum

set the memberNum of sprite gVolumeSprite to mnum


— do more stuff

updateStage

end repeat

end
```

If you have been updating your project, the volume knob should spin as you drag it.

Implementing Volume Control

We have already figured out how many degrees, from 0 to 360, the mouse is located around the dial. As we did with the slider and the bar, we can compute a **ratio** of the **current point** on the circle, measured from 0 to 360 degrees, to the **range of possible points**, 360 degrees.

We can then use this ratio to compute the new Quicktime movie volume.

To compute the ratio, we divide the degrees by the total number of degrees, 360.

```
put deg / 360.0 into ratio
```

Because *360.0* is a decimal number, *deg/360.0* is a decimal divide. The ratio will get an accurate, floating point number.

We can apply this ratio to the volume problem. Quicktime volume is determined by a Quicktime Sprite property called *the volume of sprite*. The volume of a Sprite can range from 0 (silent) to 255 (loudest).

```
put ratio * 255 into newVolume
```

After this line, *newVolume* holds the new volume of the Quicktime movie. Now we can go ahead and change it...

```
set the volume of sprite gQtSprite to newVolume
```

Putting it all together, here is the script of sprite 11, in frame 4.

```
on mouseDown

    global gVolumeSprite, gQtSprite


    put the locH of sprite gVolumeSprite into ctrH

    put the locV of sprite gVolumeSprite into ctrV


    repeat while the mouseDown = TRUE

        put the mouseH into mH

        put the mouseV into mV

        put getAngleInDegrees(ctrH, ctrV, mH, mV) into deg


        put deg / 15 into dialNum

        put dialNum + the number of member "firstDial" into mnum

        set the memberNum of sprite gVolumeSprite to mnum


        put deg / 360.0 into ratio

        put ratio * 255 into newVolume

        set the volume of sprite gQtSprite to newVolume


        updateStage

    end repeat

end
```

And, POW! You're done, right?

Well, it depends on how industrious you are. There are a couple of little bugs. You'll notice the first one if you drag the volume knob for a couple of seconds. While you are turning the knob, the slider doesn't move. We broke the slider when we made the knob. (Boy, does that sound dirty!) If you'll recall, the slider routine *setSliderByMovieTime* is called from the *exitFrame* handler in frame 4. However, while this *repeat* loop is executing, the Playback Head never moves. If the Playback Head doesn't move, no *exitFrame* events are triggered. If no *exitFrame* events are triggered, this *exitFrame* handler is never executed.

We can easily solve this problem by including a call to the handler in the mouse-down script of Sprite 11, just before *updateStage*.

. . .

```
setSliderByMovieTime

updateStage
```

. . .

You won't notice the second bug unless you are really astute and anal-retentive. While the Director movie is running, position the volume knob on the highest setting. Now open the Message Window and type

```
put the volume of sprite
```
The Message Window will answer something like

```
-- 235
```

You see the bug? The maximum volume of a Quicktime sprite is 255. The knob can't turn the movie to its maximum value!

The problem is that we are using the wrong value in the line *put deg/360.0 into ratio*. 360 is, indeed, the full range of degree values that are possible in a mathematical circle. However, the volume knob is not a mathematical circle; it's a knob. And on any knob, there is a little dead space between the highest setting and zero (Figure 6.19).

Figure 6.19 Dead space in the volume knob.

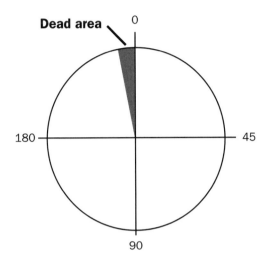

This arc doesn't have any use because the highest setting is at the bottom of the arc, and the zero setting is at the top. What happens if the mouse is in the middle of the arc? Nothing much. It's useless.

In this project, the useless arc takes up 15 degrees of the circle. We don't get a full range of degrees to spin the knob; we really get the full range less the useless part. This means our operational range goes up to 360 − 15 = 345. We should change the ratio line to

```
put deg / 345.0 into ratio
```

The final, complete, I-can-sleep-now handler is listed below.

```
on mouseDown

    global gVolumeSprite, gQtSprite


    put the locH of sprite gVolumeSprite into ctrH

    put the locV of sprite gVolumeSprite into ctrV
```

```
repeat while the mouseDown = TRUE

    put the mouseH into mH

    put the mouseV into mV

    put getAngleInDegrees(ctrH, ctrV, mH, mV) into deg


    put deg / 15 into dialNum

    put dialNum + the number of member "firstDial" into mnum

    set the memberNum of sprite gVolumeSprite to mnum


    put deg / 345.0 into ratio

    put ratio * 255 into newVolume

    set the volume of sprite gQtSprite to newVolume


    setSliderByMovieTime

    updateStage

end repeat

end
```

Chapter Summary

In this chapter, we explored Quicktime, math, and some interface widgets. Here are the highlights.

- Digital Video is hard on a computer.

- The most common codec (compressor-decompressor) for Quicktime is Cinepak.

- A Cinepak-compressed video track is made up of **key frames** and **difference frames**. A key frame contains a whole picture, while a difference frame holds only the part of the picture that is different than the previous frame.

- Quicktime and Director are like two siblings competing for their parents' attention. Both are competing for the same, limited resources of the computer like the video card, CD-ROM, hard drive, and RAM.

- You manipulate most aspects of a Quicktime movie by setting its sprite and cast member properties. Here are some of the most common ones:

  - *movieRate of sprite*

    1 for play at normal speed

    0 for stop

    − 1 for rewind at normal speed (usually results in bad performance)

  - *movieTime of sprite* The current tick (one-sixtieth of a second) of the movie.

  - *duration of member* The length, in ticks, of a digital video cast member

- Before doing anything radical to a movie, you must pause it by setting the *movieRate* of the video sprite to *0*. If you don't do this, the movie will probably stutter when played from a CD-ROM.

- To show full screen video, you generally stretch quarter-screen video (320 × 240) to full screen size (640 × 480). This technique is called Pixel Doubling.

- You can set the cursor to a custom graphic by setting the *cursor of sprite* property to a cursor Cast Member. This Cast Member must be 1-bit color, and at least 16 × 16 pixels. Only the top left 16 × 16 pixels will be used. The cursor will change only on top of the specified sprite.

- Lingo does arithmetic in a specific order. First it does *mod*, then * and /, then + and −. You can reprioritize the operations in an equation by using parentheses. The innermost parentheses will be executed first, then the outer parentheses, then the rest of the equation.

- Lingo can do two types of arithmetic: integer and floating point. Integer math uses only whole numbers, floating point uses only decimals. To turn an integer value into a floating point, use the *float()* function. To turn a decimal value into an integer, use the *integer()* function. The integer function will round off the decimal value.

Outline

Chapter Objective

Everybody who makes real multimedia needs to know about rollovers. How do you make something highlight when you roll the mouse pointer onto it? How do you make the cursor change on a "hot" Sprite? You'll find out in this project.

There are times when the Score isn't enough to animate something. We'll examine how to use Lingo to animate a Sprite.

There are times when Director isn't enough to animate something, and you have to use closely controlled Quicktime. We'll use linear lists to control playback of a Quicktime movie and synchronize it with Lingo events.

Finally, we'll take a peek under the hood and explore memory management. How does Director get an image from the disk to the screen, and how do you make that process happen as fast as possible? How does Director play sound? It all has to do with memory. Don't skip this section!

Introduction to Project

There is a very popular series of CD-ROMs for kids called the Living Books. Each CD-ROM is one children's story. Each page of the story has a few lines of text, superimposed on a cartoon scene. If the user clicks on an object in the scene, the object animates, then returns to its normal position. This interactive formula has been used in a zillion other kids' CD-ROMs. My favorite of the bunch is *Dazzeloids*, from the Voyager Co. Young kids go crazy over these CD-ROMs. I think the repeatability gives them a feeling of control in a world where they have so little.

Anyway, Director is extremely well suited for these kinds of projects. In this chapter, we'll do a page of our own. The unprogrammed file is Ch7.dir in the Chapter7 folder on the CD-ROM. The programmed version is in Ch7_done.dir.

Figure 7.1 shows the first frame.

Figure 7.1 The first frame.

Here's how the project is supposed to behave:

1. When you play the movie, the words in the upper-right corner are read aloud. As each word is read, it highlights. While this is happening, the cursor is invisible.

2. After the words are finished, the cursor appears again, and the screen sits there.

3. When the user rolls over any of the three kids, the kid is highlighted, and the cursor changes to a pointing hand.

4. If the user clicks on a kid, it animates for a couple of seconds. While the animation is playing, the cursor is invisible. When the animation is done, the screen returns to its frozen state, and the cursor is again visible.

5. When the user rolls over the bird, the bird highlights, just like the kids. However, as long as the cursor is on the bird, its wings flap.

6. When the user clicks on the bird, it animates like the kids. The cursor is hidden, and it comes back when the animation is over and the screen is frozen.

7. If the user clicks on a word, the word is highlighted and the voice says that word and only that word.

Playing with the Kids

The kids' animations are laid out in the Score and labeled "water," "baseball," and "jump," for the flower-watering girl, the baseball boy, and the jump-rope girl. Each has his or her own Sprite Channel, channels 5, 6, and 7, respectively (Figure 7.2).

In the Cast, each kid's bitmaps are grouped together. The first one for each kid is its highlight, called *flowerHil*, *baseballHil*, or *jumpHil*. Each highlight Cast Member has a yellow glow behind the kid. The other Cast Members in each kid's sequence are the cells in his or her animation (Figure 7.3).

First, some general business. In this project, we are going to loop on frame 5. I want to leave some frames at the beginning for the Quicktime movie, which we will implement later. To set up the loop, put this script into the Frame Script of frame 5.

```
on exitFrame

        go to the frame

end
```

Figure 7.2 Score with animations.

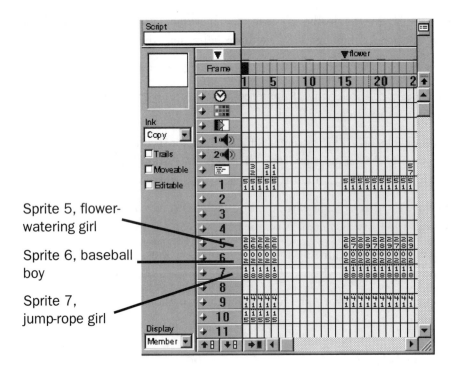

Sprite 5, flower-watering girl

Sprite 6, baseball boy

Sprite 7, jump-rope girl

Figure 7.3 The highlight cast members.

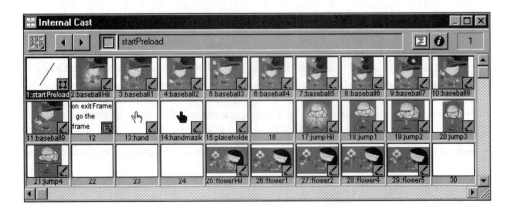

Good enough. Now let's check out which project behaviors apply to the kids:

1. When the user rolls over any of the three kids, the kid is highlighted, and the cursor changes to a pointing hand.

2. If the user clicks on a kid, it animates for a couple of seconds. While the animation is playing, the cursor is invisible. When the animation is done, the screen returns to its frozen state, and the cursor is again visible.

Let's isolate specific behaviors from these, which we can implement:

1. When the user rolls over a kid, the kid should highlight.

2. When the user rolls over a kid, the cursor should change.

3. If the user clicks on a kid, it should animate. While the animation is playing, the cursor is invisible. When the animation is done, the screen returns to normal.

Behavior 1 is a rollover, so I guess it's time we looked at rollovers.

Rolling Over Kids

There is no Lingo function that will tell you which Sprite the cursor is on. Every rollover technique tries to work around this limitation. (Actually, there is, but it's undocumented as of Director 5.0.1 which makes it risky. We'll talk about it at the end of the chapter.)There is, however, a function that tells you if the cursor is on a specific Sprite. The function, logically enough, is called *rollover*. It takes one argument, the value of the Sprite it is to test. For example, since the girl is in Sprite channel 7:

```
. . .

if rollover(7) then

        -- highlight jump rope girl

end if

. . .
```

The line *if rollover(7) then* is completely synonymous with *if rollover(7)=TRUE then*, but people generally use the shorter slang version.

We want this *if..then* to execute often because the user can roll the mouse pretty fast. We generally put rollover tests like this into an *exitframe* handler. This one should go into the Frame Script of frame 5.

```
on exitFrame

        if rollover(7) then

                -- highlight jump rope girl

        end if

end
```

Whenever you, a Lingo programmer, have to do a project that uses rollovers, it's best to come up with an overall system for handling all your rollovers, then stick to it. Since we have three kid rollovers, we are going to come up with a rollover scheme for the kids. In fact, this is my all-time favorite rollover scheme.

My Favorite Rollover Scheme

My favorite rollover scheme is a simplified version of common rollover schemes. Let's look at how this is commonly done first.

Most rollover schemes deal with puppetting and unpuppetting multiple Sprites. The script to do the highlight might look like this:

```
on exitFrame

        if rollover(7) then

                puppetSprite 7, TRUE

                set the member of cast 5 to member "jumpHil"

                updateStage

        else

                puppetSprite 7, FALSE

        end if

end
```

This is fine if you don't have many Sprites to check. When you do, though, it starts to get messy. Look at this code, as we add the baseball boy and flower-watering girl.

```
on exitFrame

      if rollover(5) then

            -- flower watering girl

            puppetSprite 5, TRUE

            set the member of sprite 5 to member "flowerHil"

            updateStage

      else

            puppetSprite 5, FALSE

      end if

      if rollover(6) then

            -- baseball boy

            puppetSprite 6, TRUE

            set the member of sprite 6 to member "baseballHil"

            updateStage

      else

            puppetSprite 6, FALSE

      end if

      if rollover(7) then

            -- jump rope girl

            puppetSprite 7, TRUE

            set the member of sprite 7 to member "jumpHil"

            updateStage

      else

            puppetSprite 7, FALSE

      end if
```

```
        go to the frame

end
```

I've implemented screens that have had 20 rollovers. Can you imagine how long the scripts get? How confusing it becomes to keep track of all the Puppets and not Puppets?

In projects like this one, it turns out that we can simplify the code a great deal. The key fact to realize is that **we only need one Puppet at any one time** because no two rollovers can happen simultaneously. Instead of dealing with multiple Puppets, we can deal with just one Puppet, in just one Sprite. Since we are dealing with just one Sprite, we only have to puppet or unpuppet it once. We can use a local variable to streamline the code even further. We've hit upon my favorite rollover scheme.

```
on exitFrame

        put empty into hiliteMember


    if rollover(5) then

            put "flowerHil" into hiliteMember

    else if rollover(6) then

            put "baseballHil" into hiliteMember

    else if rollover(7) then

            put "jumpHil" into hiliteMember

    end if


    if hiliteMember <> empty then

            puppetSprite 10, true

            set the member of sprite 10 to member hiliteMember

            updateStage
```

```
        else

                puppetSprite 10, false

        end if


        go to the frame

end
```

Let's step through this code.

The first thing the Lingo elf does as it executes the first line is create a local variable called *hiliteMember* and put an empty string into it. The next few lines, which are part of a chained *if..then..else* statement, test to see if any of the three kids' Sprites are rolled over. If one of them is, the name of that kid's highlight Cast Member is put into our variable, *hiliteMember*.

The next line, *if hiliteMember <> empty then*, checks to see if *hiliteMember* was given a value by one of the rollover tests. If it was, then *hiliteMember* contains the name of the Cast Member that should be put on the Stage, and the Lingo elf goes into the *then* clause.

The first line inside the *then* clause is *puppetSprite 10, true*. This turns sprite 10 into a Puppet. In the next line, we attach the proper highlight Cast Member to sprite 10, as determined by *hiliteMember*. Finally, we update the Stage to show the change immediately.

Why Does This Work?

It's the part of the code where we switch Cast Members that is most open to question.

```
    . . .

        puppetSprite 10, true

        set the member of sprite 10 to member hiliteMember

        updateStage

    . . .
```

The first line is pretty familiar by now. It turns sprite 10 into a Puppet. The second line seems familiar, too; it attaches a new Cast Member to sprite 10.

But how does attaching a new Cast Member to sprite 10 show a highlighted jump-rope girl, on top of the unhighlighted jump-rope girl? Wouldn't it be in the wrong position on the Stage?

Take a look at the registration point of the jump-rope girl highlight, in Cast Member *jumpHil* (Figure 7.4; the registration point is where the two dotted lines cross).

Figure 7.4 Registration point of jump-rope girl.

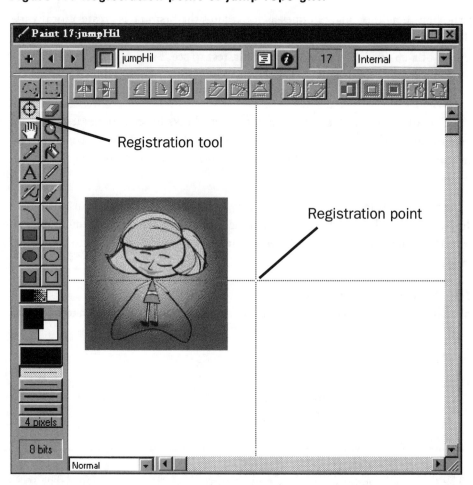

See how the registration point is off to the right of the girl's highlight image? If you lined up this point with the center of the Stage, the girl's highlight image would line up with the girl's normal image.

In this movie, sprite 10 is located at the center of the Stage. When we attach the new Cast Member to sprite 10, Director will put the highlight image on the Stage so that its registration point winds up at the exact location of sprite 10, which is, of course, the center of the Stage. The result is shown in Figure 7.5. The new image lies directly on top of the old one. The registration point (shown here for clarity) is at the center of the Stage. (By the way, the center of a 640×480 stage is 320, 240.)

The baseball boy and flower-watering girl highlights have similar registration points. Everybody lines up, and everybody's happy!

Figure 7.5 Jump-rope girl with center registration point.

The Placeholder

You might be wondering what's in sprite 10 to begin with. I generally use a very small little bitmap Cast Member. I go into the Paint Window, figure out which color is at the center of the screen, and use the pencil to make one small dot in that color. I call this Cast Member "placeholder" because it just holds the place of a Cast Member to come later (Figure 7.6).

To put this onto the Stage, I just drag it on. Then, I click on it in the Score and get its Sprite properties, from the **Modify:Sprite:Properties** menu item. I figure out exactly what the center-stage coordinates are, and I type them into the dialog box. (For a 640 × 480 stage, the center is at left: 320, top: 240.) Finally, I make sure that this Sprite is in the same frame as the rollovers, and I'm done.

Figure 7.6 Placeholder.

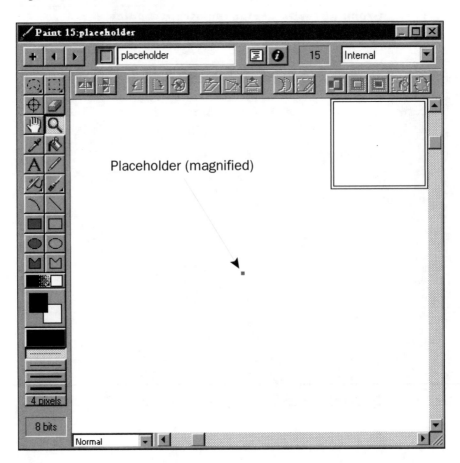

Implementing the Kid Rollovers

We are going to use a slight variation of this rollover scheme, just to give you more stuff to think about. We're going to use a couple of Lingo tricks to make the script prettier.

First, we will change the way we puppet and unpuppet sprite 10. Instead of puppetting it, changing its Cast Member, then unpuppetting it when we're done, we can take advantage of the placeholder Cast Member.

Let's turn sprite 10 into a Puppet before we get to our looping frame. Put this into the Frame Script of frame 4.

```
on exitFrame

        puppetSprite 10, TRUE

end
```

Next, let's modify our *exitFrame* script to take advantage of this idea.

Instead of putting *empty* into the variable *hiliteMember* to start with, we can put the string "placeHolder" into it. If none of the kids are rolled over, *hiliteMember* will hold the name of the placeholder Cast Member. The placeholder Cast Member is invisible to the end user, so we don't have to unpuppet sprite 10; we just have to set it to the placeholder.

Here's our first rewrite of the *exitFrame* script for frame 5:

```
on exitFrame

        put "placeholder" into hiliteMember



        if rollover(5) then

                put "flowerHil" into hiliteMember

        else if rollover(6) then

                put "baseballHil" into hiliteMember

        else if rollover(7) then

                put "jumpHil" into hiliteMember
```

```
        end if


    set the member of sprite 10 to member hiliteMember

    updateStage


    go to the frame

end
```

Notice that we were able to get rid of the second *if..then* statement. If none of the kids are rolled on, *hiliteMember* still has a valid Cast Member name. We also left out *puppetSprite 10,true*, since we are doing that in the *exitFrame* script of frame 4.

The second trick uses a new Lingo statement. Instead of using a chained *if..then*, we can use the cousin of *if..then*, the *case* statement. A *case* statement is a specialized *if..then*. **A case statement lets you test a specific variable or function for multiple values.** For example, this script will test the variable *hiliteMember*, and it will play a different sound for each kid. If *hiliteMember* doesn't have one of the three names, it shuts off whatever sound may be playing. (This is a just a code example, the movie has no sounds in it. However, sounds are available on the Web site, available as a link from **www.wiley.com/compbooks**.)

```
case hiliteMember of

    "flowerHil": puppetSound "flowerSound"

    "baseballHil": puppetSound "baseballSound"

    "jumpHil": puppetSound "jumpSound"

    otherwise: puppetSound 0

end case
```

This *case* statement could be rewritten as follows:

```
if hiliteMember = "flowerHil" then

    puppetSound "flowerSound"
```

```
else if hiliteMember = "baseballHil" then

        puppetSound "baseballSound"

else if hiliteMember = "jumpHil" then

        puppetSound " jumpSound "

else

        puppetSound 0

end if
```

The case version will execute more quickly than the *if..then* version.

My interesting trick is this: It is possible to turn the *case* statement around and use it to test one specific value against multiple functions or variables. If you put the value in the *case..of* line, you can put the function calls inside. Here's the second rewrite of the *exitFrame* handler for frame 5:

```
on exitFrame


  put "placeHolder" into hiliteMember


  case (true) of

     (rollover(5)): put "flowerHil" into hiliteMember

     (rollover(6)): put "baseballHil" into hiliteMember

     (rollover(7)): put "jumpHil" into hiliteMember

  end case



  set the member of sprite 10 to member hiliteMember

  updateStage
```

```
    go to the frame

end
```

Take a look at the *case* statement. When the Lingo elf gets to it, it sees *case (true) of*. It thinks to itself: I am going to look for a match to the value TRUE.

It goes inside the *case* statement, and it sees *(rollover(5))*. It evaluates the rollover, which returns TRUE or FALSE. Let's say the cursor is on top of the flower-watering girl, so *(rollover(5))* will return TRUE. The elf thinks "Does TRUE equal TRUE? Yes! Let's do this line!" So it executes *put "flowerHil" into hiliteMember*. When it is done with this line, it skips out of the *case* statement, and goes on with the handler.

By the way, you have to encase *rollover(5)* in parentheses for the trick to work.

Is this version "right" and the *if..then* version "wrong"? Of course not, we just have two versions, interesting for their aesthetic qualities.

Implementing Behavior B: Cursors

The next behavior we should implement is changing the cursor during a rollover. We could probably use *the cursor of sprite* property that we saw in Chapter 6, but why use the same thing twice?

Lingo has a fairly dangerous command called **cursor.** It changes the cursor to a cursor that you supply in the Cast or to one of the predefined cursors.

I said this was dangerous because the new cursor stays in effect until you issue another cursor command to change it back. If you forget to do this, the cursor will be screwed up for the rest of your program.

The following examples will change the cursor to predefined values:

```
cursor 0        -- default cursor

cursor -1       -- arrow pointer

cursor 1        -- I-Beam (like over a text field)

cursor 2        -- crosshair

cursor 3        -- crossbar
```

```
cursor 4          -- watch (Mac) or hourglass (Windows)

cursor 200        -- makes cursor invisible
```

The command is a little more complicated when you use your own custom cursor. First, you have to draw the cursor. The cursor command will take the top-left 16×16 pixel rectangular area of a bitmap Cast Member. The Cast Member **must be 1-bit,** or the command will have no effect. The registration point is the "hotspot" of the cursor (Figure 7.7).

Next, you issue the command. The *cursor* command takes one argument, the bitmap Cast Member. You must enclose the Cast Member in brackets. This line changes the cursor to the hand Cast Member, in Ch7.dir. You can type it into the Message Window while the movie is running.

Figure 7.7 Cursor with registration point.

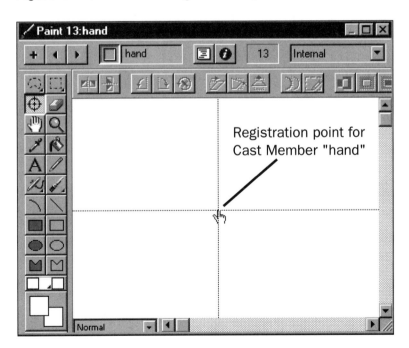

```
cursor [member "hand"]
```

You can also supply a "mask" bitmap for the cursor (Figure 7.8). Wherever the mask is black, the cursor won't be transparent. Wherever the mask is white, the cursor **will** be transparent. The mask also must be 1-bit. I have supplied a mask for the hand, to make it easier to see.

You can supply the mask argument after the first argument, inside the brackets, like so:

```
cursor [member "hand", member "handmask"]
```

Now, how should we put cursor control into our *exitFrame* script? Let's take another look at the script, as it stands now.

Figure 7.8 Handmask.

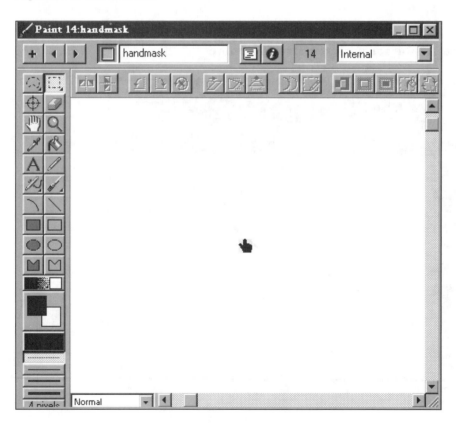

```
on exitFrame

        put "placeHolder" into hiliteMember


        case (true) of

                (rollover(5)): put "flowerHil" into hiliteMember

                (rollover(6)): put "baseballHil" into hiliteMember

                (rollover(7)): put "jumpHil" into hiliteMember

        end case




        set the member of sprite 10 to member hiliteMember

        updateStage


        go to the frame

end
```

We could probably use the same technique that we are already using with *hiliteMember*. First, we give the variable a safe default value. Next, we test our special-case conditions, to see if the variable should have a special value. Finally, we go ahead and set the property to whichever value is stored in the variable.

This is what we did with *hiliteMember*. First, we put *placeHolder* into it, because we know that, no matter what, it will always be safe to set sprite 10 to member *placeHolder*. Next, we check our special-case conditions, in the *case* statement. If a special case is met, meaning that a kid is rolled over, we put a special value into *hiliteMember*, namely, the kid's highlight Cast Member name. Finally, we set sprite 10 to whichever Cast Member name is in *hiliteMember*. It is safe to do this because *hiliteMember* always has an appropriate value.

For our special case, we can use the *otherwise* clause in the *case* statement. An *otherwise* is like an *else* : If nothing matches, the elf executes it.

For the default value, we can use the hand cursor. The value would be *[member "hand", member "handmask"]*. We could put the value into some local variable. Let's call it *newCursor*.

We can set the property using *newCursor* as the parameter to the *cursor* command. Here's how it looks:

```
on exitFrame


        put "placeHolder" into hiliteMember

        put [member "hand", member "handmask"] into newCursor


        case (true) of

            (rollover(5)): put "flowerHil" into hiliteMember

            (rollover(6)): put "baseballHil" into hiliteMember

            (rollover(7)): put "jumpHil" into hiliteMember


            otherwise: put 0 into newCursor

        end case



        cursor newCursor



        set the member of sprite 10 to member hiliteMember
```

```
       updateStage


       go to the frame
end
```

Following this code, when the user rolls over one of the kids, the value of *newCursor* is *[member "hand", member "handmask"]*. When the Lingo elf gets down to the *cursor newCursor* line, it sees

```
       cursor [member "hand", member "handmask"]
```

so the cursor turns into a hand. When the user hasn't rolled over a kid, the value of *newCursor* is 0. When the elf gets around to executing the *cursor newCursor* line, it sees

```
       cursor 0
```

which resets the cursor to the Director's plain old default cursor.

Implementing Behavior C: Connecting the Kids to Their Animations

Finally we have to answer a very modern parental question: What do kids do when you click on them? Answer: They animate in two dimensions.

The simplest way to make the kids animate is to put *play frame* commands in the *mouseDown* Sprite script on all the kids. Why not do this? Because it won't work.

The first problem is that the highlight Cast Member sticks around while the kid tries to animate. Because the highlight image in sprite 10 gets drawn on top of the image in the kids' Sprites, it'll be really hard to see the animations.

We also have to hide and show the cursor when we play an animation, and maybe do things we haven't thought of yet.

Let's route all the animation requests through a central handler in the Movie Script. Let's call this handler *playAnimation*. Here's what we'll start with:

```
on playAnimation labelName

       -- do stuff
```

```
        play frame labelName


        -- do more stuff

end
```

Let's have each of the kids call this handler when he or she is clicked. Put this in the Sprite script of sprite 5, in frame 5. This is the flower-watering girl.

```
on mouseDown

        playAnimation "flower"

end
```

This one is for the baseball boy. It goes in the script of sprite 6, in frame 5.

```
on mouseDown

        playAnimation "baseball"

end
```

Finally, this one goes in the Sprite script of sprite 7, in frame 5, the jump-rope girl.

```
on mouseDown

        playAnimation "jump"

end
```

Put these scripts in and play around with the movie. You should see the high-light-on-top-of-animation problem. How do we solve the problem? We just switch sprite 10 to the *placeHolder* Sprite before we play the animation. Here's the script:

```
on playAnimation labelName

        -- do stuff

        set the member of sprite 10 to member "placeHolder"

        play frame labelName
```

```
        -- do more stuff

end
```

Problem fixed!

Finally, we want hide the cursor. The command to do this is *cursor 200*. We want to show the cursor again after we have played the animation, which we can do with *cursor 0*. Here's the newest *playAnimation* script.

```
on playAnimation labelName

        cursor 200

        set the member of sprite 10 to member "placeHolder"

        play frame labelName

        cursor 0

end
```

We should now have fully functional kids!

That Wacky Bird

Let's recall the bird-related behaviors:

1. When the user rolls over the bird, the bird highlights, just like the kids highlight. However, as long as the cursor is on the bird, its wings flap.

2. When the user clicks on the bird, it animates, just like the kids animate. The cursor is hidden, and it comes back when the animation is done and the screen is frozen.

First, let's look at the rollover.

The difference between the bird and kid rollovers is that the bird animates as long as the cursor is on it. Each bitmap for the animation is in the Cast (Figure 7.9).

These Cast Members are different from the normal bird flaps because they have a yellow glow underneath them.

So the question: how should we make this animate? The most straightforward way would be to lay out the animation in the Score. If the rollover of bird Sprite is

Figure 7.9 Cast with highlighted bird flap.

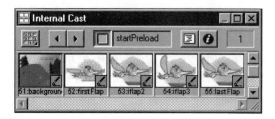

TRUE, go to the rollover animation frames. When it is FALSE, you could go back to frame 5.

By now, you should be able to tell from my tone of voice that I'm going to suggest a different way.

Implementing the Bird

I'd like to make the bird animate-during-rollover using Lingo. We have already done a little Lingo-based animation. When we have implemented Sprite drags, in Chapters 4 and 6, you could say we have been "animating" the dragged Sprites because they move across the Stage. We animated them by repeatedly setting their Sprite properties: *locH* and *locV*.

We can use a similar method to animate the bird. Instead of changing the *locH* and *locV*, though, we can change the *memberNum* of sprite 10. This will fit right into our current scheme.

If we were to implement the bird highlight in exactly the same way as the kids, meaning without animation, we could do it like this:

```
on exitFrame

    put "placeHolder" into hiliteMember

    put [member "hand", member "handmask"] into newCursor


    case (true) of

        (rollover(5)): put "flowerHil" into hiliteMember

        (rollover(6)): put "baseballHil" into hiliteMember
```

```
        (rollover(7)): put "jumpHil" into hiliteMember

        (rollover(9)): put "birdHil" into hiliteMember

        otherwise: put 0 into newCursor

    end case




    cursor newCursor

    set the member of sprite 10 to member hiliteMember

    updateStage



    go to the frame

end
```

Now we have to expand on this one line, *(rollover(9)): put "birdHil" into hiliteMember*, to make it put in the first flap Cast Member the first time, the second flap Cast Member the second time, and so on.

How do we keep track of which flap is currently displayed? We need some kind of container that will keep a value between *exitFrame* events. A container that we can always get to, no matter where we are in the movie. A container that will give us a value, and neither sleet nor snow nor freezing rain can stop it. We need a container like a **global variable**.

Let's make a global variable called *gFlapMember*. We will use it to hold the Cast Member number of the current highlighted bird flap. As always, when we use a global variable, we need to initialize it. Put this *startMovie* handler in the Movie Script:

```
on startMovie

    global gFlapMember

    put the number of member "firstFlap" into gFlapMember

end
```

Next, we have to modify the *exitFrame* handler to see the global, by adding this line:

```
on exitFrame

        global gFlapMember

        . . .
```

Now, we have to modify our *case* statement to take advantage of the variable. Here's what it looks like right now:

```
. . .

case (true) of

      (rollover(5)): put "flowerHil" into hiliteMember

      (rollover(6)): put "baseballHil" into hiliteMember

      (rollover(7)): put "jumpHil" into hiliteMember

      (rollover(9)): put "birdHil" into hiliteMember


          otherwise: put 0 into newCursor

end case

. . .
```

Instead of *birdHil* we want *hiliteMember* to get the current value of *gFlapMember*. Furthermore, we want to increase the value of *gFlapMember* by one, every time this rollover is executed. Neither one of these requests is difficult.

```
. . .

case (true) of

      (rollover(5)):     put "flowerHil" into hiliteMember

      (rollover(6)):     put "baseballHil" into hiliteMember

      (rollover(7)):     put "jumpHil" into hiliteMember

      (rollover(9)):     put gFlapMember + 1 into gFlapMember
```

```
          put gFlapMember into hiliteMember
```

```
     otherwise: put 0 into newCursor
```

```
end case
```

`. . .`

OK, let's try a test situation. Let's say that, for the first time, the user has rolled over the bird. The *exitFrame* handler executes, and the Lingo elf goes inside the *case* block. It executes *(rollover(9))* because the bird is in sprite 9.

The first line the elf executes is *put gFlapMember + 1 into gFlapMember*. Because the *startMovie* handler had already put the number of the first flap Cast Member into this global, *gFlapMember* will now have the number of the second flap Cast Member.

The next line is *put gFlapMember into hiliteMember*. The local variable *hiliteMember* will get the value of *gFlapMember*, which is the number of the second flap Cast Member. The elf will continue down the handler and end up attaching the second flap Cast Member to sprite 10. (Notice that *set the member of* will accept a member number, like 10, or a name, like "jumpHil".)

Let's say the user leaves the cursor on the bird. The *exitFrame* handler executes again, and again it goes into the *(rollover(9))* section of the case statement. This time, *gFlapMember* gets the number of the **third** flap Cast Member, which gets put into *hiliteMember* and attached to sprite 10.

The next time through, *gFlapMember* gets the number of the **fourth** flap Cast Member, which gets put into *hiliteMember* and attached to sprite 10.

The next time through, *gFlapMember* gets the number of the **fifth** flap Cast Member, and... Wait a second. There are only **four** flap Cast Members. Oops.

We have to put in a check, to make sure that *gFlapMember* doesn't get out of control. It should never go higher than the number of the last flap Cast Member.

We can do this with a simple *if..then*. After we add 1 to *gFlapMember*, we can check if *gFlapMember* is too high. If it is, we can bring it back down to the number of the first flap Cast Member. Here's the final *exitFrame* handler:

```
on exitFrame

    global gFlapMember

    put "placeHolder" into hiliteMember

    put [member "hand", member "handmask"] into newCursor


    case (true) of

        (rollover(5)): put "flowerHil" into hiliteMember

        (rollover(6)): put "baseballHil" into hiliteMember

        (rollover(7)): put "jumpHil" into hiliteMember

        (rollover(9)):


            put gFlapMember + 1 into gFlapMember


            if gFlapMember > the number of member "lastFlap" then
                put the number of member "firstFlap" into gFlapMember
            end if


            put gFlapMember into hiliteMember


        otherwise: put 0 into newCursor
    end case


    cursor newCursor
```

```
        set the member of sprite 10 to member hiliteMember

        updateStage


        go to the frame
end
```

And that takes care of that!

There's still a minor bug in our code, though. If you read the last few pages again, you might notice that the *startMovie* handler initializes *gFlapMember* to the first flap Cast Member. When you look at the code in *(rollover(9))*, the first thing to happen is that *gFlapMember* gets incremented by 1. So, the second flap is the first one to make it to the screen.

As I said, this is a minor bug. Most people would never notice it. But we're here, so we might as well get it right. All we have to do is **initialize the variable to 1 less than its first desired value**. This will come up a lot when you initialize variables. Here's the final *startMovie* handler.

```
on startMovie

        global gFlapMember

        put the number of member "firstFlap" -1 into gFlapMember

end
```

It's a no-brainer to finish off the bird. To connect the bird to its score animation, simply put this handler into the Sprite Script of sprite 9.

```
on mouseDown

        playAnimation "bird"

end
```

Speaking the Words

The words in the upper right of the screen are surprisingly functional in this project. Project behaviors 1, 2, and 7 relate to this text.

1. When you play the movie, the words in the upper-right corner are read aloud. As each word is read, it is underlined. While this is happening, the cursor is invisible.

2. After the words are finished, the cursor appears again, and the screen remains static.

7. If the user clicks on a word, the word is highlighted and the voice says that word, and only that word.

The words are not "live text" in the sense that they are bitmapped graphics that were created in Adobe Photoshop. The plain words are on the background bitmap, and the underlined versions of the words are in the Cast, one word per Cast Member.

Each Cast Member has a registration point that should be lined up with the center of the Stage, just like the kid-highlight the Cast Members.

We know that we can use a Lingo script to attach each Cast Member to sprite 10 in succession, the way we did with the flapping bird. We'll work out the details later.

At this point, we have two unsolved problems:

1. How do we play the audio of the voiceover?

2. How do we synch the displayed words to the audio?

We are programmers, and solving problems is what we do. This'll be fun.

We have four options for playing the audio. We can put the sound into the sound channel of the Score. We can use the *puppetSound* command to play a sound cast member. We can use the *sound playfile* command to play an AIFF file from disk. Or, we can play an audio-only Quicktime movie.

Our decision becomes crystal clear when we take into account our goal of synchronization. We can, using *the movieTime of sprite* property, easily find out the current point in the Quicktime movie that the user is hearing. Once you start playing a sound via *puppetSound, sound playFile,* or the Score, there is no way to know what point you are at in the sound.

If we want to synchronize something to the audio (and we do), we have to use Quicktime. See Chapter 8 for a discussion of the other three methods of playing sound.

Cast Member 3 is a Quicktime movie called "spoken.mov." It is the soundtrack for the text. It has one audio track and no video tracks. The member info dialog is configured to be initially Paused. This Cast Member is laid out in sprite channel 15 of the Score.

We already know how to set this movie playing.

```
set the movieRate of sprite 15 to 1
```

Now what is all this talk about synchronization?

Synchronizing Quicktime and Lingo

The great thing about a Quicktime movie is that it has a built-in timeline. If the user is supposed to hear the word "recess" at tick 50, Quicktime will make darn well sure that "recess" starts at tick 50.

So, here's how we can synchronize the display of the word "recess":

1. Start playing the Quicktime movie.

2. Constantly ask it for its *movieTime*.

3. When the *movieTime* is 50 ticks, display the underlined word "recess."

I know what you're thinking. You want to see the code.

First, we have to set the Quicktime movie playing. In frame 4, we might put this:

```
on exitFrame

    set the movieRate of sprite 15 to 1

end
```

In frame 5, we would put this:

```
on exitFrame

    if the movieTime of sprite 15 >= 50 then

        puppetSprite 10, TRUE
```

```
      set the member of sprite 10 to member "recess"

      updateStage

   end if

   go the frame

end
```

Notice the *if..then* test condition. It says *the movieTime of sprite 15 >= 50*, meaning if the *movieTime* is **greater than or equal to** 50. We can't test for *the movieTime of sprite 15 = 50* because we can't guarantee that this particular line of Lingo code will execute at the exact instant when the movie is at tick 50. The most we can do is hedge our bet.

So, our path seems clear. First, we have to record the starting *movieTimes* for each of the words:

ISN'T	RECESS	FUN?
0	50	76
LET'S	SKIP	SCHOOL!
105	120	140

Then, we write some sort of *if..then* statement that checks the *movieTime* against each word's start time to figure out which underlined word to display. If you think about it, this is similar to our rollover task, where we used a *case* statement instead of an *if..then*. In fact, a *case* statement is more appropriate for this situation, too.

Here we go:

```
on exitFrame

   put empty into hiliteMember

   put the movieTime of sprite 15 into mtime


   case (true) of

      (mtime >= 140) : put "school" into hiliteMember
```

```
     (mtime >= 120)  : put "skip" into hiliteMember

     (mtime >= 105)  : put "lets" into hiliteMember

     (mtime >= 76)   : put "fun" into hiliteMember

     (mtime >= 50)   : put "recess" into hiliteMember

     (mtime >= 0)    : put "isnt" into hiliteMember

  end case


  puppetSprite 10, TRUE


  set the member of sprite 10 to member hiliteMember


  go to the frame
end
```

This is another one of those times when, as the author of this book, I get to say "Sorry, bub. You don't get off that easy."

Sure, this method works. Unfortunately, it doesn't scale. What if your sentence has 30 or 40 words? Would you really want to put 30 or 40 lines into a *case* statement?

I thought not. Brace yourself, it's time to learn something new...

Linear Lists

(I'm warning you, it's late at night and I'm getting punchy. My prose might get wacky.)

Raise your hand if you know what a list is.

You, in the silly hat. Yes, you're right. A list is a collection of items that has some sort of order and generally has a name. Here's a list that we'll call "Oz."

1. lions

2. tigers

3. bears

4. dogs

5. monkeys

This list has a theme, things from *The Wizard of Oz*. (This is a great movie. Watch it again with your lover.)

If we put this into a Lingo list, the items, like "lions" and "tigers" and "bears," would be strings. (A **string** is a sequence of letters, numbers, or punctuation. In other words, a string is a piece of text.) We can put this list into a variable like this:

```
put [ "lions", "tigers", "bears", "dogs", "monkeys" ] into oz
```

The brackets *[* and *]* are necessary to envelop a list. The items inside the brackets must be separated with commas. Items that are strings have to be enveloped in quotes, but numbers must not be.

Lingo lets us manipulate this list using various built-in functions.

For example, we can ask Lingo how many items are in the list by using the *count()* function in the Message Window. You supply the function with the name of the list, in this case, *oz*.

```
put count(oz)

-- 5
```

We can ask Lingo for the fourth item in the list, like this:

```
put getAt( oz, 4 )

-- "dogs"
```

The *getAt* function takes two parameters. The first is the list that we are interested in. The second is the list position that we are interested in. *GetAt* returns the value in the specified position in the specified list. If you specify too high a position, like 834, Director will pop up an error dialog saying "Index out of range." This means that the index, 834, is higher than the maximum number of positions in this list.

We can flip that request around and ask for the position of a specified item. Check this out:

```
put getPos( oz, "dogs" )

-- 4
```

With the *getPos* function, you have to supply the name of the list and the value of the item you are looking for. The function examines each item in the list, looking for the first exact match. It returns the number of the position of the first exact match. If it doesn't find a match, it returns 0.

Heck, we can even ask Lingo to sort the list for us. All we have to supply is the name of the list. Try this in the Message Window:

```
put oz

-- ["lions", "tigers", "bears", "dogs", "monkeys"]


sort oz


put oz

-- ["bears", "dogs", "lions", "monkeys", "tigers"]
```

This is nice because we all hate alphabetizing things manually. Once you sort a list, it stays sorted unless you intentionally mess it up.

You can actually change the contents of a list. To change the value of an item, you can use *setAt*.

```
put oz

-- ["lions", "tigers", "bears", "dogs", "monkeys"]


setAt oz,5, "munchkins"


put oz

-- ["lions", "tigers", "bears", "dogs", "munchkins"]
```

The function *setAt* takes three arguments. The first is the list. The second is the index of the item that you want to change. The third is the new value of the item.

You can **add** an item to the list easily:

```
put oz

-- ["lions", "tigers", "bears", "dogs", "monkeys"]



add oz, "scarecrows"



put oz

-- ["lions", "tigers", "bears", "dogs", "monkeys", "scarecrows"]
```

You can also add an item at a specific location in the list, using *addAt*. The first parameter for *addAt* is the list, the second parameter is the position to insert the new item, and the third parameter is the item itself. Here, we add "scarecrow" to the fourth position in the list.

```
put oz

-- ["lions", "tigers", "bears", "dogs", "monkeys"]



addAt oz, 4, "scarecrows"



put oz

-- ["lions", "tigers", "bears", "scarecrows", "dogs", "monkeys"]
```

Finally, you can delete items from a list using *deleteAt*. The first parameter to *deleteAt* is the list, and the second is the position in the list to zap. Try this in the Message Window:

```
put oz

-- ["lions", "tigers", "bears", "dogs", "monkeys"]
```

```
deleteAt oz, 3
```

```
put oz
```

```
-- ["lions", "tigers", "dogs", "monkeys"]
```

```
deleteAt oz, getPos(oz, "dogs")
```

```
put oz
```

```
-- ["lions", "tigers", "monkeys"]
```

Incidentally, the lists we just talked about are called "Linear Lists." Lingo has another kind of list, called "Property Lists," that we aren't going to talk about in this book. It's a great topic for self-exploration, though!

Back to the Synch Problem

Welcome back from the land of Oz. Let's hope our foray helps with the synchronization problem. Oh, of course it does. Would I lead you astray?

Let's implement project behaviors 1 and 2.

It would be a relatively simple matter to put the *movieTimes* of each of the words into a linear list. We could store this list in a global variable. Let's be uninventive and call it *gMovieTimes*.

```
put [ 0, 50, 76, 105, 120, 140 ] into gMovieTimes
```

We could put the names of each of the word Cast Members into another list. Each word Cast Member's name is the word itself.

```
put [ "isnt", "recess", "fun", "lets", "skip", "school"] into gWords
```

Because these are global variables, we really should initialize them in the *startMovie* handler. And while we're at it, why don't we start soft-coding the number of the Quicktime Sprite, too? (By the way, you should start implementing this in the project.)

```
on startMovie

    global gWords, gMovieTimes, gQtSprite

    global gFlapMember

    put the number of member "firstFlap" into gFlapMember

    put [ "isnt", "recess", "fun", "lets", "skip", "school"] into gWords

    put [ 0, 50, 76, 105, 120, 140 ] into gMovieTimes

    put 15 into gQtSprite

end
```

Now we have to set up a few frames in the Score to work our synchronization scheme. Conveniently, I have built just the thing in frames 85–89 of the Score. Frame 85 is labeled "speakWords." (Look for yourself, if you don't believe me.)

We could have done our scheme in the first few frames, but it always seems so cramped at the beginning of a Director movie. When I have to do complicated things, I generally put them further along in the Score.

We have to play the "speakNow" sequence of frames when we start the movie, though. Why don't you put this script into the frame script of frame 2?

```
on exitFrame

    play frame "speakWords"

end
```

We, of course, have to balance this with a *play done* command. Let's put it in the frame script of frame 89.

```
on exitFrame

    play done

end
```

As of this point, the sequence of frames that the movie will play at startup is 1, 2, 85, 86, 87, 89, 3, 4...

In order for our synch-scheme to work, the Quicktime movie has to be playing, and sprite 10 has to be a puppet. It would also be nice if the cursor were hidden. Let's lay this groundwork in the frame script of frame 86.

```
on exitFrame

    global gQtSprite


    cursor 200

    puppetSprite 10,true

    set the movierate of sprite gQtSprite to 1

end
```

Finally, it's time to do some real work. Let's create an *exitFrame* handler that handles the synchronization. This script would go into frame 87.

Instead of having a long *case* statement, we can just loop through all the items in the *movieTime* list. If we find the right time, we can check that location in the word list to find the name of Cast Member to display. Here's the handler:

```
on exitFrame

    global gWords, gMovieTimes, gQtSprite


    put empty into hiliteMember

    put the movieTime of sprite gQtSprite into mtime

    put count(gMovieTimes) into numTimes


    repeat with i = numTimes down to 1

        put getAt(gMovieTimes, i) into wordTime

        if mtime >= wordTime then

            put getAt( gWords, i) into hiliteMember
```

```
        exit repeat

      end if

   end repeat




   set the member of sprite 10 to member hiliteMember



   go to the frame

end
```

The Playback Head moves and the Lingo elf executes this handler. First, it makes sure that it can see the global variables *gWords, gMovieTimes,*and *gQtSprite*. Next, it puts an empty string into the local variable *hiliteMember*. Then, it saves the current tick of the Quicktime movie into the local variable *mtime*.

Let's say that the movie is at tick 110, 5 ticks into the word "lets". So, *mtime* holds 110. Now things get interesting. The elf checks the number of items in the list *gMovieTimes*. It counts six items, and so puts a 6 into the local *numTimes*. In the next line, we set up a *repeat* loop. Instead of counting **up** from the first value to the last value, this loop counts **down** from the first value to the last. This particular loop will count down from 6 to 1.

The elf goes inside the loop. This is the first iteration, so the local variable *i* contains 6. (The letter *i* is a programmer's favorite loop variable name. We like to think that "i" stands for "iteration," but we really use it because it's easy to type.)

The elf executes the line *put getAt(gMovieTimes,i) into wordTime*. The elf puts the sixth item in *gMovieTimes*, 140, into *wordTime*. Remember, 140 is the tick in the Quicktime movie's timeline where the sixth word, "school," starts.

The next line is *if mtime >= wordTime then*. In other words, if the current point of the movie is at or after the point where the sixth word is spoken, in **other** words, if the sixth word is being spoken, *then...*

But it isn't. In our example, the current tick, the value of *mtime*, is 110. So, the Lingo elf skips to the *end if*, then to the *end repeat*, and hops back up to the *repeat with* line. It executes the loop again, and this time *i* holds a 5. In the *getAt* line, the elf puts the fifth value in *gMovieTimes*, 120, into *mtime*. And it gets rejected by the *if..then* again. *120 >= 110* is not a true statement.

The elf skips to the *end repeat*, jumps back to the beginning of the loop, then runs through with a 4 in *i*. In the *getAt* line, the elf puts the fourth value, 105, into *mtime*. The elf evaluates the *if..then*, *110 >= 105*. Eureka! The test passes, so the elf eagerly jumps into the *if..then* block.

The first inside line is *put getAt(gWords, i) into hiliteMember*. Because we know that the word in position 4 is playing, we can look up position 4 in our list of strings. After this line, *hiliteMember* gets "lets" which is the name of the cast member that has the bitmap of "let's." Ladies and germs, we have found our Cast Member!

And since we have found our Cast Member, we don't need to check items 3, 2, or 1 in the *gMovieTimes* list. In fact, we don't need to iterate through the loop again at all.

So, we don't. The `exit repeat` command throws the Lingo elf out of the loop on his little elfen butt. The next line to execute is this: *set the member of sprite 10 to member hiliteMember*

Which, thankfully, sets sprite 10 to the Cast Member for "let's." Because the Cast Member is registered for the middle of the screen, and sprite 10 is positioned in the middle of the screen, everything lines up.

The next line, *go to the frame*, executes, and this whole process happens again. It's a good thing that the elf doesn't get tired.

Eventually, the Quicktime movie will end. The way we arranged it, unfortunately, we never tell the Playback Head to go to a different frame, so the movie will just sit on frame 84 forever.

We can fix this, of course. All we have to do is compare the current *movieTime* with the *duration* of the movie. If the *movieTime* is less, then stay on the current frame. If the *movieTime* is equal to the duration, do nothing and let the Playback Head do what it does best, move forward.

Here's the final frame script for frame 87.

```
on exitFrame

    global gWords, gMovieTimes, gQtSprite



    put empty into hiliteMember

    put the movieTime of sprite gQtSprite into mtime

    put count(gMovieTimes) into numTimes


    repeat with i = numTimes down to 1

        put getAt(gMovieTimes, i) into wordTime

        if mtime >= wordTime then

            put getAt( gWords, i) into hiliteMember

            exit repeat

        end if

    end repeat




    set the member of sprite 10 to member hiliteMember


    if mtime<the duration of member(the member of sprite gQtSprite) then

        cursor 0

        go to the frame
```

```
   end if

end
```

Tackling Behavior 7

We've got one more behavior to go.

7. If the user clicks on a word, the word is highlighted and the voice says that word, and only that word.

We have already laid the foundation to solve this problem, with our lists of times in *gMovieTimes* and Cast Member names in *gWords*.

Our first problem is allowing the user to click on a specific word. I have supplied, in frame 5, six invisible-box sprites covering each word. "Isn't school fun" is covered by sprites 17, 18, and 19. "Let's skip school" is covered by sprites 20, 21, and 22.

We can easily put *mouseDown* handlers into each sprite. Put this handler into each of the word-cover sprites:

```
on mouseDown

   doWordClick

end
```

doWordClick is a handler in the Movie Script that we are about to create. The question, of course, is if all six sprites have exactly the same script, how are we going to tell which sprite was clicked? Read on.

Let's start with an empty *doWordClick* handler in the Movie Script.

```
on doWordClick

   -- do stuff

end
```

The first thing that *doWordClick* has to do is figure out which sprite was clicked. Lingo makes this very easy, in fact. A built-in function called **the clickOn** always tells you which sprite was last clicked.

If the user clicked down on sprite 18, the *mouseDown* handler on sprite 18 would execute. The only thing this does is call the *doWordClick* handler. Once inside the handler, if we check the value of *the clickOn*, we will get the number 18.

From there, we can use a *case* statement to figure out which word was clicked. Here's the code:

```
on doWordClick

    put the clickOn into clicked


    put empty into whichWord

    case clicked of

        17: put "isnt" into whichWord

        18: put "recess" into whichWord

        19: put "fun" into whichWord

        20: put "lets" into whichWord

        21: put "skip" into whichWord

        22: put "school" into whichWord

    end case


    -- do stuff

end
```

In the first line, we save the number of the clicked sprite into the local variable *clicked*. In the second line, we initialize a local variable *whichWord* with an empty string. In the *case* block, we fill *whichWord* with the actual string of the word that corresponds to each sprite number.

Now that we have the clicked word, we can switch sprite 10 for the correct Cast Member. Again, each word's Cast Member name is the word itself.

. . .

```
set the member of sprite 10 to member whichWord
```

. . .

So we have displayed the correct word's graphic. The next step is to play the piece of the Quicktime movie that plays the clicked word, and only the clicked word.

We start by figuring out the index of the word to be spoken, in the gWords list. Since we know the value we are looking for, we can use getPos. . . .

```
put getPos( gWords, whichWord ) into pos
```

. . .

This line looks through *gWords* for the first match to *whichWord*. If *whichWord* is "recess" then *pos* will get the number 2. "Recess" is the second word in the list *gWords*. We can use this position to look up a *movieTime* in *gMovieTimes*, because *gWords* and *gMovieTimes* are in the same order.

. . .

```
put getAt( gMovieTimes, pos ) into wordStart
```

. . .

Following our example, this line looks up the second *movieTime* in *gMovieTimes*. *wordStart* gets the *movieTime* of the start of word 2. We can start playing the Quicktime movie from this point.

We also need to know when to stop the Quicktime movie, since we only want to play one word. Question: When should we stop playing word 2? Answer: When word 3 starts to play. All we need to do is find the starting value of the next word.

. . .

```
put getAt( gMovieTimes, pos + 1) into wordEnd
```

. . .

Now we can play the movie. After we start playing it from *wordStart*, we can watch it continuously and stop it when it reaches *wordEnd*. Here's that code:

. . .

```
set the movieTime of sprite gQtSprite to wordStart

updateStage
```

```
set the movieRate of sprite gQtSprite to 1

repeat while the movieTime of sprite gQtSprite < wordEnd

    updateStage -- needed to keep Quicktime playing

end repeat

set the movieRate of sprite gQtSprite to 0

      . . .
```

If we throw in a *cursor 200* to hide the cursor at the beginning, and a *cursor 0* to show it again when we're done, we've got ourselves a handler!

```
on doWordClick

    global gWords, gMovieTimes, gQtSprite


    put the clickOn into clicked


    put empty into whichWord

    case clicked of

        17: put "isnt" into whichWord

        18: put "recess" into whichWord

        19: put "fun" into whichWord

        20: put "lets" into whichWord

        21: put "skip" into whichWord

        22: put "school" into whichWord

    end case


    set the member of sprite 10 to member whichWord
```

```
put getPos( gWords, whichWord ) into pos

put getAt( gMovieTimes, pos ) into wordStart

put getAt( gMovieTimes, pos + 1) into wordEnd


set the movieTime of sprite gQtSprite to wordStart

set the movieRate of sprite gQtSprite to 1

repeat while the movieTime of sprite gQtSprite < wordEnd

    updateStage -- needed to keep Quicktime playing

end repeat

set the movieRate of sprite gQtSprite to 0
```

end

OK, I'll admit it. There is a bug. A bad bug. The kind of bug you just have to fix.

If you click on the sixth word, "school," Director will pop up an ugly error dialog. The error: "Index out of range: put getAt(gMovieTimes, pos + 1) into wordEnd".

Let's step through the pertinent part of the code to figure out what's going on. Let's say that the sixth word, "school", has just been clicked.

After the *case* statement, *whichWord* contains "school". The next line displays the correct Cast Member. The next line fills *pos* with 6, which is correct. The next line fills *wordStart* with the sixth item in *gMovieTimes*, which is the start time of "school." This, too, is correct. The next line fills *wordEnd* with the seventh value of *gMovieTimes*...

There is no seventh value—*gMovieTimes* only has six items. A big, hairy, disgusting New York City cockroach of a bug.

There are lots of ways to fix this. Before trying to fill *wordEnd*, we could make sure *pos* is less than 6. Or, we can just put a seventh item into *gMovieTimes*. That would be kind of scary because other parts of the program use the same global variable. You never want to step on a different part of the program if you can help it.

We could, though, add a seventh item to *gMoviesList*, then delete it before we leave the handler. This is clean, and it gives you practice with the list operators. The seventh value should be the duration of the Quicktime movie because the last word should play through until the end of the audio. Here's the code:

```
        .  .  .

add gMovieTimes, the duration of member (the member of sprite gQtSprite)

put getPos( gWords, whichWord ) into pos

put getAt( gMovieTimes, pos ) into wordStart

put getAt( gMovieTimes, pos + 1) into wordEnd

deleteAt gMovieTimes, count(gMovieTimes)

        .  .  .
```

The first line adds the duration of the Quicktime movie to the end of *gMovieTimes*. The last line deletes the last item of *gMovieTimes*, leaving it unscathed, as if we never touched it.

Here's the final version of *doWordClick*.

```
on doWordClick

    global gWords, gMovieTimes, gQtSprite


    put the clickOn into clicked


    put empty into whichWord

    case clicked of

        17: put "isnt" into whichWord
```

```
    18: put "recess" into whichWord

    19: put "fun" into whichWord

    20: put "lets" into whichWord

    21: put "skip" into whichWord

    22: put "school" into whichWord

  end case


  set the member of sprite 10 to member whichWord


  add gMovieTimes, the duration of member (the member of sprite gQtSprite)

  put getPos( gWords, whichWord ) into pos

  put getAt( gMovieTimes, pos ) into wordStart

  put getAt( gMovieTimes, pos + 1) into wordEnd

  deleteAt gMovieTimes, count(gMovieTimes)


  set the movieTime of sprite gQtSprite to wordStart

  set the movieRate of sprite gQtSprite to 1


  repeat while the movieTime of sprite gQtSprite < wordEnd

    updateStage -- needed to keep Quicktime playing

  end repeat

  set the movieRate of sprite gQtSprite to 0

end
```

A Niggly, Unrelated Bug

You might have noticed that when you click on a word the colors go wonky in a rectangle surrounding the word. Why?

It's a Director bug (or a feature, I can't tell). When you click on an invisible box Sprite, and that Sprite has a script, Director assumes that it is a button. It also assumes that button should highlight automatically when clicked. Director tries to do this by **inverting** the colors underneath the box.

Is this stupid? Yes. Is there a way around it? Thankfully, there is. Put the following two handlers into the **Cast Member scripts** of each invisible box Cast Member. To get to an invisible box's script, click on it in the Score. Then double-click the thumbnail of the Cast Member (in the top-left of the Score Window.) This brings up the Shape Cast Member dialog box. Finally, click the Script button in the dialog.

Here are the handlers. They should go into each of the six invisible box Cast Members.

```
on mouseUp

end



on mouseDown

end
```

Yes, you're right, they do nothing. Nothing! But it solves the problem.

Managing Your Memory

Running this movie from a hard disk, you probably won't notice its sluggish behavior. Try running "Ch7_slow.dir" from the Chapter 7 folder of the CD-ROM.

The behavior you will see, unless you have a really speedy system, is that the rollover "glowing" Cast Members are slow to show up on their first appearance. After the first time, they appear immediately.

You will probably see this behavior in the animations, too. When you click on a character, the animation will be slow and jerky the first time it runs, and speedy enough the second time.

The two questions that should come to your mind are these:

1. What is going on here?

2. What can I, a Lingo-slinger, do about it?

What Is Going on Here?

The long answer starts with the section, "Under the Hood," later in this chapter. The short answer is this: disk drives are slow and RAM is fast.

Before displaying an image, Director must load it from the disk into RAM. All the Cast Members live on the disk, be it a hard disk or CD-ROM. Director doesn't like to load an image into RAM until just before displaying it. Once it is in RAM, Director doesn't like to let go of it unless the RAM is needed for some other Cast Member.

When you roll over the baseball boy for the first time, your Lingo code tells Director to display the boy's highlight bitmap. Director checks RAM and doesn't find that bitmap, so it loads it from the disk. This takes time, because disk drives are slow. Once the cast member is loaded, Director can display it straight from RAM. This is quick, because RAM is fast.

The next time you roll over the boy, Director looks for the bitmap in RAM. It finds it there and displays it immediately. This happens quickly because RAM is fast.

Repeat after me, "Disk drives are slow and RAM is fast."

The same holds true for the animations. Director displays the first frame, then has to load the second frame from the disk. It displays this image, then loads the images in the third frame from the disk. Every time it hits the disk, performance suffers. Once it is loaded into RAM, Director will try not to let go of it.

What Can I Do About It?

Lingo provides a few commands that help you help Director do the right thing.

The right thing is to load the Cast Members into RAM before the user has a chance to roll over or click anything. This way, all the finger drumming that the user has to do is all at once, up-front. When interaction is possible, all the Cast Members are in RAM, ready for instant access.

The most useful RAM-related command is *preLoadMember*. It lets you preload a cast member, **pre** meaning before Director tries to use it. The following command will preload Cast Member 2, the baseball highlight bitmap.

```
preLoadMember 2
```

This line does the same thing, using the Cast Member's name...

```
preLoadMember "baseballHil"
```

This line supplies both a starting and ending Cast Member. It will cause Director to preload all the cast members from "firstFlap" to "lastFlap".

```
preLoadMember "firstFlap","lastFlap"
```

Sometimes, if you have many Score-based animations in your movie, it is more convenient to use the *preLoad* command. This command goes through a frame or range of frames, trying to preload every Cast Member it finds in the score.

The command without any parameters, like this

```
preLoad
```

tries to load every Cast Member in the movie. If you have a lot of Cast Members, this isn't terribly viable. This next line preloads only the Cast Members on frame 4...

```
preload 4
```

You can also specify a range of frames, for example:

```
preLoad 4, 10
```

will try to preload all the Cast Members in frame 4, 5, 6, 7, 8, 9, and 10.

Remember, *preLoad* and *preLoadMember* **request** that Director load Cast Members into RAM. Director may not comply. If Director has enough RAM for 20 images, and you try to load the twenty-first, Director has to make a decision. It will throw out one of the other images to make room for yours. However, if all 20 images are displayed on the Stage, Director can't discard them. In a case like this, your twenty-first bitmap loses, and Director doesn't preload it.

Instead of trying to guess which unused Cast Member Director will choose to discard from RAM, you can be really specific and tell Director which ones to discard. If you know that you won't need Cast Member "baseballHil" for a while, you can use either of the next commands to discard it from RAM.

```
unloadMember 2
```

```
unloadMember "baseballHil"
```

You can unload a range of cast members like this

```
unloadMember 4, 10
```

The most common usage of this command takes no parameters at all. This next command tells Director to discard all the loaded Cast Members, except the ones in the current frame.

```
unloadMember
```

Director will tell you if a member is preloaded if you ask for *the loaded of member*. This code tries its darndest to preload the highlight Cast Member.

```
preLoadMember "baseballHil"

if the loaded of member "baseballHil" = FALSE then

    unloadMember

    preLoadMember "baseballHil"

end if
```

There are a few more memory management commands, but I generally don't use them. It rarely pays to create very intricate RAM management schemes because you never know what else is going on in the user's computer that may be using RAM, spinning the disk, or causing general havoc with your title.

The most common way to use memory management is this:

1. When you come to a new section of your movie, call *unloadMember* to discard unnecessary Cast Members from RAM. If the movie only has one section, don't bother.

2. Preload the Cast Members you will need.

3. Enter the section.

Implementing Memory Management in Chapter 7

To keep things simple, I always use two Cast Members, named "startPreload" and "endPreload", to book-end my important members in the Cast. Then, I call *preLoadMember* to load all the important members at once.

```
preLoadMember "startPreload","endPreload"
```

In "ch7.dir" "startPreload" is Cast Member 1, and "endPreload" is Cast Member 56. Cast Members 2 through 55 are the characters animations and highlights. If we change the frame script in frame 2, we can embed the preloading command.

```
on exitFrame

  preLoadMember "startPreload","endPreload"

  play frame "speakWords"

end
```

This version is in file "Ch7_done.dir" in the Chapter 7 folder on the CD-ROM.

The rest of this chapter aims to enrich your understanding what Director or a projector, as an application running in a computer, has to do to run your multimedia project. It should help you understand where performance bottlenecks are and how to get around them.

Under the Hood

Do you ever wonder what Director has to do when it puts a picture on the screen? There's a secret story of you and the Lingo elf somewhere in there. We just have to dig it out.

The Scene

You have given some users a projector of the Chapter 7 project. They have been running it for a while, and they have just rolled over the jump-rope girl. All the Lingo that we wrote executes and asks the Director Runtime Engine to put the highlighted jump-rope girl Cast Member onto the screen.

In this story, **you are the Director Runtime Engine**. Picture yourself as a program running on a computer. You'll be glad you did.

Here are some of the exotic locations we'll be accessing.

RAM

This is Random Access Memory, meaning you can access any piece of this memory at any time. RAM lives in silicon chips inside your computer. When the power switch goes out, the contents of the RAM chips die.

Computers only execute commands that are located in RAM. Commands that are on the disk must first be read into RAM, then executed. Any part of a program that is currently running is located in RAM.

Disk

For the following discussion, **disk** means the hard disk or CD-ROM. All Director projects live on some sort of disk. Even Shockwave movies run from the hard disk (the movie gets downloaded to the hard disk and runs from there).

Video card

For this discussion, **video card** means the place where you plug your monitor into your computer. A **video card** generally owns its own piece of RAM that represents the screen.

Director's Untold Story

You, the little Director elf that lives inside the computer, have been executing the Lingo code in the Chapter 7 project. You come to this line:

```
set the member of sprite 10 to member hiliteMember
```

As you read this line, you realize that it is asking you to put a certain Cast Member onto your screen. This isn't a problem for you; you do it all the time. Heck, you're Director.

Which Cast Member? Well, you look into the piece of RAM named *hiliteMember* and see the value *jumpHil* there. OK, so this line wants you to put some member named *jumpHil* on the screen. You can do that, no problem!

You look through the list of Cast Member names that you keep in RAM. You're looking for a Cast Member called *"jumpHil"*. Not the first one, not the second one, doo-tee-doo, here we are. Cast Member 17 is called *jumpHil*. You know you should display member 17.

Now you look in RAM for member 17. It's not there because you haven't displayed it before. You're going to have to fetch it from the Cast, which lives on disk. Bother! So now you look through the map of the movie file that you also keep in RAM, trying to find out where in the file that member 17 is. You find it in the map and get a file address for the Cast Member 17 information.

Next, you ask the operating system for the chunk of information starting at member 17's address. You are not allowed to try to talk to the disk directly; you always have to ask Mac OS or Microsoft Windows to do it for you.

Next, you wait. And wait. You can't do anything until the operating system has loaded the Cast Member from disk into RAM. So you're waiting. And waiting. Suddenly, you are active again. You look into the right place in RAM and find that it does, indeed, hold Cast Member 17!

Now that the Cast Member is in RAM, you can put it onto the Invisible Stage. The Invisible Stage is really just another place in RAM that happens to look like the Stage. To put the image of member 17 onto the Invisible Stage, you copy the bitmap information from member 17's piece of RAM to the Invisible Stage's piece of RAM.

OK, you've done your duty. It's on to the next line of Lingo.

```
updateStage
```

This command tells you to update the normal Stage with the contents of the invisible one. The Stage is really yet another piece of RAM. This time, though, the RAM lives on silicon chips inside the **video card**. The RAM on the video card is directly interpreted into dots and lines of color on your monitor. So, your final step is to copy the information in the Invisible Stage RAM into the video card's RAM.

Learning from Your Life as Director

As you might imagine, I simplified the actual process of loading and displaying a Cast Member considerably. When you see a Director title with slug-like performance, now you know what is probably happening.

As a Lingo programmer, whenever you refer to a Cast Member by name instead of number, Director has to do a lookup of that name. If the cast is large (a few hundred or few thousand members), then this lookup can start to take noticeable amounts of time. It is faster to use Cast Member numbers than names. However, with a reasonable-size cast, you'll never notice the difference, and using names allows you to move Cast Members around without having to change your scripts. Big plus.

The worst, biggest bottleneck is, of course, disk access. Video card RAM is fast. Normal RAM is not quite as fast. The hard disk is really, really not fast. The CD-ROM is extremely not fast. And a modem-Internet link is so not fast we won't even discuss it until the Shockwave chapters.

The more information you need to read off the disk, the slower the operation will be. Let's look at some variations of a quarter-screen, 320 × 240 pixel image, and how much room it takes on disk and in RAM.

If a Cast Member is 320 pixels wide and 240 pixels tall, then it takes up 320 × 240 = 76,800 pixels. If it is an 8-bit Cast Member, meaning it uses 1 byte to represent 1 pixel, then this bitmap takes up 76,800 × 1 = 76,800 bytes, or 76,800 / 1024 = 75k of RAM.

If it is a 16-bit Cast Member, meaning it uses 2 bytes to represent a pixel, it will take up 76,800 × 2 = 153,600 bytes or 153,600 / 1024 = 150k of RAM. If it is a 24-bit bitmap, meaning 24 / 8 = 3 bytes per pixel, it would take up 76,800 × 3 = 230,400 bytes or 225k of RAM.

From a double-speed CD-ROM drive, which has a theoretical speed limit of 300k per second, you could load just a little more than one quarter-screen 24-bit image in one second.

The formula for the size of a bitmap is as follows:

```
pixels wide * pixels tall * bits per pixel / 8 / 1024 = size in kilobytes
```

This is the size that the bitmap takes up in RAM once it is loaded by the operating system. The image takes up a little less space on the disk because Director uses minimal compression on bitmaps in the cast. The image will take up a great deal less space in a Shockwave movie because Afterburner heavily compresses a normal Director movie when it makes a Shockwave version. For details, check out Part IV: Shockwave.

Yes, it **is** difficult to accurately figure out how long an image will take to load, especially since the operating system might be doing other things when you make your request, and might not serve you until it is good and ready.

Copying the information of a Cast Member from its place in RAM to the Invisible Stage is fairly fast. Copying it from the Invisible Stage to the real Stage is very fast on modern computers. However, neither step is instantaneous.

If you move around 10 Puppet Sprites and update the Stage once at the end, you probably won't notice any slowness. You can even do this repeatedly with decent performance. If you update the Stage between every individual movement, though, performance will suffer greatly because 10 stage updates is 10 times slower than 1 stage update.

When Memory Is Your Enemy

Three words invoke fear and terror in any multimedia programmer's heart: "Out of Memory."

Sometimes you'll see this message in a Director error dialog. Usually, though, the problem is more insidious than that, and you'll have to diagnose it from the symptoms.

Usually, your program slows down to a crawl. The hard disk and the CD-ROM are both accessed so much they seem to thrash. Animations that used to run at 10 frames per second start to jerk, and accomplish only one or two frames every couple of seconds. Pictures fail to show up on screen. Big, white, rectangles appear where bitmaps were supposed to be. Sounds don't play, or they stutter unbearably when they do. Sometimes, though this is rare, the whole program crashes.

What Is Going on Here?

RAM is a finite resource on any computer. As of late 1996, most multimedia developers target a Mac or PC with 8MB of RAM. The operating system generally needs 2MB or 3MB megabytes to run. The Director projector needs around 1.5MB just to run. On the Macintosh, Sound Manager needs at least 500k of free space, not given to any program, or it can't make sound.

This leaves about 3MB to hold all your graphics, sounds, text, scripts, and Score.

If you have a screen with many animations, and/or looping sound and/or a huge cast with lots of text and Scripts, 3MB can fill up pretty quickly.

Once this RAM is used up, Director can't find room to load another graphic. It tries to throw out an unused Cast Member. If all the Cast Members are being used, though, it can't throw anything out. Sometimes, it just gives up on the new graphic.

Even if it does throw out a few currently unused Cast Members, what happens when it gets to the next frame of the animation, and the Cast Members it has to use were thrown out? It has to load them from the disk again. And it has to find more RAM to load them into, so it has to throw something else out.

Other types of Cast Members suffer from RAM crunch, too. If you try to play an embedded sound, using *puppetSound* or just putting it into the Score, Director has to load the entire sound into RAM before it can start playing it. If there isn't enough room for the entire sound, Director just gives up on playing it and you hear silence.

The formula for the size of a sound is as follows:

```
channels * samples per second * length * bits per sample /
8 / 1024 = size in k
```

The most common multimedia sound format is 16-bit 22.05kHz mono. In a 16-bit digital sound, each sample is recorded in a 16-bit number. 22.05kHz means 22,050 samples per second. If the sound were 30 seconds long, then it would take up

```
1 * 22,050 * 30 * 16 / 8 / 1024 = 1,292k
```

This one sound would take up about 1MB of RAM. If there wasn't 1MB free when you tried to play it, you would hear only silence.

The **most** insidious memory problem is caused by, and I shudder to utter the words, **virtual memory**. The creators of both the Macintosh and Windows realized that users would sometimes need more RAM than they actually had in their machines. They adopted an old operating system trick, in which they disguise a part of the hard disk to look like additional RAM. That's why it's called **virtual** memory.

Virtual memory is a trade-off: you get to run with more "RAM" but the fake RAM runs really, really, really slowly compared to real RAM. This is an acceptable trade-off if you are using spreadsheets or word processors. Unfortunately, though, it kills multimedia titles like ebola.

If the user has VM turned on, there is no real way for Director to know if it is loading a Cast Member into real RAM or fake RAM. If it winds up loading into fake RAM, it is the slowest of all possible scenarios. Each byte in the Cast Member is read from the disk file, into a holding area in real RAM, then written to the hard disk fake RAM. You never know how much real RAM is in the machine, so it is impossible for you or Director to get predictable performance. Ack. Ask your users to turn it off.

Making Friends with Memory

Figure out how much RAM your target machine will have. If you are building a kiosk, for example, you can decide always to spec 32MB of RAM. If you are building a consumer CD-ROM, maybe put "16mb recommended" on the box. If you are stuck with 8MB, be happy about 8MB.

Take RAM considerations into account when you design user interfaces, animations, sound environments, and so on. Designing a CD-ROM screen that plays 80 cells of 16-bit bitmaps while looping a minute-long audio loop is just not a good idea. **Design with the target system's limitations in mind**. A modest design that actually works is usually better received than an ambitious design that chokes.

If you need to do long animations, consider making them into Quicktime movies and putting them into the animating part of the screen. Beware, though. Creating a playable Quicktime movie that composites seamlessly with a Director graphical screen is a tricky undertaking. If you're going to use Quicktime, try working a graphic frame into the screen design, so the graphics don't have to composite seamlessly.

Avoid Lingo scripting schemes that necessitate a huge volume of Lingo, because all the Lingo in a movie is always held in RAM. I once saw a movie that had 30,000 lines of Lingo code. A smart programmer named Mitch Grasso cut this down to about 3,000 lines of code and **increased** the functionality. The program ended up running much faster, and in much less RAM.

Finally, you can use the Lingo memory-management commands to try to make projects behave the way you would like. These commands can markedly improve performance, but they can't help you at all if your design is too ambitious for your target machine.

CD-ROM Considerations

CD-ROMs are less desirable than hard disks for two reasons:

1. They are slower.

2. The head mechanism moves more slowly.

A single-speed CD-ROM can read, at most, 150k per second. These days, 4 × CD-ROM drives are ubiquitous and can read a theoretical 600k per second. A normal internal hard disk can read at least 1,024k per second, and more often around 2,048k per second. If you are trying to load all the cells of an animation, or the highlights of a complex screen, the difference between reading from a CD-ROM and a hard disk can be night and day.

The **head** of any mechanical disk drive is the component that actually moves across the disk, reading information bit by bit. On a hard disk, the head can go from one location to a faraway location, and back again, very quickly. This is why you can play a Quicktime movie from one location on a hard disk and preload Cast Members from another part of the hard disk, both at the same time.

On a CD-ROM drive, the head is much slower. If you try to do the same Quicktime + preloading trick, it is likely that the head won't be able to move back and forth between the two locations fast enough to keep the Quicktime movie playing back smoothly. Your only option is to preload the Cast Members before playing the Quicktime movie.

And don't even think about playing two Quicktime movies at once from a CD-ROM. It won't work.

Macintosh versus Windows Performance

On the Mac, virtual memory is an option that you can ask users to turn off via a simple control panel. In all versions of Windows, VM is a fact of life that you just have to live with. This makes Windows playback inherently less predictable than Macintosh playback.

On the other hand, Windows 95 multitasks much more smoothly than 1996 versions of Mac OS. If you are trying to play a Quicktime movie or sound file while animating the screen, you will tend to see smoother animation on a Windows 95 machine.

On yet another hand, Macintosh disk and CD-ROM input/output work better than Windows. You can get away with playing a Quicktime movie from the CD-ROM while reading something else, perhaps another Quicktime movie, from the hard disk. Windows 95 will let you do this on a decent Pentium.

Try to do any of these fancy tricks on a Windows 3.1 machine and you will be sorry. Windows 3.1 can read the CD-ROM, read the hard disk, or let Director run, but not do any two at once. It also seems really slow to switch among the three tasks.

Performance is always best when you use 8-bit graphics, especially when running with the monitor set to 8-bit mode, sometimes called 256-color mode. You can get away with 16-bit or 24-bit color if the project doesn't use much animation and if slow performance isn't a problem. Bear in mind, though, that Director for Windows 3.1 doesn't support 16-, 24-, or 32-bit color modes.

The Great Unknown

No matter how smart a programmer you are, no matter how much experience you have, no matter how little time you have before your ship date, **there is no way to know how your project will perform on another machine until you test it.**

One of the stupidest and deadliest traps that Director developers fall into is programming a project completely on one platform, then trying to "port" it to another platform. I have seen this most often when a Mac-based shop waits until the last few days of a project to "see how it runs in Windows." Sure, I've done it, you've done it, but it isn't sane. This is dumb, and if you operate this way, you deserve the calamity that will befall you.

Macintosh, Windows 3.1, and Windows 95 are three completely different, alien universes. Director does its best to hide the differences from you, but you are a fool if you have blind faith in Director. Director for Windows 95 will have different problems than Director for Window 3.1 or Director for Macintosh or Director for Power Macintosh. There is no accurate way to predict how your program will like each of these platforms.

While you are developing, if you come up with an interesting scheme or a neat hack, test it immediately on the other platforms. If it doesn't work well, you'll have a chance to come up with a new cross-platform trick or decide to use different tricks on each platform. This is the only realistic, not-stupid way to do cross-platform development.

We'll revisit the cross-platform problem in Part IV.

A Parting Trick

Remember I mentioned an undocumented rollover trick? Here it is: to get the number of the sprite that is currently rolled over, use *rollover()* without any parameters. For example:

```
on exitFrame

        put rollover()

end
```

will constantly put the number of the rolled-over sprite into the Message Window. This is not an official function, and might be dropped at any time by any version of Director. Use it at your own risk.

Chapter Summary

- The *rollover(spriteNum)* function returns TRUE if the cursor is on top of sprite *spriteNum*, and FALSE if it isn't. This example beeps continually while the cursor is on top of sprite 8.:

```
on exitFrame

   if rollover(8) then

       beep

   end if

end
```

- You can change the cursor to a predefined cursor using the *cursor* command, like so:

```
cursor 0    -- default cursor

cursor -1   -- arrow pointer
```

```
cursor 1     -- I-Beam (like over a text field)

cursor 2     -- crosshair

cursor 3     -- crossbar

cursor 4     -- watch (Mac) or hourglass (Windows)

cursor 200  -- makes cursor invisible
```

- You can change the cursor to your own, custom cursor with the *cursor* command. You give it two arguments, the member of the cursor bitmap and the member of the mask bitmap. The mask is optional. Both bitmaps must be 1-bit and at least 16×16 pixels. This example changes the cursor to a hand while rolled over sprite 8.

```
on exitFrame

    if rollover(8) then

            cursor [member "hand", member "handmask"]

    end if

end
```

- You can use a cousin of *if..then* called *case..of*. You can use this to compare one variable to many values. It is more compact and efficient than using a chained *if..then* statement. The following code fragment prints the name of the operating system that you are running.

```
case the platform of

    "Windows,16"     : put "Windows 3.1"

    "Windows,32"     : put "Windows 95 or NT"

    "Macintosh,68k" : put "Mac OS on  Quadra/Centris or lower"

    "Macintosh,PPC" : put "Mac OS on Power Macintosh"

end case
```

- The formula for the size of a bitmap is as follows:

```
pixels wide * pixels tall * bits per pixel / 8 / 1024 = size in kilobytes
```

  This is how much space the image takes up in RAM. On disk, it will be slightly compressed. In an Afterburned Shockwave movie, it will be highly compressed.

- The formula for the size of a sound is as follows:

```
channels * samples per second * length * bits per sample / 8 / 1024 = size
in kilobytes
```

- Director has a data type called a *linear list*. It is a list of similar items, such as strings or numbers. You create a list by putting a value into a variable surrounded by brackets. The items should be separated by commas.

```
put ["Neuromancer","Count Zero","Mona Lisa Overdrive"] into books
```

  The variable *books* now holds three strings, which are titles of novels by William Gibson. You can put an empty list into *books* like this:

```
put [ ] into books
```

- There are several functions for accessing items in a list. Here are a few:

  count(*list*) returns the number of items in *list*

  getAt *list,index* returns item *index* of the list

  getPos *list,value* returns the index of the first item that matches *value*

  sort *list* sorts the list in ascending order

  setAt *list,index,value* sets the item *index* in *list* to *value*

  add *list, value* adds a new item to *list*, with value *value*

  addAt *list,index,value* adds a new item of *value* in list *list* at index *index*

  deleteAt *list,index* deletes item at index *index* of *list*

- You can manipulate RAM with a few Lingo commands that load and unload Cast Members from RAM.

  preLoad *first,last* attempts to load every Cast Member in frames *first* through *last*.

preLoadMember *first,last* attempts to load every Cast Member from *first* through *last* in the Cast.

unloadMember *first,last* attempts to unload every Cast Member from *first* through last.

unloadMember attempts to unload all Cast Members from RAM.

A Small, Encarta-like Database

Chapter Objective

Director makes a really bad database engine. Nevertheless, everybody in this business, sooner or later, has to create a database in Director. In this chapter, we create a small database of musical terms, which you could apply to many CD-ROM, online, or kiosk situations.

At the heart of any database is a great deal of text. We'll cover many uses of text, in programming and displaying information. We'll learn how to search, dissect, and play with text. We'll also take a hard look at how to play sound in many forms. We'll examine some useful interface tricks, like opening a new window with Movie-In-A-Window and using pull-down menus. Finally, we'll learn how to read and write files to the disk, using the FileIO Xtra.

Introduction to Project: Musical Database

This project lets the user browse through a small database of musical termi-nology. The records in the database sometimes have related pictures and sound. Figure 8.1 shows the first frame of the project.

Figure 8.1 The first frame.

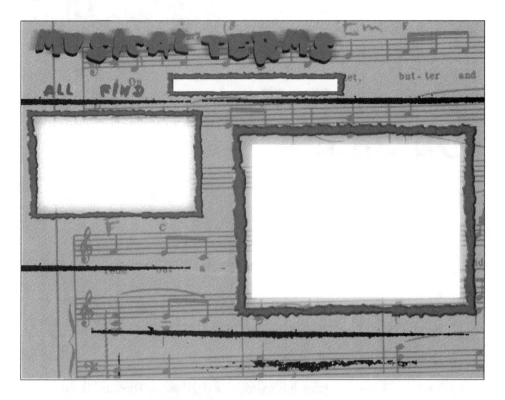

The top box accepts a find string. The box on the left is for pictures, and the box on the right is for text. Here's how the project is supposed to work:

1. When the user gets to the screen, it holds no data. The user can also type a string into the find box.

2. When the user clicks Find, the program searches the database. If any matching records are found, they are displayed in a list, in a new, floating window. The find string is also displayed in this window. If the find string was empty, the user is presented with an error message.

3. If the user clicks on an item in the pop-up window's **hitlist,** the appropriate record is displayed in the main window. The text-box of the window contains the textual information, with the title bold, in large text.

4. If a picture is associated with this record, the picture is displayed. If a sound is associated with this record, the Play button appears.

5. Initially, the Save Hitlist menu item is disabled. If the Hitlist window is open, all the menu items are enabled.

6. Choosing **Save Hitlist** from the **File** menu lets a user save the current hitlist, using a Save As dialog. Choosing **Open Hitlist** from the **File** menu lets the user open a previously saved hitlist from a file, using a File Open dialog.

Play a little bit with Ch8_done.dir in the Chapter8 folder on the CD-ROM to get a feel for this project. When you are ready, bring up the unprogrammed version of the movie from file Ch8.dir and read on.

Defining Database

The word "database" means many things to many people. It should mean only one thing to us.

What we are going to build is a modified version of a "flat-file" database. This kind of database is based on the set-of-index-cards metaphor. In this metaphor, each piece of information is held on an index card with containers for text. Each container on the index card has a name. The index card for our project might have containers called "TERM," "PICTURENAME," "SOUNDNAME," and "DESCRIPTION." A filled-out index card might look like Figure 8.2.

The most common task for a database is searching for specific text. When our database searches for a specific piece of text, it must compile a list of index cards that contain the string. It will do this, simply, by looking at each index card, or record, in the database and checking its "TERM" and "DESCRIPTION" fields to see if it contains the search text.

Figure 8.2 Index cards.

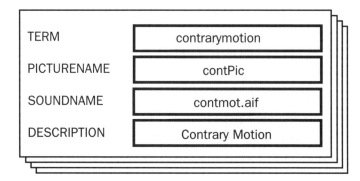

The approach we will take in this chapter works well with small databases, with maybe 300 records, tops. Trying to search 1,000 or more items with this method will be slow, annoying, and memory-intensive. Also, even though it is possible to simulate other database metaphors with Lingo, such as "relational" or "object-oriented" metaphors, you'll be fighting an uphill battle.

If you want to create a large or sophisticated database, you should use an Xtra as an external database engine for your Director project. The most popular relational database Xtra, a version of which ships free with Director, is called FileFlex. Perhaps a better choice is another database Xtra called V12. Both are available from the World Wide Web. For links, check the Xtra page in Macromedia's site, at **www.macromedia.com.**

We won't be using FileFlex in this chapter, but we will use the FileIO Xtra, so you'll learn the basics of what Xtras are and how to use them. After that, tackling FileFlex or V12 won't be much of a problem.

Before we can really figure out how to implement a flat-file database in Director, we really have to understand how to deal with text in Director. The next couple of sections deal with text manipulation. You should try many of the examples yourself, in the Message Window.

Text Containers

To be useful, text in Director must usually be **contained**. Director gives us three containers for textual information: **text** Cast Members, **field** Cast Members, and **variables**.

Text Cast Members

A text Cast Member lets you type text into it while you are authoring. However, when you deliver your product, running in a Shockwave movie or Projector, it becomes a bitmap. Yes, that's right, Director takes your nice, editable, modifiable text and turns it into a static, stupid, unchangeable bitmap. (You can pop back into authoring mode if you really need to change it.) For most functions in multimedia programming, text Cast Members are unbelievably lame.

In their favor, text Cast Members don't require the user to have the same font that you do because they are saved in bitmapped format. Also, Director can anti-alias this text for you when it creates the bitmap of the text. This can save production time over anti-aliasing text in Photoshop, especially since Director can import word processing files in RTF format. (Although Director tends to crash if you try to import large RTF files.)

Text Cast Members are mostly useful for displaying text that doesn't have to be changed for any reason at runtime. They are really awful for Shockwave movies because a bitmapped image of a piece of text is much, much bigger than the plain old text information.

To create a text Cast Member, choose the menu item **Insert: Media Element: Text.**

Field Cast Members

A field contains text—real text, with editable characters, modifiable data, and font and style information. You can enter text into a field in authoring mode or runtime mode, and you can change any aspect of the field's contents from Lingo. Fields can be placed on the Stage, just like Text Cast Members. When Director displays a field on the Stage, it uses the host computer's fonts and type services to draw the text onto the screen.

Fields have their downsides, though. Text in a field is never anti-aliased, so it generally kills a "designed" feel of a screen. Also, because fields render text on the fly during runtime, they are at the mercy of the fonts installed on the end-user's machine. If you use a non-standard font in a field, the text may show up in a random font. (Use a standard font if you can.)

To create a field, choose the menu item **Insert: Control: Field**. A new field will appear in the Cast, and the field will be initially placed on the Stage.

In Director 4, fields were much more buggy, inflexible, and slow than they are now. In an effort to address this, Macromedia invented text Cast Members in Director 5. Why didn't they add features to fields, like anti-aliasing, preferred or embedded fonts, or RTF importing? Who knows? My guess is that they were in a hurry, and the text Cast Member was a quick way to quiet the critics.

I really don't like text Cast Members. Maybe you can tell.

Variables

As I mentioned in Chapter 6, variables, both local and global, can contain strings. **String** is a programming term for a piece of text.

Variables, in many ways, are the purest containers for text information. When a variable holds a string, it remembers only the sequence of characters that make up the text. Because they cannot be displayed, variables do not remember any style information, like bold or italic, or any font information, like Helvetica or Times.

Text versus Fields versus Variables

As you might imagine, each type of text container has different uses.

When you simply want to display text at runtime, which cannot be changed once it leaves your computer, and you are not worried about disk space, text Cast Members are a good choice.

If you need to display **live text**, meaning text that is drawn on-the-fly at runtime, you have to use fields. The nice thing about a field is that you can manipulate it with Lingo.

Whenever you are manipulating text with Lingo, unless style information is important, you should probably put the text into a variable. Accessing a variable is amazingly quick, compared to accessing a field. A very common sequence is to take the text from a field, put it into a variable, manipulate it, then put it back into the field for display.

Programming with Text

Lingo has a myriad of facilities for dealing with text, (and no facilities for dealing with text Cast Members, so we won't talk about them anymore). These facilities tend to help you with a few overall tasks, like storing text in containers, combining strings, using special characters, or accessing just part of a sting.

Storing Text in Containers

The first question that might come to your mind is "How do I put a string into a container?" Pretty darn simple, it turns out.

```
put "We are not alone." into credo
```

In this command, we use the *put..into* command to put a string value, *We are not alone.*, into a variable, *credo*. Yes, this is the same *put..into* command we have been using since Chapter 4.

We can actually use the same command to put a string into a field. Let's say we have a field in Cast Member 2, called "credo." Then

```
put "We are not alone." into member "credo"
```

would stuff member 2 with the sentence *We are not alone.* If the field was on the Stage in the current frame, the words would appear onstage. If Cast Member 2 was empty when this line executed, it would turn into a field and accept the string.

Notice the quotation marks. Whenever you hard-code a string in Lingo, you must enclose it in quotes, otherwise the Lingo elf tries to interpret the string as a Lingo command. This really confuses the silly Lingo elf.

As we have done before with numbers, you can use a variable to put a value into another variable, like

```
put "We are not alone." into txt
```

```
put txt into credo
```

or into a field Cast Member, like

```
put "We are not alone." into txt
```

```
put txt into member "credo"
```

The commands to put a value into a variable are pretty slangy, as I mentioned in Chapter 5. To demonstrate, all the following commands are completely equivalent to *put "We are not alone." into member "credo"*.

```
put "We are not alone." into field "credo"
```

```
put "We are not alone." into member 2
```

```
put "We are not alone." into field 2
```

```
set the text of field "credo" = "We are not alone."
```

```
set the text of member "credo = "We are not alone."
```

```
set the text of field 2 to "We are not alone."
```

```
set the text of member 2 to "We are not alone."
```

When you use the *set..to* command to deal with fields, you must specify *the text* property of the Cast Member. I recommend using *put..into* whenever you deal with text.

Combining Strings

Lingo has four **operators** that deal with adding one string to another. (An operator is a Lingo phrase that does an **operation** on data.)

The operator **&** attaches one string directly to the end of another. You put it between two string values, like this:

```
put "Here's to "&"you," into myString
```

Type this line into the Message Window, then type

```
put myString
```

The Message Window should answer

```
-- "Here's to you,"
```

This means that the variable *myString* contains the characters *Here's to you,*. You use the quotes to let the Lingo elf know that *Here's to* and *you* are not supposed to be Lingo commands.

Lingo has a **&&** operator, which also attaches one string to another. However, this operator adds a space between the two strings. After the last two lines, if you type this

```
put myString&&"Mrs. Robinson." into myString
```

```
put myString
```

The Message Window will return...

```
-- "Here's to you, Mrs. Robinson."
```

Notice the space after the comma?

There are two more operators, but they are words instead of punctuation. The **before** operator puts a string before another, like this:

```
put "And " before myString
```

```
put myString
```

```
-- "And here's to you, Mrs. Robinson."
```

This is functionally equivalent to the following:

```
put "And "&myString into myString
```

Finally, **after** puts one string at the end of another.

```
put "Get over the sixites." after myString
```

```
put myString
```

```
-- "And here's to you, Mrs. Robinson. Get over the sixties."
```

This is the same as

```
put myString & "Get over the sixties." after myString
```

Special Characters

As you may have noticed, the practice of putting a string between quotes presents some problems, like "How do you put a quotation-mark into the string?" And "How do you create a multiline string?" Lingo has some special keywords that represent these awkward characters. For example, the ***return*** keyword adds a return character to a string. Try this sequence in the Message Window:

```
put "line 1" & return & "line 2" into myString

put myString

-- "line 1

line 2"
```

Don't get this mixed up with the *return* command, which you use to return values in custom handlers.

Similarly, you can embed a quotation mark using the ***quote*** keyword.

```
put quote & "Four score and seven years ago."&quote into myString

put myString

-- ""Four score and seven years ago.""
```

You can also put an empty string into a variable or field. Lingo uses the word ***empty*** to signify a string with no characters. A slang version uses two quotes, "". Both of the following lines fill the variable *myString* with an empty string.

```
put empty into myString

put "" into myString
```

Accessing Parts of a String

Lingo has many interesting ways of accessing just one part of a string. Let's fill a variable, then dissect it in various ways.

```
put "I'm a doctor, not a programmer." into rant
```

The variable *rant* now holds the text *I'm a doctor, not a programmer.* In the following examples, type the Lingo into the Message Window. The results are listed after the Lingo.

The first way to dissect a string is to grab just one character...

```
put char 7 of rant
```

```
-- "d"
```

The letter *d* is the seventh character in *rant.* Spaces, returns, punctuation, and tabs all count as characters.

You can also grab a range of characters...

```
put char 5 to 9 of rant
```

```
-- "a doc"
```

This example returns characters 5, 6, 7, 8, and 9 of the string inside *rant.*

The next way to dissect a string is by the word.

```
put word 4 of rant
```

```
-- "not"
```

The Lingo elf assumes that everything between spaces makes up a word (a *return* counts as a space). The Lingo elf determines a word only by spaces, not by punctuation, as you can see by the next example. (Notice the comma attached to the end of the word.)

```
put word 3 of rant
```

```
-- "doctor,"
```

Of course, you can also specify a range of words.

```
put word 3 to 5 of rant
```

```
-- "doctor, not a"
```

The next way to dissect a string is by line. Let's put a multiline string into a variable called *ranting.*

```
put "1."&rant&return&"2."&rant&return&"3."&rant into ranting
```

```
put ranting
```

```
-- "1.I'm a doctor, not a programmer.
```

```
2.I'm a doctor, not a programmer.
```

```
3.I'm a doctor, not a programmer."
```

We can dissect a specific line or range of lines like this:

```
put line 2 of ranting
```

```
-- "2.I'm a doctor, not a programmer."
```

```
put line 2 to 3 of ranting
```

```
-- "2.I'm a doctor, not a programmer.
```

```
3.I'm a doctor, not a programmer."
```

The Lingo elf sees everything between *return* characters as a line. It cares not for word wrapping or screen display. Only *return* characters count.

Finally, Lingo has a dissection style that only a programmer could love. Instead of using a space to separate chunks like *word..of*, or *return* characters like *line..of*, there is another way to dissect a string that uses a *comma*, called *item..of*. Usually, you don't use *item..of* for English text, but for lists of strings. For example:

```
put "Monica,Phoebe,Rachel,Chandler,Ross,Joey" into friends
```

```
put item 4 of friends into favoriteFriend
```

```
put favoriteFriend
```

```
--"Chandler"
```

The cool thing about *item..of* is that you can change the character that separates items. There is a system-wide property called *the itemDelimiter* that you can change to any character you want. If we wanted to, we could use something as random as "o" to separate items. (Remember to always save the original delimiter and to reset it after you are done.)

```
put the itemDelimiter into oldDelim
```

```
set the itemDelimiter to "o" -- letter o
```

```
put "Monica,Phoebe,Rachel,Chandler,Ross,Joey" into friends
```

```
put item 3 of friends into friendGibberish

set the itemDelimiter to oldDelim

put friendGibberish

-- "ebe,Rachel,Chandler,R"
```

You need this property, usually, when the items in your list might have commas in them. In a case like this, you can use a weird control character or punctuation mark as a delimiter.

Every piece of a string that you can grab with these operators is called a **chunk** of the string. *char..of*, *word..of*, and *line..of* are called **chunk expressions** because you use them to specify which chunk of a string that you want.

If you ask for an out-of-bounds chunk, you will get an empty string. For example, if I asked for word 794 of rant, I would get back an empty string.

```
put word 794 of rant

-- ""
```

You can't **mix and match** types of chunk expressions. There is no way to say "give me word 4 to char 100 of rant."

However, you **can** subdivide chunks. Try the following examples:

```
put word 3 of line 2 of ranting

-- "doctor,"
```

```
put word 7 of line 2 to 3 of ranting

-- "3.I'm"
```

```
put char 3 of line 2 to 3 of ranting

-- "I"
```

Counting Chunks

The Lingo elf will count the chunks in a string for you. Remember our variable *rant?*

```
put rant
```

```
-- "I'm a doctor, not a programmer."
```

Lingo will tell you how many characters are in *rant.*

```
put length(rant)
```

```
-- 31
```

Lingo will also tell you how many words are in *rant.*

```
put the number of words in rant
```

```
-- 6
```

It'll even tell you how many lines are in *rant.*

```
put the number of lines in rant
```

```
-- 1
```

You can get tricky and find the number of characters in "doctor."

```
put length(word 3 of rant)
```

```
-- 7
```

Modifying Chunks

You can change any aspect of a string in variables or field Cast Members.

You can change a character in a string like so:

```
put "D" into char 7 of rant
```

```
put rant
```

```
-- "I'm a Doctor, not a programmer."
```

You're not limited to changing just one character. You can insert a whole string into the space of one character. The Lingo elf just inserts your new string at the specified position and makes the changed string longer. Watch.

```
put rant
```

```
-- "I'm a Doctor, not a programmer."
```

```
put "Pr" into char 7 of rant
```

```
put rant
```

```
-- "I'm a Proctor, not a programmer."
```

You can modify and insert words and lines this way, too.

If you want to get rid of chunks, you can just delete them.

```
delete word 3 to 5 of rant
```

```
put rant
```

```
-- "I'm a programmer."
```

The Cast as Database

So, how do we use our new knowledge of strings to implement a database?

If you think about it, the Cast itself is a database. It has index card records (Cast Members) with containers (the media asset inside the Cast Member). Each record can have a number (the member number) and a name (the name of the Cast Member). We should be able to put this insight together with our new knowledge of strings to design a workable database.

The easiest technique, which—for once—we will use, is to make one field Cast Member = one record. We can put each index card container into a line of the field. A typical record might be a field Cast Member called "Barform" and contain this text:

```
Bar form.pic
```

```
barform.aif
```

```
Bar form
```

```
A form with 3 sections, the first one being repeated. (AAB)
```

For every field, the first line will always be the Cast Member name of the picture, the second line will always be the filename of the audio file, the third line will be the full name of the term, and the fourth and following lines will be the description.

If we wanted to get the sound file associated with this record, we could get it like this:

```
put line 2 of field "Barform" into soundFileName
```

If we wanted to access the description of this record, we could get it like this:

```
put the number of lines in field "Barform" into numLines

put line 4 to numLines of field "Barform" into description
```

We can get any other piece of information in this record similarly.

The database of musical terms is already created for you in Ch8.dir, starting at Cast Member 100. Records that don't have pictures have an empty first line. Records that don't have audio have an empty second line.

Displaying the Text of a Record

The display area for the record's text is the big white box on the right side of the screen. This box should display the name of the term in 18-point type, followed by a blank line, followed by the description in 12-point type. All this text should be in Helvetica on the Macintosh and Arial in Windows.

The display area is covered by a field Cast Member called "displayField," in Sprite Channel 5. Whenever we want to display a record, we are going to fill this field with the text from the record. Because this field is attached to a Sprite on the Stage, the text inside it will appear immediately on the screen.

Let's write a handler that takes a record field's member name or member number and displays it onstage. Let's call it, oh, I don't know, *displayRecord*?

```
on displayRecord recID

   -- do stuff

end
```

The first thing that *displayRecord* should do is put the text of the field specified by *recID* into a variable. Remember, variables are much faster to access than fields.

```
put field recID into rec
```

Now, the local variable *rec* holds the contents of the record.

The next step is to extract a piece of information from the text in *rec* and put it into a holding variable. We will deal with the picture and sound elements of the record later in this chapter, so lines 1 and 2 don't interest us now. We just want to grab the title.

```
put line 3 of rec into holding
```

Next, we want to put a blank line after the title. We append one *return* character to end the line, and another to insert a blank line. We also want to append the description to our new variable. The description is contained in the fourth line to the last line of *rec*.

```
put the number of lines in rec into numRecLines

put return & return & line 4 to numRecLines of rec after holding
```

And, finally, put the variable *holding* into the display field to show up on-screen.

```
put holding into field "displayField"
```

The whole handler, up to this point, looks like this:

```
on displayRecord recID

    put field recID into rec

    put line 3 of rec into holding

    put the number of lines in rec into numRecLines

    put return & return & line 4 to numRecLines of rec after holding

    put holding into field "displayField"

end
```

If you type this into the Message Window,

```
displayRecord "Barform"
```

the result should look something like Figure 8.3.

Now that we've got the basic mechanism working, we have to make it pretty.

Figure 8.3 The result.

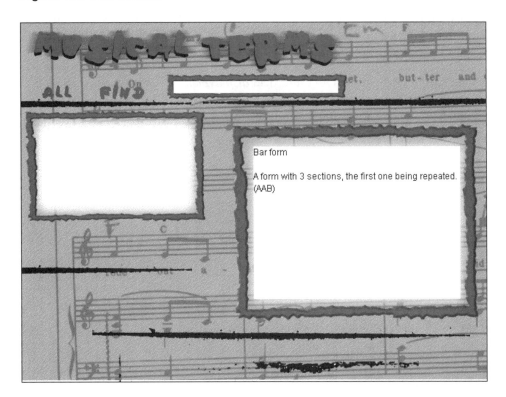

Styling Text

In fields, text has a style or combination of styles: plain, **bold**, *italic*, or <u>underline</u>. Text also has a font, like Helvetica or Arial, and a font size, like 18-point.

We can set the size of an entire field using *the fontSize of field* property.

```
set the fontSize of field "displayField" to 12
```

This line sets the whole field *displayField* to 12-point type. Lingo also lets us set the font and styles for a specific chunk of text. We don't set a Sprite property or Cast Member property, but something we might call a **chunk property**.

```
set the fontSize of line 1 of field "displayField" to 18
```

This line changes the font of line 1 of *displayField* to 18-point. It leaves the rest of the field alone. The next line changes the style of line 1 to bold.

```
set the fontStyle of line 1 of field "displayField" to "bold"
```

If we wanted the style to be bold and italic, we could set *the fontStyle* to *"bold,italic"*. You can't combine anything with the "plain" style, for obvious reasons.

When *displayRecord* puts text into field *displayField*, we want the text to be in a specific font: Helvetica on the Mac or Arial in Windows. (The reason for these choices: Macs always have a Helvetica font; Windows always has an Arial font, and the two look pretty similar.)

We can use a special system-wide property here, called *the platform*. In the Message Window, type:

```
put the platform into myPlatform
```

The value of *myPlatform* will depend on your computer and operating system. There will be two items in the resulting string. The first item will be "Macintosh" or "Windows," depending on your system.

On the Mac, if you have a Quadra-class computer or lower, item 2 will be "68k." If you are running on a PowerMac, item 2 will be "PowerPC."

In Windows, item 2 will be "16" if you are running Windows 3.1. If you are running Windows 95 (or Windows 96, Windows NT, or later), item 2 will be "32." This, obviously, means 16-bit or 32-bit Windows.

Getting back to our problem, we need to set the font of field *displayField* to the proper font for the system on which it is running. We can do it with a simple *if..then*.

```
if item 1 of the platform = "Windows" then

   put "Arial" into defaultFont

else

   put "Helvetica" into defaultFont

end if


set the font of field "displayField" to defaultFont
```

> **N O T E**   None of the font or styling properties has any effect on an empty field. Always put some text into a field, if only a space, before setting the font, size, or style of a field.

Displaying the *Styled* Text of a Record

We can incorporate the styling tricks we just learned into our *displayRecord* handler. There is just one more trick you should know.

Unfortunately, changing the contents or styles of text inside a field doesn't go through the Invisible Stage. If a field is on the Stage, it will show the results of any change as soon as you make it, without waiting for an *updateStage*. This is one of the most annoying, stupid weirdnesses Director has.

This means that if you put text into field *displayField*, you will see the text immediately. If you then set the first line to 18-point, the 12-point line will be replaced by the 18-point version. If you change the font, the font will change on-screen. **The user will see every step happening on-screen.** The end-result feels unprofessional and slightly disappointing, like watching a magician in slow motion.

It would be nice if we could just style the text in each record's data field. When it came time to display the records, we could just grab the text data, styles and all, and display it. Of course, Director lacks this feature, too.

There are only two workarounds that I know of. The first, which is a little complicated, is to have two display fields. While the first is on screen, you change and style the second. When you are done styling, you puppet the second one into the Sprite of the first. The next time you need a display field, you use the first one, which isn't currently on display.

The other workaround, which doesn't look as nice but is easier to program, is simply to hide the Sprite that is attached to the display field while you do the styling. When you are done, you show the Sprite. Each of the 48 Sprite Channels has a property called *the visible of sprite*, which can be TRUE or FALSE, 1 or 0. You can hide any Sprite in the channel like this: *set the visible of sprite 5 to FALSE*. You can show it again like this: *set the visible of sprite 5 to TRUE*. Putting it all together, our new *displayRecord* handler displays a good-looking, styled text field.

```
on displayRecord recID

    set the visible of sprite 5 to FALSE
```

```
updateStage


put field recID into rec

put line 3 of rec into holding

put the number of lines in rec into numRecLines

put return & return & line 4 to numRecLines of rec after holding

put holding into field "displayField"


-- style it

if item 1 of the platform = "Windows" then

    put "Arial" into defaultFont

else

    put "Helvetica" into defaultFont

end if


set the font of field "displayField" to defaultFont

set the fontstyle of field "displayField" to "plain"

set the fontSize of field "displayField" to 12


set the fontSize of line 1 of field "displayField" to 18

set the fontStyle of line 1 of field "displayField" to "bold"


set the visible of sprite 5 to TRUE

updateStage

end
```

Now, if you type this into the Message Window

```
displayRecord "barform"
```

you should see Figure 8.4.

We have a few more basic mechanisms to create before we have a working application.

Searching the Database

Here's the most important question in any database: "What happens when you click **Find**?"

In our database, we are going to look through each and every record field, trying to match a specific search-string which the user has typed. If a field contains the search-string, it's title will be added to a list of all matching fields. Because a matching field is often called a **hit**, we'll call this list a **hitlist**. At some point, this list will be presented to the user, but we'll deal with that later.

Figure 8.4 Main screen with styled bar form record showing.

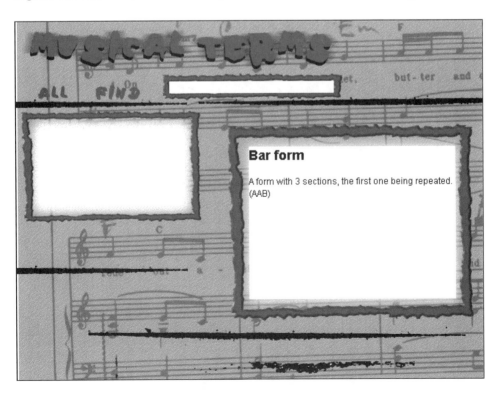

We should start by creating a handler in the Movie Script to gather the list of hits.

```
on doSearch keyString

    -- do stuff

end
```

Next, we need to come up with a method to check a field for a specific string. This is surprisingly easy to do. This code fragment checks to see if field *barform* contains the string "sections".

```
if field "barform" contains "sections" then

    put "It's a hit!"

end if
```

It is a small step to wrapping this *if..then* with a *repeat..with* loop that checks every record field in the cast. The first record field is preceded by an empty field called *startDatabase*. The last is followed by an empty field called *endDatabase*. This is an easy technique to soft-code Cast Member numbers.

```
    . . .

    put the number of member "startDatabase"+1 into startField

    put the number of member "endDatabase"-1 into endField


    repeat with i = startField to endField

        if field i contains keyString then

            -- compile hitlist

        end if

    end repeat

    . . .
```

Now we have to figure out what to put in the hitlist. To the user, the hitlist should appear as a list of musical terms. If the user clicks on a term, that term will be displayed on the main screen.

So, every time we find a hit, we have to store the full text of the title of the musical term (line 3 of the record). To implement the click-term-and-display-record function, we also have to remember how to get to this record. We can store either the name of the Cast Member or its number. Although it is slower to look up a Cast Member by name than by number, names are more robust because the Cast Member doesn't have to be in the same place for a name to still find it. Because we will be saving and loading hitlists from disk, it would be nice to not assume that the database will be exactly the same the next time the hitlist is loaded. We can do that only with member names.

Each item in the hitlist is going to have a string that is the musical term and a string that is the Cast Member name. In what kind of variable will we store this list?

Well, we could use the solution that we came up with for the Quicktime-synchronization problem in Chapter 7. We used two **linear list** variables, each holding a specific piece of information for every item. To get the *movieTime* for the third word, we checked position 3 in the *movieTime* list. To get the text of the third word, we checked position 3 in the word list.

In our hitlist situation, one list could hold the musical terms, and the other could hold the Cast Member names. To show hit 3 to the user, we could display item 3 of the musical terms list. To display the record corresponding to hit 3, we could look up item 3 of the Cast Member name list.

Or, we can play a little trick and use just one list.

Let's say that each item in the list is a string. This string is made up of two items, separated by a comma. The first item is the title of the musical term, which we will eventually display to the user. The second is the name of the Cast Member that holds the record for the term. Following this method, the list:

```
["Bar Form,barform"]
```

has one item, the string *Bar Form,barform*. The first item of the string, *Bar Form,* should be displayed to the user. The second item of the string, *barform,* is the name of the Cast Member for the barform record.

Let's implement this method in code.

The first step is to initialize a variable with an empty list. An empty string is represented by ""; an empty list is represented by []. The following line sets a local variable called *hitlist* to an empty list.

. . .

```
set hitlist = []
```

. . .

Next, we can start filling out the inside of the *if..then*. The first thing to do is put together the string that will become the item.

. . .

```
if field i contains keyString then

    put line 3 of field i into itemString

    put the name of member i into item 2 of itemString

end if
```

. . .

Now, we want to add *itemString* to *hitList*. Because we want to add it to the end of the list, we can use the *append* command. The first argument to this command is the list variable, and the second is the new item. *Append* just sticks the new item to the end of the specified list.

. . .

```
if field i contains keyString then

    put line 3 of field i into itemString

    put the name of member i into item 2 of itemString

    append hitlist, itemString

end if
```

. . .

At the end of this handler, let's put the whole hitlist into the Message Window. We can't properly display it until we get the Movie-In-A-Window stuff going, so this is our only chance for a while to make sure it is working.

Also, we are going to need to keep the hitlist around in a global variable, when we get the Movie-In-A-Window working. Let's call this variable *gHitlist* and set it in this handler. We're also going to need to remember the *keyString*. Let's put it into a global variable called *gKey*.

Here's the whole handler, as it stands.

```
on doSearch keyString

    global gHitlist, gKey

    put the number of member "startDatabase"+1 into startField

    put the number of member "endDatabase"-1 into endField

    set hitlist = []


    repeat with i = startField to endField

        if field i contains keyString then

            put line 3 of field i into itemString

            put the name of member i into item 2 of itemString

            append hitlist, itemString

        end if

    end repeat


    put hitlist into gHitlist

    put keyString into gKey

    put hitlist

end
```

Try it out. In the Message Window, type

```
doSearch "form"
```

You should get this result:

```
-- ["Bar form,Barform", "Binary form,Binaryform", "Melody,Melody",
"Opera,Opera", "Tempo,Tempo"]
```

Connecting the Find Button

It won't be too hard to connect the **Find** button to our new search mechanism.

An invisible-box in sprite 7 covers the **Find** button (supplied by Yours Truly). A field Cast Member called *findField* is attached to sprite 6, which covers the find text-entry area. It's *Editable* property is TRUE, so the user can type text into it. The script for this button must simply send the text of the field to the *doSearch* handler. (Well, it also has to make sure the field is not empty, or *doSearch* might get confused.)

Here is the Sprite Script for sprite 7, the **Find** button.

```
on mouseUp

    if field "findField" <> empty then

        doSearch field "findField"

    end if

end
```

Implementing the All Button

Our mechanism to select all of the records should be the same as our search mechanism. The only difference is that we won't be searching for anything.

Copy and paste the *doSearch* handler. Change the name of the new handler to *showAll*, and delete the *keyString* parameter. Take out the *if..then* statement inside the *repeat with* loop. Finally, because there is no key string, put "All Terms" into the global variable *gKeyString*.

This handler should go in the Movie Script of Ch8.dir.

```
on showAll

    global gHitlist, gKey

    put the number of member "startDatabase"+1 into startField

    put the number of member "endDatabase"-1 into endField

    set hitlist = []


    repeat with i = startField to endField
```

```
        put line 3 of field i into itemString

        put the name of member i into item 2 of itemString

        append hitlist, itemString

    end repeat


    put hitlist into gHitlist

    put "All Terms" into gKey

    put hitlist

end
```

Finally, we have to connect the **All** button to this handler. There is an invisible box in sprite 8 of Ch8.dir that covers the **All** button. This Sprite Script should go on it.

```
on mouseDown

    showAll

end
```

At this point, you should be able to do searches and show all the records. The results will show up in the Message Window, for now.

You might try searching on words that you know are in the database. Good candidates are "form," "note," or "tone."

The next step is to implement the floating window with the displayed, clickable hitlist. To make this happen, we have to learn about Movie-In-A-Window functions.

Movie-in-a-Window

All the projects we have worked on so far interact with the user through the Stage. What's the big deal about the Stage? In reality, it is just a normal window, like a window in your word processor or spreadsheet. Your movie just happens to be attached to it.

With this in mind, the folks at Macromedia invented the Movie-In-A-Window concept to extend Director's capabilities. You can open multiple windows, the idea goes, as long as there is a Director movie attached to each one.

They were so insistent about this idea that there is no *create window* command. Creating a window, giving it a name, and attaching a file to it are all part of the same, seminal act. If you have Ch8.dir open, the following line creates a window attached to the file Hitlist.dir, which is in the same folder. (You can type this in the Message Window.)

```
set the filename of window "Hits" to "hitlist.dir"
```

Look at this line two or three times. *set the filename of* generally implies that you are going to set the property of something that exists. But this floating window doesn't exist yet!

set the filename of window "Hits". Again I say, this floating window, which we insist is called "Hits," doesn't exist yet!

to "hitlist.dir" supplies the name of the movie file to attach to this non-existent window.

Even though it doesn't seem to make sense, this is the Lingo syntax to create a new window. Creating it and setting its *filename* property happen simultaneously.

When you create a window like this, it is initially invisible. To make it visible, you "open" it.

```
open window "Hits"
```

This will make the window magically appear. To hide the window, you "close" it.

```
close window "Hits"
```

Even though the window is invisible after you close it, it still exists. It's just hanging out like the Invisible Man. You can bring it back at any time by opening it again.

If you ever want a list of the movies-in-windows that currently exist, you use *the windowList* system property.

```
put the windowList

-- [(window "Hits")]
```

To actually kill the window, you use the *forget* command.

```
forget window "Hits"

put the windowList

-- []
```

You can change the style of the window using the *windowType* property.

```
set the windowType property of window "Hits" to 49
```

This command sets the *windowType* of the floating window to type 49, a floating toolbox-like window. Even in a language that has come so far, there are still really bizarre little warts, like this property. The number on the end can be any integer from 1 to 16, or number 49. Couldn't the Macromedia people just name the window types? I guess not. Your best bet is to try out each different number and see the style of window it produces. I'm not sure how long these types will stay the same, so I can't include a list of them. Here's a creepy thought. The windows in your Director project can actually **communicate**. Don't worry too much, though. They will only tell what you let them tell.

Windows talk to each other via the *tell* command. The *tell* command takes two arguments. The first is the name of the window that should receive the message, and the second is the message itself. The message can be a Lingo command, but it is usually the name of a custom handler in the receiver's Movie Script.

If our window "Hits" had a handler called *freakOut*, the Stage could send this message to the window.

```
tell window "Hits" to freakOut
```

If the Stage had a handler called *shutUp*, the window could send this back.

```
tell the Stage to shutUp
```

Alas, these handlers don't exist, so we'll have to make do with our less colorful project.

Opening the Hitlist Window

The first thing to realize is that we will be referring to our window "Hitlist" quite often. It would be worth our while to soft-code the name in a global variable, in case we want to change it later. Let's call it *gHitsWindow* and initialize it in a *startMovie* handler in Ch8.dir.

While we're at it, let's initialize the global variables *gHitlist* and *gKey* from the *doSearch* handler, too.

```
on startMovie

    global gHitlist, gKey, gHitsWindow


    put [] into gHitlist

    put empty into gKey

    put "Hits" into gHitsWindow

end
```

Next, let's create a Movie Script handler that creates and displays the "Hits" window. Let's call it *displayHitsWindow*, just because we're in a logical mood today.

```
on displayHitsWindow

    -- do stuff

end
```

Before we create the new window, we should delete any window that is hanging around. (The second time the user does a *find*, the first window might be hanging around.) We can use a Lingo function called *windowPresent*. It takes one argument, the name of the window, and returns TRUE if the window exists or FALSE if it doesn't. If it does exist, we want to *forget* it.

```
    . . .

    if windowPresent(gHitsWindow) then

        forget window gHitsWindow

    end if

    . . .
```

Next, we can create (or re-create) the window and attach to it the movie that was created for the purpose, Hitlist.dir.

```
   . . .
set the filename of window gHitsWindow to "hitlist.dir"
   . . .
```

Before we show the window, we should set it up. We can *tell* it to execute a handler that we will actually implement in the next section. The handler will be called *displayHitlist*.

We should also set the *windowType* of the window now. Let's make it a toolbox-type window, number 49.

```
   . . .
tell window gHitsWindow to displayHitlist

set the windowType of window gHitsWindow to 49
   . . .
```

Now that the new window is ready, we can make it visible.

```
   . . .
open window gHitsWindow
   . . .
```

From here on, the window can take care of itself. Here's the final *displayHitsWindow* handler.

```
on displayHitsWindow

   global gHitsWindow


   if windowPresent(gHitsWindow) then
      forget window gHitsWindow
   end if


   set the filename of window gHitsWindow to "hitlist.dir"
```

```
tell window gHitsWindow to displayHitlist

set the windowType of window gHitsWindow to 49


open window gHitsWindow
```

end

Before we're done, we should connect *displayHitsWindow* to the rest of our code. Because this handler must be called whenever the user does a new search, the *doSearch* handler should probably call it. Here's the modified *doSearch*.

```
on doSearch keyString

    global gHitlist, gKey

    put the number of member "startDatabase"+1 into startField

    put the number of member "endDatabase"-1 into endField

    set hitlist = []


    repeat with i = startField to endField

        if field i contains keyString then

            put line 3 of field i into itemString

            put the name of member i into item 2 of itemString


            append hitlist, itemString

        end if

    end repeat


    put hitlist into gHitlist
```

```
put keyString into gKey

put hitlist
```

displayHitsWindow

```
end
```

Because the "Hitlist" window should also change when the user hits the **All** button, we should put a call to *displayHitsWindow* into *showAll*.

```
on showAll

    global gHitlist, gKey

    put the number of member "startDatabase"+1 into startField

    put the number of member "endDatabase"-1 into endField

    set hitlist = []


    repeat with i = startField to endField

        put line 3 of field i into itemString

        put the name of member i into item 2 of itemString

        append hitlist, itemString

    end repeat


    put hitlist into gHitlist

    put "All Terms" into gKey

    put hitlist
```

displayHitsWindow

```
end
```

Implementing the Hitlist Window

Opening the Hitlist Window is nice, but will behave? Not yet; you'll get error dialogs. We have to make it behave.

The Hitlist Window has the following behaviors:

1. When opened, it shows the current key string and hitlist.

2. When opened, the first hit in the list is selected, and the corresponding record is displayed on the Stage in the movie Ch8.dir.

3. If the user clicks on a hit in the hitlist field, that line of the field gets highlighted and the corresponding record is shown on the Stage in the movie Ch8.dir.

Save the current movie and open Hitlist.dir. Remember, your copies of Hitlist.dir and the Ch8.dir must be in the same folder on your hard disk.

The first frame of the movie looks like Figure 8.5.

This movie has two field Cast Members. The first is called *keyField* and is meant to hold the key string. It is attached to sprite 3 and takes up the small white box at top.

Figure 8.5 The first frame.

The second is called *hitsField* and is meant to contain the musical terms in the hitlist. It is attached to sprite 5 and takes up the large white box on the Stage. If you click on a musical term in this field, it should highlight and cause the main movie, on the Stage, to display the clicked record.

You'll notice that the Stage size of hitlist.dir is smaller than the normal 640 x 480. The size of the Stage now is the size of the window it will appear in later. In other words, this Stage is the right size to appear floating above our normal 640 x 480 background.

Where do we start? Well, it seems logical to start with the one handler that we know this movie is supposed to have, *displayHitlist*. Since Ch8.dir is going to *tell* this movie to execute *displayHitlist*, we better make sure the handler exists.

The handler must accomplish three tasks:

1. Fill in the key string field.

2. Fill in the hitlist field.

3. Choose the first hit, and tell the Stage to display the corresponding record

Task 1
Let's start of with the familiar skeleton, in the Movie Script of hitlist.dir.

```
on displayHitlist

    -- do stuff

end
```

Task 1 is easy. We have a global variable that contains the key string, *gKey*, and a field meant to hold it, Cast Member *keyField*. The Lingo isn't a big deal.

```
on displayHitlist

    global gKey

    put gKey into field "keyField"

end
```

Done!

Task 2

Task 2 will require more thought. We want to extract the musical term string from each item in our global variable *gHitlist*. Each string should go in its own line in the field.

This implies that we will have to do two things. First, we will have to loop through each item in *gItemsList*. Second, we'll have to compile a string as we iterate through the loop.

To do these two things, we'll have to figure out how many items are in *gItemList*, and initialize a local variable to compile the string into.

```
on displayHitlist

    global gKey, gHitlist


    put gKey into field "keyField"


    put count( gHitlist ) into numItems

    put empty into buildString

        . . .
```

Next, we need to set up the loop.

```
        . . .

    repeat with i=1 to numItems

        -- do stuff

    end repeat

        . . .
```

Every time we pass through the loop, we want to grab an item from *gHitlist* and save it in a variable.

```
        . . .

    repeat with i=1 to numItems
```

```
    put getAt( gHitlist, i ) into itemString

    -- do stuff

  end repeat
```

    . . .

We only really want the first item of each string, which contains the title of the musical term. So, we extract it from *itemString*.

    . . .

```
repeat with i=1 to numItems

    put getAt( gHitlist, i ) into itemString

    put item 1 of itemString into musicalTerm

    -- do stuff

  end repeat
```

    . . .

Finally, we want to put the musical term into the correct line of the *buildString* variable.

    . . .

```
repeat with i=1 to numItems

    put getAt( gHitlist, i ) into itemString

    put item 1 of itemString into musicalTerm

    put musicalTerm into line i of buildString

  end repeat
```

    . . .

Once the loop is done, we should put the string we have built into the field that is waiting for it.

```
        . . .

    put buildString into field "hitsField"

        . . .
```

Here's what the whole handler looks like so far.

```
on displayHitlist

    global gKey, gHitlist


    put gKey into field "keyField"

    put count( gHitlist ) into numItems

    put empty into buildString


    repeat with i=1 to numItems

        put getAt( gHitlist, i ) into itemString

        put item 1 of itemString into musicalTerm

        put musicalTerm into line i of buildString

    end repeat


    put buildString into field "hitsField"


    -- do stuff

end
```

If you want to test it, open Ch8.dir again. Run the movie, and type this into the Message Window:

```
doSearch "form"
```

This will execute the *doSearch* handler that we implemented previously. The first result this shows is the list *gHitlist* in the Message Window.

```
-- ["Bar form,Barform", "Binary form,Binaryform", "Melody,Melody",
"Opera,Opera", "Tempo,Tempo"]
```

Next, it calls the handler *displayHitsWindow*, which opens Hitlist.dir in a new floating window and tells it to execute *displayHitlist*, which we just created. Finally, the window gets "opened" and becomes visible.

The final result of that line in the Message Window should be the Hitlist Window opening up with the correct key string and the hitlist filled in!

Task 3

Task 3 needs to persuade the Stage to display the record associated with the first hit. This isn't that hard. The movie on the Stage, Ch8.dir, already has a handler called *displayRecord* that will display any record. All we need to do is *tell* the Stage which record to display.

Because we'll need to trigger this behavior in a couple of different places (in *displayHitlist* and when the user clicks on the hitlist,) let's put this behavior into a handler all its own.

```
on displayHit hitNum

   -- do Stuff

end
```

The parameter *hitNum* will be the number of the hit in *gHitlist*. To display the first hit, you would call *displayHit 1*. To display the fifth hit, you would call *displayHit 5*.

Given this number, all the handler has to do is grab that item string from *gHitlist*, extract the Cast Member name from the string, then *tell* the Stage to display that item. Here's the whole handler.

```
on displayHit hitNum

   global gHitlist


   put getAt( gHitlist, hitNum ) into itemString -- grab item

   put item 2 of itemString into mname -- extract member name
```

```
    tell the Stage to displayRecord mname

end
```

Notice that, because this handler tells the Stage to do something, you can test it only while Hitlist.dir is running in a floating window. You can't test it while you are authoring Hitlist.dir.

Now, all we have to do is put a call to *displayHit* in *displayHitlist*.

```
on displayHitlist

    global gKey, gHitlist


    put gKey into field "keyField"

    put count( gHitlist ) into numItems

    put empty into buildString


    repeat with i=1 to numItems

        put getAt( gHitlist, i ) into itemString

        put item 1 of itemString into musicalTerm

        put musicalTerm into line i of buildString

    end repeat


    put buildString into field "hitsField"


    displayHit 1

end
```

Open your version of Ch8.dir again, and press Play. Try doing a few finds. The list of hits will be listed in the floating Hitlist Window, and the first hit will be displayed on the Stage.

Re-open your version of Hitlist.dir to continue.

Implementing the Click-on-the-Hitlist Function

If you look way, way back at our behavior list, you'll see that the user is supposed to be able to click on a line of the hitlist field and see the record that he or she clicked on displayed in the main window.

We can implement this with the help of a special Lingo function called *the mouseLine*. This function tells you which line of text the cursor is currently on top of. It **doesn't** tell you which **field** the cursor is on, but we can figure that out from context.

Here's the context: If we check the *mouseLine* when the user clicks on field *hitsField*, we can be pretty sure that the cursor is on top of field *hitsField*. You can't click on something from across the screen.

Once we figure out which is the correct line of the field, we have figured the correct item in *gHitlist*. Remember, each line of field *hitsField* directly corresponds to an item in *gHitlist*. So, to implement this behavior, all we have to do is put this handler into the Sprite Script of sprite 5, which is attached to field *hitsField*.

```
on mouseDown

    displayHit the mouseline

end
```

> **N O T E** Director has a few other functions, like *the mouseWord*, the *mouseItem*, and the *mouseCast*, that can help you implement hot text. We aren't going to do that in this project, but you should look them up if you are going to do hot text. (If you're wondering, "hot text" is text that does something when clicked.)

Scrolling

When you have to scroll only one field at a time, as we do, Lingo makes it really easy. A command called *scrollByLine* takes as arguments the field Cast Member and the number of lines you want to scroll.

We could scroll our *hitlist* field **forward** one line like this:

```
scrollByLine member "hitsField", 1
```

We could scroll it **back** one line like this:

```
scrollByLine member "hitsField", -1
```

There are already invisible box Sprites on our scroll-back and scroll-forward arrows, in sprites 10 and 11, respectively.

Because we want them to scroll continuously as long as the mouse button is pressed, we should wrap these statements in *repeat while* loops. Put this handler on the Sprite Script of sprite 10...

```
on mouseDown

  repeat while the mouseDown

    scrollByLine member "hitsField", -1

  end repeat

end
```

And put this one on sprite 11.

```
on mouseDown

  repeat while the mouseDown

    scrollByLine member "hitsField", 1

  end repeat

end
```

There's a Cast Member property in fields called *the scrollTop*. It will tell us the number of pixels that the field is scrolled. When the hits field is not scrolled at all, *the scrollTop of member "hitsField"* is 0. (We're going to need to know this in the next section.)

Showing the Selection

If you play with the finished version of the movie, Ch8_done.dir, you will notice that a black bar appears in the hitlist whenever you click a hit. It looks like Figure 8.6.

This "selection" is an interesting Director trick. It looks like a normal selection, like one you might see in a word processor, but it isn't. In fact, it is a black-filled rectangle, drawn with the toolbar, in sprite 7. The ink-mode on sprite 7 is **reverse**, so it shows

Figure 8.6 Black bar appears when you click a hit.

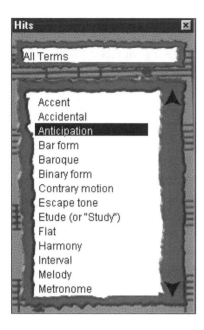

the white pixels underneath it as black, and the black pixels as white. (**Reverse** does really bizarre things with colors, so it is good that the field is on a white background.)

The selection bar, as we'll call it, starts out at *locV* -100. This means that it is not even on the Stage, effectively invisible. When a hit is chosen for display, we have to move the selection bar on top of the correct line of the "Hits" field.

This is a bit involved, so let's create a handler designed specifically to select lines. Let's call it, duh, *selectLine*.

```
on selectLine lineNum

    -- do stuff

end
```

The parameter *lineNum* takes the number of the line to select.

Here's the situation. There is a field called *hitsField* in sprite 5 that contains one or more lines of text. We need to position sprite 7, the selection bar, on top of line *lineNum* of this field. To do this, we will need to figure out the *locV* of line *lineNum* of this field.

We will do this in a couple of steps.

The first step is to figure out how many pixels line *lineNum* is from the top of the field Cast Member. Lingo gives us a function to do this, called *linePosToLocV*. This function takes two parameters, the member and the line number.

. . .

```
put linePosToLocV(member "hitsField", lineNum) into fromTopOfField
```

. . .

Now the local variable *fromTopOfField* holds the number of pixels between the top of the field Cast Member and the top of line *lineNum* of the field. However, since a Cast Member doesn't have a location on Stage, this isn't a stage coordinate. We still need to do some work to get that *locV*.

(Notice that we had to say *member "hitField"* instead of *field "hitField"*. It is a subtle difference. The Lingo word *field* actually refers to *the text of member*. When a function has to operate on the actual Cast Member instead of the text inside it, you have to say *member*.)

The value returned by *linePosToLocV* is offset by *the scrollTop* of the member. In order to get an accurate number of pixels from the top of the scrolled field, we have to subtract *the scrollTop* to *fromTopOfField*.

. . .

```
put fromTopOfField-the scrollTop of member "hitsField" into fromTopOfField
```

. . .

The second step is to use the current value of *fromTopOfField* to compute a screen location.

At this point, *fromTopOfField* holds the pixel location of line *lineNum*, relative to the top of the field, as it is currently scrolled. In order to get the *locV*, we have only to add this value to the coordinate of the top of the field Sprite.

. . .

```
put the top of sprite 5 + fromTopOfField into selBarLocV
```

. . .

Now, we are ready to turn sprite 7 into a Puppet and set its location.

. . .

```
puppetSprite 7, TRUE

set the locV of sprite 7 to selBarLocV

updateStage
```

. . .

Here's our *selectLine* handler, as of now.

```
on selectLine lineNum

    put linePosToLocV( member "hitsField", lineNum) into fromTopOfField

    put fromTopOfField-the scrollTop of member "hitsField" into fromTopOfField

    put the top of sprite 5 + fromTopOfField into selBarLocV


    puppetSprite 7, TRUE

    set the locV of sprite 7 to selBarLocV

    updateStage

end
```

We have to connect the rest of our code to *selectLine*. First, whenever a new hit is selected, its line should be selected. Let's put a call to *selectLine* into *displayHit*. While we're here, we should save the current *hitNum* into a global variable. (We're going to need it soon.)

```
on displayHit hitNum

    global gHitlist, gHitNum


    put getAt( gHitlist, hitNum ) into itemString

    put item 2 of itemString into mname
```

```
selectLine hitNum

put hitNum into gHitNum


tell the Stage to displayRecord mname
end
```

Finally, whenever we scroll field *hitsField*, the selection-bar has to be moved. Let's say we have line 2 of field *hitsField* selected. Now, we scroll the field up one line. Unfortunately, we didn't move the selection-bar up a line, so it looks as if line 3 is selected because it has scrolled into line 2's old position.

To avoid this problem, we have to call *selectLine* whenever we scroll the field. This is why we saved the current hit in the global variable *gHitNum* just now.

The new Sprite Script for sprite 10 is:

```
on mouseDown

    global gHitNum


    repeat while the mouseDown

        scrollByLine member "hitsField", -1

        selectLine gHitNum

    end repeat
end
```

And the Script on sprite 11 is:

```
on mouseDown

    global gHitNum


    repeat while the mouseDown

        scrollByLine member "hitsField", 1
```

```
        selectLine gHitNum

    end repeat

end
```

Open movie Ch8.dir again and try the whole shebang. Do some Finds, perhaps on "form," "note," or "music." Play with the scrolling and the selecting.

Bugs? What Bugs?

I see two bugs.

1. Clicking on the selection-bar (or double-clicking on a line) causes an "Index Out of Range" error.

2. The selection-bar doesn't disappear when the field is scrolled too far up or down. Instead, it appears on top of the background graphic.

Stomping Bug 1

What is going on here?

When you click on the selection-bar in sprite 10, sprite 10 doesn't capture the *mouseDown* or *mouseUp* events because it doesn't have a *mouseDown* or *mouseUp* handler. The *mouseDown* event goes to the Sprite underneath it, which is the hitlist field in sprite 5.

Sprite 5's *mouseDown* handler is triggered. This handler works using the *mouseLine*, which keeps track of which line of any field is rolled over.

Unfortunately, no line of a field is rolled over right now. The mouse is over the selection-bar. So, *the mouseLine* returns –1.

Then we go into *displayHit*, which, among other things, executes this line:

```
    put getAt( gHitlist, lineNum ) into itemString
```

The value of *lineNum* comes from the *mouseLine* that was originally clicked, which is -1 right now. This line asks Director for the -1th item of *gHitlist*. *GetAt* can't give you a negative item, so it causes an "Index Out of Range" error.

Phew! We can fix this at the root of the problem. We can capture that first click on the selection-bar and keep this whole chain of events from happening. To capture a mouse click, all you have to do is put a *mouseUp* and a *mouseDown* handler into the Sprite Script of the selection-bar, in sprite 7

```
on mouseDown

    nothing

end



on mouseUp

    nothing

end
```

Stomping Bug 2

Basically, the selection-bar doesn't know where the on-screen boundaries of the field are, so it goes above and below them, according to our computations. We have to tell it where the boundaries are.

The top boundary of the *hits field* in sprite 5 is *the top of sprite 5*. The bottom boundary is *the bottom of sprite 5*. If the new location that we calculate is above the top boundary, or at or below the bottom boundary, the selection-bar should effectively disappear. To make it disappear, we can set it to an off-screen location, like a vertical position of –100.

Here is the revised *selectLine* handler:

```
on selectLine lineNum

    put linePosToLocV( member "hitsField", lineNum) into fromTopOfField

    put fromTopOfField-the scrollTop of member "hitsField" into fromTopOfField

    put the top of sprite 5 + fromTopOfField into selBarLocV



    if selBarLocV < the top of sprite 5 then

        put -100 into selBarLocV

    else if selBarLocV >= the bottom of sprite 5 then
```

```
    put -100 into selBarLocV

  end if


  puppetSprite 7, TRUE

  set the locV of sprite 7 to selBarLocV

  updateStage

end
```

As of right now, the database should be functional. Take a breather, play with the program, and relax before you move on. I know I'm going to!

We are done with Hitlist.dir. Save the latest version of it, then open Ch8.dir again. We will be working with this file from now on.

Showing the Pictures

A few of the records in the database have pictures associated with them. All the available pictures are bitmap Cast Members, starting at member 80.

If a record has a picture associated with it, the first line of the record field will be the name of the picture Cast Member. Figure 8.7 is the text of member *Contrarymotion*.

The first line, *contPic*, is the name of the graphic Cast Member that should be displayed when this record is displayed.

Figure 8.7 Contrarymotion Cast Member.

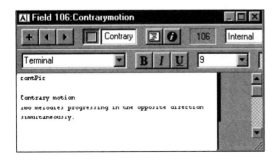

In the Score, there is an invisible box in sprite 3 that covers the picture-display box on the left side of the Stage. To display a picture, we have to turn sprite 3 into a Puppet, then change the attached Cast Member to the picture. We have switched Cast Members like this several times in the last few chapters.

This is an ability that we should add to our *displayRecord* handler. It should check the first line of the record. If it is not empty, we should switch the specified Cast Member into sprite 3. If it is empty, we should make sure that sprite 3 is not puppetted, so it won't display any picture at all.

Here is the new *displayRecord* handler.

```
on displayRecord recID

    set the visible of sprite 5 to FALSE

    updateStage


    put field recID into rec

    put line 3 of rec into holding

    put the number of lines in rec into numRecLines

    put return & return & line 4 to numRecLines of rec after holding

    put holding into field "displayField"


    -- style it

    if item 1 of the platform = "Windows" then

        put "Arial" into defaultFont

    else

        put "Helvetica" into defaultFont

    end if


    set the font of field "displayField" to defaultFont
```

```
set the fontstyle of field "displayField" to "plain"

set the fontSize of field "displayField" to 12


set the fontSize of line 1 of field "displayField" to 18

set the fontStyle of line 1 of field "displayField" to "bold"


set the visible of sprite 5 to TRUE


-- show picture if it exists

put line 1 of rec into picName

if picName <> empty then

    puppetSprite 3, TRUE

    set the stretch of sprite 3 to FALSE

    set the member of sprite 3 to member picName

else

    puppetSprite 3, FALSE

end if


updateStage

end
```

Director and Sound

You can make sound in a Director project via two basic mechanisms: Director audio and Quicktime audio. We covered Quicktime audio in Chapter 6, so here, we will talk about Director audio.

Director for Windows has four internal audio channels. This means that it can play up to four sounds at one time (as long as Quicktime isn't playing audio already).

Director for Macintosh has no real limit on the number of audio channels, except for the performance of the machine. The more audio channels, the slower the performance you can expect. You won't know how many channels work for you until you test.

Sound in the Score

The first and easiest way to play Director sound is by importing a sound Cast Member and putting it into the sound channels of the Score. Whenever the Playback Head enters a frame that has sound in the sound channels, it will start to make noise.

puppetSound

The second way is to use a new command: *puppetSound*. This command takes two arguments. The first one is the number of the channel in which you want this sound to play (1–4 in Windows, 1—a big number on the Mac). The second argument is the Cast Member name or number that contains the sound.

If we had a sound Cast Member called "scream," we could play it in Sound Channel 4 like this:

```
puppetSound 2, "scream"

updateStage
```

You should always throw in the *updateStage* to make sure the sound starts playing as soon as possible.

If you want to stop the sound playing in channel 4, you can shut it off by putting a zero in the second argument.

```
puppetSound 2, 0

updateStage
```

You can, at any moment, check to see if a certain channel is busy playing a sound. Lingo gives us a function called *soundbusy* that takes one argument, the number of the channel that you want to check. The function returns TRUE if a sound is playing, and FALSE if not.

The following code fragment checks to see if sound channel 1 is already playing a sound. If it is, the sound is stopped. Finally, it plays a new sound in channel 1.

```
if soundbusy(1) = TRUE then

    puppetSound 1, 0

    updateStage

end if
```

```
puppetSound 1, "scream"
```

If the sound Cast Member, in this case "scream," is a linked sound, the sound will be read continuously from the disk until it is done playing. If the sound was embedded, the entire sound will be read into RAM before the system tries to play it. If there isn't enough free RAM to hold the entire sound, the sound simply won't play. (By the way, it is common practice to preload sound Cast Members, so they will play immediately.)

Another of the dangers in using *puppetSound* is that you become responsible for that Sound Channel, the same way you become responsible for a Sprite Channel when you use *puppetSprite*. If you have puppetted Sound Channel 1, and the Playback Head is on a frame with something in Sound Channel 1 of the Score, then the Score sound won't play. When you are done manipulating a Puppet Sound Channel, always turn it off with *puppetSound channel,0*.

Sound playFile

Director can also play a sound file directly from disk, without importing it into the Cast. Director can play AIFF files on the Mac and in Windows. In Windows, it can also play WAV files.

To play a sound from a file, you use the *sound playFile* command. It takes two arguments, the number of the desired sound channel, and the filename of the sound.

```
sound play file 1, "scream.aif"
```

If the sound file is not in the same directory as the Director movie, you must supply a full pathname and filename in the second parameter. For a detailed discussion of pathnames, see Part IV of this book.

The Dangers of Sound

A couple of dangers apply to all three kinds of Director sound. For starters, you can't play Director sound and Quicktime sound at the same time. This does work on the Mac, but doesn't work in Windows. Whichever software starts playing sound first, **Director** or **Quicktime**, will block the other from being able to play sound until it is done. See Chapter 6 for a more detailed explanation.

It is also dangerous to play multiple, linked sounds from a CD-ROM. Playing multiple, linked sounds is fine if all the sounds are on the hard disk. However, CD-ROM drives can't handle reading from multiple, scattered locations on the CD fast enough to play more than one sound. If you must play two sounds, one or both of them should be embedded, so that they will play directly from RAM.

Implementing Sound in the Database

If a record has an associated sound, the name of the sound file will be in line 3 of the database field. This record, "Harmony," has a related sound file called *harmony.aif* (Figure 8.8).

Our *displayRecord* handler must do two things if the record has a sound: It must show the **Play** button, and it must load the name of the sound file into a global variable. Later, the *mouseDown* script of the **Play** button Sprite will use this global variable to play the sound.

There is an invisible box in sprite 4, ready to be switched to the bitmap Cast Member *playBtn*. The code is straightforward.

Here is the **final** version of *displayRecord*.

Figure 8.8 Harmony Cast Member.

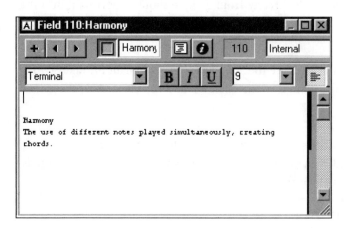

```
on displayRecord recID

    global gSndFile

    set the visible of sprite 5 to FALSE

    updateStage


    put field recID into rec

    put line 3 of rec into holding

    put the number of lines in rec into numRecLines

    put return & return & line 4 to numRecLines of rec after holding

    put holding into field "displayField"


    -- style it

    if item 1 of the platform = "Windows" then

        put "Arial" into defaultFont

    else

        put "Helvetica" into defaultFont

    end if


    set the font of field "displayField" to defaultFont

    set the fontstyle of field "displayField" to "plain"

    set the fontSize of field "displayField" to 12


    set the fontSize of line 1 of field "displayField" to 18

    set the fontStyle of line 1 of field "displayField" to "bold"
```

```
set the visible of sprite 5 to TRUE


-- show picture if it exists

put line 1 of rec into picName

if picName <> empty then

    puppetSprite 3, TRUE

    set the stretch of sprite 3 to FALSE

    set the member of sprite 3 to member picName

else

    puppetSprite 3, FALSE

end if


-- check for sound

put line 2 of rec into sndFile

if sndFile <> empty then

    -- display play btn and fill global

    puppetsprite 4,true

    set the stretch of sprite 4 to false

    set the member of sprite 4 to member "playBtn"

    put sndFile into gSndFile

else

    -- hide play btn and empty global

    puppetSprite 4,false

    put empty into gSndFile

end if
```

```
    updateStage
```

```
end
```

After the record is displayed, the **Play** button appears on the Stage. If the user clicks it, the sound file should play.

All the sounds are contained in AIFF files, located in the AIF folder, inside the Chapter8 folder. When you copied the Chapter8 folder to your hard disk, the AIF folder should have come along for the ride.

Because the sound files aren't in the same folder as our Director movie, we must supply a fully qualified filename to the *sound playfile* command. A fully qualified filename has a complete path to the file, plus the filename. These are two examples of fully qualified pathnames.

- e:\working\chapter8\aif\harmony.aif—Windows

- My Hard Disk:Working:Chapter8:AIF:harmony.aif—Macintosh

Notice the backslash that separates Windows folders and the colon that separates Macintosh folders.

The value of our global variable *gSndFile* is, in our example

```
"Harmony.aif"
```

So, how do we get from here to there?

There is a function in Lingo called *the pathname*. It returns the full pathname of the current Director movie. Type *put the pathname* into your Message Window, while your Ch8.dir is loaded.

In Windows:

```
put the pathname
```

```
-- "e:\working\chapter8\"
```

On the Macintosh:

```
put the pathname
```

```
-- "My Hard Disk:Working:Chapter8:"
```

Based on the platform, our code will have to put together a fully qualified filename based on *the pathname* and *gSndFile*.

Here is the final handler for the Sprite Script of sprite 4, the **Play** button.

```
on mouseDown

    global gSndFile


    if gSndFile <> empty then

        if item 1 of the platform = "Windows" then

            put the pathname & "AIF\"&gSndFile into fullSndFilename

        else

            put the pathname & "AIF:"&gSndFile into fullSndFilename

        end if


        if soundbusy(1) then

            puppetSound 1,0

        end if


        sound playfile 1, fullSndFilename

    end if

end
```

Director and Menus

Not many multimedia titles use the menu bar anymore, for good reasons.

The menu bar is always drawn using a system font, which tends to look ugly against the graphic-designed, anti-aliased look and feel of most multimedia interfaces.

Also, the menu bar tends to take on weird colors when you install a custom palette. The Windows System Palette is custom on the Mac. The Macintosh System Palette is custom in Windows. The menu bar is going to look a little strange on at least one platform.

A menu bar also takes up 20 or more pixels at the top of the screen. At 640 × 480 pixels, there isn't much screen real estate to spare for a menu bar.

However, some people like them. And so we use a small menu bar here.

To make a menu bar in Director, you first define it in a text field. Each menu in the field looks like this:

```
menu: menuName

item 1|handlerName

item 2|handlerName

item 3|handlerName
```

After the *menu:* keyword, you type the name of the menu. For a File menu, the line would look like this:

```
menu:File
```

The lines beneath are items that go in this menu. On the left side of the "|" character is the name of the item, the way it should show up in the menu. On the right of the "|" character is the script that will execute if the item is chosen. Usually you use a call to a handler. If we had a menu item called "Find Harmony," it might be defined in a menu like this:

```
menu:File

Find Harmony|doSearch "harmony"
```

There are many special characters, a couple of which are important. On the Mac, the "@" character denotes an Apple menu, which you define like this:

```
menu: @
```

On both platforms, the item (- defines a horizontal line.

On both platforms, you define a speed key (accelerator) for the item with a slash and a letter, after the item name. Here's how you might define a normal File menu. It has speed keys 'S' for Save, 'O' for Open, 'W' for Close, and 'Q' for Quit.

```
menu: File

Open/O|doOpen
```

```
Save/S|doSave
```

```
Close/W|doClose
```

```
(-
```

```
Quit/Q|quit
```

Let's say this was in a field Cast Member called *fileMenu*. We could make it the current menu bar with the *installMenu* command.

```
installMenu member "fileMenu"
```

We could get rid of the menu bar with this command.

```
installMenu 0
```

Let's say that no files are currently open. We want to dim or disable the Save and Close menu items because they are inappropriate without a file to save or close. We could take care of this by setting a property of the menu items.

```
set the enabled of menuItem 2 of menu "File" to FALSE
```

```
set the enabled of menuItem 3 of menu "File" to FALSE
```

Implementing Menus in the Database

If you look at Cast Members 21 and 22 of Ch8.dir, you'll see two menu bar definitions, one for Mac and one for Windows. The only difference is that the Macintosh version has an Apple menu.

```
Cast member macMenu
```

```
menu:@
```

```
menu:File
```

```
Open Hitlist/O|openHitlist
```

```
Save Hitlist/S|saveHitlist
```

```
(-
Quit/Q|quitCast
```

```
member
```

```
winMenu
```

```
menu:File
```

```
Open Hitlist/O|openHitlist

Save Hitlist/S|saveHitlist

(-

Quit/Q|quit
```

We will implement the handlers *openHitlist* and *saveHitlist* in the FileIO section, coming up in a few pages.

The menu bar should be installed as soon as Ch8.dir starts running, so let's put the command into the *startMovie* handler.

```
on startMovie

    global gHitlist, gKey, gHitsWindow


    put [] into gHitlist

    put empty into gKey

    put "Hits" into gHitsWindow


    if item 1 of the platform = "Windows" then

        installMenu "winMenu"

    else

        installMenu "macMenu"

    end if

end
```

The second item in the File menu, **Save Hitlist**, is really only appropriate when the Hitlist Window is open. When it isn't, it should be disabled.

It's always good practice to centralize access to any shared resource, such as menus, Quicktime, etc. Since we will want to disable and enable the **Save Hitlist** menu item from a couple of places, we should envelop the functions in a couple of handlers. Let's call them *disableSave* and *enableSave*. These go in the Movie Script of Ch8.dir.

```
on disableSave

        set the enabled of menuItem 2 of menu "File" to FALSE

end

on enableSave

        set the enabled of menuItem 2 of menu "File" to TRUE

end
```

Since the items should be disabled when the movie starts playing, we should add a call to *disableSave* into the *startMovie* script.

```
on startMovie

        global gHitlist, gKey, gHitsWindow


        put [] into gHitlist

        put empty into gKey

        put "Hits" into gHitsWindow


        if item 1 of the platform = "Windows" then

                installMenu "winMenu"

        else

                installMenu "macMenu"

        end if


        disableSave

end
```

But where do we enable it again? And if the user closes the window, how will the Lingo elf know to disable it?

Turns out, there are a couple of events that would be perfect for this purpose. They are called whenever a window opens or closes. They are named, obviously, *openWindow* and *closeWindow*.

Open hitlist.dir for editing. Put these handlers into the Movie Script.

```
on openWindow

    tell the stage to enableSave

end
```

```
on closeWindow

    tell the stage to disableSave

end
```

The last pieces of the project are the *openHitlist* and *saveHitlist* handlers that we referenced in the menu bar definitions. Director has no capabilities to load or save text files, so we are going to have to learn about Director Xtras.

Extending Director with Xtras

Extend both your arms, and spread them apart as wide as you can.

This is what your computer can do.

Now bring your arms together so that your palms are about six inches away from each other.

This is what Director can do.

A modern personal computer is an amazingly capable workhorse. A Mac or PC can do amazing things, from storing large databases to rendering in 3D to video conferencing. No single program or authoring tool could ever hope to encompass all of that vast functionality.

Understanding this, Macromedia gave us the Director **Xtra**.

An **Xtra** is a piece of software that adds capabilities to Director that aren't part of the basic Director application. They are very much like plug-ins for Adobe

Photoshop or QuarkXPress. If you need a capability that isn't part of Director's normal command set, chances are you can find or write an Xtra to add it.

An Xtra is written in C++ by a C++ programmer. It is then packaged into a nice little file and generally posted to the Internet. You, as a Lingo programmer, can generally download the Xtra and incorporate into your project, perhaps for a fee. **Most Xtras are listed at Macromedia's site, www.macromedia.com.**

There are four types of Xtras that work with Director.. **Tool Xtras** add tools to the Director authoring environment. **Sprite Xtras** add new types of Sprites to Director. **Transition Xtras** add new kinds of frame transitions to Director.

And then there are **Lingo Xtras**. This type of Xtra adds new commands and capabilities to Lingo, which is why I like them so much. If you need to manage a big database, you can use the FileFlex or V12 Xtras, which add databasing commands to Lingo. If you need to print, you can use the PrintOMatic Xtra, which adds printing commands to Lingo. If you need to record audio, you can use the Sound Xtra, which adds sound recording commands to Lingo.

And if you need to read or write files, you can use the **FileIO Xtra.**

We are going to explore the FileIO Xtra a little, in relation to our current project. Along the way, though, you'll learn things you can apply to any Xtra.

At the time of this writing, you have to download the FileIO Xtra from the Macromedia website, **www.macromedia.com.**

The FileIO Xtra

Your Director project needs outside assistance to work with files and disks. This is why you need the FileIO Xtra.

An Xtra is not cross-platform. When you acquire an Xtra, you generally need four versions of it, for Windows 3.1 (16-bit), Windows 95 (32-bit), Macintosh 68k, and Power Macintosh. Often, the 68k and Power Macintosh versions will be combined into the same "fat-binary" file. (Read Chapter 13 for more information on cross-platform issues.)

The filenames for the versions of FileIO are:

Windows 3.1	**fileio16.x16**
Windows 95	**fileio.x32**

Macintosh 68k

PowerPC   **FileIOXtraFat**

Except for the names of the files, all the actual commands are the same. Variations will arise in the differences between Windows 3.1 filenames, Windows 95 filenames, and Macintosh filenames, but we'll deal with those as they come up.

On your hard disk, there is a folder in the Director folder called Xtras. If you place the proper Xtra (check the table above) into this folder, FileIO will be loaded and ready to go as soon as you restart Director.

However, you can also open an Xtra from Lingo. This is a preferable method if you want to use the Xtra's capabilities only once in a while. You use the *openxlib* command, which takes the filename of the Xtra as an argument.

Open the Message Window. Put the correct version of FileIO (check the table above) into the same folder as the currently open movie. Then use the *openxlib* command to load it. This line opens the Windows 95 version

```
openxlib "fileio.x32"
```

You can make sure that FileIO was loaded by checking the list of all opened Xtras. Type this into the Message Window

```
showxlib
```

You'll see a list something like this

```
-- XLibraries:
--    Xtra: FileFlex
--    Xtra: PrintOMatic_Lite
-- "*Standard.xlib"
--    XObject: FileIO          Id:1020
--    XObject: SerialPort      Id:200
--    XObject: XCMDGlue        Id:2020
-- "fileio.x32"
--    Xtra: FileIO
```

If you look at the last couple of lines, you'll see the XLibrary file fileio.x32, and the Xtra it contained, FileIO. From now on, we'll just refer to FileIO, which is the software entity that was loaded when we opened its container file, fileio.x32.

Now that you have opened the Xtra, there's a bunch of new functionality waiting for you. It takes a little understanding to use it correctly, though.

To access any of FileIO's functionality, you send **messages**. You can find out all the messages that any Xtra understands by sending the *mMessageList* message. Every Lingo Xtra supports the *mMessageList* message.

```
put mMessageList (xtra "FileIO")
```

You should see something like this...

```
-- "xtra fileio -- CH May96

new object me -- create a new child instance

-- FILEIO --

fileName object me -- return fileName string of the open file

status object me -- return the error code of the last method called

error object me, int error -- return the error string of the error

setFilterMask me, string mask -- set the filter mask for dialogs

openFile object me, string fileName, int mode -- opens named file. valid modes:
0=r/w 1=r 2=w

closeFile object me -- close the file

displayOpen object me -- displays an open dialog and returns the selected
fileName to lingo

displaySave object me, string title, string defaultFileName -- displays save
dialog and returns selected fileName to lingo

createFile object me, string fileName -- creates a new file called fileName

setPosition object me, int position -- set the file position

getPosition object me -- get the file position
```

```
getLength object me -- get the length of the open file

writeChar object me, string theChar -- write a single character (by ASCII code)

to the file

writeString object me, string theString -- write a null-terminated string to the

file

readChar object me -- read the next character of the file and return it as an

ASCII code value

readLine object me -- read the next line of the file (including the next

RETURN) and return as a string

readFile object me -- read from current position to EOF and return as a string

readWord object me -- read the next word of the file and return it as a string

readToken object me, string skip, string break -- read the next token and return

it as a string

getFinderInfo object me -- get the finder info for the open file (Mac Only)

setFinderInfo object me, string attributes -- set the finder info for the open

file (Mac Only)

delete object me -- deletes the open file

+ version xtraRef -- display fileIO version and build information in the message

window

* getOSDirectory -- returns the full path to the Mac System Folder or Windows

Directory

"
```

We'll use only a few of these messages. To find out what they all do, check out the FileIO documentation. The next paragraph gives a quick road map of how to read this output, but don't worry too much if it doesn't make sense. The documentation is easier to understand.

The first word on each line is the name of the message. The rest of the words in the line specify arguments to the message. The first word in the argument is the type of argument. The second word is the name of the argument. The argument *object me* is the *instance* of the Xtra.

(This won't make sense until later, but the "+" means that message should be sent to the Xtra, not an instance of the Xtra, and the "*" means that the message is available like a plain old Lingo command as long as the Xlibrary is open.)

Don't worry if that wasn't clear. I included it just for the technically masochistic among you.

To use most of FileIO's features, you have to create a FileIO **instance**. A particular FileIO instance can become attached to one particular file. Once this attachment is complete, you can read from, write to, or delete that file. If you want to have more than one file open at a time, you can create multiple instances of FileIO.

The FileIO Xtra is like Fox Mulder's sister on the X-Files. She is a real human being, but you never see her in the show. You only know about her because Fox and Dana speak her name every now and then.

However, the aliens **cloned** her, and her clones actually appeared in an episode. Even though she, the original, doesn't have direct power to manipulate the plot, her clones, with all her knowledge and abilities, do. **Instances** of FileIO are like the **clones** of Mulder's sister. They have all the power, but they come from a template.

The following line creates an instance of FileIO and puts it into the variable *someFile*. Type it into the Message Window.

```
set someFile = new( xtra "fileIO")
```

The variable *someFile* now contains an instance of FileIO, a clone of the original. You can send messages to the instance in this variable, and it will actually do things. File and disk things.

Say you were going to save a file. You first need to ask the user for a filename, which is usually done through a platform-specific File Save dialog box. FileIO will do this for you if you send the *displaySave* message to our new instance of FileIO.

```
set newFilename = displaySave (someFile, "Save file as:", "default.txt")
```

The first parameter to *displaySave* is a variable containing an instance of FileIO. It is this instance that is doing the dirty work of displaying the dialog. The second parameter is the prompt for the user. The third string is the default filename to offer the user.

The variable *newFilename* now has a fully qualified filename, the name that you entered before you clicked **Save**. If you clicked **Cancel** instead, *newFilename* will be empty.

Now that we have a filename, we can create the file.

```
createFile(someFile, newFilename)
```

This will create the file on disk. Before we can use it, though, we have to open it.

```
openFile(someFile, newFilename, 0)
```

The first argument to *openFile* is the instance of FileIO, the second is the filename of the new file, and the third is the open mode. Supply a 0 if you want to be able to read and write to this file, a 1 if you only want to read, and a 2 if you only want to write.

Now that the file is open, we can write a string to the file.

```
writeString(someFile, "This is my sample file text.")
```

The first argument to *writeString* is the instance, and the second is the string.

Now that we're done, we can close the file.

```
closeFile(someFile)
```

Finally, we can zap and destroy the instance of FileIO.

```
set someFile = 0
```

This is obviously the technique that we will use to save a hitlist to disk. We will use a similar technique to load a hitlist from a saved file.

Implementing *Save Hitlist*

We just covered most of what we'll need to add this feature. We have to put it into a handler called *saveHitlist*, so that the menu item will invoke it correctly. It should go in the Movie Script of Ch8.dir.

Here's the handler.

```
on saveHitlist

  global gHitlist


  case the platform of

     "Windows,32": put "fileio.x32" into xtraFilename

     "Windows,16": put "fileio.x16" into xtraFilename

     "Macintosh,68k":

     "Macintosh,PowerPC": put "fileIOXtraFat" into xtraFilename

  end case


  openxlib xtraFilename

  set someFile = new(xtra "FileIO")


  set filename = displaySave(someFile,"Save hitlist as:","hits.txt")

  if filename = empty then

     return

  end if


  createFile(someFile, filename)

  openFile(someFile, filename, 0)


  writeString(someFile, string(gHitlist))


  closeFile(someFile)

  set someFile = 0
```

```
    closexlib xtraFilename

end
```

I added a couple of tricks that we didn't discuss in the last section. I used a *case* statement to figure out the correct filename of the Xtra, based on the platform. I threw in an *if..then* that kicks us out of the handler if the user clicked **Cancel** in the Save dialog.

Finally, I slipped in a way to convert the linear list into a string.

```
    . . .

    writeString(someFile, string(gHitlist))

    . . .
```

You can convert one type of value to another by stating the type, as above. If I wanted to turn the string "1234" into an integer, I could do this:

```
        put integer("1234") into myInteger
```

Similarly, I turned the list into a string with *string(gHitlist)*.

This trick will prove useful in the next section, when we reconstitute the list from a text file.

Implementing *Open Hitlist*

This isn't a hard feature either. All we have to do is open the file, read it into a string, then reconstitute the string. The structure of *openHitlist* will be very similar to *saveHitlist*.

We start with the skeleton.

```
on openHitlist

    -- do stuff

end
```

Next, we have to open FileIO and create an instance. This comes straight from *saveHitlist*.

```
    . . .

    case the platform of
```

```
"Windows,32": put "fileio.x32" into xtraFilename

"Windows,16": put "fileio.x16" into xtraFilename

"Macintosh,68k":

"Macintosh,PowerPC": put "fileIOXtraFat" into xtraFilename

end case


openxlib xtraFilename

set someFile = new(xtra "FileIO")

    . . .
```

Now we can ask the user to find the file. This will display the platform-specific Open dialog box. The only parameter *displayOpen* takes is the instance of FileIO.

```
    . . .

set filename = displayOpen(someFile)

if filename = empty then

    return

end if

    . . .
```

If the user clicks **Cancel** in the dialog, *filename* will be empty, and the handler should stop executing. That's what the *if..then* is for.

This next piece of code opens the file for reading and reads the entire file into the variable *fileString*.

```
    . . .

openFile(someFile, filename, 1)

set fileString = readFile(someFile)

    . . .
```

Since *fileString* now contains the entire contents of the file, we don't need to keep it open. You should always close a file as soon as you're done with it.

. . .

```
closeFile(someFile)

set someFile = 0

closexlib xtraFilename
```

. . .

Finally, we have to reconstitute the list that is hiding as a string. We can do this with the *value* command, which looks for the non-string value hiding inside a string. We'll load *gHitlist* with the resulting list.

```
put value(fileString) into gHitlist
```

Now that we have a new *gHitlist*, we can invoke our normal mechanism for displaying a hitlist!

```
displayHitsWindow
```

Here's the final handler.

```
on openHitlist

    global gHitlist


    case the platform of

        "Windows,32": put "fileio.x32" into xtraFilename

        "Windows,16": put "fileio.x16" into xtraFilename

        "Macintosh,68k":

        "Macintosh,PowerPC": put "fileIOXtraFat" into xtraFilename

    end case


    openxlib xtraFilename
```

```
set someFile = new(xtra "FileIO")


set filename = displayOpen(someFile)

if filename = empty then

    return

end if


openFile(someFile, filename, 1)

set fileString = readFile(someFile)


closeFile(someFile)

set someFile = 0

closexlib xtraFilename


put value(fileString) into gHitlist


displayHitsWindow

end
```

> **N O T E**   Using *value()* to reconstitute a list from a string can be tricky. The string that contains the list must be properly formatted, which happens automatically if you used *string()* to create the string from a list. However, you must make sure that none of the items in the list contains quotation marks, or the value function will get confused and return *<void>* instead of your list. Commas and some other weird characters can cause problems also.

Chapter Summary

- Director has three kinds of text containers: Text Cast Members, Field Cast Members, and variables.

- A Text Cast Member is only editable during authoring. When run from a projector or in a Shockwave movie, only the bitmaps image of the text is available. The actual text information is not available for manipulation by Lingo.

- A Field Cast Member can be edited at any time, and can be manipulated by Lingo. Since the text is live, the font you specify must be available on the destination computer.

- Variables can contain text, but no styling information such as font, size, or text style.

- You can manipulate text in variables or fields with several operators.

  & combines two strings

  && combines two strings with a space between them

  before inserts a string into the beginning of another

  after appends one string to another

- You can specify chunks of text using chunk operators.

  char a specific character or range of characters in a string.

  word a word or range of words in a string. Words are separated by spaces or return characters.

  line a line of range of lines in a string. Lines are separated by return characters.

  item an item or range of items in a string. Items are delimited by a comma, unless you change *the itemDelimiter* system-wide property.

- You can manipulate styling information in a Field Cast Member by setting field properties. These properties also work on specific chunks of text.

  the font the typeface of text

  the fontSize point size of text

  the fontStyle plain, bold, italic, underline

- There are two commands to play sound from Lingo.

  puppetSound channel, member Plays sound from Cast Member *member* in the specified channel. This takes over the channel, though, so you should eventually release the channel and stop the sound with *puppetSound 0.*

  sound play file channel, filename Plays an audio file from the disk in the specified channel. You can play AIFF files on the Mac and in Windows, and WAV files in Windows.

- **soundbusy(channel)** is a function that returns TRUE if *channel* is currently playing a sound or FALSE if it isn't.

- To create a pull-down menu, you first define it in a field. The format is:

```
menu:First Menu Name

item 1|message to send from item 1

item 2|message to send from item 2

menu:Second Menu Name

item 1|message to send from item 1

item 2|message to send from item 2
```

- You create a menu by calling *installMenu* with the name of the field that contains the definition. To clear the menu bar, use *installMenu 0.*

- A Director Xtra is a plugin for Director that extends its capabilities. There are four types of Director Xtras: Tool, Sprite, Transition, and Lingo. Lingo Xtras are meant to be manipulated from Lingo.

- You will need a different Xtra for every platform. On the Mac, sometimes both Xtras come in the same file.

- To use a Lingo Xtra, you first open the file that it comes in using *openxlib*. Then, you create an instance of the Xtra using *new*. You manipulate the instance of the Xtra by sending it messages. Finally, you clear the variable that contains the instance and close the Xtra file by calling *closexlib*.

- You can save files, load files, choose files. and do other disk and file related things using the FileIO Xtra from Macromedia.

Part Three
Shockwave

Introducing Shockwave

Chapter Objective

In this chapter we begin our introduction to the world of Shockwave. We'll cover a wide territory as we bridge the worlds of multimedia and the Internet. Starting with an overview of the relationship between Internet and multimedia, you'll build an understanding of where Director and Shockwave fit into the bigger picture. We'll briefly cover some of the central technical areas such as URLs, HTML, browser options and plug-ins, and last but not least, Shockwave itself.

This chapter is not intended to be a complete introduction and reference to the Internet and World Wide Web. There are literally hundreds of books and many excellent Web sites that address these subjects in more detail than we can here (see the Online Resources section at the end of this chapter for the names of a few good places you might want to try).

By the end of this chapter you should have a good understanding of the overall picture of what Shockwave is, and how it works, and you should be prepared for the rest of this section as we begin building Shockwave movies.

The World Wide Web Before Shockwave (B.S.)

Long before there was this thing called Shockwave, there was the Internet, the international network of networks that arose from modest beginnings back in the 1960s as way to keep researchers in touch with one another. An outgrowth of the Cold War, it was originally funded by the military and built to withstand enemy (read: nuclear) attack. For the next 20 years, as it grew from its original four computers to tens of thousands, it also spread from its academic and military roots to a much wider commercial and general-public audience. But during this time the Internet remained primarily a way to send electronic mail, transfer documents, and conduct online discussion groups. Very functional and very text-centric.

Then, in 1989 the Internet was given a whole new look with the introduction of the World Wide Web (the year it was proposed by a fellow named Tim Berners-Lee at a research facility in Geneva). It was to the Net as the Macintosh was to DOS: a sophisticated, easy-to-use, powerful technology that made it vastly more accessible to a wide audience.

The Web's structure is familiar to most of you by now: Built on what's known as a client/server model, users run a client program, the Web browser, to access documents made available on server computers running a Web server program. The typical Web document is a text file whose content has been formatted using a system of tags known as the HyperText Markup Language, or HTML. Web browsers know how to interpret this simple language and can format and display the contents accordingly. Web pages and Web sites are connected to one another through the use of hypertext links embedded in the documents.

Figure 9.1 is a typical Web page as displayed in Microsoft's Internet Explorer browser.

Because Web browsers are usually run on graphically oriented operating systems, such as Microsoft Windows, the Macintosh, or the UNIX X-Window system, they have the ability to display more than just text. In the early days of the Web, that is, up until just last year, the primary forms of "multimedia" found on Web pages were images. The two most widely supported image formats were GIF (Graphic Interchange Format) and JPEG (Joint Photographic Experts Group). Nearly all Web browsers have the built-in ability to display these image formats.

When it came to other forms of media online, such as sound and video files, browsers lacked the capability to handle most of these formats. Instead, they relied on separate playback programs that operated in conjunction with, but outside of,

Figure 9.1 An example Web page displayed in Microsoft's Internet Explorer.

the browser itself. These programs that assist the browser with various data formats are known as **helper applications**.

Using these "helper apps" was, and still often is, not a pretty process. They work on a *download-and-play* model. In this model, Web sites provide links to video and audio files (Quicktime, MPEG, AIF, WAV, and other formats), users download these files, then, if they don't already have a playback application for this format they must locate and download an appropriate helper application, and finally they play the data back in this other program outside of the browser. A bit clumsy.

Starting with Navigator version 2.0 in the fall of 1995, Netscape introduced a much more powerful and better integrated way of doing the same thing: plug-ins. Plug-ins allow application developers to build custom components that extend the basic capabilities of the browser (just as Photoshop plug-ins enhance its capabilities and Director Xtras do for it). The most common use of these plug-ins are playback and display of various multimedia data types. Most of the older helper applications are now being superseded by newer plug-ins that perform essentially the same functions but do so in a much more seamless fashion right within the main window of the browser itself.

Third-party developers have since created more than 150 different plug-ins for a whole range of purposes. They support data formats like Quicktime, AIF and WAV audio files, spreadsheets, PDF files, VRML, dozens of image formats, and an ever growing array of multimedia formats. Oh, yes, there's this one called Shockwave that plays back compressed Director movies. Right there in the middle of a Web page. Very nice.

In addition, many of the newer network-aware multimedia tools and plug-ins (including Shockwave 5) have begun to employ techniques designed to avoid the long, annoying delays for users waiting for a whole file to download. These methods are usually referred to as **streaming**. It's very convenient. You listen to the audio or watch the video *as* it downloads to your computer (in real-time). For audio it's like having a new form of radio or a free online jukebox: Pick the song you want to hear and hear it almost immediately. In Chapter 11 we'll build a movie that uses Shockwave's streaming audio capabilities.

So What Is Shockwave?

Shockwave is Macromedia's technology that enables the publishing of Director movies over the Internet. It is like having the elves of the Director runtime engine work within the confines of a Web browser. Rather than creating projectors for Windows or the Mac you're creating projectors for browsers (independent of any operating system).

The first version of Shockwave appeared shortly after the plug-in-capable Netscape 2.0 was released. It was one of the very first plug-ins available and received a good deal of press coverage at the time (not to mention visibly boosting the price of Macromedia stock immediately after it was released). A second version of Shockwave was released in the summer of 1996. This version is often called Shockwave 5 because of its close support of, and integration with, Director version 5.

An historical side note: During the second half of 1995, Macromedia's internal code-name for its Internet development efforts was Shockwave. It wasn't originally intended to be the name given to the final product. But once the development community got hooked on beta versions of this catchily named product and it received a tremendous amount of media publicity, Macromedia decided to keep the name. Actually, Macromedia now uses the term Shockwave more generally to apply to the lineup of technology for Internet-enabling each of their major applications. In addition to Shockwave for Director there is also Shockwave for Freehand, Shockwave for Authorware, and the recently introduced Shockwave Imaging for xRes.

Where Do You Get Shockwave?

You typically get Shockwave in one of two ways: either on the Director CD-ROM or by downloading it from the Macromedia Web site (see the Resources section at the end of the chapter for the URL of this site as well as other pointers to useful Director-related resources online). The most recent version of Shockwave is always available from their Web site. In addition, Macromedia posts beta (that is pre-release, in-progress, sometimes-buggy) versions of upcoming Shockwave releases on their site as well.

What does it cost? Nothing. If you get it on the Director CD-ROM it's included in the cost of the package. If you download it from the Macromedia Web site it's free also. Macromedia's business model is not to make money by selling Shockwave plug-ins but to promote widespread use of its technology and thus continue to encourage more developers to purchase its suite of development tools. Remember, unlike Java, Shockwave is a proprietary "standard." The more users demand Shockwave-enabled Web sites, the better it is for one company in particular, Macromedia.

How many users have it? As of the end of 1996 Macromedia expects 20 million users to have Shockwave. This includes both users who have obtained the plug-in from their Web site and those who'll get the plug-in as part of their browser itself. For example, Macromedia and Netscape have agreed that Shockwave will become a core content type for Navigator. This means that it will ship as part of the standard browser package and thus be installed along with the browser itself. Macromedia has also signed deals to distribute Shockwave with numerous partners including

Microsoft (Shockwave will ship with pre-installed versions of Windows 95 on most new PCs), Apple (as part of its Internet Connection Kit), and both America Online and CompuServe (each will ship its customers Shockwave as part of its communications software).

The Two Faces of Shockwave: Production and Playback

Shockwave really exists in two parts. On one side is what the developer needs, which is a program called Afterburner; on the other side is what the user needs, which is the Shockwave browser plug-in. Web surfers do not need to be concerned with this thing called Afterburner (or even Director, for that matter). All they need is the plug-in. Developers, on the other hand (that's us), need to have both halves of the equation. Here's the formula:

Production Side
Director + Afterburner = Shockwave Movie
Shockwave Movie + HTML = Shocked Web page

Web Surfer's Side
Web browser + Shockwave plug-in = Shockwave-ready browser
Shockwave-ready browser + Shocked Web page = Fun

Afterburner is a Director Xtra whose sole purpose is to compress Director movies so that they download more quickly across the Internet. The Shockwave plug-in is a browser extension that knows how to decompress these movies and play them back within the context of a Web page.

Figure 9.2 is an example of the Shockwave plug-in playing back a Director movie in the Netscape browser. Notice how well it's integrated into the Web page and is displayed just as standard Web graphics would be. The key difference is that this is a fully interactive multimedia movie with working buttons, animation, and sound.

In addition, as part of Shockwave, several new Internet-related commands have been added to the Lingo language (which is, after all, what we're learning about). The new Lingo commands provide the ability to do such things as get Web pages, load movies, and retrieve files, all across the Internet. In this section we'll refer to these new commands as NetLingo.

Figure 9.2 Sample Shockwave movie.

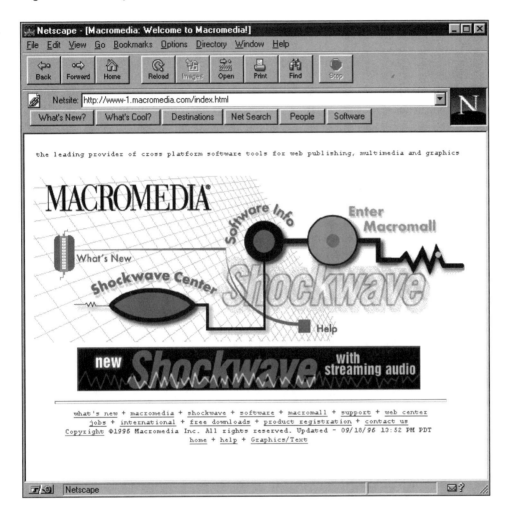

There you have it, the three main pieces of the Shockwave puzzle: Afterburner, the Shockwave plug-in, and NetLingo. Now let's look at how these pieces then fit into the wacky and dynamic world of Web browsers.

Two Browsers, Two Flavors of Shockwave

Sure, there are more than two vendors that develop browser software to let you surf the Web. But, there are only two that really matter: Netscape's Navigator and Microsoft's Internet Explorer. All the rest are only bystanders in the real browser war.

Netscape had an early lead in the browser market, releasing Navigator 1.0 by the end of 1994. Microsoft was asleep at the wheel on the information superhighway and got off to a very late start. They didn't really get their browser act together until the summer of 1996 with the release of Internet Explorer 3.0 (it seems Microsoft's magic number is "3," the release version by which their software is truly usable). Since the near-simultaneous release of version 3.0 of both browsers, Web surfers have had their choice of two very powerful tools for accessing the Internet. And, as you probably know by now, both have the ability to playback Shockwave movies.

For Netscape Navigator version 2.0 and later, the Shockwave plug-in, once downloaded and installed, is the answer. With Internet Explorer version 3.0 and later, the answer is a little more complex on one hand, and much simpler on the other. Let me explain. Because Internet Explorer has the ability to use existing Netscape-compatible plug-ins, it's possible to just use the Shockwave plug-in for Netscape to play-back movies in Internet Explorer. But this is not the recommended approach. Why? Because a much more powerful solution exists for this browser. It's called Active Shockwave.

Active Shockwave is a modified version of the Shockwave plug-in (and, therefore, the Director runtime engine) that Macromedia has developed for Internet Explorer. It's designed to be compatible with the new Microsoft-sanctioned standard it calls ActiveX. This standard is the latest incarnation of Microsoft's OLE (Object Linking and Embedding) operating-system level architecture for Windows. Windows 95 is currently the only platform that supports ActiveX, but Microsoft has pledged support for the Macintosh and UNIX as well.

Just as plug-ins extend the browser, ActiveX controls provide a way to extend the operating system. Third-party software developers can create controls (which are actually small executable programs) that can be integrated into other applications in order to extend their capabilities. ActiveX controls can work with any program that adheres to this standard, not just browsers. Internet Explorer is one such application that knows how to speak with and use ActiveX controls (it's likely in the future that Netscape will support these controls as well). Active Shockwave is one of hundreds of controls compatible with this standard.

Why is this better than a plug-in? First of all, and perhaps most importantly, it has a very straightforward installation process. ActiveX controls know how to install themselves dynamically, directly into the browser. Also, once the control is installed, its performance and integration with Internet Explorer is better than with the plug-in version.

> **NOTE** As Microsoft has a inherent preference (or is that a bias?) to releasing its software for the Windows 95 and NT platforms before supporting other operating systems, the Macintosh version of Internet Explorer 3.0 was not due until the fourth quarter of 1996 (three to four months after the Windows version). By the time you read this, the Mac 3.0 version may be available so check back at Microsoft's Web site for more details: http://www.microsoft.com/ie.

In this section of the book we'll use the term "plug-in" as the general way of referring to both the Netscape-compatible plug-ins (the original form of Shockwave) and the Internet Explorer-compatible ActiveX controls. In this book we will address the issues you'll face in making sure your Shockwave-ready pages can deal with both browsers. Fortunately, in many ways this is not a big deal. But there are a few gotchas and differences that we'll point out along the way.

> **NOTE** Since Netscape's introduction of its plug-in standard other browsers have begun to support these plug-ins as well. This standardization is similar to how a number of applications, including Director, support the Photoshop plug-in standard for graphics tools. Here's a list of browsers supporting Shockwave plug-ins as of this writing: Internet Explorer 3.0 and greater, Netscape Navigator 2.02 and 3.0 (and greater), Attachmate's Emissary, and Netmanage's WebSurfer (check with Macromedia's Web site for the latest browser compatibility list).

Unlike Shockwave movies or Java applications, plug-ins are platform-specific. With Shockwave, and all other plug-ins, you need a different version for each platform on which you wish to run it. And at that point you're at the mercy of each third-party plug-in developer and its ability and willingness to develop tools for each platform. Most vendors support both the Macintosh and Windows with their plug-ins. Shockwave currently supports the Macintosh (PowerPC and 68K) and Windows 3.1, Windows 95, and Windows NT 3.5.1 and 4.0.

Once the Shockwave runtime system is installed in either plug-in or ActiveX form, your Director movies should be ready to go. The key is that the *same* Shockwave movie plays back **identically in both browsers** (that is, barring any bugs in Macromedia's implementation of either Shockwave player). This is a good thing. As Macromedia continues to port the runtime engine to additional platforms, it will only improve as an all-round cross-platform multimedia system (fulfilling their stated goal of "author once, play anywhere").

Before we go on to create Shockwave-enhanced Web pages we need to take a quick review of a few fundamental Internet concepts we'll need to know. We'll look at URLs (the way in which Internet resources are identified), HTML (the language of Web pages), and the importance of bandwidth.

URLs Explained

URLs, you seem to see them everywhere now: in advertisements, on television, billboards, radio (OK, you can't *see* them there), and they're even on beer bottles. These ubiquitous identifiers are to the world of the Internet what phone numbers are to the telecommunications world and street addresses are to the Post Office. They uniquely identify the location of something in cyberspace. That something could be an organization's home page, a single file intended for downloading from an FTP site, a user's electronic mail address, or a particular Usenet newsgroup.

As is typically the case in computer jargon, a URL is an acronym, this time for Uniform Resource Locator (sometimes referred to as an "Earl," as in "What's the earl for their site?"). Don't worry, most people don't know what this really stands for. And don't have to. What is important is knowing how URLs work because we'll be using them in programming our Shockwave movies. Let's take one apart.

```
http://www.macromedia.com/shockwave.html
```

URLs have three main parts:

1. Protocol to use

   http://

2. Internet domain name for the Web server

www.macromedia.com

3. Path to the desired file

/shockwave.html

These correspond to the three things a browser needs to know: how to get there, where to go, and what specific thing to get once you're there.

How to Get There

The letters http: mean that the HyperText Transfer Protocol (HTTP) is the method to use in retrieving this resource (HTTP is the basic communications protocol upon which the Web is built). Technically, this part of the URL is called the scheme. Besides http, the most common schemes are: ftp (the FTP protocol); mailto (for electronic mail messages); gopher (yes, the Gopher protocol); and news (NNTP news protocol).

Where to Go

The Internet domain name, www.macromedia.com, specifies the server on which this resource is located. An optional part of the domain name is the **port number** identifying exactly where on that server to connect to. So sometimes you'll see an address like http://www.company.com:8080/index.htm where 8080 is a port number.

What to Get Once You're There

The path and filename, **/shockwave.html,** identify where on this server to find the file you're looking for. The part from the first slash to the last is the path [in a UNIX-like syntax using forward slashes, similar to how the PC uses backslashes (\) and the Mac uses colons (:) to divide directories or folders]. The last part is the name of the file itself. Remember: Case usually matters when dealing with the path and filename. Thus, /dirA/shockwave.html is different from /dirA/ShockWave.html.

The key here is that URLs are an excellent general-purpose way of identifying a wide variety of online resources.

The are three basic "types" of HTTP URLs: complete, relative, and absolute. The URL shown above is complete because it specifies the full address to that resource. Simple enough. Relative URLs, on the other hand, specify just part of the address. Its location is relative to the document in which it is specified (usually an HTML page). An example of a relative URL is **file2.html**. An absolute URL specifies the entire path to this file but does not include the protocol or the domain name: /topdir/seconddir/file1.html.

> **TIP** I don't know about you, but I hate typing more than I have to. Here's a typing-reduction trick to try. Most browsers now allow you to type in addresses without specifying the entire URL. Experiment with your browser to see how little of the address you can get away with. For example, both Netscape Navigator and Internet Explorer will figure out that if the address you enter starts with www that you probably want to use HTTP as the protocol for getting there. Additionally, some newer versions of Netscape allow just the company name to be entered; it will add the http://www prefix and the .com suffix. So typing just macromedia in the location box would be a shorthand way of saying http://www.macromedia.com. Much, much easier.

Why do you care? Because in general you want to use relative URLs wherever possible within your HTML pages and Shockwave movies. They not only reduce typing, they make URLs more manageable. For example, if you have 17 HTML pages and four Shockwave movies in a directory on a Web server and you move them to a different directory, all non-relative addresses in those files will have to be updated to reflect this change. This is extra work. That's bad. We'd rather be creating new Shockwave movies than retyping URL links in our old ones.

HTML and Shockwave

Now that we've looked at how to specify the location of a Web page, we should quickly review what's in one. A Web page is a text file that consists of some content whose formatting is described through the use of a simple markup language called HTML (the HyperText Markup Language).

In HTML, a set of commands known as tags tells the browser how to display the text, images, and other data in the page. Tags are identified by the angle brackets surrounding them (the less-than, <, and greater-than, >, symbols). Tags often come in pairs in order to delimit the beginning and end of a particular area to be formatted (where the second, or closing, tag begins with a slash character, /). For example, the pair of tags used to specify a highest-level heading would be: *<H1>My Heading</H1>*. A Web page consists of many sets of such tags describing such things as: headings, paragraph breaks, font sizes, hypertext links, and image placement.

Often these tags will refer to other files that are to be included as part of this page. (Remember that the Web page itself is just text; the images and other media exist in completely separate files. This is different than most self-contained Director movies where the assets often become loaded into the movie file itself.) The process goes as follows: the browser downloads the Web page you've requested (**pagex.html**); it then reads through the file searching for HTML tags to give it instructions; when it finds tags referring to other files (like the *IMG* tag used as *<IMG SRC="myimage.gif">*) it then makes another request to the Web server asking for this file as well; it then continues through the HTML file repeatedly making individual requests back to the server each time it finds references to other files included in this page. This means that for even a single Web page the browser may make a dozen or more requests back to the Web server asking for all the various components that make-up that page.

Over the recent past a number of new tags have been added to the HTML standard. The most notable to Shockwave developers is the *EMBED* tag. This tells the browser to embed, or include, an external data file such as a Shockwave movie at a particular location within the page (which, as noted above, involves another trip back to the server to get this file). This tag, along with the even more recent *OBJECT* tag, are the two ways in which Web pages can incorporate Shockwave movies.

Here's a complete HTML page that displays a Shockwave movie (in the next chapter we'll go into HTML and Shockwave integration in more detail):

```
<HTML>

<HEAD>

<TITLE>A Minimal Shockwave Demo</TITLE>

</HEAD>

<BODY>
```

```
<EMBED SRC="mymovie.dcr" WIDTH=300 HEIGHT=50>

</BODY>

</HTML>
```

Here we see the use of five basic HTML tags (four of which are used in pairs):

- *HTML*: identifies this as an HTML document

- *HEAD* and *BODY*: separate the document into its two major sections

- *TITLE*: gives the document a title (which the browser will display in its title bar)

- *EMBED*: says to include this file, mymovie.dcr, and give it a 300 x 50 rectangle in which to be displayed ("dcr" is the standard Shockwave file extension)

When the browser encounters the *EMBED* tag it says, "Look, here's a piece of data I have to include in this page." It then goes out and downloads this file. Once the file has been retrieved it then says, "Do I know how to display this thing? No. OK, has a plug-in been registered with me that says it can handle files of this type? Yes. Great, I'll set aside a 300 x 50 pixel area in my window for displaying this thing, I'll load that plug-in, and then hand off this file to it so it can deal with it." Then, the Shockwave plug-in takes over, loads the movie, and displays right there in the middle of the Web page. The user can then interact with the movie just as he or she would with a projector-sized version of the same. When the user goes on to another page the browser unloads both the movie and the plug-in and proceeds to get that next page.

That's all there is to it. One of the best things about HTML is how easy it is to write. Just a simple text editor, a few commands, and you're set. Many of the pros use little more than that—no fancy tools required.

Shockwave versus Java

About the same time that Shockwave hit the scene so did a new programming language called Java. Java was developed by Sun Microsystems as an object-oriented language well suited for distributed, online, networked applications. Both of these technologies have gained wide acceptance. Since then, developers have often had to choose, or sometimes just debate, which of these two tools were best for their needs.

At times this has appeared as some sort of religious war. "My language is better than your language." It shouldn't be. These are two separate technologies, each designed for different, but overlapping purposes. In many ways it's like the offline discussions that occur regularly about should a given CD-ROM be developed using Director or C++. It depends.

The comparison here is between a multimedia authoring tool and a general-purpose programming language. One has a HyperTalk-like scripting language, and the other uses a C++-like syntax. Both are supported on a wide variety of operating systems. Relevant factors include what type of experience the developers have, what level of programming expertise is available, the time constraints, the nature of the application, and so on. If it's a multimedia application and/or you have experience with Director then the choice leans toward Director. If you're building an online multiuser spreadsheet application then the choice would likely be Java.

As a matter of fact, just before this book went to press, Macromedia and Netscape announced an agreement on a new technology they called Fireworks. Fireworks will provide multimedia extensions to Java programmers based on Macromedia-developed technology (the Director engine perhaps?). So it may be that, in the end, developers will be able to use the best of both these technologies without resorting to an either-or decision.

Bandwidth, Evil Bandwidth

Before we go off and build gigantic, CD-ROM-quality Director movies for the Internet we need to discuss the problematic issue known as bandwidth.

Just a few short years ago, CD-ROM developers used to complain incessantly about how darn slow single-speed CD drives were. How great it would be to get more than 150 kilobytes of data per second delivered to our multimedia application. Then came double-speed drives (giving 300KB/s throughput) and things got much better. Not great, but better. Then came the Web, and things got worse. Much worse. At least as far as throughput was concerned, this was orders of magnitude slower.

In the online world, throughput is known as bandwidth: the speed at which data can be transferred through your connection. As you're probably aware, the average speed at which most home users are connected to the Internet is 14.4 or 28.8kbps. Notice the small b in that measure. That's kilo-BITS per second. Not bytes. This translates to approximately 2KB (kilobytes) per second. And don't forget, in most situations this is the maximum data rate, and actual real-world throughput can often be much less than that.

Therefore, the average modem-enabled Web surfer has a throughput rate that is one-hundredth of the speed of a single-speed CD-ROM drive. One-hundredth! That makes compression all the more important than it ever was. Thus, the need for Afterburner. Afterburner often compresses Director movies somewhere between 40 and 70 percent of their original size (an approximate 2:1 compression ratio). This translates to a proportional savings in each user's download time.

TIP A good rule of thumb to use in estimating download times is a rate of 1KB/sec as the base measure. This is the average throughput of a 14.4 modem (and it is what a 28.8 modem gets on a subaverage or busy connection). This means if you have a 60KB Shockwave movie you can expect the average dial-up user to wait for one minute for this single file to download to his or her computer. If you wish to be very optimistic you can halve this time to approximate a good speed for a 28.8 modem. The key is to put yourself in the shoes of your online visitor when creating and sizing your movies to ask "Would I wait (staring at my browser) X seconds or even X minutes for this movie to download? Or would I hit the Stop button?" This is ultimately a very important question.

Besides the bandwidth issue, the second major issue in designing for Shockwave (and online in general) is latency. Latency refers to the delay between the time you ask for something and the time the request is heard on the other end. Latency only compounds the bandwidth issue.

The Internet is a patchwork collection of smaller networks. Hundreds of individual networks each with their own size and performance characteristics are all tied together with the online equivalent of duct tape. Transmission speeds vary widely within and across these various networks. Thus, how quickly you can get a file from a particular server out on the Internet is a factor of many variables including: your connection speed (is it a 14.4 baud modem, a 28.8 modem, or an ISDN line?), the quality and access speeds available from your Internet Service Provider (ISP), the current overall Net load (is there a lot of other traffic?), the number of intermediate networks between you and your destination, and finally, the connection speed of the server at the other end. It's a complex process, one in which these are only some of factors that influence how long you'll wait to get a Web page or transfer a file at any given time. The moral is that it's usually unwise to count on high-performance throughput.

By using tools like Afterburner developers can help minimize the evils of limited bandwidth. This is certainly not the last time we'll look at issues of bandwidth: Throughout this part of the book this subject will reappear. Unfortunately.

Online Resources

The following section outlines some of the most useful Web sites available to assist you in developing your Director and Shockwave movies.

Browser Information

http://www.netscape.com Netscape Corporation's home page. Download Navigator and the Shockwave plug-in from here. Plenty of information and links on Web development topics.

http://www.microsoft.com/ie Microsoft's Internet Explorer home page. Can download their browser from here. Extensive IE-related resources and guides.

http://www.browserwatch.com An excellent place for all sorts of browser-related news and links. Comprehensive list of plug-ins. Covers Netscape, Internet Explorer, and other browsers.

Director Information

http://www.macromedia.com Lots of Shockwave and Director resources. Get the plug-in and the ActiveX control here. Get Afterburner and the streaming audio Xtras here. Includes Shockwave development guides (see below).

http://www.mcli.dist.maricopa.edu/director/ "Director Web": Has loads of resources on Director and Shockwave. Includes sections on Object-Oriented programming in Lingo, Xtras and XObjects, demos, code snippets, and digests from Direct-L (the Director mailing list). Shockwave tidbits include the Shockwave Frequently Asked Questions list (the FAQ).

Shockwave Information

http://www.macromedia.com/shockwave/index.html Macromedia's main Shockwave page. Includes links to the latest version of Afterburner, the Shockwave Developer's Guide, and a Support Area.

http://www.macromedia.com/shockwave/audio/audio.html The Shockwave Audio Developer's Guide. Shows how to get Audio Xtras and create the audio files. This site also provides a complete reference for the new Lingo streaming audio commands.

http://www.macromedia.com/shockwave/new/vanguard/ Macromedia's index to who's on the "Shockwave Vanguard." Includes links to many sites, often music related, that use Shockwave's streaming audio.

http://www.shocker.com Links to hundreds of Shockwave-enabled sites. Alphabetically listed and searchable database. You can subscribe to the associated Shocker mailing list with updates of Shockwave news, tips, and sites.

http://www.webcontent.com/shocker/digests/index.html#search A terrific searchable index of the digests from the Shocker Mailing list.

Multimedia Information

http://viswiz.gmd.de/MultimediaInfo/ One of the best lists of links to multimedia resources on the Net. Fully categorized.

HTML & Web Site Construction

http://www.netscape.com/assist/net_sites/ Netscape's guide to "Creating Net Sites." Resources for HTML authoring, HTML extensions, Gif89a, Javascript, imagemaps, and more.

http://www.netscape.com/eng/mozilla/2.0/relnotes/demo/target.html TARGET tag reference. Useful when programming with NetLingo like gotoNetPage.

http://www.netscape.com/assist/net_sites/frames.html FRAMES reference. Again, useful in HTML authoring and NetLingo programming.

http://www.microsoft.com/workshop/ Microsoft's Site Builder Workshop. The ActiveX Control Pad is available for download from this site. Lots of material but is often very Windows-centric (no surprise). Still very useful.

http://hoohoo.ncsa.uiuc.edu/cgi/overview.html The CGI (Common Gateway Interface) specification for allowing external (gateway) programs to interface with Web servers. Includes a good overview, detailed specification and sample CGI programs.

http://home.netscape.com/assist/net_sites/html_extensions_3.html. Reference for HTML 3 extensions including client-side imagemaps.

http://home.netscape.com/eng/mozilla/Gold/handbook/javascript/index.html
Netscape's resources for JavaScript. Includes both a programming introduction and reference.

Chapter Summary

In this chapter we introduced the fundamental concepts and technology behind Shockwave. Some of these items were historical background, others conceptual background, and some were technical:

- The early developments in multimedia on the Internet and World Wide Web

- What *helper applications* are: separate programs that work in conjunction with a Web browser to help it manage data types it doesn't have the built-in ability to handle

- What *Shockwave* is: Macromedia's technology for publishing Director movies over the Internet

- The two sides of Shockwave: the production side and the playback side

- The three main pieces of Shockwave: Afterburner, the plug-in, and NetLingo

- What *Afterburner* is: a Director Xtra that compresses Director movies to a smaller file size so they download more quickly across the Internet

- What *browser plug-ins* are: dynamically loadable programs that extend the capabilities of the browser to handle new types of data

- How plug-ins work: the browser loads them at runtime and they display data directly into a Web page within the browser's main window

- The two flavors of Shockwave: the Netscape-compatible plug-in and the Internet Explorer-compatible Active Shockwave control

- What *HTML* is: the HyperText Markup Language used in formatting the contents of documents on the Web

- The basics of how to use *the EMBED tag* to incorporate a Shockwave movie into a Web page

- Some of the key differences between *Shockwave and Java*: one is a cross-plat-form, multimedia authoring tool with Internet-enhanced capabilities; the other is a general-purpose, cross-platform programming language designed for online applications

- What *bandwidth* is: the speed at which data can be transferred to a given online connection, and why it is important: we want the smallest file size possi-ble for our Shockwave movies (so users are willing to wait for them to be downloaded over their limited-bandwidth connection)

- That the throughput (or bandwidth) of the average Internet connection is one-hundredth the speed of a single-speed CD-ROM drive. Very slow!

Creating Shockwave Movies

Chapter Objective

In this chapter we'll take what we've learned about Lingo and add in some Shockwave, Afterburner, and a little HTML to construct an interactive, fully shocked Web page. By the end of this chapter you'll be familiar with all the key steps necessary to create Shockwave movies for the Internet.

Our project for this chapter is an interactive, dynamic imagemap allowing users to visit selected Web sites using our Shockwave-enabled navigation bar. We'll tackle this problem in two exercises:

1. Go through the process of creating a simple, rollover-based Shockwave movie and integrating it into a Web page.

2. Make it really functional by using the new network-enabled Lingo commands.

During the course of building this project we'll address many of the most important Shockwave development issues.

The Shockwave Development Process

There's a basic flow to developing in Shockwave that differs from the process we've followed so far. Here's how it goes:

1. Plan.

2. Build the movie.

3. Compress the movie with Afterburner.

4. Write the HTML.

5. Test in browser locally.

6. Upload to Web site.

7. Test over the Net.

8. Repeat steps 2–7 as necessary (optimizing, debugging, and fine-tuning).

Up until this point we've been concerned with steps 1 and 2: movie planning and construction (along with some of step 8's debugging and refinement process). Steps 3–7 are unique to creating Shockwave movies. Even those steps that we looked at previously are handled somewhat differently when building a Shockwave movie; we'll look at those differences in this chapter. Note that there are additional substeps within each stage, especially step 2, and it's possible to change the order somewhat (for example, the HTML could be written before the movie is constructed).

Shockwave Movie Project:
The NavMan Navigation Bar

Our first Shockwave project is designed to be very simple. We'll build it in two main exercises:

Exercise 1: Integrating a simple rollover-sensitive Shockwave movie into a Web page.

Exercise 2: Adding the ability to load other Web pages into a separate browser frame by clicking on the movie's hotspots.

The first exercise introduces no new Lingo concepts. The goal is to cover each of the various steps necessary in building any Shockwave movie without complicating the issue. Many a developer has run into stumbling blocks just getting started with this patchwork of tools—Director, Afterburner, HTML editors, Web servers, browsers, and plug-ins—and making them all get along. By the end of this project it should be clear to you how this whole process works and where the pitfalls are.

The second exercise takes our movie and makes it into a useful tool by adding the ability to jump to other Web pages. We then have an interactive Shockwave implementation of a more traditional (and very static) imagemap or navigation bar. (On the Web an **imagemap** is an embedded GIF or JPEG image that responds to mouse clicks on a per-region basis. Each region is assigned its own URL and can thus lead to different actions. Typical actions are loading of other pages or running a CGI script on a server.) In our Shockwave movie we'll add this capability through Sprite handlers that use the new network-based Lingo command *gotoNetMovie*.

Figure 10.1 shows what the final version of the movie looks like.

Our Shockwave movie is contained in the upper frame of the browser. When you roll the mouse over any of the buttons an animated surfer appears beneath it. By clicking on one of these images you'll cause the browser to load that site's home page into the lower frame.

To try the completed Shockwave version of the movie, load the Web page Ch10fram.htm in the Chap10 directory on the CD-ROM into your Shockwave-enabled browser. If you wish to try the same completed version in Director, open the file Ch10done.dir from the same directory (note that you cannot use the Lingo network extensions from within Director—we'll discuss this later in the chapter). The unscripted, Lingo-free version that we'll start with is named Ch10.dir.

Planning the Movie

The first thing to understand about developing movies for Shockwave is the importance of planning. Sure, you've heard it before. But in this case the issue concerns keeping in mind the ultimate goal of your movie. It's not a CD-ROM. It's a Web page. They are not the same thing. It sounds simple, but you'll occasionally hear someone say "Yeah, just take your Director movie and convert it." And that may work. But it's not always so straightforward. The conversion isn't just in the movie itself; it's also in the conceptualization of how it's to be designed and built. The

Figure 10.1 The final movie.

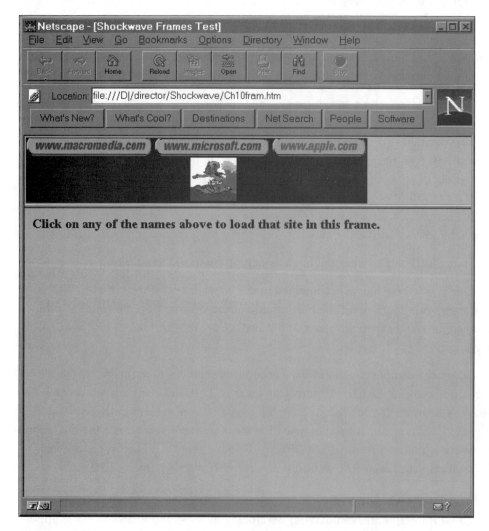

Web is a different medium with its own distinct characteristics (such as very low bandwidth). We want to address these factors from the beginning.

For example, let's look at the plan for our first project. Ultimately what we want from this movie are mouse-sensitive interactivity, the ability to navigate to other Web pages by clicking on a Sprite, small size, and effective Web page integration. The inter-activity we can achieve by using the type of *rollover*-based Lingo we've used before, and the navigation we'll get by using the new NetLingo commands. Then at that point we still need to consider size, integration, and any Shockwave-specific issues.

In addressing the size issue we want to accommodate the needs and expectations of our audience. Who is the audience? In this case it's average Net surfers often connecting through dial-up modems. Therefore, size matters. Many GIF-based navigation bars and imagemaps range in size from 10 to 30KB each. And that should be our goal: to give Net surfers a more highly interactive and fun experience than with an ordinary imagemap but not make them wait longer to get it.

Second, let's consider how we plan to integrate this movie into our Web page. Our goal is to use this as a navigation bar that fits within a single, horizontal browser frame. This Web page integrated design impacts the movie's dimensions, its background, its palette, and its behavior. This is in contrast to traditional Director movies that like to operate on their own, occupy the whole screen, and essentially take-over the computer. Here, in the context of a Web page, the Shockwave movie is just one piece of the puzzle.

Third, we'll need to keep in mind the differences in capabilities between a Shockwave movie and a Director movie. For example, some Director and Lingo features have been disabled in the interest of security, and others are not yet available. In general this is not a major obstacle because only a limited number of features are not available in Shockwave 5, but it is still worth considering up front. Chapter 11 includes a brief outline of disabled Director features.

Setting the Stage

Open the file Ch10.dir in the Chap10 directory on the CD-ROM. The movie contains all the Cast Members we'll need for this project and the Stage is empty (Figure 10.2).

We'll begin with one of the first questions that needs to be answered before creating any Shockwave movie: What should its dimensions be? We don't want to begin creating Cast Members or positioning Sprites on the Stage until we've decided on its size. As you've seen, most Director movies are designed for playback at a standard 640×480 resolution. That's fine for CD-ROM titles but it won't work for Shockwave movies. They have to share the screen (and the computer) with other programs, most notably the browser itself. Look at the example in Figure 10.3.

As you can see, with a typical browser window on a 640×480 screen the maximum size remaining for a Shockwave movie is somewhere around 600×400 pixels (or even 400×300 for those Web surfers who size their browser windows in a vertical, portrait orientation). And that's only if you want the movie to fill the entire remaining space: If you wish to have HTML text, images, or other elements visible

Figure 10.2 The Directory environment with all the Cast Members and the empty Stage.

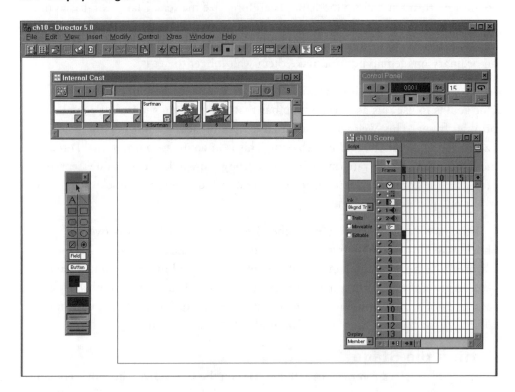

along with your Shockwave movie then, of course, the movie size will need to be decreased further. Finally, one other problem that arises when creating Shockwave movies with large Stages is just that: size. The Stage then needs to be filled with something. Often this can translate into larger graphics and bigger files, which in turn lead again to longer download times.

When choosing the appropriate size for our navigation bar we don't want to use more screen real estate than we need to. Following the model of most horizontally oriented navigation bars we'll make our movie 480 pixels wide by 90 pixels high. This will allow the movie to fit nicely within our planned horizontal window frame.

So let's change the movie's size. Select Movie/Properties from the Modify menu (or use Cmd-Shift-D on the Mac or Ctrl-Shift-D on Windows) to bring up the dialog box shown in Figure 10.4.

Figure 10.3 The browser.

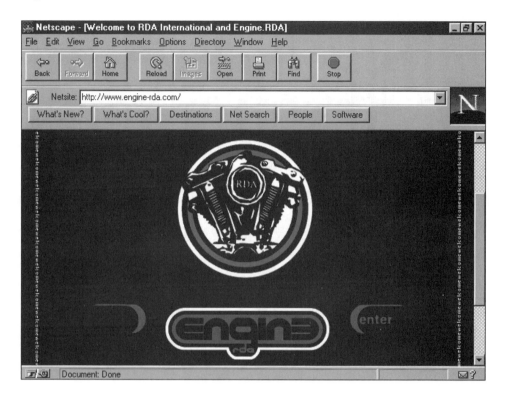

In the Stage Size fields of Width and Height enter our new dimensions of 480 and 90, respectively. Select OK to close the dialog box. The Stage is now resized to our desired horizontally oriented shape. (If it is not centered in your window and you would like it to be, go to the File/Preferences/General menu option and make sure Stage: Center option is selected.)

With that detail out of the way we can begin putting the movie together. First, we need to set the background. For simplicity's sake (and to save on file size) we'll use a solid black background. Again, from the Movie Properties dialog, use the Stage Color item to select black as background color for this movie.

Next, drag each of the Cast Members 1 through 3 onto the Stage and position them side-by-side, as shown in Figure 10.5. Select all three Sprites in the Score Window and set the ink to Background Transparent.

Figure 10.4 Movie properties dialog box.

Adjusting Width and Height settings
in the Movie properties dialog box.

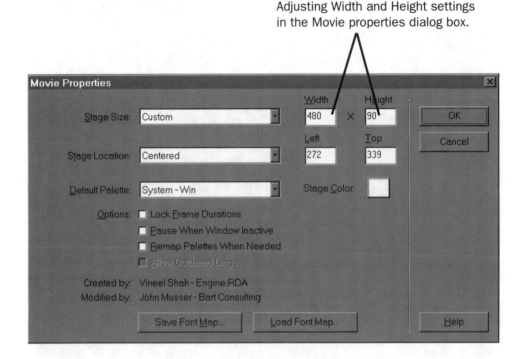

The last visual component of this movie we need to set up is the Net surfer. He's been created as a Film Loop in Cast Member 4. What's a Film Loop? It's a type of Cast Member that acts a multi-image animation. This can be very convenient because it allows you to treat a series of related images, like two images of a man surfing, as a single Sprite. When you use a Film Loop in a movie it automatically sequences through its individual images without your having to swap images in and out

Figure 10.5 Cast Members 1 through 3.

manually. You create one by laying out a related sequence of bitmap Cast Members in a single Sprite Channel across a series of frames. Then select those cells in the Score and choose Film Loop from the Insert menu. A dialog box asks you to name the new Film Loop and when you select OK the Film Loop appears in the Cast Window.

In this movie the Film Loop has already been created for you. Drag the Net surfer Film Loop out onto the Stage and center it beneath the first button on the left.

Now we need to prepare for making it appear and disappear. Remember that we don't want it to appear under this button, or any others, until the user actually moves the mouse over each button's Sprite. We'll do this using a standard Director trick of moving the Sprite completely off the Stage. By initially positioning this Sprite outside the visible field of view (off to stage-left) it's effectively out of sight until we use Lingo to move it where we want (underneath whichever button the user has rolled over). It's just like in real theater where actors remain just off to the left or right of the Stage until it's their turn to be on.

Select the surfer Sprite and bring up the Sprite Properties dialog box. Change the Left location entry to be –100, but leave the Top location at its current setting. The negative offset means move the Sprite 100 pixels from the left-hand side of the Stage (which is horizontal offset 0). When you select OK to close this dialog box you'll see that this Sprite no longer appears on the Stage. But how do you know it's still there? Because it still appears in the Score in Channel 4. You can select and modify this Sprite from there.

In the Score Window, copy these four Sprites across to frames 2 and 3. This allows Director to do its housekeeping initializations and cleanup in frames 1 and 3 and we can safely add our Lingo in frame 2.

Adding Interactivity

Now it's time to add some interactivity to our movie (which means it must be time for some Lingo). Because this first exercise is intended to introduce Shockwave and not any new Lingo we'll use the type of rollover techniques we've used before.

Start by adding a new frame handler to frame 2 (where all the interaction will occur) and enter the following code:

```
on exitFrame

  if (rollover(1)) then
```

```
        set the locH of sprite 4 to 90

    else if (rollover(2)) then

        set the locH of sprite 4 to 260

    else if (rollover(3)) then

        set the locH of sprite 4 to 410

    else

        set the locH of sprite 4 to -100

    end if

    go the frame

end
```

This code checks to see if the mouse is over any of the Sprites-acting-as-buttons that we're interested in. Three *if* statements check Channels 1, 2, and 3 to see if the cursor is over that Channel's Sprite. If so, it moves the hidden Film Loop Sprite into the correct location on the Stage under this button (note that you may want to change the *locH* offsets to match your placement of the buttons on the stage). If none of the *rollover* calls returns TRUE then we'll just move the surfer Sprite back off to the left of the Stage. We then keep looping in the frame until the user leaves this Web page (and thus our movie). This is all the interactivity that we'll need for the first version of the movie.

Note that using *go the frame* here is pretty important. Shockwave movies are different than Director movies in that they don't automatically loop back to the beginning once they reach the last frame. This is one of those little differences you need to be aware of. Because most real Director movies use Lingo for navigation rather than relying on the built-in looping this isn't usually a problem. Just keep this in mind if you make a small Shockwave movie that doesn't seem to respond in the browser—it could have just run to the end and stopped.

If you now play this movie you'll see that, well, this doesn't work. Why not? Because we haven't puppetted Sprite 4, and so Director dutifully ignores our Lingo instructions to change its position. We can easily remedy this situation by adding a *puppetSprite* call once at the beginning in the *startMovie* Script (we never have to unpuppet this Sprite because throughout the movie we want it under Lingo control).

Add a new Movie Script and enter the following code:

```
on startMovie

   puppetSprite 4, TRUE

end
```

At this point if we run the movie it should behave as we expect and the surfer should do his thing under each of the buttons. If all is working well, then recompile all Scripts and save the movie (a very important step).

This type of quick testing while in Director is important: Before proceeding to the next step of using Afterburner always try to test the movie first. It's much easier to debug and diagnose problems within the Director environment than it is once the movie's inside a Web page. In Shockwave development the testing process is broken into two parts. This is the first stage. The second comes later when we test the movie as it runs within the browser. We'll look in more detail at Shockwave debugging issues in Chapter 11.

Once the movie seems to be functioning as we expect it's time to move on to the next step: compressing the movie with Afterburner.

Movies on Fire
(or Learning to Burn with Afterburner)

As you recall from our earlier discussion, on the Web bandwidth is king. Nothing influences the design of multimedia for the Web more than the obsession with optimizing performance to live within the constraints imposed by the online world's ridiculously limited throughput. This means the smaller, the better. This is where Afterburner comes in.

Afterburner is a Director Xtra whose job is to compress Director movies down to as small a size as possible. (In addition it protects your movie just as creating protected movies and projectors does.) As we saw in Chapter 9, it's one part of the overall Shockwave puzzle: Afterburner is used on the production side in making the movie Web-ready, and the Shockwave plug-in is used in a browser to play that movie back. (If you don't have Afterburner installed on your system see the section below on how to do so.)

Making Director Afterburner-Enabled

Before you can make shocked movies you need to make sure Afterburner is properly installed on your system. Prior to Director 5, Afterburner was a separate executable that was run outside of the Director environment. Starting with version 5, however, this was changed; now Afterburner is an Xtra accessed via Director's Xtras menu. If you don't already have this installed then follow the steps outlined below.

1. *Get the Afterburner Installer.* The best way to obtain the most recent version of Afterburner is to download it from the Macromedia Web site (www.macromedia .com). Follow the links to the Shockwave section and then into the Developer's section. Download the compressed Afterburner setup file to your local machine (perhaps best done to a temporary or scratch folder—you'll probably want to erase this file once the setup is complete).

2. *Run the Installer.* Run the downloaded executable. Follow the instructions given by the setup program. Once this is done, Afterburner should be present in the appropriate Xtras folder on your system (underneath the Director folder).

3. *Startup Director.* Once Afterburner is installed and you launch Director you will notice that two items have been added to the bottom of the Xtras menu (Figure 10.6)

The last menu item invokes the Afterburner Xtra, allowing you to save the current movie as a compressed .dcr file, and the item above it allows you to set options for compressing audio in your movie (which we will review in Chapter 11). Director is now ready to burn Shockwave movies for you.

Moving Forward

Before we send our movie through Afterburner let's review some Shockwave-compatible vocabulary. Compressing a movie through Afterburner is sometimes referred to as "burning," as in "Did you burn the movie yet?" The output of burning is often called a "burnt" or "shocked" movie and a "shocked" Web page or site is one containing shocked movies.

Two nit-picky things you must do prior to sending any movie through Afterburner are:

Figure 10.6 Xtras menu with Afterburner.

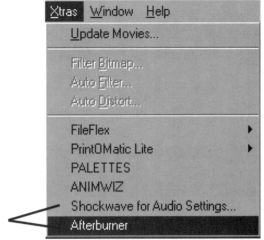

After installing Afterburner, these two items will show up in the Xtras menu.

1. Recompile all Lingo scripts.

2. Save the movie file.

If need be, recompile the scripts (by selecting Recompile All Scripts from the Control menu) and save the file now.

With the movie open in Director, select Xtras/Afterburner from the menu. The standard Save File dialog box appears (Windows or Mac), asking you to specify a name for your compressed movie. The suggested filename ends in .DCR (the C is for Compressed), just as the conventional file extension for Director movies is .DIR. The Windows version is shown in Figure 10.7.

As you can see, there are not a lot of options presented at this point. All you do is choose the name of the .dcr file to be created, and that's it. Afterburner does the rest. It's not that you don't have any options; it's just that you've exercised them in the decisions you made in constructing your movie. That's why planning a Shockwave movie is so important. You don't have a dozen options available at the end where you can say "Oh, yeah, by the way, set these seven options so it'll be small and fast. Thanks."

On the other hand, tweaking your movie *is* usually an option. If the shocked movie is too large, slow, or otherwise doesn't behave as expected, you can always go

Figure 10.7 Save File dialog box.

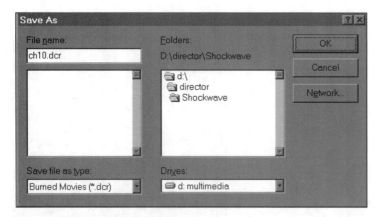

back, modify the movie, burn again, and so on. This is a very common process. Things rarely turn out just right on the first try. Don't be afraid to fine-tune your Shockwave creation. Many of the best techniques used by the experts were discovered in just such a fashion. Some call this iterative refinement; others call it trial-and-error; and to others it's just called multimedia authoring.

Back to our project. Save the movie with the suggested name, Ch10.dcr, in a folder of your choice. Once you select Save, a dialog box will appear showing Afterburner's progress in compressing and saving the file. The larger the movie, the longer the compression takes. For this movie, on a decent computer, it only takes a few seconds.

By the way, the folder you save this file in is important inasmuch as we'll be putting other related files in this same location—specifically, the HTML Web page for this movie.

> **NOTE** Once a movie has been compressed with Afterburner it cannot be opened in Director. You can still open the original .DIR movie but not the compressed .DCR (which is similar to what happens with projectors—you can't open and edit them). If you later find bugs in your movie or wish to make changes to it you'll need to go back to the original DIR movie and recompress it once you've made your changes.

HTML Meets Shockwave

As I briefly mentioned earlier, HTML is pretty simple. It's a way of describing the visual layout of pages of text, images, and other media through the use of tags.

Web browsers know how to read these tags and display the data accordingly. Standard tags are available to describe many basic page layout operations: specifying headings, paragraphs, image locations, hypertext links, and so on. For a good overview of HTML and other useful references on the subject see the links outlined in the Resources section at the end of Chapter 9.

An HTML file is just plain old ASCII text, the kind you can edit with nearly any text editor such as Notepad on Windows or SimpleText on the Mac. That's what we'll do now. Open your favorite text editor and enter the following text:

```
<HTML>

<HEAD>

<TITLE>A Shockwave Rollover Bar</TITLE>

</HEAD>

<BODY>

<EMBED SRC="ch10.dcr" WIDTH=480 HEIGHT=90>

</BODY>

</HTML>
```

Now save this file out as Ch10.htm in the same folder in which you saved the shocked version of the NavMan movie (Ch10.dcr).

That's essentially the minimalist set of HTML needed to get a Shockwave movie into a Web page (and, as you can see, it doesn't take much). The part we're most interested in is the *EMBED* tag. As noted in Chapter 9, this is what causes our Shockwave movie to be loaded, or "embedded," into the page. The tag, first recognized by Netscape Navigator starting in version 2.0, identifies external data to be displayed on the Web page through the use of a plug-in. This same syntax is recognized by Internet Explorer as well.

The browser itself uses the *SRC* attribute of the *EMBED* tag to determine the name of the file to load (the *SRC*, *WIDTH*, and *HEIGHT* items are called attributes; they are arguments or properties of the *EMBED* tag). It then checks for the extension of that file, "dcr" in this case, and matches that against its list of registered plug-ins. Each registered plug-in has one or more associated file extensions that it says it can handle. When the browser finds an extension that matches, it then loads the appropriate plug-in (if it's not already loaded), and gives it the file to display. It sets aside a 480×90 pixel area for it to draw in and let it do its thing. When the user leaves this page the browser unloads both this file and the plug-in.

From that point forward, an ongoing negotiation and delicate dance occurs between the browser and the plug-in. They don't always get along. Occasionally the two want to draw on the same area, or the plug-in doesn't always get redraw messages, or it doesn't get keyboard input when it should, and so on. Over time these incompatibilities have lessened, but they still exist. Also keep in mind that this is fresh-out-of-the-box technology. It may not always work as advertised. The Shockwave plug-in has come a long way in the short time it's been available, but it is still a work in progress.

Installing the Shockwave Plug-in for Netscape Navigator and Internet Explorer

Before Netscape Navigator can load a Shockwave movie, it must have the Shockwave plug-in installed. Here are the basic steps to follow to get and install the plug-in:

1. Download the compressed version of Shockwave setup program from the Macromedia Web site. Follow the links to Shockwave and download the file to your local machine (currently the plug-in is located at http://www.macromedia .com/shockwave). Once the file is downloaded, exit Navigator.

2. Run this executable. It automatically decompresses to the Shockwave setup program. Follow the instructions given. This should install the necessary plug-in files under your Netscape Navigator folder.

3. Restart Navigator. (Netscape recognizes that having to exit and re-start the browser is laborious and error-prone. It's likely that this process will be significantly streamlined with the release of Navigator 4.0.) Find a shocked Web page to try.

For the latest updates to this process as well as detailed installation instructions check the download section of the Macromedia Web site.

With Microsoft's Internet Explorer (IE 3.0) the process of installing Shockwave is already streamlined. Just start up IE, go to the Shockwave section of the Macromedia site, and follow the link to the ActiveX Control for Shockwave. Once there, the Active Shockwave main page informs you that "The Shockwave for ActiveX control is now installing." Through the use of the new HTML *OBJECT* tag (which we'll discuss later), the browser automatically recognizes that it needs a new ActiveX control to display the Shockwave file on this page. It uses the URL specified in the *OBJECT* tag to go retrieve the Active Shockwave control. At this point the browser begins displaying a progress bar to the user while it downloads Active Shockwave (which can, unfortunately, take quite some time—it's a very large file).

Once the Shockwave files have been downloaded to the local computer IE displays the dialog box shown in Figure 10.8

If you select OK to this, the control installation completes, the control automatically loads into the browser, and the page you were hoping to see now magically loads with the movie.

Figure 10.8 Certificate dialog box.

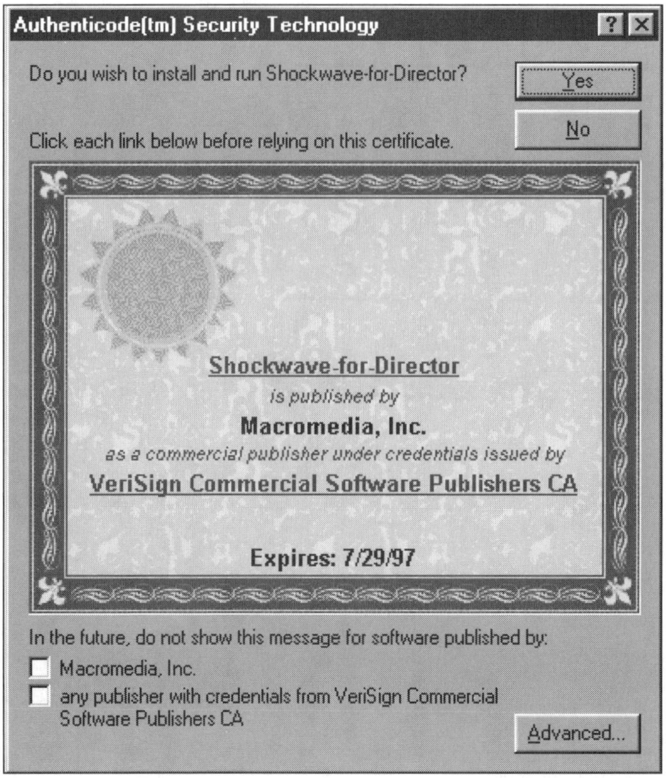

Loading It onto the Browser

Now that we have the movie, the HTML, and the plug-in ready, it's time to load it into the browser. Start up Navigator and choose "Open File..." from the File menu or start Internet Explorer and choose "Open" from the File menu. Enter the full path and name of the HTML file you just created. If the plug-in is correctly installed your shocked movie should load. Figure 10.9 shows what our movie looks like in Netscape Navigator.

Figure 10.9 Movie displayed in Netscape Navigator.

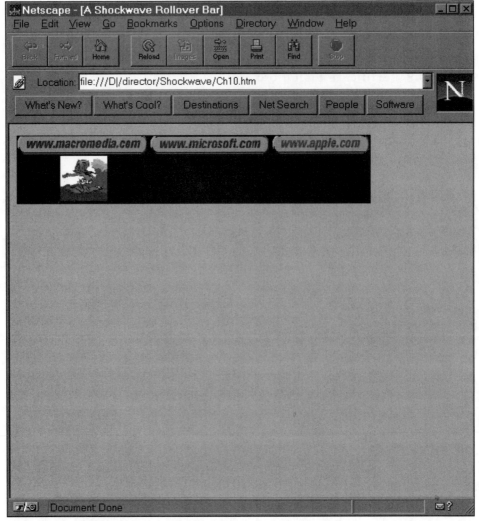

As you roll the mouse over the movie's Sprites they should respond with the animated man.

That's a big step. We've constructed the movie, made a Web page for it, and tested it locally in a browser. Not bad. That takes us up through the first five steps of creating Shockwave movies.

Now is a good time to mention a couple of other tips that may save you time during the development of your Shockwave movies:

1. You may want to add a Bookmark in your browser that points to this page. That way you can quickly get to, test, and experiment with your movie (during development you'll often find yourself running both Director and a browser at the same time while switching back-and-forth between them). You can always remove the Bookmark later.

2. The browser will allow you to open a movie without using HTML. You can use the Open command from the File menu to directly read in your Shockwave movie. The browser will identify the file type based on its extension (.DCR) and load the Shockwave plug-in. (Sometimes the HTML will be necessary because you may want to use it to pass special parameters to your movie. This will be true for our movie in Chapter 11.)

3. Both browsers support drag-and-drop of files. That means you can just drag a movie file from the Finder (on the Mac) or Explorer (on Windows) directly into the browser's main window. It will load the movie just as above.

4. The Shockwave plug-in can read normal Director files as well as burned Shockwave movies. Anywhere you would refer to a .DCR file you can use a .DIR or .DXR file as well: from the menu, drag-and-drop, and HTML. You can use this to save the Afterburner step during early browser testing of the movie.

What Does Afterburner Do?

Afterburner's main purpose is to compress Director movies. As you've seen, it's simple to use: Select it from the Xtras menu, select a filename, and you're done. But what happens to the movie during that compression process?

When you think about it, most non-text data transmitted over the Internet is compressed: GIF images, JPEG images, RealAudio, and Quicktime—each of these has its own internal data compression formats. In addition, other types of data files that don't use internal compression (such as word processor documents) are normally compressed with some archiving tool like ZIP or STUFFIT before being sent across the Internet. It's nearly all compressed in some fashion. Sometimes it's even compressed twice, like a ZIPed Quicktime movie.

Compression of any data is usually done in one of two forms: *lossy* or *lossless*. Lossy compression uses sophisticated algorithms to throw away some of the information from the original source data in order to save on size. In so doing it loses some of the quality of the original data. Lossy compressors are often tailored to the type of data being compressed, such as video or audio information (so that they can be "smart" about reducing the information that is least "needed"). The Cinepak codec for Quicktime video (codec meaning: COmpressor/DECompressor) is a good example of a lossy compression scheme: The video quality degrades somewhat, but in return we can get larger window sizes, smaller file sizes and a data rate that allows playback from a CD-ROM. It's a trade-off between image quality and size reduction.

Lossless compression, on the other hand, is just that: lossless—it doesn't permit any of the data to be lost. The data is exactly the same before and after compression. Lossless compression algorithms are used by all archive programs like ZIP. You don't want to get out fewer bits than you put in. If your spreadsheet unzipped with a few of the digits missing, you would have a serious problem.

The original Afterburner used a lossless compression scheme. The movie that was decompressed by the Shockwave browser plug-in was exactly the same as it was before being sent through Afterburner. Afterburner for Shockwave 5 uses both lossy and lossless compression. With the addition of compressed streaming audio Afterburner allows you to use lossy compression on this data. As we'll see in Chapter 11, the degree of compression (and, therefore, the amount of data loss and degradation in sound quality) can be selected when the movie is burned. The graphics data is still compressed using lossless algorithms.

Using the EMBED Tag

Let's look in more detail at the HTML *EMBED* tag used to incorporate Shockwave movies into a Web page. This tag accepts a number of parameters that you should know how to use. (Note that the *EMBED* tag is used to specify data types that the browser doesn't have the built-in capability to handle. Some of the parameters to this tag are shared by all plug-ins, such as *SRC*, but others are specific to the data type being embedded. For example, the Quicktime plug-in supports parameters such as *AUTOPLAY* and *LOOP*. The discussion here refers to those parameters relevant to embedding Shockwave movies.)

Any time this tag is used at least three attributes must be specified: *SRC*, *WIDTH*, and *HEIGHT*. All other *EMBED* tags attributes are optional. Table 10.1 summarizes this tag and its attributes.

Table 10.1 EMBED Tag Attributes

Parameter	Example Usage	Description
SRC	SRC = "mymovie.dcr"	Specifies the URL of the movie to embed. Can be any valid HTTP URL (relative, absolute, or complete).
WIDTH	WIDTH = 300	The width of the movie in pixels.
HEIGHT	HEIGHT = 100	The height of the movie in pixels.
PARAMETER	MYTAG = "loop"	Allows any user-defined parameters. Can be read-in with the new NetLingo HTML parameter access commands.
TEXTFOCUS	TEXTFOCUS = onStart	Specifies when and if the movie should begin accepting keyboard input. Three possible values are:
		onStart: Accept keyboard input as soon as the movie is loaded into the Web page.
		onMouse: Start accepting input after the user has clicked inside the movie window with the mouse. (This is the default setting if you don't specify any TEXTFOCUS option.)
		never: All keyboard input is ignored.
PALETTE	PALETTE = foreground	Determines whether or not to us this movie's palette instead of the browser's palette. Two possible values are:
		foreground: Make this movie's palette the foreground palette and therefore override the browser's palette. (This is the default if you load the movie into the browser without any HTML.)

continued

Table 10.1 *Continued*

Parameter	Example Usage	Description
		background: Don't override the browser's palette with this movie's palette. (The default if you use the EMBED tag to include the movie.)
BGCOLOR	BGCOLOR = #FF0000	Specifies the hexadecimal RGB value of the background color to display in the movie's rectangle while the browser downloads the file. Works the same way as the BGCOLOR parameter to the HTML BODY tag. Each color value (Red, Green, Blue) can range from 00 to FF. Therefore, white would be #FFFFFF, black is #000000, and pure green would be #00FF00.

Some advice on the available *EMBED* parameters:

1. You almost always want to use the *BGCOLOR* parameter. Setting the background color helps integrate your movie with the surrounding Web page.

2. Be careful when using the *PALETTE* parameter. It's usually best to allow the browser and plug-in to take their normal course when displaying your movie (the browser uses its own palette and normally dithers all graphics to this set of colors—we'll discuss this further in Chapter 11). If you use a custom palette in your movie and specify that the plug-in should make it the foreground palette the results may be undesirable. The browser's palette management may become confused, other images on the page could be displayed with the wrong colors, the browser may not revert to the correct palette when you leave the page, and so on. Remember that your movie is not the only thing on-screen. Caveat emptor.

3. The URL given in the *SRC* attribute of the *EMBED* tag can be either a full, absolute, or relative URL (as was done here).

Wondering what happens if you happen to enter the wrong values for *WIDTH* and *HEIGHT*? It depends. Netscape will crop the movie to the size if it is smaller, and you will get extra space around your movie if you specify a size that's too large (it will position the movie in the upper-left corner of that area). Internet Explorer will behave similarly, the differences being that the lower-right portion of the movie will display if too small a size is specified and it will try to center the movie in the display area if the size is larger than the movie. Not surprisingly, therefore, it's always best to match these to the dimensions of your movie.

You'll want to be aware of one other important aspect of the *EMBED* tag: You can use it to pass data directly to your Shockwave Movie. Shockwave 5 added a set of three commands that let you access the values of parameters placed in this tag. For example, given the following *EMBED* tag:

```
<EMBED SRC="Ch10.dcr" WIDTH=480 HEIGHT=90 NEWURL="http://www.microsoft.com">
```

you can now use the new *externalParamValue* function to retrieve your own parameters you place in this tag. Here, we created a parameter NEWURL and could call *externalParamValue("NEWURL")* to retrieve the string http://www.microsoft.com. This can be very useful. You can pass in data values for Lingo variables, URLs to access, names of sounds to play, flag settings, and so on. You can make your Shockwave movies more reusable by including the same movie on multiple pages and then passing in page-specific information via the HTML. We'll revisit the use of this command in Chapter 11.

Troubleshooting Tips

If you're having trouble loading and displaying your Shockwave movies in your browser the following tips may be of help:

- Set the disk cache and memory cache sizes to 8MB or more.

- In Netscape, select the About Plug-ins item from the Help menu. This should list all the currently installed plug-ins. Make sure Shockwave is listed.

- In earlier versions of Shockwave, putting a movie inside an HTML table caused problems.

- Check the HTML syntax and the *EMBED* tag parameters.

NavMan 2: Using the *gotoNetPage* Command

We're now ready to make our first Shockwave movie really do something useful (watching the surfer come-and-go gets old pretty quickly). We'll use the new *gotoNetPage* Lingo command to make our movie serve as a functional navigation bar.

This will not require significant changes to our movie. All we need to do is add a short Sprite Script to each of the three button Sprites. Each Script will use *gotoNetPage* to load a different Web page.

In the same Ch10.dir movie we used before, in Frame 2 add the following Sprite Script in Channel 1:

```
on mouseUp

  gotoNetPage "http://www.macromedia.com"

end
```

The argument to the *gotoNetPage* command is the URL of the Web page to retrieve. Once the browser has retrieved this page it then *replaces the page containing this movie*. This means our movie will be unloaded at that time (so will the Shockwave plug-in).

It's important to be aware that this movie continues to play until the specified Web page has been retrieved and that no warning is given to our movie when that page arrives. This means there is no "Hey, I'm about to unload your movie!" message from the browser. As noted earlier, latency and bandwidth constraints both mean that getting and loading this new page will not happen as instantaneously as it would on your local machine.

When programming online applications it's always safest to assume that things will take longer than expected. For example, it's possible in the movie we've created for the user to click on one of the Sprites asking for a Web page. So we obediently call *gotoNetPage* asking for that page. Meanwhile, the user gets impatient, or maybe wasn't sure he or she really clicked on the Sprite, or maybe has a change of heart. So that user clicks another Sprite. And then clicks the original one again just for good measure. Things can get pretty confused. Therefore, we want to program defensively.

   Defensive programming in this case could be done in a number of ways. One
way is through better interface design, where we let the user know the page is on its
way. But this won't prevent users from madly clicking away. Another method is to
allow the user to select only one Web page. To do so you'd add a global state flag
variable that is set to TRUE once the user has chosen to load a Web page (set right
after any of the *gotoNetPage* calls). Then, in any of the Sprite Scripts you would
check to make sure this flag was not TRUE before loading any other Web pages
(you don't have to implement this code now):

```
on mouseDown

   global gLoading

   if (gLoading = FALSE) then

      gotoNetPage "http://www.acme.com"

      set gLoading = TRUE

   end if

end
```

   We won't add this code here because once we begin using this movie with
HTML frames we won't mind if users keep changing their mind and selecting a second page before the first has arrived. Our movie will just remain in a separate
browser window, happily loading new pages into the other browser frame.

   The next thing we do want to program now is very similar code to the other two
buttons. The only difference is that each refers to a different destination Web site.
In Channel 2 of Frame 2 use this code:

```
on mouseUp

   gotoNetPage "http://www.microsoft.com"

end
```

   And for Channel 3 use this code:

```
on mouseUp

   gotoNetPage "http://www.apple.com"

end
```

One other note about *gotoNetPage*: If the URL given is a relative URL it's considered relative to the location of the Shockwave movie on the server, not the location of the Web page in which the .DCR file is embedded (which may not be in the same directory). This could cause the page not to be found by the browser if you are keeping the HTML and Shockwave movies in different locations (a good argument for keeping them both in the same directory). This caveat applies to all the URLs specified using NetLingo commands.

Recompile the scripts and play the movie. Everything seems fine until you go to click on any of the buttons. When you do you'll get a dialog box like the one shown in Figure 10.10.

Director 5 does not recognize the *gotoNetPage* as a legal Lingo command. As a matter of fact, it doesn't know about any of the Shockwave Lingo extensions and will complain when you call any of them. This is a problem. Eventually Macromedia will fully integrate the Shockwave extensions into the authoring environment, but until then this problem will continue to give us Shockwave developers headaches.

Because Director 5 doesn't recognize these commands some sections of our movie can be tested only in a browser. We'll do that now. Take the movie and send it through Afterburner, overwriting the previous version of the Shockwave file. Make sure you're currently online (meaning connected to the Internet via dialing in or through a dedicated connection) and load the file in the browser (with File/Open to read the local HTML file). Now try to click on the buttons in the movie. What you should see, after a couple of seconds' delay, is your Shockwave movie's page replaced with the home page of the site you requested. This is very good; we're almost done.

Figure 10.10 Dialog box with "Handler not defined."

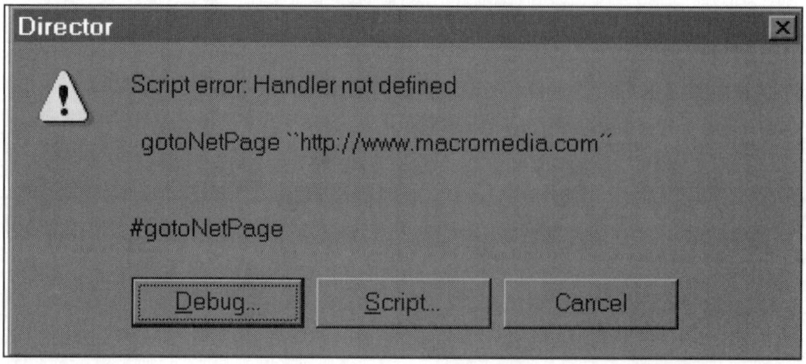

Uploading and Testing Your Movie from a Server

Now that we know our movie works as expected, it's time to actually try running it from a real-live Web server. This includes the last three steps of the Shockwave development process: uploading the file to the server, testing it over the Net, and refining or making any necessary changes to the movie. In addition, the first time you want to deliver Shockwave movies from your Web server you'll need to make sure that the server has been configured to do so. See the accompanying section for more on this process.

Making Your Web Server Shockwave-Aware

Some minor modifications must be made to your Web server to enable delivery of Shockwave movies to visiting Web surfers. This is usually a simple configuration change and can be performed by you or by your local Webmaster. Here's a quick review of the modifications needed.

The primary change is letting the Web server know that Shockwave movies have a MIME type of "application/x-director" and a file extension of ".dcr." What's a MIME type, you ask? Of course, it's yet another acronym: Multipurpose Internet Mail Extensions (MIME). This standard was initially used for allowing non-textual information such as multimedia data to be added to Internet mail messages. It has since been adopted for use by Web servers and Web browsers as a way to identify and coordinate transfer of different types of data between them.

MIME types specify any type of data in two parts: a content type and a subtype. Common types, sometimes known as categories, include application, image, and other. Each category contains a set of relevant subtypes. For example, within the image category are subtypes such as gif, jpeg, and bmp. The syntax for describing MIME types is "type/subtype" so for example a GIF file is represented as "image/gif." Since we want the Web server to recognize Shockwave movies as a new type of data we need to tell the server about this new type in terms it under-stands: MIME. And so somewhere in each server's configuration is a table of MIME types into which the new type "application/x-director" should be added. We also tell the server to identify these files by their .dcr extension. Usually this is done by editing a text file (srm.conf for NCSA servers and mime.types for a Netscape server) or using a dialog-box interface to make this change (as in Microsoft's Internet Information Server or the Mac-based WebSTAR server). That's usually all it takes to make a Web server deliver Shockwave movies.

Somehow, someway, you need to get this Shockwave movie, Ch10.dcr, loaded onto your Web server. This is normally fairly easy to do, but it can be tricky the first couple of times until you've got the kinks worked out of the process. Unless you're running a Web server on the same machine that you're authoring on (unlikely for most people) you'll need to use a transfer program to copy your Shockwave movie onto the correct machine. You may want to check with your system administrator about: the recommended way to transfer the files (usually using some form of FTP program), where the files should go, and to make sure the server is properly configured to deliver the movies.

When transferring Shockwave movies it's important to make sure you're using the "binary" or "binary raw" mode. This ensures that the file is not modified during transmission. You'll also want to transfer the Ch10.htm file to the same directory on the server (which is normally uploaded in an ASCII or text mode, not binary).

Final Tests

Once the files have been uploaded to the proper location on the server and the server has been configured to deliver Shockwave movies it's time for the final tests. Bring up the browser and enter the full URL for the Ch10.htm page on your server. If each of the configuration and transfer steps succeeded then the page should appear in the browser now, just as it did when we tested it locally.

Congratulations, you've now been through the complete Shockwave development process! All eight steps from beginning to end, and now your movie is online for the whole world to see.

Using HTML Frames with Lingo

The last thing we'll do in this project is to enhance our movie by using HTML frames to put our movie inside of one frame and then load the chosen Web sites into a separate frame. HTML frames allow the main browser window to be divided into multiple separate regions with each frame referring to a different URL. This allows our Shockwave movie to remain loaded and visible in a narrow horizontal strip at the top of the browser window while completely different Web sites are loaded into the larger frame below it. Adding this capability to our movie is relatively straightforward all we need is one change to the Lingo and some additional HTML.

The *gotoNetPage* command takes an optional second parameter: a target. This lets you load the page in a separate frame or a new browser window. Just as the *HREF* linking tag in HTML allows a *TARGET* attribute, this command works the same way (for more information on the *TARGET* attribute see the Resources section at the end of Chapter 9).

The values for this parameter can include the name of an existing window or frame or can specify a new window, as shown here:

```
gotoNetPage "page3.html", "_blank"
```

We'll use this feature in our movie. With the same movie you've been working on open in Director, edit the Sprite Scripts for each button. Add a second argument to each *gotoNetPage* call, as shown below (this snippet shows the code for the Microsoft button):

```
gotoNetPage "http://www.microsoft.com", "mainbody"
```

What this says to the browser is to load this page but load it into the frame named "mainbody." Once you've added this same second argument for each of the three button Sprites you're done. Now recompile the scripts, save the movie, and burn it again to the same .DCR file.

The Web pages we'll need for this movie consist of three small HTML files. The first page will be the frame document, which includes the other two pages, each in its own window frame. The HTML needed to create a frame document is fairly straightforward (at least for the simple case we'll be using here). Again, using your favorite text editor, enter the HTML code that follows and save it out as Ch10fram.htm.

```
<HTML>

<TITLE>Shockwave Frames Test</TITLE>

<FRAMESET ROWS="90,*">

<FRAME SRC="Ch10.htm" NAME="navman" SCROLLING="NO" NORESIZE MARGINWIDTH=0

MARGINHEIGHT=0>

<FRAME SRC="Ch10body.htm" NAME="mainbody" >

</FRAMESET>

</HTML>
```

Here, the *FRAMESET* tag is placed in the HTML instead of the *BODY* tag because this page contains only other pages it has no "body" to speak of. It tells the browser that this file includes other HTML documents that are to be displayed as individual frames. Note the closing *</FRAMESET>* near the end of the document.

The *ROWS* attribute says to divide the frames into horizontal rows and also specifies how to space them. The number 90 says make the top frame 90 pixels in height, and the asterisk after the comma means let the other frame occupy whatever height is left over (depending on the user's current sizing of the browser). There is a corresponding *COLS* attribute that could have been used if we wanted to divide the page vertically, perhaps using a vertically oriented navigation bar. We chose 90 here to correspond to the height of our Shockwave movie.

Within the *FRAMESET* tags are nested two *FRAME* tags, each specifying a single frame in the set. The first one identifies, via the *SRC* parameter, which HTML file to display in this frame, what name to identify it by, and that it should not display scrollbars or allow the user to resize this frame. The second frame specifies the HTML page to display in the larger frame and gives it a name of "mainbody." This name should look familiar to you, no? It is the same name we specified in the second argument to our *gotoNetPage* call from the Lingo above. It's important that these names match exactly or the browser won't load the pages into our frame as we hope.

Nothing special needs to be done to the pages we're including within our frames. The first one is just the same page we had used earlier, and the second one is just a "filler" page containing a simple text message. It's displayed there only until the user clicks on one of the buttons in the navigation bar, at which point that page is replaced by the home page of the chosen organization. The Ch10body.htm file (in the same directory) should contain the HTML that follows:

```
<HTML>

<BODY>

<H3>Click on any of the names above to load that site in this frame.</H3>

</BODY>

</HTML>
```

Once the HTML files have been created and placed into the same folder you're ready to test this in the browser. Open the Ch10fram.htm file in the browser, either locally or over the Net (once all of the files have been uploaded to your server). Click on any of the movie's buttons and the corresponding pages should load in the frame below.

That's it, you've completed every step of the Shockwave development process, including using new NetLingo commands and HTML frames. The rest of this chapter will fill in a couple of details on how to use the *OBJECT* tag so you can get the most out of Active Shockwave.

Using the OBJECT Tag

To benefit from Internet Explorer's ability to automatically download and install the Active Shockwave control we need to change our HTML to use the new *OBJECT* tag. This tag will eventually be recognized by all browsers (it has been adopted by the W3C, the World Wide Web Consortium) and works very much like the plug-in tag. Its purpose is to identify an "object" that the browser is to include at some location. In the future, the object specified could be anything from a GIF image to spreadsheet or a Shockwave movie. Essentially it provides a superset of the *EMBED* tag's functionality.

Here's an example of the *OBJECT* tag you can use to include the NavMan movie into an IE 3.0 compatible page...

```
<OBJECT CLASSID="clsid:166B1BCA-3F9C-11CF-8075-444553540000"

CODEBASE="http://active.macromedia.com/director/cabs/sw.cab#version=5,0,1,61"

WIDTH=480 HEIGHT=90 NAME="sw" ID="sw">

<PARAM NAME="SRC" VALUE="CH10.DCR">

</OBJECT>
```

Yes, it's not nearly as simple and readable as the *EMBED* tag, is it? This tag demands much more information than the *EMBED* tag, but in return you get at least one very powerful benefit: automatic installation and updating. There is enough information included here to allow the browser to determine what ActiveX control is required, what version of that control is needed, and where to get it if it's not already present on the user's system.

In terms of how to write this HTML the key is copy-and-paste. You'll never type or be expected to remember the first two parameters to this tag, but since you'll always use the same values each time it's best to borrow the *CLASSID* and *CODEBASE* parameter text from an existing (and working) HTML page (like the one included on the CD-ROM). Microsoft also gives away a tool called the Microsoft Control Pad (Figure 10.11) that helps you add controls and their *OBJECT* tags to HTML files. See the Resources section for more information on where and how to get this free (yes, more free online software) program.

Note that unlike the *EMBED* tag, the *OBJECT* is used in pairs with an opening <*OBJECT*> tag along with its attributes, any number of intermediate <*PARAMETER*> tags, and finally the closing </*OBJECT*> tag.

Figure 10.11 Microsoft Control Pad.

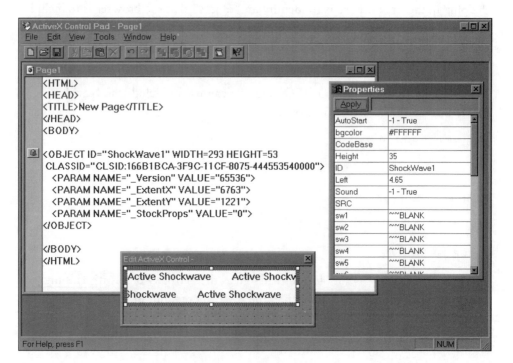

What do these parameters mean? The *CLASSID* is special form of URL that is necessarily complex because it designates a completely unique identifier for this type of object (in this case, the identifier for Active Shockwave control). This identifier must not conflict with the identifier for any of the potentially infinite number of ActiveX controls available. The *CODEBASE* parameter tells the browser from where it can download this control if it's not already installed. Table 10.2 summarizes the parameters available for this tag.

Table 10.2 Parameters for the OBJECT Tag

Parameter	Example Usage	Description
CLASSID	CLASSID = "clsid:166B1BCA-3F9C-11CF-8075-444553540000"	A special URL identifying an implementation for the object. The example to the left identifies this object as a Shockwave movie.
CODEBASE	CODEBASE = "http://active.macromedia.com/director/cabs/sw.cab#version=5,0,1,61"	A URL specifying the location for the code that implements this object type. The browser uses this to automatically download and install the Active Shockwave control.
ID	ID = "shockmov"	A document-wide identifier for this object.
WIDTH	WIDTH = 400	The horizontal size given to the movie in the browser window.
HEIGHT	HEIGHT = 100	The vertical height given to the movie.
NAME	NAME = "Shockwave"	Allows the object to be included as part of a FORM block. The browser will send the NAME and value along with the other form data when "submit"ed. Rarely used for Shockwave movies.

One of the restrictions on the Active Shockwave control is that when using the *OBJECT* tag only the parameters in Table 10.3 are recognized and available inside the movie from Lingo.

Table 10.3 Object Parameters Recognized in Lingo

Parameter Tag	Description
NAME="SRC" VALUE="movie URL"	The only required parameter. Identifies the movie to load.
NAME="swURL" VALUE="URL"	A URL you may want to use with a NetLingo command.
NAME="swText" VALUE="text string"	A generic way to pass a text string into the movie.
NAME="swForeColor" VALUE="colorCode"	A colorCode you can use to set an object's foreground color.
NAME="swBackColor" VALUE="colorCode"	A colorCode you can use to set an object's background color.
NAME="swFrame" VALUE="frameName"	The name of an HTML frame that can be used as a target.
NAME="swColor" VALUE="objectColor"	Can be used to specify the color of an object.
NAME="swName" VALUE="theName"	Specifies a name to be used in the movie. Can be a user name or other value.
NAME="swPassword" VALUE="userPassword"	Specifies a password that might be used with the user name above.
NAME="swBanner" VALUE="bannerText"	Text that can be used as a banner or for other display or use in the movie.
NAME="swSound" VALUE="soundName"	Identifies a sound to be played (filename or URL perhaps).
NAME="swVolume" VALUE="volumeLevel"	Usually a volume-level value from 1 to N (as in the Lingo command "set the soundLevel to 5").
NAME="swPreloadTime" VALUE="theTime"	Specifies the preload time to use for a streaming audio file.
NAME="swAudio" VALUE="audioFile"	Specifies the name or URL of an audio file to play.

continued

Table 10.3 *Continued*

Parameter Tag	Description
NAME="swList" VALUE="listValues"	Comma-separated list of values.
NAME="sw1" VALUE="sw1value"	Author-specific parameter. There are 9 of these available: "sw1" to "sw9".

No law says you have to use any of these tags as described except for the SRC tag (or else it won't find the movie), but try to use them as recommended (we'll show you how to do so in Chapter 11). This parameter set was designed to give a representative set of the types of parameters developers might want from within a movie. This restriction also means you do not have an unlimited number of parameters you pass to your movie (not that you *wanted* that many). It's up to your movie to read these values in and use them as you see fit.

These must be used in between the *OBJECT* and */OBJECT* tags as part of the *PARAM* tag:

```
<PARAM NAME="swText" VALUE="Today's Secret word is: Swordfish">
```

It can be difficult to use both the *EMBED* and *OBJECT* tags in the same Web page. Browsers can get confused. Some sites inform users that they're optimized for one browser or the other. Other sites use more sophisticated methods such as dynamically determining which browser a surfer is using when the user hits their site and then give the user different Web pages based on the browser. These pages could include the *EMBED* tag, the *OBJECT* tag, or maybe just include an image if they can determine that the browser won't support plug-ins or Shockwave. This is what the Macromedia site currently does for its home page (which includes Shockwave movies). You can experiment by logging into the same site with both Navigator and Internet Explorer and then use the browser's View/Source option to look at the HTML for that page. This can be very enlightening.

One approach that you can use as a way of covering both browsers with the same HTML is to nest the *EMBED* tag within the opening and closing *OBJECT* tags as follows:

```
<OBJECT CLASSID="clsid:166B1BCA-3F9C-11CF-8075-444553540000"

CODEBASE="http://active.macromedia.com/director/cabs/sw.cab#version=5,0,1,61"

WIDTH=480 HEIGHT=90 NAME="sw" ID="sw">

<PARAM NAME="SRC" VALUE="Ch10.dcr">

<EMBED SRC="ch10.dcr" WIDTH=480 HEIGHT=90>

</OBJECT>
```

As new versions of Shockwave are released the identifiers used in the *CLASSID* and *CODEBASE* tags may need to be updated if you wish to use the newer releases. The best way to stay tuned to these developments is by regularly visiting Macromedia's Web site and seeing what's new in the Director and Shockwave sections.

Chapter Summary

In this chapter we made our first big step into the world of Shockwave. We built our first Shockwave-enabled Director movie, connected it to some HTML, and put it up on the Web. Doing this included learning the following:

- The eight primary steps in the Shockwave development process—Plan, Build, Compress, Add HTML, Test Locally, Upload, Test over the Net, Repeat

- How to create movies using Stage sizes smaller than 640 × 480

- Using rollover functions and film loops to create an animated navigation bar

- How to use Afterburner to compress movies for Shockwave

- How Afterburner works and the different types of compression algorithms it uses: lossy and lossless

- The basic HTML necessary to create a Web page for Shockwave

- The *EMBED* tag and its parameters

- How to install Shockwave for Netscape and Internet Explorer

- Time saving Shockwave development tips

- Configuring a Web server for Shockwave

- How to upload Shockwave movies to a Web server

- How to test Shockwave movies locally and over the Net

- The *gotoNetPage* command, which causes the specified page to be retrieved and loaded into the browser and which either replaces the current Web page or is loaded into a specific browser frame

- HTML frames and the *FRAME* tag

- Using the new *OBJECT* tag for Active Shockwave HTML

11

Advanced Shockwave

Chapter Objective

This chapter continues our journey into the depths of Shockwave and the more advanced capabilities of the new NetLingo. The centerpiece of this chapter is our project: a "You Don't Know Jack"-like trivia game built for Shockwave. In constructing this movie we'll use a number of the advanced, asynchronous NetLingo commands. This will be a much larger project than our first Shockwave movie. As we did last time, we'll build this in two phases: the first exercise builds the basic game, and the second exercise enhances the game with streaming audio.

By the end of this chapter you should have a good understanding of how to construct sophisticated, Internet-savvy Shockwave movies.

The Eight Types of NetLingo Commands

With the release of Shockwave for Director 5 there are eight types of new Lingo commands providing network functionality. Table 11.1 summarizes these new commands.

Table 11.1 New Lingo Commands from Shockwave for Director 5

Type	Commands, Functions, and Elements
Starting Operations	gotoNetPage url, target gotoNetMovie url getNetText url preloadNetThing url
Status of Operations	netDone() netError()
Results Retrieval	netTextResult() netMIME() netLastModDate() getLatestNetID()
Canceling Network Operations	netAbort
Message Display	netStatus string
Parameter Access	externalParamCount(n) externalParamName(n) externalParamValue(n or string)
Preferences	setPref prefName, prefValue getPref(prefName)
Streaming Sound	URL preLoadTime preLoadBuffer play/stop/pause state duration percentStreamed percentPlayed bitRate getError() getErrorString()

Some of these commands were introduced with the initial version of Shockwave (sometimes called version 4), and others were added with Shockwave 5. During the course of building our next project we'll use commands from most of these groups. Note that at the present time the primary reference manual for these commands is located on the Macromedia Web site. In future releases of Director these commands will be integrated into its help system, just as the authoring environment will integrate the commands themselves.

Understanding Asynchronous NetLingo Commands

Before we begin building our trivia game we need to take a look at how the new Lingo network extensions work and how they differ from the Lingo you've used before.

Thus far, nearly all of the Lingo we've encountered has behaved in what's known as a "synchronous" fashion. For example, when you issue the command *beep* you expect the sound to play nearly immediately; when you say *go frame "X,"* the Playback Head is there by the time this Lingo command returns; and so on. When the command returns, the operation is complete. These commands finish "in sync."

This is not the case with many of the high-latency (meaning "a-bit-too-slow") network-based commands you'll be using with the new NetLingo. Many of these fall into the category of what are known as "asynchronous commands." That is, they don't complete what you tell them to do when you tell them to do it. They don't finish in-sync. Why not? Because of the inherent delays in sending and receiving information online. When your Lingo code returns from calling a command such as *getNetText* the operation is started but it doesn't finish until some point in the future. Asking for, checking-on, and finally getting results from across the Internet in Lingo is often a multipart process.

Let's start by looking at how the *getNetText* command operates. This command typifies the flow of asynchronous operations in Shockwave:

1. Start operation.

2. Check status till done.

3. Retrieve results.

This sequence is the key to proper use of many of the asynchronous commands. As you've seen, in the online world things often take much longer than we would like. For example, here's what happens when you issue a NetLingo call to get a file from a Web server out on the Internet:

- The plug-in talks to the browser and asks it to retrieve this file

- The browser then locates the correct Web server

- It asks the server for the file

- The Web server finds the file and starts sending it back

- The browser meanwhile waits for all the file's data to arrive

- Once all the pieces have arrived the browser then gives it back the plug-in

- And finally the plug-in can open that file and begin playing the movie

All of this can take many seconds (or minutes if the file is large). In most cases, it would be undesirable to have your Lingo program just sit there waiting for this one command to complete. That's why the retrieval process is broken into multiple steps.

Let's look at a simple example of how the NetLingo commands can be used to perform this type of sequence. Say we want to retrieve a text file from across the Internet to use in our movie. This could be to display it on the stage, to set variables, or for anything our movie might need (such as the answers for our trivia game). Regardless of what we want to use the text for, we get it as so:

1. **Start operation**

```
getNetText "http://www.acme.com/mydata.txt"
```

This sends an HTTP request across the Internet (by way of the browser) asking for the file we specify with the given URL. This command returns nearly immediately even though text hasn't yet been retrieved.

2. **Check status till done**

```
on exitFrame

    if netDone() then

        processResults

    end if

end
```

A new Lingo function, *netDone*, allows you to check the status of a pending network request to see if it's complete. If the operation is still outstanding, that is, the results have not fully arrived, then this function returns FALSE. When all the data for the given file has been retrieved *netDone* then returns TRUE: The network operation is done.

In the example above we use an *exitFrame* event handler to check the status of this command and act accordingly. Immediately after calling *getNetText* why not do something like the following?

```
repeat while netDone() = FALSE

end repeat
```

Because this is usually bad. Why? At that point we're being a CPU hog. Shockwave does a lot of vital processing, like downloading a file, only when the playback head moves. Getting stuck in this repeat loop could hang the movie forever. Nor do we give ourselves a chance to respond to user's mouse clicks and other input. Our program is more flexible, interactive, and polite to other applications if we use a Frame Script instead.

Once *netDone* returns TRUE we can safely get the results of our initial request.

3. **Retrieve results**

```
set s = netTextResult()

put s into field "Message"
```

The *netTextResult* function returns the complete contents of the specified file as a single string. At this point we could parse the string into the pieces we want, keep it around for future use, or send it straight to the Stage, as we did here.

A couple of things to note about the *netTextResult* function: (1) If you call it before calling *getNetText* or before any results have been returned you'll get an empty string, ""; (2) Calling this after calling *getNetText* but before *netDone* returns TRUE may return part of the file or may not (which you usually don't want to do).

So this is the central process: You execute the command, the movie continues on, then you regularly check back to see if the asynchronous operation is done; when it is, you check for errors (which I'll show you how to do later) and get the results.

> **NOTE** The *getNetText* command can only retrieve files by accessing them through a Web server. That is, you cannot use this command to directly read files from your local file system. Macromedia has disabled this command from reading local files directly because of security concerns that we'll look at later in this chapter. What this means is that you can test and debug this command only when you have access to a Web server—either by being online or by running a Web server locally.

Exercise 1:
A "You Don't Know Jack"-like Trivia Game

To demonstrate Lingo programming using these new Shockwave commands (and to have some fun in the process) we'll build a game. This will be a "You-Don't Know Jack"-style trivia game in which each day's puzzles can be downloaded from the Internet. In addition, the puzzle's clues can be heard in real-time using Shockwave's new streaming audio functions.

For those of you who haven't had the chance to play "You Don't Know Jack," it's a very successful trivia game on CD-ROM developed by a company called Jellyvision. It's fun to play and has a great sense of humor. The graphics are very modest, but the game makes excellent use of audio. It's a good starting point for our network-based game because we can build the core game with a minimum of graphics (thus saving download time), it can make use of dynamically updated content (giving it a reason for being online), and its extensive use of audio ties into our goal of using the new streaming audio Lingo commands.

Planning the Game

Our Shockwave version of the game, which we'll call "You Don't Know Mac," will implement one of the more dynamic sections of the real game called the "Jack Attack." When this portion of the game starts an audio clue is given that hints at the types of word pairs to expect (such as "The First Family's Furry Friends"). The player must then match-up a given word (such as "Nixon") with an appropriate matching word (like "Checkers") while not mismatching it with decoy incorrect words (like "Spot" or "Fido"). The potential matching words fly by one at a time, giving the player a few seconds to decide if this is a correct match. Each segment includes five words to be matched. A point value is assigned to each word. Answering correctly adds that value to the player's total score, and each wrong guess is subtracted from the player's running total.

For our implementation of the game we want to design the experience for the online environment:

- The puzzles and clues will be stored in a separate text file on our server so they can be updated regularly (perhaps drawing from yesterday's headlines).

- We'll use the *getNetText* and related calls to get this data from the server.

- We'll minimize the download overhead by keeping the size of our graphics small through effective use of dynamic text and shape Cast Members (meaning we won't pre-render all the text and graphics as they do in the real game).

- The Stage will be a modest 320 × 240, again in the interest of minimizing download time.

- We'll need to integrate a set of streaming audio files for our puzzle clues. These will be stored as external files on our server.

- An HTML file must be created to incorporate the game.

- We may want to use parameters for the *EMBED* tag to make our file more flexible and reusable.

- We have to come up with a way to store the user's score locally.

This is a lot to do, so let's get started by opening the Ch11.dir movie from the Chap11 folder on the CD-ROM. The Score Window for this movie is shown in Figure 11.1.

The Ch11.dir file has all the Cast Members we'll be using for this movie and has a partially completed Score. Because we have a lot to cover in this exercise we won't go over the details of placing the Sprites on the Stage, creating the Markers, and the other early production-oriented steps. You know how to do this by now, so it's been done for you in Ch11.dir.

Figure 11.1 The Score Window.

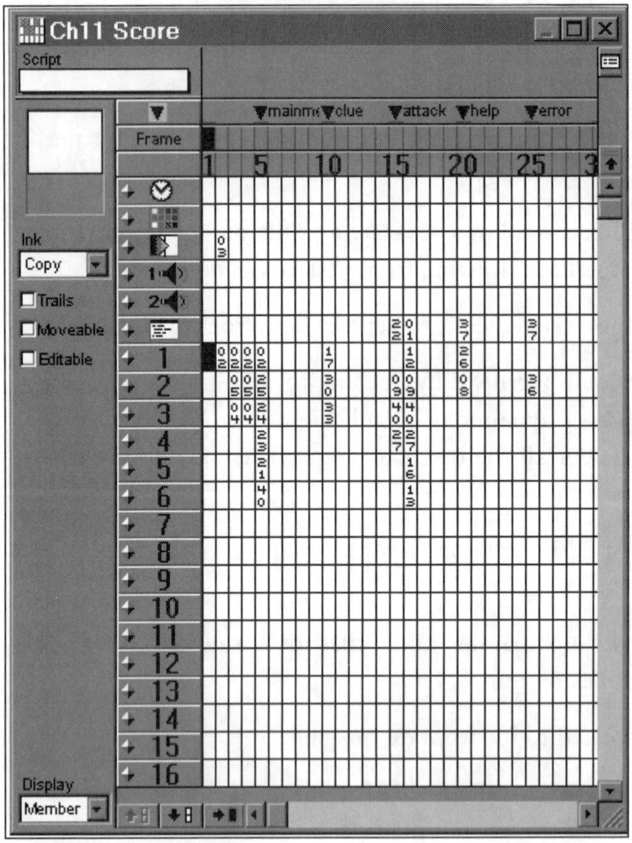

```
Ch11 Score
Script
                    ▼        ▼mainme ▼clue   ▼attack ▼help  ▼error
           Frame
                    1    5     10     15     20     25    3
     ⊘
     1 ◀))
     2 ◀))
     ▤
     1
     2
     3
     4
     5
     6
     7
     8
     9
    10
    11
    12
    13
    14
    15
    16

Ink
Copy
□ Trails
□ Moveable
□ Editable

Display
Member
```

Using *getNetText*

The first thing we want to program is getting today's puzzle data when we start the movie. At the bottom of the first frame of the game, the title screen, we'll display a text message and a dynamic progress indicator letting users know that we're downloading today's questions.

Then, by using the *getNetText* command we can get the puzzle data from across the Net directly into our movie. As outlined above, we'll perform this operation in three steps: Initiate the retrieval, check its status, get the results. We'll start getting the data in one frame and then loop in the following frame until the data arrives.

Double-click the Script Channel in frame 3 and add this Frame Script:

```
on exitFrame

    getNetText ("jackdata.txt")

    puppetSprite 2, TRUE

end
```

This handler initiates retrieval of the file jackdata.txt. Because we've used a relative URL the browser will look for this file in the same directory on the server from which we loaded our Shockwave movie. The *puppetSprite* command is used to put under Lingo control a Sprite we'll animate to indicate progress.

Then in frame 4 double-click on the Script Channel to add this Frame Script:

```
on exitFrame

    if ( netDone() = TRUE ) then

        readPuzzleData

        puppetSprite 2, FALSE

        go "mainmenu"

    else

        updateProgress

        go the frame

    end if

end
```

What this script does is loop on frame 4 until the puzzle data file has been fully retrieved (it's a very small file, so it shouldn't take long to fetch). While it's waiting, it calls a handler we'll write named *updateProgress*. Once *netDone* returns TRUE telling us that the file has arrived, we call another handler, this one named *readPuzzleData*. There we'll take the contents of this file and use it to initialize our game. After that handler returns we then turn off puppetting of the progress indicator Sprite. And finally, after we've read the data, we move on the frame labeled mainmenu where the user can begin to play.

In general, it's important to let users know when a network operation is in progress (lest they start hitting the browser's Stop or Back buttons to leave our seemingly stalled movie). Just as all browsers have some sort of spinning, rotating or otherwise moving icon to let users know that it's working on their behalf, we'll move a simple red dot across the stage to do the same thing (the dot's a circular Shape Cast Member). In a Movie Script add the following code:

```
on updateProgress

    if (the locH of sprite 2 < 320) then

        set the locH of sprite 2 to (the locH of sprite 2) + 2

    else

        set the locH of sprite 2 to 0

    end if

end
```

This function is called on each frame from the script above. All it does is move the horizontal position of the Sprite across the bottom of the Stage letting the user know activity is occurring.

Before we add the code for the *readPuzzleData* handler we should take a quick look at what the contents of a puzzle data file looks like. Below is the contents of the jackdata.txt file:

```
First Families' Furry Friends

pets.swa

Nixon;4;Spot;Pushinka;Ralph;Checkers;Bart

Dole;2;Fala;Leader;Fido;Chief;Boots

Clinton;3;Tiger;Dick;Socks;Tom;Scotty

Ford;5;Topper;Lassie;Sam;PeeWee;Liberty

Bush;1;Millie;Ref;Allie;Tipper;Bob
```

The first line of the file contains the puzzle's clue. The second line contains the URL of the SWA streaming audio clue to play. The next five lines are the puzzles themselves. Semicolons separate the three parts of each puzzle. The first part is the word to be matched (this will be displayed in the center of the screen); the second part is a number identifying which of the following items is the correct answer; and the remainder of the line is the five words the user can try to match with the center word.

Let's add the handler to read this file. In the same Movie Script used above add the *readPuzzleData* handler as follows:

```
on readPuzzleData

    global gWordSets, gSwaClue

    set puzzdata = netTextResult()

    set the text of member "clue" to line 1 of puzzdata

    set gSwaClue to line 2 of puzzdata

    set gWordSets = []

    repeat with i = 3 to 7

        add gWordSets, line i of puzzdata

    end repeat

end
```

As you can see, this is a much more complex handler. This is called when *netDone* returns TRUE, telling us that the jackdata.txt file has been retrieved from the Web server. The first thing we do here is use the *netTextResult* function to assign the full contents of that file to the variable *puzzdata*. Then, the rest of this handler takes this string apart and assigns each piece to the appropriate variable or Field. The first line of the file is assigned to the Field "*clue*" where it will be displayed to users when they begin to play. The second line, the URL of the streaming audio file, is saved into the global variable *gSwaClue*. And the last section of the handler assigns each of the rest of the lines of the file to an array called *gWordSets*. This array will contain the five sets of words that make up each question.

Adding Error Handling

There is an implicit, and somewhat unsafe, assumption made in the *exitFrame* handler we added to frame 4. It assumes that our data was successfully retrieved from the Net when *netDone* returned TRUE. But as anyone who's ever surfed the Web knows, files do not always arrive as hoped. What we should do here is add some error checking to verify that the data arrived without any problems.

We can do this by using the NetLingo call *netError*. This function returns OK if no error occurred, otherwise it's a string describing the error. We can add this to frame 4's Frame Script as follows:

```
on exitFrame

    if ( netDone() = TRUE and netError() = "OK" ) then

        readPuzzleData

        puppetSprite 2, FALSE

        go "mainmenu"

    else if (netError() <> "") then

        puppetSprite 2, FALSE

        go "error"

    else

        updateProgress

        go the frame

    end if

end
```

This change adds calls to *netError* in two locations. First, it calls the *readPuzzleData* handler only if both *netDone* is TRUE and *netError* says the operation was successful. Second, if the previous condition is not true it checks to make sure *netError* hasn't returned some other string telling us there's been an error. If it returns an error string we go to the Marker labeled "error" where we give users an error message and ask them to reload the movie if they want to try again.

Another option you might use would be to save a default or fall-back set of game data in a Field Cast Member and use its contents for the puzzles if the network read failed. This would allow the game to function even if there was a problem getting the data from the server. Just something to consider.

At this point we've completed our first big step in programming this game. We've used the asynchronous NetLingo commands to get today's puzzles.

Here are a couple of things to keep in mind when using the these NetLingo commands:

- The *getNetText* command cannot read a file locally from the user's computer. This is to keep your Shockwave movie from reading a user's file and uploading it to the server, which would be low down and dirty.

- Remember that the default value for *netDone* is TRUE. If you call this before you've invoked any asynchronous operation you'll get a value of TRUE (which means it's important not to depend on this call until after an asynchronous operation has started).

- You can invoke a CGI script on a server through any of the NetLingo commands that take a URL. CGI, which stands for Common Gateway Interface, is the standard mechanism for launching programs on a Web server. These programs can perform actions such as querying a database and will return those results to you. For example, if your server had a CGI program that checked a database for past players' high scores and returned them as a string, you could use the following *getNetText* request to retrieve those results into your Shockwave movie:

```
getNetText "http://www.myserver.com/highscores.cgi"
```

The details of CGI programming are beyond the scope of this book, but you can visit some of the online Web resources listed at the end of Chapter 9 for more details on how this works or to begin programming CGI yourself.

Programming the Game's Main Menu

The next thing we have to do is add the interactivity and navigation functions to the main display screen (located at the "mainmenu" Marker). This screen gives the user his or her main choices in the game. Users can get help, save their score, or begin the Mac Attack. Each of the buttons on this screen (Field Cast Members actually; they take up less space than bitmaps) have already been laid out for you. All you have to do is add the Lingo. We'll start with the simplest code and work our way up to the more complex.

Add a Frame Script to frame 5 that keeps the Playback Head at this spot until the user makes a choice:

```
on exitFrame

    go the frame

end
```

Then, at the same frame, select Sprite channel 3 and add this code by clicking on the Script Preview button:

```
on mouseUp

    go "help"

end
```

This jumps the user over to the Help screen when the Help button is clicked. There we've added a Field with text that explains the rules of the game. Although the help text is included as part of the movie we could have chosen to include the instructions as part of the HTML text in which this movie is embedded. Always keep this in mind when designing your Shockwave movies—remember that text, images, and other related information can be presented to the user as part of the surrounding HTML context as well as inside your movie.

At frame 20, the Help screen, we'll add a Sprite Script to the "Go Back" button in Channel 1. Click on the Script Preview button to add the following script:

```
on mouseUp

    go "mainmenu"

end
```

This will simply return the users back to the frame from which they just came.

A note on fonts: As you're aware, a Shockwave movie can be played back on both the Mac and the PC. This means that any Field text will be displayed using the font originally assigned to it or with the closest appropriate matching font for that platform. Beware, this can cause trouble if no corresponding font is available. In this movie all the Fields' fonts have been set to Arial on Windows, which

Director maps to Helvetica on the Macintosh. This is a safe choice because these fonts come standard on both platforms. You could also address this issue in Lingo by using *the machineType* or *the platform* to determine which system the movie's currently running on and then set the font and the fontSize properties of each Field accordingly.

Using the New Shockwave Preferences Functions

Next, we'll add the handler to save the user's score. In this way each time the user plays the game his or her score can be read from this file in order to create a cumulative, ongoing, total score. To implement this we'll use the new NetLingo *setPref* and *getPref* functions added with Shockwave 5. These allow us to save data to a text file on the user's local disk and read it back later. (And yes, it's just a plain text file so users are free to cheat by later editing the file and boosting their score.)

Go to frame 5 and select the Cell in Channel 4. This is the Sprite for the Save Score button (the button is actually just a Field Cast Member saying "Save"). Add the following Sprite Script here:

```
on mouseUp

    global gScore

    setPref "dontknow.txt", string(gScore)

end
```

The *setPref* function takes two arguments: The first is the name of a file we'll write to, and the second is the complete contents of that file. It all happens in one call; we can't make multiple writes to this file with each one appending to the end. If we wanted to put lots of information into this file we'd need first to build-up a single string that contained all of the data we wished to save and then make the one call. Of course, this is not a problem for us here because all we want to save is a single score value.

How do we read this back out? With *getPref*. When? Well, next time the user loads our Shockwave movie. This means we want to add some Lingo to the *startMovie* handler to get this value so that it gets called each time the movie begins. Add a Movie Script with this Lingo...

```
on startMovie

    global gScore

    set s = getPref("dontknow.txt")

    if (not voidP(s)) then

        set gScore = integer(s)

    else

        set gScore = 0

    end if

    put string(gScore) into field "score"

end
```

Here you're using the *getPref* function to read the value of the score file. If the file doesn't exist *getPref* returns void. This could happen because this is the first time they've played or they haven't saved a score yet. If we did read a value from this file we use it to initialize the global variable *gScore*, else we just set the beginning score to zero. We then use this value to update the "score" Field the user will see on the Stage.

Where does this file get saved? In the so-called Preferences folder underneath the Shockwave support folder (which in Netscape is underneath the plug-ins folder). On the Mac this is often something like Macintosh HD:Netscape folder:Plug-Ins:NP-PPC-Dir-Shockwave folder:Prefs. Under Windows 95 this might be c:\Program Files\Netscape\program\plugins\np32dsw\prefs. For security reasons this is the only folder on the user's local disk you're allowed to write to and read from in a Shockwave movie. It's assumed this is restrictive enough to prevent security breaches. You can create as many files in this directory as you wish. The only malicious problem a Shockwave movie could cause the user with this would be to fill up their hard disk with useless text files.

The last bit of navigational Lingo we need to add now is the Sprite that sends the user off to actually play the game. In frame 5 select Sprite channel 2 and add this code by clicking on the Script Preview button:

```
on mouseUp

  go "clue"

end
```

This moves the Playback Head to the frame labeled "clue," which is where the user is shown the clue for today's game. Move the Playback Head to frame 10 now to see this screen.

If you remember, back in our handler *readPuzzleData* we used the first string read from the puzzle's data file to initialize a Field Cast Member named "clue." Here's where that Field appears in our movie: in the center of the Stage on this Frame. The only other Sprite on the Stage here is a Field used as a button which reads "Begin Attack." We'll add a Sprite Script to this Shape Cast Member in Sprite channel 2 that will take the user to the game:

```
on mouseUp

    go "attack"

end
```

This moves the Playback Head to the "attack" Marker where the Mac Attack begins. And not a moment too soon.

Playing the Game: The Mac Attack Screen

All the real action in this game happens once the player arrives at the frame labeled "attack." Here's where the user actually plays the game. It's the most complex frame in this movie.

Again, in the interest of saving download time, this frame uses no bitmap Cast Members. It uses only Shape and Field Cast Members. We'll use Fields to display the word to be matched in the center of the Stage, the potential matching word that we'll move across the Stage, and the message given to the user after each guess. Although this lacks some of the visual appeal of Bitmap Text fields, such as anti-aliasing, it makes for a much smaller movie.

Most of what goes on in this section is manipulation of Text Fields, checking if the user's guesses are correct, and giving feedback to users. None of this programming uses any new NetLingo so we won't review that code here (it's all in the

Ch11done.dir movie on the CD-ROM). Examine the code on the CD-ROM; it has extensive comments to let you know how it works.

Once the user has tried to match answers for each of the five word sets the game automatically brings him or her back to the main menu. At that point the user can choose to save the game or play again (and yes, the score just keeps going up and up; feel free to add the code to handle this more robustly and prevent rampant cheating).

The Lingo you've written, combined with the existing code for the Mac Attack, is all the programming you'll need for this exercise. Recompile all Scripts and save the Director movie as Ch11.dir. Then run it through Afterburner to save it as Ch11.dcr.

Adding the HTML and Testing the Game

Now that the Director and Lingo portions are done it's time to write the HTML for our game. We'll make it very simple, using essentially the same HTML we did in the last chapter. Enter the following text into your favorite text editor:

```
<HTML>

<HEAD>

<TITLE>You Don't Know Mac</TITLE>

</HEAD>

<BODY>

<EMBED SRC="ch11.dcr" WIDTH=320 HEIGHT=240>

</BODY>

</HTML>
```

Now save this file as Ch11.htm in the same folder as your Shockwave movie. Upload both of these files and the jackdata.txt file from the CD-ROM to your Web server. It's time to try the big online test.

Start your browser and load the Ch11.htm file from your Web server. This should: bring-up the game, dissolve-in the title screen, load the game data, and bring you to the main menu. From there you can go on to the help screen or save your score (which, until we add the code to play the game, will be zero).

Debugging Shockwave

There is a minute possibility that things won't go perfectly the first time (unfortunately, it would be a wild chance if everything worked perfectly the first time). Because some of this movie can only be tested from the server, the debugging process becomes tougher. If problems such as Script errors appear you may want to keep both your browser and Director open at the same time. That way you can test in the browser, fix in Director, reburn the movie, upload again, then reload into the browser, and so on. And, yes, running both of these memory-intensive programs at the same time is a good argument for using a development machine with a lot of RAM.

When you make a change to a Shockwave movie and then reload it into the browser it may not appear to have taken the changes you made. If you find yourself looking at your movie in the browser and saying "Hey, didn't I change that?" you may have to clear the browser's memory and disk caches in order to force it to load the new version of the movie.

Browsers are designed to help save you time when surfing the Web by maintaining what's known as a local disk cache. Each time the browser gets an HTML page, an image, or other file for you from across the Internet, it not only displays it to you, it saves it into a file on your local hard disk (each browser has options you can set to specify how much disk space to set aside for this cache). This can be a very effective time-saving measure because it means when you revisit pages (even just by hitting the back button) or go to pages from a site that uses common elements, the browser won't have to go out and transmit those files across the Internet again. The downside to this when developing Shockwave movies is that it sometimes will go get a cached version of your movie when, in fact, you want it to go get the new version instead.

You can explicitly ask the browser not to cache files for you at all, and you can also ask it to clear out its cache. For example, in Netscape this is done using the Options/Network Preferences menu choice, selecting the Cache tab, and then choosing the Clear Now buttons for both the Disk and Memory cache (the **memory cache** refers to whatever the browser still has loaded into RAM since you launched it for this session; the Mac version doesn't have an option to clear this). Browsers can be very finicky about caching.

Shockwave Integration Advice

One of the biggest problems with all plug-ins, including Shockwave, is graceful handling of the Web page for those users without the plug-in or who are using a browser that doesn't support plug-ins at all. As a Web page designer you need to remember that your audience includes those who are not yet fortunate enough to have Shockwave. You want them to be happy visitors to your Web site as well. Although there are many ways to address this issue, none of them are completely satisfactory. Below is a summary of the primary ways currently available for handling this situation. Each has its own problems and limitations (and improving browser/plug-in integration is certainly one of the areas that all browser vendors will be addressing in the near future).

Give the user shocked and unshocked versions of your page or site to choose from. This option is first in the list because none of the others solves the problem in a completely satisfactory or cross-browser friendly fashion. Don't force the users to have Shockwave or not see your site at all—this probably defeats your larger purpose for being online. Often you can offer GIF or JPEG image equivalents that are comparable to what the user would otherwise see via Shockwave. For example, the Macromedia site offers users without Shockwave the option to see a GIF-based version of their home page (which looks very similar to the Shockwave version but lacks some of the playful interactivity). Users may also deliberately choose to see the vanilla version because they wish to avoid the delay of downloading the glorious Shockwave rendition (and waiting for the browser to load the plug-in itself).

Use the NOEMBED tag. This tag exists for the benefit of older or less sophisticated browsers that don't recognize the *EMBED* tag. It is normally placed immediately after the corresponding *EMBED* tag:

```
<EMBED SRC="file.dcr" WIDTH=480 HEIGHT=90>

<NOEMBED>

<IMG SRC="myimage.gif" WIDTH=480 HEIGHT=90>

</NOEMBED>
```

Any valid HTML may be inserted between the *NOEMBED* tags: images, text, and so on. Here's the idea underlying this tag: Browsers by design are supposed to ignore HTML tags they do not understand. They don't say "Hey, Mr. User, what the heck's this strange tag doing in here!" They just say "What's this? I think I'll just skip it." So, when the folks at Netscape added the *EMBED* tag they also added its partner, the *NOEMBED* tag. If an older, or non-*EMBED* aware, browser encounters the *EMBED* tag, it will skip both it and the *NOEMBED* tag (which it also doesn't recognize), but it will recognize the HTML between the *NOEMBED* tags. This it reads and displays. *EMBED*-aware browsers, on the other hand, will skip whatever is in the *NOEMBED* tags. Convoluted, but true.

Use Javascript to smooth over the rough edges. Javascript is a small HTML-centric programming language introduced with Netscape 2.0; it has since also been adopted by Internet Explorer (although with enough minor differences to cause compatibility woes). Javascript programs are included as part of the text within an HTML document. The following short script writes the *EMBED* tag into the HTML document (this code will be executed, and therefore insert the *EMBED* tag, only if the browser understands Javascript and presumably supports plug-ins as well).

```
<SCRIPT LANGUAGE="JavaScript">

      document.write('<EMBED SRC="Ch11.dcr" WIDTH=480 HEIGHT=90>');

</SCRIPT>
```

The biggest caveat with this approach is that it can get in the way as often as it helps. Script bugs, browsers without Javascript, and Javascript implementation differences all conspire to make this solution imperfect. (Some very good resources on Javascript programming and HTML are listed at the end of Chapter 9.)

Additionally, with Navigator 3.0, Netscape added an array called *navigator .plugins[]* to Javascript. Some developers have begun using this array to address the problem of missing plug-ins, but again the results have been mixed. For most users it's no better to get a error dialog box from some Javascript that didn't work as expected than it is to get a missing plug-in message.

Provide a link to get the plug-in. You can help those users who don't have the plug-in but may want to get it by pointing them in the right direction. This can be done by simply including the Shockwave GIF image shown in Figure 11.2 in your page with a HTML hypertext link to Macromedia's Shockwave download page.

Figure 11.2 Get Shockwave GIF image.

The user can then go off, get and install the plug-in, and perhaps even return to your page and play the movie.

Also, be careful about putting Shockwave movies on your home page. This can be a turn-off for many of your visitors. You don't want to discourage users from seeing any of your site simply because your home page was too much trouble for them (either because they don't have the plug-in or don't want to wait for the movie to download).

Exercise 2: Adding Streaming Audio to the Game

Now that "You Don't Know Mac" is up-and-running it's time do to what most developers eventually do: add more features. For us, the new feature's going to be the addition of streaming audio clues to the game. By the time we're done our game will have an announcer who automatically reads each day's clue to the player. This is the main goal of the second exercise. We'll begin by introducing the technology behind streaming audio and how it works. With that background out of the way, we'll go over each step in the process of creating the streaming audio files, importing them into Director, and programming them from NetLingo.

An Introduction to Streaming Audio

One of the biggest issues faced by Web developers, and Shockwave developers in particular, is that difficult problem of the amount of time it takes for a file to download before the user can actually see it or use it. This is the infamous download-and-play model that we discussed earlier. It's how loading a Shockwave movie basically works: The browser requests the file, waits until it's completed the download, then the plug-in begins to play it back. What can be done about this? Well, one of the best answers so far has been the introduction of a new set of technologies that do something known as 'data streaming' or just 'streaming.'

Data streaming addresses the download-and-play issue by actually playing-back the data *as it downloads* to the computer. This approach works very well for linear media-based data types like sound and video. Shockwave can play back the first second of sound even as it downloads the second second (that's 2nd second.) As it plays the second second of audio, it's simultaneously downloading the third second of sound. This process continues until the sound is finished or the user interrupts it.

Before starting to play the sound, Shockwave preloads a bit of the file into a piece of memory called a preload buffer. Let's say we set this buffer to hold three seconds of sound. As Shockwave plays the sound, it might experience a delay in getting the next piece of data. As long as the delay is less than 3 seconds, the sound will not be interrupted, and the user will never notice the delay.

With streaming audio, even if it's a 5-minute interview clip you're able to hear the whole thing without waiting. Streaming methods are also the basis for similar new Net technologies such as using the Internet as a cheap telephone and Internet-based videoconferencing system.

To make this work you need both production and playback tools (each of which Shockwave now provides). First, on the production end this requires software capable of generating one of these streaming-compatible data formats. Likewise, on the receiving end, you need a playback engine that knows how to capture, decompress, and interpret this data. In between the two ends are the data format and transmission method—both of which are geared toward high compression rates and are designed to deal with the inherent bandwidth limitations of the Internet and lost data.

Macromedia's first implementation of streaming technology was introduced with Shockwave 5. This technology is scalable, which means that compressed audio files can be tailored to meet the needs of varying connection speeds (so that users with a dedicated fast T1 connection, at 1.5Mbs, can enjoy much higher quality audio clips, but that users with 14.4 modems can still access lower-bandwidth versions of the same audio). The only catch to this is that the mathematically intensive nature of the work means that the user's system must have a Floating Point Unit (FPU) on board to assist in these calculations (Pentiums, most 486s, PowerMacs, and other systems have these).

The compression rates achievable with this codec vary according to the usual trade-offs we make when using a lossy compression algorithm. Quality is inversely related to transfer rate or size. The maximum compression ratio Macromedia claims can be achieved is 176:1, which would be suitable only for scratchy voice recording. Buffering parameters can be set to fine-tune the amount of preloading of the stream that's done. This can help smooth out the rough spots or gaps in transmission (with slow connections often requiring a larger buffer size).

How to Create Streaming Audio Files

Shockwave 5 supports two forms of compressed audio: internal and external. External audio files can be both compressed and streamed. Internal audio Cast Members can be compressed but not streamed.

To create external streaming audio files, identified with an .swa extension, you'll need to download the necessary Xtra from the Shockwave section of Macromedia's Web site. Once you've downloaded and installed the Xtra for your platform (Mac or PC) you're ready to create the .swa files. Rather than go into elaborate detail on the production process here (this is a Lingo book, after all) we'll briefly outline the core steps in converting audio to an .swa format.

On the Mac, here's how the process works from within SoundEdit 16 (there are other sequences you can use; this is just one example): Select File/New to create a new audio buffer and then File/Import to read-in the file you wish to use (usually an AIF file). Next, select the Shockwave for Audio Settings from the Xtras menu. Then select a bit rate: 16kbps is good for 28.8 modems and 8kbps for 14.4 speeds. Close the settings dialog box and choose Export from the File menu, and specify a format of .SWA file from the Export Type drop-down. Name the file, save, and you're done.

On Windows select "Convert WAV to SWA..." from the Xtras menu in Director. Click on the "Add Files" button to select one or more .wav files to be converted. You can also select a Bit Rate, an Accuracy Level and a destination folder. Once you click on the "Convert" button each of the files selected is sent through the converter and you're done.

Adding External Streaming Audio Files to Your Movie

Once you've created the SWA files it's time to import them into Director and program them from Lingo (for this movie we've provided the pets.swa file on the CD-ROM). The first step is to add a streaming audio Cast Member by selecting "Other/SWA Streaming Xtra" from the Insert menu (Figure 11.3).

Assign the name "swa clue" to this Member, as shown in Figure 11.4.

Notice that Director doesn't know the name of the file that's used for this sound. The only way Director knows the name of streaming audio files is when we tell it through Lingo. We'll do that in the next section.

Figure 11.3 Insert menu.

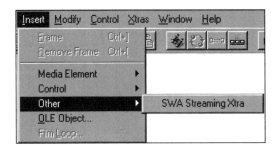

Programming Streaming Audio

When the user selects the Mac Attack button we want to do a few things: We want to go to the frame labeled "clue," start playing the streaming audio clue, wait for the sound to finish, then go on to the "attack" frame and play the game. Playing the streaming audio requires four steps: specifying the URL of the file to play, setting the preload buffer's size, preloading some of the audio, and finally playing that audio back.

The first step is to set the URL of the streaming audio file to play. SWA Cast Members have a *URL* property that can be accessed and set. Remember, when we created this Cast Member we told it nothing about the file itself. The only way to establish which file to play is through this NetLingo property. This is very important; without setting this property to a valid URL you'll never hear anything because Shockwave will have no idea where to find the file.

The next step is to set the preload buffer size. This is the number of seconds of audio that the playback system preloads into memory before actually playing back the sound. For slower connections you'll want to increase this amount and for faster connections reduce it—ranging from 2 to 4 seconds for a 28.8 connection up to 5 or 7 seconds on a slower 14.4 modem.

Figure 11.4 Cast Member of imported sound.

Once the size for the buffer has been set, the third step is to do the actual pre-loading. This is done with the *preLoadBuffer* command, which takes the name of the Cast Member to preload.

And, finally, you'll issue the *play* command to begin streaming playback. This may pause a moment while the preloading occurs.

Because we already have code that jumps us to the "clue" frame what we'll need to do is add to it the NetLingo that begins playing the audio. Change the Sprite handler for Channel 2 in frame 5, the "Play Game" button, to the following:

```
on mouseUp

    global gSwaClue

    set the URL of member "swa clue" = gSwaClue

    set the preLoadTime of member "swa clue" = 5

    preLoadBuffer (member "swa clue")

    play (member "swa clue")

    set the text of member "loading" to "Loading audio..."

    go "clue"

end
```

Because it will take a few seconds for the streaming audio to begin playback you may want to again let the user know that something's in progress. How to this time? We'll just show the user a simple Field Cast Member that tells them we're "Loading audio...." The last command in this handler then moves the Playback Head to the "clue" Marker, at which point the user can both see and hear the clue.

At that frame you should monitor of the progress of the streaming audio. The following code will help:

```
on exitFrame

    if (the percentStreamed of member "swa clue" > 99) then

        set the text of member "loading" to ""
```

```
    end if

    if (the percentPlayed of member "swa clue" > 99) then

        go "attack"

    end if

    go the frame

end
```

In this handler two other streaming audio properties are used: The *percentStreamed* property tells us how much of the file has been streamed across the Internet to our movie, and the *percentPlayed* then tells us what percentage has completed playback. Each begins as zero and eventually increases up to 100 percent. When the file is done streaming we clear the "loading" message and when it's done playing we move the Playback Head to the "attack" Marker.

What happens if the player decides to hit this before the audio clue has finished streaming? We could just let it continue to play, but that wouldn't give us a chance to explore a couple of other streaming audio NetLingo commands we want to use. In this case, we'll stop the sound if the user presses the button while the sound is still playing.

Move the Playback Head to frame 10, the one labeled "clue." Select the Cell for Sprite 2 in this frame and click on the Script Preview button to edit this Sprite Script. Edit the Script to read as follows (you'll be adding to the already existing script):

```
on mouseUp

    if (the state of member "swa clue" = 1 or the state of member "swa clue" =

3) then

        stop (member "swa clue")

    end if

    go "attack"

end
```

What you're doing here is checking the *state of member* property of the streaming audio Cast Member to see if it's still preloading or playing. If the audio is not done playing we use the *stop* command to stop playback. This property can be one of the values in Table 11.3.

Two other new streaming audio Cast Member properties accessible from NetLingo are the *duration* and *bitRate*. Each of these can be read but not set.

Note that if you wanted to be thorough and allow the user to adjust the volume or to mute the sound you could use existing Lingo sound functions to do so. Changing the volume for .swa files can be done just as it is for other sounds by setting Lingo's *the soundlevel* property.

Using the NetLingo Parameter Access Functions

We can do a few things to the existing game to make it much more flexible. Have you spotted any? One of the best changes we can make to improve the movie's flexibility and reusability is to not hard-code the name of the game's puzzle data file. Back in frame 3 we have a Frame Script that asks *getNetText* to get us the file jack-data.txt. This means the only way to change the game's puzzles is to update this one file. While this is certainly better than building the puzzles into the movie itself we have more flexible alternatives we can use.

By using the new *externalParamValue* function we can use tags in our HTML page to tell the movie which puzzle data file to use. This means we can use the same movie in different Web pages, each page pointing to a different data file. Or we could also use Javascript to dynamically generate HTML tags that reference a

Table 11.3 Values for State Property

Value of state property	Meaning
0	Stopped
1	Pre-loading
2	Pre-loading is done
3	Playing
4	Paused
5	Done
9	Error

particular puzzle file based on a user's choices (we won't get into this option here). Using this NetLingo function lets the HTML and your movies work together. This, in turn, opens up a range of possibilities.

The only place we'll make a change to the Lingo will be in that Frame Script in frame 3. Go to that frame now and double-click on the Script Channel. Edit the Script to look like the following:

```
on exitFrame

    if externalParamName("swURL") = "swURL" then

        getNetText(externalParamValue("swURL"))

    else

        getNetText("jackdata.txt")

    end if

    puppetSprite 2, TRUE

end
```

The *if* statement calls the NetLingo function *externalParamName* to see if the *EMBED* tag for our movie included a parameter named "*swURL.*" If it does, then we use the *externalParamValue* function to read-in the value associated with that parameter. This value becomes the URL argument to *getNetText* used to get today's puzzle data. If the enclosing HTML doesn't use this parameter we'll just use the jackdata.txt file we've used before.

To use this feature you can change the *EMBED* tag in Ch11.htm file as follows:

```
<EMBED SRC="Ch11.dcr" WIDTH=320 HEIGHT=240 swURL="jackdata.txt">
```

With this HTML the movie would read the parameter named "*swURL*" and find that we should use the string "jackdata.txt" as the URL for our puzzles. This allows it to be easily changed to tvshow.txt or sports.txt or any other trivia sets you want to create.

Note that the name we've chosen for the parameter was "*swURL.*" We could have chosen to call it anything, even "*JACKURL*" or "*PUZZFILE,*" but by using "*swURL*" we're making sure our parameter names will work with both the *EMBED* and *OBJECT* tags. As we saw in the previous chapter, the *OBJECT* has a limited set of parameters it allows us to use, and "*swURL*" is one of them. This means our Lingo code won't have to change if we later include the same movie in a page that uses the *OBJECT* tag.

Compressing the Sound Effects

The final game includes a couple of sound effects we play back when the user makes a right or wrong guess in the game. We can choose to compress these internal sounds in our movie. These won't stream, but they will consume less space and help decrease the download time of our game. Select the Shockwave for Audio Settings item from the Xtras menu to bring-up the dialog box shown in Figure 11.5.

Make sure the Enabled option is checked. Next we need to select the Bit Rate to use: a smaller rate saves space but trades off quality, and a higher rate, of course, means higher quality but consumes more space. Choose 32 KBits/second from the scrolling list. Select OK to close the dialog box. Next time you run Afterburner on this movie these settings will take effect and all your audio Cast Members will be compressed.

Completing the Game

Now you've finished all the Lingo you'll need for the streaming audio clues. Recompile all Scripts, Save your movie, and send it through Afterburner. You don't need to change the HTML, but you do need to upload the new movie as well as the audio file "pets.swa" from the CD-ROM. Make sure to upload the .swa file in a Binary or Raw mode.

Figure 11.5 Audio dialog box.

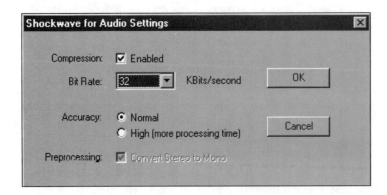

Once these files have been uploaded it's time to fire-up the browser and load the Ch11.htm file from your server. You won't notice any changes until you get to the "clue" frame. Then you'll see the browser's status bar showing a progress message like the one shown in Figure 11.6.

Figure 11.6 Loading status message.

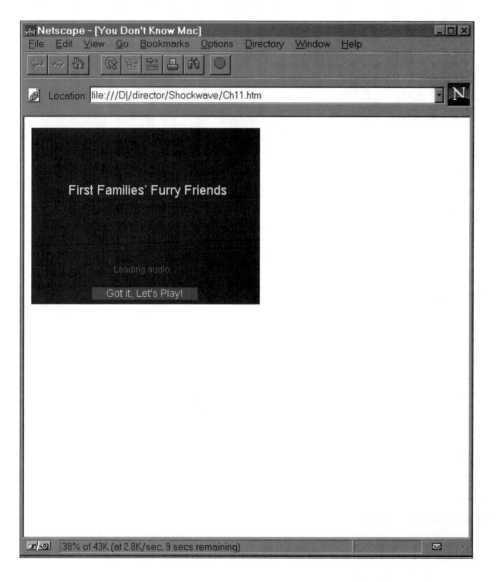

This is a good thing. It means the streaming audio has been found and is beginning to preload. Depending on the value you gave for *preloadBufferSize* this will load some percentage of the file before you begin to hear it playing back. Once you hear the audio playing you'll know you've successfully made it into the real-time streaming audio world.

And that's it! You've finished "You Don't Know Mac!" In so doing you've learned about and used a variety of most important new NetLingo commands. The rest of this chapter will review a few noteworthy Shockwave topics these exercises didn't get a chance to cover.

Using Multiple Simultaneous Network Operations

In the design of "You Don't Know Mac" you may have noticed that at any one point in time there was never more than one network operation in process. This helped keep the programming simple and our game easier to develop, debug, and maintain. These are all good things. But at times in your future Shockwave adventures you may have reason to want to perform more than one network operation at once. Because retrieving data from across the Internet can take time, letting the browser retrieve two or more files at a time for you can be very efficient.

NetLingo will let you run more than one asynchronous operation at a time. The only catch is that you must be diligent in identifying and tracking each operation. For example, take the following (problematic) code:

```
getNetText "questions.txt"

getNetText "answers.txt"
```

In some handler you've made two consecutive calls to *getNetText*. NetLingo and the browser can handle this. But now what do you do if you want to put the contents of these files into the correct fields on the stage? You call *netTextResult,* of course. But wait, the results of what? Are you getting the question text or the answer text? Hmmm.

Well, the solution to this type of problem is to use the *getLatestNetID* function after starting each asynchronous operation. The following code shows one way you could make this work:

```
global gAnswersID, gQuestionsID

getNetText "answers.txt"
```

```
set gAnswersID = getLatestNetID()

getNetText "questions.txt"

set gQuestionsID = getLatestNetID()
```

You'll need one or more global variables (or a list) in which you'll keep track of the identifiers that Shockwave has assigned to each operation. These identifiers are unique positive integers. Most of the NetLingo functions accept an optional argument in which you may specify one of these ID values. For example, while you check to see if either of these operations are complete (as in an *exitFrame* handler) you could do the following:

```
if netDone(gAnswersID) then put netTextResult(gAnswersID) into field "Answers"

if netDone(gQuestionsID) then put netTextResult(gQuestionsID) into field

    "Question"
```

These IDs give you a way to distinguish each operation and act accordingly. It's the key to successfully handling more than one network operation at a time.

> **NOTE** There's a limit to the number of simultaneous asynchronous NetLingo requests you can have outstanding. For Shockwave running under Netscape the default maximum is four. Although it is possible for the user to increase this limit (by changing the Connections setting in Navigator's Options/Network dialog box) it's not recommended that you depend on this number being higher.

Using *gotoNetMovie*

Even though we didn't use the *gotoNetMovie* command in either of the Shockwave projects in this book, it can be a very useful command in many circumstances. Just as the Lingo *go movie* and *play* commands can launch another Director movie, the *gotoNetMovie* can launch one Shockwave movie from another. It's used in very much the same way, the difference being it takes a URL as its first argument. Here's an example of its usage (using a relative URL):

```
gotoNetMovie "movie2.dcr"
```

Calling this command causes the named Shockwave movie to be downloaded and launched within the same space as the current movie. There are a few things to note about this command:

- The launched movie plays back in the same display rectangle as the caller. This means that you should make sure both movies have the same stage size.

- It takes time before the next movie begins playing. The browser must retrieve the complete movie before it begins playback.

- The current movie continues to play until the next movie arrives. This should be planned for in the calling movie (such as by preventing the user from launching the second movie multiple times).

- No notification is given to the calling movie when it is unloaded (just as is the case with *gotoNetPage*).

Here's one other tip: Global variables are not cleared when a second movie is launched with *gotoNetMovie* and thus can be shared across movies. (This is not the case when going from movie to movie in different Web pages using *gotoNetPage*. But, in that case you could use the preference settings functions to work around this limitation. Before calling *gotoNetPage*, save any necessary variables out to a preferences file, then read them back from this file later, either from another movie in the new page or from this same movie if it's re-loaded at a later time.)

The *gotoNetMovie* command also provides a useful way to partition your movies into sections that can be downloaded individually. Movies can thus appear more quickly and the user won't have to wait for movie segments they may never wish to see. It can also be used for small starter or stub movies that download quickly, display an image or animation, and then immediately call the larger main movie.

One of the clever ideas hidden in this command is its ability to begin playback at a marker within the specified movie. You may know that in HTML you can link to an offset within a Web page through the use of a *fragment identifier*. In the following URL

```
<A HREF="page1.html#section2">See Section 2</A>
```

the *#section2* fragment identifier refers to a *<A NAME="#section2">* tag located at some offset within the file page1.html. As it turns out, this is closely analogous to the way in which markers work in an ordinary Director movie: They specify offsets. The developers at Macromedia realized this when they created the *gotoNetMovie* command, and so you can use a URL like this one

```
gotoNetMovie "mymovie.dcr#marker2"
```

to begin playback of this movie starting at the Marker labeled "marker2." This can be a very handy feature and can make your Shockwave movies much more flexible.

The Problems with *preloadNetThing*

Another new NetLingo command that we haven't discussed is *preloadNetThing*. *preloadNetThing* is the kind of command that sounds like a good idea. It's the NetLingo equivalent of existing Lingo commands for preloading data such as *preLoad* and *preLoadMember*. But rather than loading them into RAM it loads the files onto the local hard disk from across the Internet. The *preloadNetThing* command takes a single argument, the URL of the file you wish to preload. The thing asked for can be any valid online resource: a Web page, a GIF image, another Shockwave movie, and so on. This file is then asynchronously fetched for you and stored as part of your browser's local disk cache. Then, if the user chooses to access that data it can be displayed without waiting because the browser just reads it from the local cache.

On the low-bandwidth Internet, preloading data can be even more beneficial than off a normal CD-ROM. The problem is that it doesn't always work the way we would like. It is important to first understand how it's supposed to work. For example, say you have a small Web page named "mypage.html" that includes a link to a large GIF image, "bigimg.gif." You might think the following code would be a good way to speed up the user's next operation:

```
preloadNetThing "mypage.html"
```

But this won't save the user much time. When this operation is completed the only thing cached on the user's hard disk will be a 2KB HTML file. This command downloads only the file you specify, not any files referenced within that file. In this example, it would be strategically wiser to specify the GIF file for preloading, not the small HTML file.

> **NOTE** The browser has the final say in how long this file remains in its cache. If the browser's cache is full and it decides that it wants to make space by clearing-out the file you just downloaded, so be it. Shockwave has no control over how the browser manages its cache.

Certainly this command has its uses, but it still has some kinks to be worked out. Future releases of Shockwave (and browsers) will certainly continue to improve and refine the functionality of this and perhaps other preloading commands.

Cross-Platform versus Cross-Browser

When creating and distributing ordinary Director movies it's vitally important to test your movie thoroughly. If you are producing a Mac and Windows CD-ROM this means creating projectors for both platforms and then testing, again and again, on a variety of machines on both operating systems (especially on Windows). This may mean Windows 3.1, Windows 95, a PowerMac, a 68K Mac, a machine with 8MB of RAM, and one with 32MB of RAM, different sound cards, different display cards, different video depths, and so on.

With Shockwave this issue is no less important. As a matter of fact, it can even get a bit more complicated. Why? Because you still have to make sure it runs on both the Mac and Windows, but now it has to run under different browsers as well. Primarily you should test your movie under each version of Netscape Navigator from 2.0 upward and each version of Internet Explorer later than 3.0. The odds are that it should run the same in all of them, but the only way to be really sure is to try it out. They might treat HTML parameters slightly differently, the plug-in might behave a bit differently than the Active Shockwave control, the performance might vary, or a number of other variables can influence the outcome.

With IE and the Active Shockwave control you may also want to test the automatic installation via the *CODEBASE* tag to make sure that it's working as expected. You're not responsible for having to host or serve the ActiveX control files themselves; you just need to make sure your HTML points to the correct location at the Macromedia site so the browser can find them.

This testing also usually means making sure it integrates into the HTML properly. This can be as simple as making sure that it is loaded and positioned properly in the page. It can also mean checking that it looks right in context, that the other elements on the page work with the movie, and that there aren't layout problems or palette issues. In order to test your *NOEMBED* tags, Javascript, or other integration techniques you may have used, be sure to try out your Web page using browsers that don't support plug-ins and those that do support them but don't yet have Shockwave installed.

Director Features Disabled in Shockwave 5

When a properly configured Web surfer visits a page that contains a Shockwave movie that movie is automatically downloaded and played on their system. Normally this is a good thing. But what might happen if that movie was created by some malicious, ill-intentioned developer? Could it erase files on your system? Could it search your hard disk for something it was interested in?

It is primarily for these sorts of reasons that a small subset of the Director functionality and some Lingo commands have been deliberately disabled from within a Shockwave movie. Additionally, some commands have been disabled that might be problematic in a browser-based environment (such as movie-in-a-window commands and menus).

The types of disabled commands are often file and system-level commands. Table 11.4 lists examples of the disabled commands.

Table 11.4 Disabled Commands

Command Type	Examples	Comments
File Import and Save	importFileInto, saveMovie	These could violate security restrictions.
Movie-in-a-Window	open window, close window	Difficult to manage and coordinate with the browser.
Resources	openResFile, closeResFile	More security issues.
Printing and menus	printFrom, installMenu	Difficult from within the browser environment.
Clipboard	pasteClipboardInto	So Shockwave movies cannot send whatever information might happen to be in your clipboard at any given moment—a copy-and-pasted password perhaps—up to your server.
System	quit, restart, shutdown	You can see why you wouldn't want to download a movie that did any of these.
System paths	getNthFileNameInFolder, moviePath	Not implemented because these would allow you to gather information about the user's system.
External File Access	openCastlib, openXLib	Many of these work but are restricted to the support folder.

The list of disabled or missing features is a moving target—with each Shockwave release more features have been enabled, such as external file links and Xtras, and others, like frame targeting, have been added. The Macromedia Web site has a detailed list of the currently disabled Lingo commands and Director features.

Other Tips That Didn't Fit Anywhere Else

Here are some more tips for working with Shockwave:

- Be very careful when using multiple Shockwave movies on a single HTML page or frame set. Audio conflicts, memory issues, display issues, and other perils can arise.

- Be aware of those situations when Shockwave may not be the most appropriate choice for your goals. For example, if you just want to animate an image, your best choice is probably to use a GIF89a animation. Every nail need not be hit with the Shockwave hammer.

- You can read the contents of a CD-ROM from your Shockwave movie by using its ability to link to external casts. Shockwave 5 can reference these external assets as long as they are in the Shockwave "Support Folder" (the folder containing the Shockwave plug-in). In this folder you can create an alias on the Mac or a shortcut on Windows 95 to an external cast on your CD-ROM (the alias should have the same name as the original external cast).

- Don't loop in a frame in which you call *gotoNetPage* or *gotoNetMovie*. If you do so you run the risk of calling these repeatedly, which you probably don't want to do. Make the call to one of these functions, then immediately move to the next frame.

- Palette handling is as much an issue in Shockwave as it is in normal Director movies. Be cautious. Most browsers including Netscape and Internet Explorer use an 8-bit palette consisting of 216 colors. Unless you use the *EMBED* tag's foreground attribute (which is risky) Netscape will remap your colors to this palette. Fortunately these colors correspond very closely to the Mac palette (and aren't too far from the Windows palette). You can also use a Netscape-compatible palette and import it into your Movie if you wish. On the Xtras menu in Director is a PALETTES item. Selecting this will open the Palettes Cast, which includes a Netscape-compatible palette that you can insert into your movie.

- External and linked assets referenced in a movie are not downloaded automatically. This is part of Shockwave's security restrictions. The user, or some other software the user "trusts," must be responsible for putting these files (or their shortcuts or aliases) into the Support Folder.

- You can pass data between movies or pages by passing the data to a CGI script on the server (which then sends it on to the next movie in the HTML or makes it available via another CGI).

One Last Tip

You can have fun with any Shockwave movie even before it loads. It turns out that the Macromedia logo that's shown by the plug-in while the movie downloads isn't so static (Figure 11.7). If you move the mouse toward it you'll see that it begins to run away as you get too close. You can chase it all the way around the plug-in window. Then when you catch it and click on it you'll get a little text-based show displaying in multicolor glory the names of many of the Macromedia developers behind the product. Great fun at parties. Figure 11.7 The "Easter Egg" screen.

Chapter Summary

This chapter took us a long way into the world of Shockwave development. In building our online trivia game we learned the following:

- The eight types of NetLingo commands:

  Starting operations

  Status of operations

  Results retrieval

  Canceling network operations

  Message display

  HTML Parameter access

  Preferences

  Streaming audio

- The difference between the synchronous and asynchronous Lingo commands

- The basic three-step process used with the asynchronous commands: initiate the operation, check the status till data is ready, retrieve the results

Figure 11.7 The Easter Egg screen.

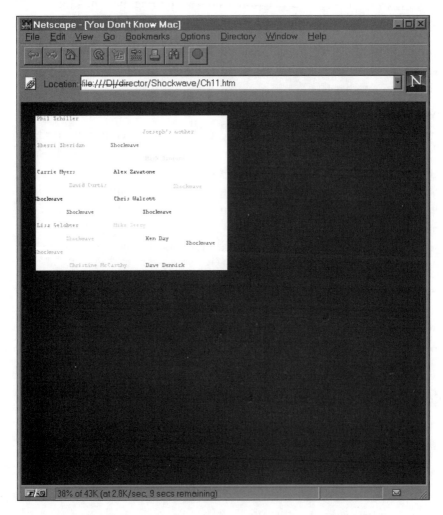

- How to use *getNetText* to retrieve text files from across the Internet

- That the *netDone* function can be used to monitor the status of a network operation in progress

- Using *netTextResult* as the function called to retrieve the results of a *getNetText* call

- The two types of compressed audio for Shockwave: internal and external

- How to create external .SWA streaming audio files and import them into a Shockwave movie

- How to use the streaming audio Lingo commands to play these files back:
  - *preloadTime* and *preloadBuffer* are used together to pre-load the sound from across the Net
  - *set the URL of member* specifies the URL or the streaming audio file to play
  - *play* is called to begin playback
  - *the state of member* identifies if the audio is preloading, playing, done, or in error
  - *externalParamName* and *externalParamValue* functions can be used to read *EMBED* tag parameters directly from the HTML page

- The steps used to compress internal sound effects

- The methods used to issue and track multiple simultaneous NetLingo operations and the importance of using the *getLatestNetID* function

- Use of the *gotoNetMovie* command, which replaces the current movie with the specified movie

- How *preloadNetThing* is supposed to work and why it doesn't always work as expected

- Important cross-platform and cross-browser considerations in Shockwave development

- The Director functionality and Lingo commands disabled in Shockwave movies

- Where to find Shockwave's hidden "Easter Egg" screen

Part Four

Shipping Your CD or Kiosk

Chapter

12

Projectors, Platforms, and Products

Chapter Objective

As fun as it is to make Director projects on your machine, you eventually have to give it to somebody else. If you are going to deliver your product on CD, hard disk, or floppy disk, this chapter will help you.

I've tried to include just what you need to know about every platform you might deliver on.

What's a Projector?

Not everyone who buys your product is going to have purchased Director and installed it on his or her machine. Since Macromedia couldn't figure out how to pull this off, it has given us the ability to make a projector.

A **projector** is an application, like a word processor or spreadsheet. It combines Director's runtime engine with a movie or movies. You can take Ch8.dir and turn it into a self-running application.

To make a projector, first save the movie you are working on. Choose File:Create Projector, which brings up a dialog box. Select the .DIR file that you want to make self-executing, and press Create. It will ask you for a filename, then it will build the application.

Not all your product's movies have to go into a projector. A movie-turned-projector can use *go to movie* or *play movie* just like any other movie.

Now that you are making real applications that will run on real computers and real operating systems, you have to worry about real problems that any other real programmer always worries about.

The Somebody-Is-Stealing-My-Code Worry

Shipping and delivering Director movies are beneficial for your customers. Not only do they get to experience all your cool multimedia, they can open up your DIR files and see how you did it.

Director provides two ways to hide your hard work from prying eyes. The first way is to turn your movie into a projector. There is no way to open a projector and look at its code.

The second way is to protect your movie. Protecting a movie rips out all the Scripts and changes the extension from .dir to .dxr. There's no way for any curious hacker to open the file in Director and peek around. Make sure you keep the originals, though, because there is no way for you to open the file and peek around, either.

To protect a movie, choose Xtras:Update, then click Protect and choose your DIR file.

Multiplatform Worries

The biggest worry is that you might have to deal with four platforms:

- Windows 95/NT

- Windows 3.1

- Macintosh 68k

- Macintosh PowerPC (a.k.a Power Macintosh)

There are differences between all four platforms that you need to know.

> **NOTE** In the following discussion, Windows 95 applies to all the operating systems that Microsoft has announced plans for through 1997. Some configurations of NT have had trouble running Director programs, but that difficulty will, we hope, be a bad memory by the time you read this.

Windows Worries

There are certain things to worry about in any Windows product. There are also things to worry about specifically in cross-platform products, meaning those that run in Window 3.1 and Windows 95.

As time progresses, bothering with Windows 3.1 will become less and less important. Some of my clients, though, will still be using it throughout 1997. A few end users I know haven't upgraded either. Until these people all go away, which could easily be in our lifetimes, most Director products will have to run on both.

16-bit versus 32-bit

Windows 3.1 runs in 16-bit mode, which means that the machine instructions that it uses are 16-bits, or 2 bytes, each. All other modern versions of Windows, such as Windows 95, run in 32-bit mode, which means that the instructions that they understand are 32-bits, or 4 bytes, long.

What does this mean to you? Well, it means that your 32-bit projectors crash under Windows 3.1. It also means that your 16-bit projectors will run more slowly under Windows 95, and possibly not at all under Windows NT. Windows 95 has a nice "16-bit compatibility" feature, which means it bends over backward to run 16-bit applications. NT is not so accommodating.

A proper Windows product has one projector for 16-bit Windows and one for 32-bit Windows. If you are in a pinch on disk space, you could probably get away with just a 16-bit version because it will run in some fashion on both Windows 95 and Windows 3.1.

You decide which type of projector to create by clicking the Options button when you make a projector. Choose Windows 3.1 or Windows NT and 95 from the menu.

Xtras, because they are written in C++ and compiled into machine instructions, care about running in 16 or 32 bit mode. If you make a 32-bit projector, you must have a 32-bit version of the Xtra. If you make a 16-bit projector, you must have a 16-bit version of the Xtra. No tricks can get around this rule.

Quicktime for Windows also comes in 16-bit and 32-bit flavors. A 16-bit projector needs 16-bit Quicktime, and a 32-bit projector needs 32-bit Quicktime. A projector won't even admit the existence of the wrong flavor of Quicktime.

Filenames and Pathnames

Windows 95 can use long filenames, names with up to 255 characters. Pathnames can get really long.

Windows 3.1, built on clunky old DOS, is restricted to eight-character-long filenames. A filename can have an additional three-character extension to specify the type of file. A valid movie filename is

chapter8.dir

Director files always have the ".dir" extension, unless they are protected (see below) in which case they will have the ".dxr" extension. Shockwave movies have the ".dcr" extension.

This filename restriction applies to 16-bit projectors, even if they happen to be running in a 32-bit operating system like Windows 95.

Additionally, the CD-ROM format that Windows reads is called ISO 9660. It doesn't like any filenames longer than 8.3 characters. This means that long filenames die on CD-ROM.

For this reason, it is a good idea to name every file in your project with 8.3 character names. Make no exceptions, except for files that will show up on the Macintosh but not under Windows.

Windows Installation

You cannot ship a Windows CD-ROM without writing an installer.

It's important, so I'll say it again.

You cannot ship a Windows CD-ROM without writing an installer.

Why? Because Windows users won't have a clue about running your program if you don't. The CD-ROM will sit in the drive, untouched, for decades.

There are clear and important standards for installers:

1. The installer must be called *setup.exe* and be on the root of the CD-ROM.

2. The installer takes over the screen.

3. As files are copied to the hard disk, a progress gauge progresses.

4. Just before finishing, the installer must create an icon for the user to launch the program. Windows 3.1: A Program Manager group and item. Windows 95: An icon in the Start Menu.

5. If the product requires Quicktime, the installer must launch the Quicktime for Windows installer.

6. It would be nice if it would install an "Uninstall" icon.

There are many installer-authoring applications on the market. We generally use InstallShield from Stirling Technologies. It's pretty standard, and it does the job. The distribution license is free, but the product itself is pricey.

Windows 3.1 versus Windows 95 Installation Worries

You knew this wouldn't be easy.

A 16-bit application, one that can run under Windows 3.1, can access only 8.3 character filenames, no matter which operating system is running. This goes for installers, too.

So, either you write two installers, 16- and 32-bit, or you write one 16-bit installer and hope that the Windows 95 users won't find it weird that they can't type more than 8 characters.

Who has time to write two installers? Not most multimedia people. Most 16-bit/32-bit Director projects use one 16-bit installer.

Windows 95 has an AutoRun feature that will automatically launch an application from the CD-ROM when the CD-ROM is inserted. It's a great feature, but it is really tough to implement unless you have written a 32-bit installer.

Which program do you automatically run? The installer? Then the user has to re-install every time he or she sticks in your CD. Do you autorun your projector? Where is it? It was supposedly copied to the hard disk, but the user was able to choose its location, so you don't know where it is. You could run it from the CD-ROM, but it would be dog-slow.

Most multimedia developers don't implement AutoRun, unless you've got a C programmer hanging around.

Why would Microsoft design a feature like AutoRun if it was so hard to use? Well, for most applications, it isn't so hard to use. You see, Windows 3.1 uses special text files to keep track of configurations, called INI files. The main config files are called WIN.INI and SYSTEM.INI. When you install your projector, you create a file called, perhaps, MY_PROJ.INI. In this file, which lives in the same directory as your projector, is the drive letter of the CD-ROM drive. It is relatively straightforward to read an INI file using FileIO. More about this later.

Windows 95 doesn't like INI files. It has a whole new configuration system, called the Registry. Unfortunately, 16-bit installers can't access the Windows 95 registry, and 16-bit and 32-bit Director projectors can't either. For Director applications like ours, the Registry is dead. That's what makes AutoRun so darn difficult to implement.

Finding Other Director Movies

OK, you've copied your projector over to some unknown folder on the hard disk. The user double-clicks the projector. It does its little song and dance, and then it executes *go to movie* to go to the big movie on the CD.

But, um, where's the movie on the CD?

While you were developing, your hard disk was letter E. Your projector always said *go to movie "E:\MAIN.DIR"*. You burned a CD and tried it on your friend's computer, whose CD-ROM drive was letter E. Everything was great.

Now you've shipped your product and you are sitting with your other friend, Bubba, who was silly enough to actually buy your product. He installs the application, launches it from the Start Menu or Program Manager, and sees

A big, fat dialog box asking "Where is file E:\MAIN.DIR?"

You see, Bubba's CD-ROM drive is letter F. Oops.

What your installer has to do is write an INI file, as we discussed above, into the same Directory as the projector. This INI file must contain the drive letter of the user's CD-ROM drive. When your projector runs, it must use FileIO, as discussed in Chapter 8, to read in the file and extract the drive letter from the text. Once it has this, it can combine the letter with the name of the movie and supply this new, correct filename to the *go to movie* command.

In order for this to work, of course, the installer must also copy the FileIO Xtra. It must be the 16-bit or 32-bit version, whichever matches your projector.

So, when your friend Bubba installed your projector, the installer also should have written a file called Product.ini to the same directory. When Bubba launches the projector, it reads in Product.ini, extracts the letter D, and puts it into a variable called *driveLetter*. Now it's ready to execute a command like:

```
go to driveLetter&":\MAIN.DIR"
```

which will find the correct movie and open it!

There is an alternate method. Your installer writes an INI file to the same directory. The INI file must be called Lingo.ini. When the projector runs, it reads this file and executes the Lingo code contained in it. You put Lingo code inside it that will put the drive letter into a global variable. You combine this global variable with the filename to go to a movie.

Finding Linked Cast Members: The searchPath
Windows projectors must deal with yet another sneaky problem.

Here's the situation. When you were developing your project, you imported a Quicktime movie called Video.mov. It ran fine, played fine, wonderful. If you had gone to its Cast Member Info dialog, you would have seen the filename was

```
E:\MEDIA\QT\VIDEO.MOV
```

Do you see the problem?

Now we're with Bubba again. The DIR file that played the movie was copied to the hard disk. Bubba clicks the Show Video button in your interface, which goes to the Director file on the hard disk. What does he see?

A big, fat, ugly dialog box that says "Where is E:\MEDIA\QT\VIDEO.MOV?"

Remember, his CD-ROM drive is letter F. Oops again.

When the Runtime Engine tries to play the Quicktime movie, all it knows is the pathname and filename with which the movie was imported. It looks there, finds nothing, then puts up a dialog box asking poor Bubba for help.

You can save Bubba from this nightmare by adding to *the searchPath*.

The searchPath is a system-wide global variable. It is a linear list that holds a bunch of pathnames. When the Runtime Engine can't find a linked Cast Member like a Quicktime movie, linked sound, or linked graphic, it looks for the missing file in all the folders listed in *the searchPath*. Only then does it put up the big, fat, ugly dialog box.

You can add a path to *the searchPath* with the *append* command. The same projector that saved Bubba before can save him again. Since the variable *driveLetter*, from our previous example, holds the correct drive letter of the CD-ROM drive, we can easily add the Quicktime directory to *the searchPath*. This would go before the *go to movie* statement.

```
append the searchPath, driveLetter&":\MEDIA\QT\"
```

Remember, though, that additions to *the searchPath* have no effect until you go to another Director movie. That's why you usually do this in the very first movie that runs, preferably the one that gets turned into a projector.

Here's the whole Bubba-saving handler that might go into the last frame of a movie-turned-projector.

```
on exitFrame

    put readINIFile("Product.ini","cd-rom", "drive") into driveLetter

    append the searchPath, driveLetter&":\MEDIA\QT\"

    go to driveLetter&":\MAIN.DIR"

end
```

This movie-turned-projector is called a stub. Its only purpose in life is to launch MAIN.DIR on the CD-ROM. I always use stubs instead of important movies when I make projectors, so I don't have to remake the projector every time I change the important movie.

A more fully-fleshed installer-and-stub-projector example is in the Chaptr13 folder on the CD-ROM. In fact, it is the installer and stub for the Lingo & Shockwave Sourcebook CD-ROM.

Macintosh Worries

There are fewer things to worry about on the Mac, but the few that are there can trip you up badly.

68k versus Power Macintosh

There are two distinct flavors of Macintosh although they both share the same (more or less) operating system. The first, older, flavor of Macintoshes is based on the Motorola 68000 processor, hence the term 68k. The newer, zestier flavor is based on the IBM/Motorola PowerPC processor, hence the name, Power Macintosh.

Similar to the Window 16- versus 32-bit issue, there is a 68k versus PowerPC issue. Both processors understand 32-bit instructions, but they understand different 32-bit instructions. This means that a PowerPC projector won't run on a 68k Mac.

However, a 68k projector will run on a Power Macintosh, albeit slower than a native PowerPC projector would. If you are in a pinch or just don't care, create a 68k projector.

The Macintosh operating system, called MacOS, plays compatibility tricks that bend over backward to let Power Macs run 68k software. These tricks take time and resources away from the system, so there is less time to give to your projector. Power Macs are fast enough, though, that this often doesn't matter.

You decide which type of projector to create by clicking Options when you make a projector. Choose from Standard Macintosh which means 68k, Power Macintosh Native which means PowerPC, and All Macintosh Models.

All Macintosh Models is a nice choice because it combines both types of projectors into the same application file. This kind of application is called Fat Binary, since it is fat and has binaries (don't ask me, I don't work for Apple). This file can be launched from either type of Mac. When it is launched on a 68k Mac, it will run 68k instructions. When it is launched from a PowerPC Mac, it will run PowerPC instructions. Nice.

However, it does make the size of the application bigger and asks the user to dedicate more hard disk space to your title. Your call.

Xtras care about PowerPC versus 68k. A PowerPC projector can access only a PowerPC Xtra. A 68k projector can access only a 68k Xtra. A Fat Binary projector can access only a PowerPC Xtra when running on a PowerMac, and only a 68k Xtra when running on a 68k Mac.

Most Xtras for the Mac are Fat Binary Xtras, which may be used on either platform.

Memory Worries

The way Windows uses RAM, you are never quite sure how much RAM your projector has at its disposal. If it doesn't have enough, it will slow to a crawl as half your program winds up in Virtual Memory.

There are different worries on the Mac. A Macintosh application requests a certain amount of RAM. When the user launches the application, if there isn't sufficient RAM available, the user is warned or asked to stop.

You set this amount by clicking on the projector file in the Finder and choosing File: Get Info. The resulting window has three editable fields: a Comments field that we care nothing for, a Minimum size field, and a Preferred size field. The latter two fields have numbers in them.

These numbers represent amounts of RAM, in kilobytes. The Minimum size is the smallest amount of available RAM that is acceptable to run the application. The Preferred size is the amount of RAM that the application would really like when it runs. If the amount of available RAM falls between the Minimum and Preferred amounts, the application will get all the rest of the available RAM and launch. If the available RAM is bigger than the Preferred amount, then the application will get just the amount it asked for, and it will leave the rest free.

Here's a problem: You never know how much RAM your projector will need. You can guess all you like, but you'll never really know.

You'll never know. Never.

Nope.

The best you can do is experiment with different RAM settings and watch your projector. If it doesn't have enough RAM, it will slow down, preloading won't work, pictures might fail to load, sounds might fail to play. Or, you might see **really** strange behavior. Work down until you see weird happenings, then work up until it seems comfortable.

There are, of course, complications.

The amount of RAM a PowerPC or Fat Binary projector wants is higher than a 68k projector. Yes, it gets more complicated. The amount of RAM that a PowerPC or Fat Binary projector wants when Virtual Memory is turned off is higher than what the same projector wants when Virtual Memory is turned on. With Director 5.0.1, the amount is 938k more.

Think about this. Our user, Bubba, clicks on the projector icon and chooses Get Info. He reads the product's instructions, which tell him to turn off Virtual Memory so the Quicktime will run better. He does this, restarts the machine, and looks at the Get Info dialog again. The numbers in the boxes are now 938k bigger.

You try to write that ReadMe file.

The next complication: When the projector takes up all the remaining RAM, some system functions begin to suffer. Sound will start to drop out or not play, and Quicktime will start hitching like there's no tomorrow. You should try to leave about 500k free and let your projector take up the rest.

The final complication: There is a Create Projector option called Use Temporary Memory. If Director uses up its allocated RAM, it will probably want more. If you checked this option when you made the projector, Director will now look outside itself, see the available memory, and use it to store more of its own stuff. There will be less and less free memory left, which might lead to the problems of the last paragraph.

Figuring out exactly how much RAM to request can drive a programmer insane. But when things work, they work beautifully.

Macintosh Installation

Here's an arguable statement: You don't always need an installer on the Macintosh.

No, really, you don't. It is generally considered OK simply to have a folder on the CD that the user drags off to the hard drive. If the product needs Quicktime, you should put Quicktime, Quicktime PowerPlug, Quicktime Musical Instruments, and Sound Manager into another folder called Put In System Folder, which the user can copy if he or she likes.

Macintosh doesn't have the same requirements, like creating a Start Menu icon or writing an INI file, that Director does. All a Mac user really needs is the file.

An nice touch with this type of delivery is to embed instructions in the CD's Finder Window itself. The trick is to copy a 32×32 pixel rectangle from a paint program, then paste it onto the icon of an empty folder, in the Get Info window.

For an example of these techniques, take a look at the CD-ROM included with this book on a Macintosh.

If you have a complex installation process, it is appropriate to create an installer. In one project that I worked on, we had a low-memory and a high-memory version of the projector. We also had minimal and large install versions for each of the projectors. We decided it wasn't right to force the user to pick between four different folders. We wrote an installer.

There are several installer-authoring applications on the Mac market, but the good ones, like StuffIt InstallerMaker, have unrealistic licensing fees for CD-ROMs. Do some shopping. Also check out Apple's installer and DeveloperVISE.

Finding Other Director Movies

Here's a tip: When you are developing a CD-ROM product on a Mac, name your hard drive the name of the final CD-ROM, set up its final directory structure, and don't change it for anything. This will cut your potential bugs by 20 percent.

Finding a Director movie on the CD-ROM is easy because the CD has a name instead of a drive letter. If the CD was called "Sourcebook CD" you could say

```
go to movie "Sourcebook CD:Main.dir"
```

If the CD was loaded, this line will always find the correct movie, on any Mac, anywhere. As long as you are not fickle about how you name your CD, you'll be fine.

When you specify every volume and directory like this, leaving no room for error, you are specifying an absolute pathname.

Finding Linked Cast Members: The searchPath

This absolute pathname capability also helps out with our linked Cast Member problem. When you import a Quicktime movie on the Macintosh, Director records the entire absolute path and filename to the file. For example, the filename for a Quicktime movie might be

```
Sourcebook CD:Media:QT:Video.mov
```

When Director tries to find this Quicktime movie, as long as the CD is in the drive, Director will find it. This is a very happy thing.

Developing on One Platform and Delivering on Another

Whichever platform you are doing the most development on is your product's native platform. Every other platform is alien, and it must be approached with caution.

After making sure you have all the right versions of the Xtras, projectors, Quicktime, and so on, you start to fall into Director's weird cross-platform behavior, and the natural differences between platforms start to emerge.

Text

For example, Macintosh and Windows come with different fonts. There are some similar fonts, like Arial and Helvetica, but they are slightly different sizes and look a bit different.

Also, the Mac and Windows character sets are different, so that nice smart-quote on the Mac will end up as an "o" with a squiggly line over it in Windows. Bullets? Forget 'em.

You can try to map fonts and characters automatically using a special file called Fontmap.txt. There is a sample Fontmap.txt in your Director folder. In the Movie Properties dialog box, you click Load Fontmap, then point it at the file. When the movie is run on an alien platform, Director will use the guidelines in the font map to translate fonts, sizes, and characters.

You're working in Windows 95. You import a Quicktime movie, with the filename

```
E:\MEDIA\QT\VIDEO.MOV
```

Now you copy the Director movie and Quicktime movie over to the Mac side. You burn a CD, Director tries to find the movie, and you get the dreaded dialog asking where E:\MEDIA\QT\VIDEO.MOV is.

Director isn't always smart enough to realize that it is on the Mac now, and that it should change the backslashes in the Quicktime filename to colons, before looking for it. Or even figure out that the Macintosh doesn't use drive letters.

The workaround? Put this in your Macintosh stub:

```
append the searchPath, "Sourcebook CD:MEDIA:QT:"
```

This will force Director to start looking at the QT folder before it asks the user to find the file.

Here's a more common case. You import a Quicktime movie on the Mac with the filename

```
Sourcebook CD:Media:Qt:Video.mov
```

When you run the Windows projector and it tries to find the movie, you get "Where is file Sourcebook CD:Media:Qt:Video.mov?"

To solve this, add a *searchPath* to the correct directory.

Finally, and I know this sounds wacky, open the DIR file and save it again in Windows before copying it back to the Mac and burning the CD. Really, it does the trick sometimes. I'm not kidding.

When your brain starts to fry, just remember: Director usually doesn't make sense.

Part Five
Conclusion

13

Conclusion

Creating multimedia is a hugely imaginative, fulfilling, passionate, annoyingly detailed, tiring, often frustrating experience. It requires that you know something about graphic design, media production, and computer programming.

Well, now you know something about computer programming!

Seriously. If you have worked through much of the book, you have developed some real multimedia. The only thing that separates you from most of the other Lingo programmers out there is the walls of your apartment. Hit the pavement!

If you don't feel ready, then make yourself ready. Take an idea that has been floating around at the back of your head, and implement it. It doesn't have to be beautiful or polished. It just has to challenge you, stretch your knowledge, and help you have fun.

That is, of course, the crux of the matter. Creating multimedia is qualitatively different from designing databases on Wall Street. Multimedia is about fun, both for the end-user and for the developers. If you aren't having fun, you aren't creating great multimedia.

If you aren't having fun, sit back in your chair and meditate for a second. Remember that John Musser and Vineel Shah, the two guys who wrote that book that you spent so much time with, think that you really should be having fun.

Because that's what life (and computer programming) is all about.

What's on the CD-ROM?

What's on the CD-ROM?

This CD-ROM contains all of the projects that we build in the book. Chapters 2, 3, 4, 6, 7, 8, 10, and 11 have projects.

You must already have access to Macromedia Director for Windows or Macintosh, version 5.0 or later.

The graphics and animations on this CD-ROM are for your educational use only. Use them to learn Lingo, but do not use them in paid projects, or projects that will be distributed online or via recordable media.

The Lingo source code, however, is yours to use in any way you like.

Hardware Requirements

If your computer can run Director comfortably, you can use the projects on the CD-ROM. These are rough minimum configurations:

Windows 3.1

486dx, 8mb RAM, CD-ROM drive, SVGA 256 color video

Windows 95

486dx, 16mb RAM, CD-ROM drive, SVGA 256 color video

Macintosh, System 7.1 or better

68040 or better, 8mb RAM, CD-ROM drive, 640 × 480 256 color video

Power Macintosh, 16mb RAM, CD-ROM drive, 640 × 480 256 color video

Installing the Software

Windows 3.1

From Program Manager, Select File, Run, and type **X:\SETUP** (where **X** is the correct letter of your CD-ROM drive)

Windows 95

From the Start Menu, select Run, and type **X:\SETUP** (where **X** is the correct letter of your CD-ROM drive)

Macintosh

Drag the "Sourcebook" folder from the CD-ROM to your hard disk. Drag the "Drag over System f" folder onto the System Folder of your hard drive. Restart the Macintosh. Make sure the CD-ROM is in the drive, then double-click the "Sourcebook" icon from your hard disk.

Using the Software

This will install the "Sourcebook" application to your hard disk, and QuickTime software for playing digital video. The "Sourcebook" application is a projector that presents an interface for browsing the projects from each chapter.

As you work through the chapters, you should manually copy the chapter folder from the CD-ROM to your hard disk. Windows users will have to uncheck the "Read Only" flag on the DIR files after they have been copied to the hard drive.

Windows 95

From the desktop or Explorer, right-click on the file. Choose "Properties" from the menu. Make sure "Read Only" is not checked.

Windows 3.1

From the file manager, click on the file. Choose "Properties" from the "File" menu. Make sure the "Read Only" box is not checked.

User Assistance and Information

The software accompanying this book is being provided as is without warranty or support of any kind. Should you require basic installation assistance, or if your media is defective, please call our product support number at (212) 850-6194 weekdays between 9 am and 4 pm Eastern Standard Time. Or, we can be reached via e-mail at: **wprtusw@wiley.com**.

To place additional orders or to request information about other Wiley products, please call (800) 879-4539.

Index

& operator, 294–295
&& operator, 294

A

abort command, 143
ActiveX, 372–373, 401, 417–418, 458
addAt command, 256
add command, 256
Adobe Premier for Windows, 154
Afterburner, 370, 380, 395–398,
   403–404
after operator, 294–295
AIF audio files, 368
alert command, 36–37
All button, 312–313
America Online, 370
Animation
  bird, 244–249
  expressive skull, 21–110
  inserting frames in, 23
  kids, 223–244
  looping, 15–18, 30, 33
  menu for playing, 21–22, 27–37
  RAM limits and, 280
  smiling skull, 9–18
Animation codec, 151
append command, 474

Argument, defined, 12
Arithmetic, 189–192
Assets, defined, 5
Asynchronous commands, 425–428
Authoring Environment, 5–6
AutoRun feature, 471–472

B

Bandwidth, 379–381, 395
beep command, 11–12
before operator, 294
BGCOLOR, 406
Bitmaps, 277–278, 290
bitRate property, 450
<BODY> tag, 378
Bookmarks, 403
Bozo message, 28, 35–37
Buttons
  bug related to, 270
  database, 312–313, 340, 343–344
  Shockwave, 393, 394, 395

C

Cancel, 357, 358
case..of statement, 132–133, 234–236,
   240, 246–247, 284, 357

Cast, 5, 300–344
Cast Members
  attaching scripts to, 17–18, 24–26, 33, 34,
    46, 138
  database pictures as, 335–336
  field, 291, 292, 448
  Film Loop, 392–393
  finding linked, 473–475, 478–479
  loading into/unloading from RAM,
    271–274, 275–278
  memory limits and, 279
  names vs. numbers for, 276–277
  naming of, 135
  placeholder, 232
  properties of, 107, 188, 191, 450
  Quicktime, 155–158, 159, 182–183
  rollovers and, 229–231, 232, 237
  Shockwave, 392–393, 446, 447, 448, 450
  sound, 338, 339
  SWA (streaming audio), 446, 447,
    448, 450
  text, 290–291, 292
Cast Member Scripts, 30–31, 118–119, 120
Cast window, 5, 6, 155–158
CD-ROMs, 222
  bandwidth and, 379–380
  delivery on, 470–475, 477–480
  digital video on (Quicktime), 149–151,
    169, 172
  disadvantages of, 281
  Macintosh vs. Windows with, 282
  sound from, 340
  speed of access, 277, 281
CGI programming, 435, 461
char..of operator, 296
checkIntersections() function, 136–138
Chunks, 298–300, 303
Cinepak codec, 151–152, 172, 404
CLASSID parameter, 416, 417, 420
Click-on-the-hitlist function, 327
Close menu item, 346
closeWindow event, 349
closexlib command, 362
CODEBASE, 416, 417, 420, 458
Codec, 151
Color, 152, 270, 345
COLS attribute, 414

Command, defined, 12
Compression
  of audio files, 445, 446, 452
  lossy/lossless, 404, 445
  Quicktime, 151–152, 153, 404
  Shockwave, 278, 380, 395–398, 403–404,
    445, 446, 452
CompuServe, 370
Conditions, 52–54, 62–64, 94, 97–99,
    124–127, 129–130
Control Panel Window, 50
count() function, 254
Counting down, 129, 260
Cursor, 225, 236–241, 243, 266, 284
cursor command, 236–241, 283–284
Custom functions, 136–138, 142
Custom handlers, 81–90, 113, 135–142, 144

D

Database
  chunks in, 298–300, 303
  creating in director, 300–344
  defined, 289–290
  pictures in, 335–337
  records, 300–303, 305–307, 325–327
  searching, 307–335
  sound in, 340–344
  strings in, 293–298
  text in, 290–293, 301–307, 429
delay command, 30
deleteAt command, 256–257
Delivery concerns, 469–480
Difference frames, 152, 172
Digital video, 147, 149–151
Director, 3–7
  audio, 337–344
  Cast Member loading/unloading by,
    275–276
  features disabled in Shockwave 5, 458–460
  multiple play statements and, 109–110,
    118–119
  projector memory requirements, 279
  Quicktime compared to, 154–155
  Shockwave compared to, 389
  Web site information on, 381
Direct to Stage option, 157, 158

disableSave handler, 348–349

Disks, 275, 355

displayHit handler, 325–327, 331

displayHitlist handler, 317, 321–325

displayHitsWindow handler, 316, 317–318

displayRecord handler, 301–303, 305–307, 325, 336–337, 340–343

displaySave message, 355

Division (arithmetic), 190–191

doSearch handler, 308, 311, 312, 316, 318–319, 324

Downarrow, 182, 185

doWordClick handler, 263–270

Dragging, 51–91, 199–202, 205–207

duration property, 450

E

"Easter Egg" screen, 461, 462

else if statement, 131–132

<EMBED> tag, 377, 378, 399, 404–407, 419–420, 442–443, 451, 460

Empty strings, 295

Enable Preload (Quicktime), 158

enableSave handler, 348–349

end repeat command, 52–54, 94, 95

Error handling, 433–435

Event handler scripts, 14–18, 21–38, 46, 138, 142–143, 144, 179. *See also* Custom handlers; *specific event handlers*

Events, defined, 14

Execution point, 7

exit command, 129, 142

exitFrame event handlers, 15–17, 27, 30, 33

exitFrame events, 15–17, 27

exit repeat command, 127–129

externalParamName function, 451

externalParamValue function, 450–451

F

FALSE, 125–126

Fast Forward, 168–174, 180–181, 197–198

Field Cast Members, 291, 292, 448

Fields, creating, 291

FileFlex, 290, 350

FileIO Xtra, 350–355, 358, 472–473

File Menu, 6

File menu, database, 289

Filenames, 470

Files

in database, 350–355

from Internet for Shockwave, 425–428, 441

saved by Web browser, 441, 457

Film Loop, 392–393

Find button, 312

Fireworks, 379

Float() function, 192

Fonts, 303–305, 436–437, 479

forget command, 314–315

Fragment identifiers, 456

Frame labels, 23, 29, 135

Frame rate, changing, 50

Frame Scripts, 16–18, 27, 33–34, 118, 120, 427

<FRAMESET> tag, 414

<FRAME> tag, 414

FTP protocol, 375

Full-screen Quicktime, 181–187

Functions, 47–48, 136–138, 142. *See also specific functions*

G

Generalizing scripts, 83–90, 108–109

getAngleDegrees handler, 209–212

getAt() function, 254

getLatestNetID function, 454–455

getNetText command, 425–428, 430–433, 435, 450, 451, 454–455

getPos() function, 255

getPref function, 437, 438

gFlapMember variable, 245–249

GIF, 442, 460

Global space, 174, 176

Global variables, 83, 174–181, 193–194, 245–249, 315–316

go loop command, 33, 34

Gopher protocol, 375

go to frame command, 13–15, 17, 22–23, 31–32, 35, 116, 119–120, 123

go to movie command, 117, 123

gotoNetMovie command, 387,
    455–457, 460
gotoNetPage command, 408–410, 413, 460
go to the frame command, 30, 47–48
gQtSprite variable, 179–180
Graphics codec, 151

H

Hard–coding, 175
Hard disk, 277, 279–280
<HEAD> tag, 378
HEIGHT parameter, 405, 407, 417
Helper applications, 367
Help screen, 436
Hiding code, 468
hiliteMember variable, 229, 233–234,
    239–240, 247
Hitlist, 289, 307–311, 317, 321–325,
    327–335, 347–348, 355–361
Hitlist window, 315–327, 347
Hot text, 327
HTML (HyperText Markup Language), 366,
    376–378, 382, 398–400, 404–407,
    412–420, 442–443, 450–452, 456
<HTML> tag, 378
HTTP, 375–376, 405

I

ID, 417, 454–455
if..then command, 62–64, 97–99, 124–127,
    130–133, 199–202, 225–226, 229, 234,
    252
IMA compression, 152
Imagemap, 387
INI files, 472–473
Initializing, 177–179, 249
Installation, 400–401, 470–473, 477–478
installMenu command, 346
Instances, FileIO, 354–355, 358
Integer() function, 192
Internet, 366, 380–381, 425–428
Internet Explorer, 366, 367, 372, 373,
    400–401, 402, 443
Intersecting Sprites, 64–71, 91, 96–97,
    136–137, 140–141

Invisible Stage, 56–59, 123
item..of operator, 297

J

Java, 378–379
Javascript, 443, 450–451, 458
JPEG, 442

K

Key frames, 152, 172, 173

L

Latency, 380
Life, meaning of, 484
Linear lists, 253–257, 357
line..of operator, 297
Lingo, defined, 7
Lingo elf, 7
Lingo Xtras, 350
Living Books, 222
Local variables, 83–87, 100, 133–135, 167,
    171, 173, 174, 229, 233–234, 247
Logical operators, 126–127
Looping, 15–18, 30, 33, 52–54, 59–60, 62,
    94–97, 99, 108, 116, 127–129

M

Macintosh
    database with, 304, 338, 339, 340,
        345–346
    delivery concerns, 475–480
    FileIO Xtra with, 350, 351
    menu bars with, 345–346
    for playback, 281–282
    Quicktime for, 153–154, 173
    Shockwave for, 374, 436–437, 446, 460
    sound with, 279, 338, 339, 340, 446
    Web browsers for, 373, 441
Memory. *See* RAM; Virtual memory
Memory cache, 441
Menu bars, 344–347
Message Path, 27
Messages, with FileIO, 352–355
Message Window, 11

MIME types, 411
mMessageList message, 352
mnum variable, 107
mouseUp event, 14, 27
mouseUp event handlers, 24, 26–27, 30, 32, 35, 36–37
moveFace event handler, 79–102, 138–141
Movie-In-A-Window, 313–315
Movies, navigating between, 117, 123, 455–457
Movie Scripts, 27, 35–38, 82–83, 138, 143, 144
movieTime, setting, 202–205
mtime variable, 171, 173
Multimedia, sources of information on, 382

N

name of member property, 107
NAME parameter, 417
Naming, 83, 133–134, 135, 179
Navigation, 12–14, 22–23, 116, 117, 119–120, 123
Navigation bar, 408–410
netDone() function, 427, 435
netError() function, 434
NetLingo, 370, 423–428, 437, 455. *See also specific commands*
Netscape Navigator, 368, 369, 372, 400, 402, 441, 443
netTextResult() function, 427, 433
new(), 355
NNTP news protocol, 375
<NOEMBED> tag, 442–443, 458

O

<OBJECT> tag, 377, 401, 415–420, 451–452
Open Hitlist, 289, 357–361
openHitlist handler, 347, 357–361
openWindow event, 349
openxlib command, 351
Operators, 126–127, 293–296
Options (Quicktime), 157
otherwise clause, 240

P

Painter problem, 105–110
PALLETTE, 405–406, 460
Parameters, 87–90, 138–142
<PARAM> tag, 419
Parsing, defined, 46
Pathnames, 339, 343–344, 470
pause command, 30
pausing, of Quicktime movies, 165
PDF files, 368
percentPlayed property, 449
percentStreamed property, 449
Photoshop, 290, 373
Pixel-doubling, 181–187
Placeholder, 232, 233
Platforms, 282–283, 373–374, 458, 467–480. *See also specific platforms*
playAnimation handler, 241–243
Playback Head, 12–14, 30, 119–120
Play button, 340, 343–344
play done command, 117–119, 258
Play Every Frame (No Sound) (Quicktime), 157
play frame command, 107, 108, 109–110, 116–120, 241, 258
Play Looping, 10
play movie command, 117, 123
Plug-ins, 368, 370, 373–374, 400, 442–444
Port number, 375
Power Macintosh, 350, 351, 475–476, 477
Power switch, 160–163, 179–180
Preference functions, 437–438
preLoadBuffer command, 448, 454
preLoad command, 272
preLoadMember command, 271–272, 273–274
preloadNetThing command, 457
PrintOMatic Xtra, 350
Projectors, 467–479
Property, defined, 44
Protecting movies, 468
puppet of sprite property, 122
puppetSound command, 250, 338–339
puppetSprite command, 43–44, 121–123, 394–395, 431

Puppet Sprites, 41–52, 86, 121–123, 162–163, 226–229, 233, 331, 336, 394–395, 431
put command, 44
put..into command, 84, 133, 292–293

Q

Quicktime, 147–219
  Cast Members, 155–158, 159, 182–183
  compression, 151–152, 153, 404
  delivery concerns, 477, 478–480
  dialog box, 156–158
  plug-ins for, 368
  primer, 147–155
  sound, 150, 152–153, 154–155, 250–263, 339–340
Quotation marks, 134–135, 293, 295
quote keyword, 295

R

RAM, 270–281, 476–477
Rate option (Quicktime), 157
readPuzzleData handler, 432–433, 439
Records, database, 300–303, 305–307, 325–327
Registration points, 73–78, 100–102, 230–231, 237
repeat loop, with Quicktime, 170, 172, 200–201
repeat while command, 52–54, 59–60, 62, 92–94, 124–127, 129, 199
repeat with command, 94–97, 99, 108, 129–130
return command, 136–137, 295
return keyword, 295
Reverse ink-mode, 328–329
Rewind button, 163–168, 180
rollover() function, 225, 283
Rollovers, 182–183, 225–249, 283, 388, 393–394
Rotating dial, 207–217
ROWS attribute, 414
RTF files, importing, 290
Runtime Engine, 6, 7, 26–27

S

Save Hitlist, 289, 356–357
saveHitlist handler, 347, 356–357
Save Hitlist menu item, 347–348
Save menu item, 346
Score, 5, 7
Score Window, 5, 6, 12, 15
Script Channel, 15–16
Script Pop-up Menu, 34, 35
Script Preview Button, 16, 17, 18
Scripts. *See also specific types of scripts*
  defined, 7, 11
  duplicating, 33–34, 80, 108
  types of, 26–27
Script Window, 16–18, 33
Scrolling, 327–328
searchPaths, 474, 478–479, 480
Selection bar, 328–329, 332, 333–335
selectLine handler, 329–333, 334–335
setAt command, 255–256
set command, 45–46, 133
setMovieTimeBySlider handler, 202–205
setPref function, 437
setSliderByMovieTime handler, 194–198, 216
set..to command, 45, 133, 293
Shockwave, 365–463
  Active Shockwave, 372–373, 401, 417–418, 458
  Cast Members, 392–393, 446, 447, 448, 450
  compression, 278, 380, 395–398, 403–404, 445, 446, 452
  debugging, 441–444
  description of, 368–369, 370–371
  development process steps, 386
  Director compared to, 389
  Director features disabled with, 458–460
  "Easter Egg" screen, 461, 462
  installing plug-in, 400–401
  interactivity in, 393–395
  Java compared to, 378–379
  loading movies, 402–407, 412
  multiple movies on single HTML page, 460
  obtaining, 369–370

stage size, 389–393

streaming audio with, 444–454

text containers with, 290, 291

Web site information on, 381–382

"You Don't Know Mac" game, 428–440, 444–455

showAll handler, 312–313

Show Controller option, 157

Shrinking, 186–187

Simultaneous network operations, 454–455

Slang commands, 116, 130–131, 293

Slider-bar, 149, 187–207, 216

snum variable, 86–90, 99

Soft-coding, 175–179

Sorting, of lists, 256

Sound

    accessing file from database records, 301

    in database, 340–344

    with digital video, 150, 152–153, 154–155

    with Director, 337–344

    memory requirements, 279

    with Quicktime, 150, 152–153, 154–155, 250–263, 339–340

    rollovers and, 234–235

    with Shockwave, 444–454

    size formula, 279

    sources for, 234

    streaming audio, 368, 444–454

    synchronization of, 250–263

    on World Wide Web, 366–367, 444–454

soundbusy() function, 338

Sound Manager, 279

sound playfile command, 250, 339, 343

Sound Xtra, 350

sprite..intersects function, 64–65, 140–141

Sprites, 24–26. *See also* Puppet Sprites

    databases and, 305, 330–331, 332

    determining last clicked, 263–264

    flashing, 122

    intersecting, 64–71, 91, 96–97, 136–137, 140–141

    properties of, 44, 66–68, 72–73, 107, 122, 160–174, 182–183, 185, 187–189, 191–192, 196, 199–200, 214–215, 250, 305–306

    Quicktime, 159–168, 182–184, 185, 214–215

rollovers and, 232

Shockwave, 393, 394, 431, 449

updateStage command and multiple types of, 124

Sprite Scripts, 34–35, 46, 118–119, 120

Sprite Xtras, 350

SRC, 405, 406

Stage, 4, 389–393

startMovie handler, 177, 178

state of member property, 450

stop command, 450

Streaming, 368, 444–454

string(), 360

Strings, 134–135, 293–298

Stubs, 474–475, 479–480

Style, of text, 303–305

Synchronization, sound, 250–263

Sync to Soundtrack, 157

T

TARGET attribute, 413

tell command, 315

Testing, 282–283, 395, 410, 412, 458

Text, in database, 290–293, 301–307, 479

Text Cast Members, 290–291, 292

TEXTFOCUS, 405

the clickOn function, 263–264

the cursor of sprite property, 182–183, 185

the duration of member property, 188, 191

the fontSize of field property, 303

the fontStyle of field property, 303

the frame function, 47–48

the itemDelimiter property, 297–298

the left of sprite property, 196, 199–200

the memberNum of sprite property, 66–68, 107, 122

the mouseCast function, 327

the mouseH function, 48, 49

the mouseItem function, 327

the mouseLine function, 327

the mouseV function, 48, 49

the mouseWord function, 327

the movieRate of Sprite property, 160–163, 165, 169–170, 173–174

the movieTime of Sprite property, 163–168, 171–172, 187–189, 191–192, 250

the pathname function, 343–344
the platform function, 142
the platform property, 304
the right of sprite property, 199–200
the scrollTop property, 328
the searchPath variable, 474–475,
    478–479, 480
the soundlevel property, 450
the stretch of the sprite property, 72–73
the visible of sprite property, 305–306
the volume of sprite property, 214–215
the width of Sprite property, 188
<TITLE> tag, 378
Tool Xtras, 350
trackNextKeyTime() function, 173
Tracks, in Quicktime movies, 151
Transition Xtras, 350
Transmission speed, 380–381
TRUE, 125–126

U

unloadMember command, 272–273
Unload menu (Quicktime), 158
Uparrow, 182–183, 185
updateProgress handler, 431–432
updateStage command, 58–60, 123, 124,
    165, 170–171, 278, 338
URLs, 374–376, 387, 401, 405, 406
    CLASSID, 416, 417, 420
    with gotoNetMovie command, 455, 456
    with gotoNetPage command, 409, 410
    with streaming audio, 447, 451

V

value() command, 359, 360
Values, putting in, 84, 133
Variables, 83–87, 94–95, 129–130,
    133–135, 179, 291–292. *See also*
    Global variables; Local variables;
    Parameters
Video card, 275, 276, 277
Video for Windows, 153–154
Video menu (Quicktime), 157
Virtual memory, 279–280, 281, 476
voidP() function, 141

Volume knob, 207–218
VRML, 368
V12 Xtra, 290, 350

W

WAV audio files, 368
Web browsers, 366–367, 372–374, 381,
    400, 402–407, 441, 457, 458
Web pages, 366, 370, 374–378, 382,
    387–389, 398–400, 404–407, 412–420,
    442–444
Web servers, 366, 411–412
Web site construction, sources of
    information on, 382
WIDTH parameter, 405, 407, 417
windowList property, 314
windowPresent function, 316
Windows, creating and manipulating,
    314–317
Windows (operating system)
    database with, 304, 345–346, 350, 351
    delivery concerns, 469–475, 479
    menu bars with, 345–346
    for playback, 281–282
    Quicktime for, 153–155, 173, 174
    Shockwave for, 370, 374, 436–437, 446,
        460
    sound with, 337, 339, 340, 446
Windows NT, 304, 374, 469
Windows 3.1, 282, 304, 350, 351, 374,
    469–472
Windows 95, 282, 304, 350, 351, 370, 374,
    460, 469, 471–472
Windows 96, 304
Windows System Pallette, 345
windowType property, 315, 317
word..of operator, 296
Words, speaking of, 250–270
World Wide Web, described, 366
writeString command, 355

X

Xtras, 290, 349–355, 370, 469–470, 476.
    See also specific Xtras

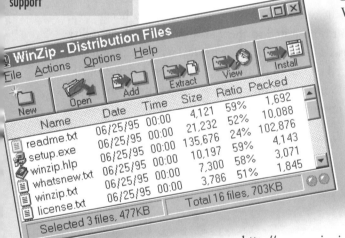

CUSTOMER NOTE: